GERMAN SOCIAL DEMOCRACY

1905–1917

GERMAN SOCIAL DEMOCRACY

1905–1917
The Development of the Great Schism

By

CARL E. SCHORSKE
Wesleyan University

HARPER TORCHBOOKS
Harper & Row, Publishers
New York, Evanston, San Francisco, London

This work is Volume 65 in the Harvard Historical Studies.

GERMAN SOCIAL DEMOCRACY 1905–1917

First HARPER TORCHBOOK edition published 1972

This book was originally published in hardcover by Harvard University Press. It is here reprinted by arrangement.

STANDARD BOOK NUMBER: 06–1316873

*To the Memory
of My Parents*

PREFACE

No political parties of present-day Germany are separated by a wider gulf than the two parties of labor, one democratic and reformist, the other totalitarian and socialist-revolutionary. Social Democrats and Communists today face each other as bitter political enemies across the front lines of the cold war; yet they share a common origin in the Social Democratic Party of Imperial Germany. How did they come to go separate ways? By what process did the old party break apart? How did the prewar party prepare the ground for the dissolution of the labor movement in World War I, and for the subsequent extension of Leninism into Germany? To answer these questions is the purpose of my study.

The development of the schism within the body of the old party provides the theme of the work; the history of the late German Empire, its setting. I have attempted to illuminate the internal dynamic of the split in the light of the external political and economic pressures which forced it forward. The final breakup of the party under the hammer blows of war was but the consummation in event of a complex process of slow change. Of this process the historical actors were themselves only half aware. In party disputes arising out of concrete problems of the prewar years, the Social Democrats only gradually developed the divergent factional attitudes which were to govern their behavior in the crises of war and revolution.

In tracing the schismatic development, I have had to abandon the widely held view that the rise of reformism provides the only key to the breakup of Social Democracy. Reformism was surely one of the dynamic factors in the split. After 1905, however, its growth was paralleled by the rise of a new revolutionism, as hostile to the traditional tactic of the Social Democratic Party as the revisionists were to its theory. Under the pressure of events, these two wings, both minorities in the party, became its vital elements. The dialectic between them polarized the party at the expense of the champions of Social Democratic tradition in theory and political practice as that tradition became increasingly irrelevant to the historical life of the twentieth century.

The controversies which culminated in the schism took place at three different levels: ideas, tactics, and organization. A study of their interaction must thus partake of the character of intellectual, political, and sociological history. I have utilized any of these approaches only where it contributes to an understanding of the total process of schismatic development. My focus has led me to exclude otherwise significant aspects of the party's history. Relations with the socialist parties of other countries, for example, are considered only where they had an effect on the split. There is no treatment of the "social imperialists," interesting though they are to the intellectual historian, since they remained mavericks without real influence on the party's policy before 1914. The oft-studied political history of the party during the war years is presented only as a kind of ultimate projection and resolution of prewar tendencies and tensions. On the same principle of concentration on the schism, I have explored developments well outside the Social Democratic camp where these have had divisive repercussions within it.

Method and scope, then, have been determined by a single aim: to lay bare the process whereby the greatest socialist party of the prewar world fell into disunity — a disunity fraught with fateful consequences for European civilization, even to our own day.

My erstwhile colleagues in the German Research Section of the Office of Strategic Services stimulated my original interest in this undertaking. To two in particular, Professors Felix Gilbert and Franz L. Neumann, I owe an immense debt of gratitude: as my constant counsellors, they have offered close and trenchant criticisms of my work. Professors Norman O. Brown, Hajo Holborn, Karl W. Kapp, Leonard Krieger, and Sigmund Neumann have helped me to grapple with many a knotty problem. Those who have known Professor William L. Langer both as teacher and friend will understand the depth of my gratitude to him, not only for the rigor of his training and the soundness of his advice, but also for the warmth with which he cultivates the intellectual independence of his students.

While the Social Science Research Council and the Rockefeller Foundation extended generous financial assistance, Wesleyan University kindly gave me leave to carry on the work. Mrs. M. Gilbert Burford, Mrs. Ellen D. Heye, and Miss Marilyn Kwayauskas performed yeoman service at the typewriter. To all of these, my warmest thanks. My wife helped the work to its completion by her resolute refusal to discuss the Social Democrats during our leisure hours and by her equally resolute handling of the drudgery connected with the preparation of the manuscript.

Middletown, Connecticut   C. E. S.
February 1954

CONTENTS

PART I

THE REFORM TACTIC CHALLENGED, 1905–1907

PART II

THE CONSOLIDATION OF THE RIGHT, 1906–1909

CONTENTS

GERMAN SOCIAL DEMOCRACY

1905–1917

ABBREVIATIONS

Internationaler Sekretär, *Bericht, 1905* — Internationaler Sekretär der Gewerkschaftlichen Landeszentralen, Hrsg., *Internationaler Bericht über die Gewerkschaftsbewegung, 1905* (Berlin, 1907).

Luxemburg, *Werke* — Rosa Luxemburg, *Gesammelte Werke,* ed. Paul Frölich 3 vols. (Berlin, 1925–1928).

N.Z. — *Neue Zeit* (Stuttgart, 1893 *et seq.*).

Prot. S. P., 1905 — *Protokoll über die Verhandlungen des Parteitages der Sozialdemokratischen Partei Deutschlands, 1905* (Berlin, 1906).

Reichstag Debates — *Stenographische Berichte der Verhandlungen des deutschen Reichstages* (1871 *et seq.*).

Schulthess, 1905 — *Schulthess' Europäischer Geschichtskalender,* ed. Ludwig Reiss and successors (Munich, 1906).

S.M. — *Sozialistische Monatshefte* (Berlin, 1898 *et seq.*).

PART I

THE REFORM TACTIC CHALLENGED
1905–1907

Chapter I

BACKGROUND: THE ERFURT SYNTHESIS
AND THE RISE OF REFORMISM

i. Toward a Revolutionary Socialist Party

It was a peculiarity of German development, influencing the whole course of German labor history, that the middle class was unable to bid for political power before capitalism had already entered its industrial phase. In the Revolution of 1848, the working class, small though it was, made its debut on the political stage simultaneously with the revolutionary bourgeoisie. Although little organized, the workers in certain industrial areas already manifested a sense of class interest separate from that of the middle class. Socialist doctrine, however primitive in character, appeared at the same time. The middle-class leaders of the Revolution of 1848 recoiled from the revolution they had conjured up, and, leaving political power in the hands of the aristocracy, placed their hope for the achievement of a constitutional order in legal methods.

In the period of reaction which followed, the new-born labor movement in Prussia was thoroughly repressed. The right to organize was denied by law, while in the expanding industrial economy labor and capital moved into ever deeper conflict. Nevertheless, anti-capitalist feeling did not yet assume a revolutionary form. The middle-class Progressive Party of Prussia carried on its fight for parliamentary government in the "time of conflict" in the 1860's. Democratic ideas were still common coin in the middle and working classes, even though divergent class interests were mutually recognized.

In 1863, when the Prussian constitutional crisis was at its height, Ferdinand Lassalle founded his General German Workers' Association. Socialism and democracy were bound in indissoluble union in the Association's program, wherein the goal of socialism (the establishment of producer coöperatives by the state) was to be achieved through the introduction of democracy. The peculiar triad of social forces in Germany was reflected in Lassalle's effort to win Bismarck's support for his plans on the basis of their mutual antipathy to middle-class liberalism.

It was not until 1868–1869 that Marxian socialism acquired institutional form in the Social Democratic Labor Party, under the leadership of Wilhelm Liebknecht, a disciple of Marx, and the young Saxon, August Bebel. It is significant that the new party was established at the very time when the Progressive Party was splitting under the impact of Bismarck's first blows for national unification. The strong secessionist right wing of the Progressives, nucleus of the National Liberal Party of the empire, abandoned the fight against Prussian authoritarianism in exchange for the achievement of German unity by blood and iron. Bismarck's success in drawing a large part of the middle class further away from its democratic heritage meant that the working class would find its aristocratic and bourgeois enemies not divided as before, but in coalition. With this changed social alignment, the ideas of revolution, democracy, and socialism coalesced once more, and the Marxian synthesis of these elements found its expression in the Eisenach program of the new party. The Eisenacher differentiated themselves from the Lassalleans not only by their revolutionary gospel but also by their anti-Prussian, *Grossdeutsch* views on unification.

With the establishment of the Reich in 1871, the two rival socialist parties began to draw closer together. As the divisive question of national unification receded into the background, Lassalleans and Eisenacher found a common interest in defending the workers' standard of living in the face of the price rises which accompanied the post-war boom.[1] At a conference held in Gotha in 1875, the two parties merged to form the Socialist Labor Party of Germany under a program more strongly influenced by Lassalle than by Marx. The Gotha program called for the abolition of the iron law of wages through the "cooperative control of collective labor," and pledged the party to work "with every legal means for the free state." The party listed among its immediate demands universal suffrage and the secret ballot, direct legislation by the people, full civil liberties, freedom of association, and various legislative actions for the reform of working conditions.[2] To the intense annoyance of Karl Marx, the Gotha program contained none of his analysis of economic development, no word of revolution, and no clear indication of the class character of the state.[3] The Eisenach leaders showed that, insofar as they had understood Marx, his doctrine was worth less to them than the achievement of unity in the labor movement for the pursuit of critical democratic objectives.

Not until Bismarck unleashed his fury against them did the German Socialists become really receptive to Marxism. Bismarck's repressive acts, in force from 1878 to 1890, compelled the Socialists to use illegal means to preserve their movement. The revolutionary temperature of the party rose during the eighties. At the first congress-in-exile (Wyden, Switzerland, 1880), the Socialists unanimously voted to strike from their program the clause stating that they would pursue their aims "by all legal means."[4] At Copenhagen three years later, the congress declared the party to be revolutionary, with "no illusions" concerning the realization of its goal by parliamentary methods.[5] During this time of troubles, the urban working class became increasingly alienated from the state. The vote polled by the Socialists reflected the change in mood; it rose from 311,961 in 1881 to 1,427,298 in 1890.[6] Within the Socialist Labor Party, there

[1] Harry J. Marks, "Movements of Reform and Revolution in Germany from 1890 to 1903" (Ph.D. Dissertation, Harvard Univ., Cambridge, Mass., 1937), 2.

[2] Felix Salomon, *Die deutschen Parteiprogramme* (4th edition, Leipzig and Berlin, 1932), II, 40–42.

[3] Cf. Karl Marx, *Critique of the Gotha Program* (New York, 1933), *passim*.

[4] Marks, *Reform and Revolution*, 7.

[5] *Ibid.*

[6] Johannes Ziekursch, *Politische Geschichte des neuen deutschen Kaiserreiches* (Frankfurt a. M., 1930), III, 54; Paul Hirsch and Bruno Borchardt, *Die Sozialdemokratie und die Wahlen zum deutschen Reichstage* (Berlin, 1912), 24–25.

developed a left-wing revolutionary opposition verging close to anarchism in its condemnation of parliamentary action as a futile instrument in the advancement of the proletarian cause.[7]

These developments combined to force forward the question of a revision of the party program. The party leadership, fearing to provoke the government into intensifying or prolonging the persecution, resisted any radicalization. Although empowered by the party congress of 1887 to draft a new program, the leaders produced nothing by the time of the first congress after the lapse of the Anti-Socialist Laws (Halle, 1890).[8] Only when the party again enjoyed legal status was the work taken up in earnest, to culminate in the Erfurt program of 1891, which served the reorganized Social Democratic Party until the collapse of the German Empire.

The Erfurt program enshrined Marxism as the official gospel of German Social Democracy. Marxist theory, as its adherents recognized, was singularly appropriate to the historical moment. By its distinction between the objective historical conditions necessary to achieve socialism and the subjective will of the proletariat required to bring it about, Marxism made possible a reconciliation of the revolutionary rancor engendered in the Social Democratic rank and file during the persecution, and the need for a reformist tactic in a fundamentally non-revolutionary period. Engels made the most of the opportunity. In *Neue Zeit,* the theoretical organ of the party, he published Marx' *Critique of the Gotha Program,* previously withheld from the membership.[9] Engels' accomplice in this action was Karl Kautsky, *Neue Zeit*'s editor.

Kautsky was the principal architect of the new program.[10] The son of a Czech nationalist father and a German mother, Kautsky had been attracted to socialism in his student days at Vienna. At the age of twenty-five, he cast his lot with German Social Democracy as an editor of its newspaper-in-exile in Switzerland. Four years later, in 1883, Kautsky founded *Neue Zeit,* the first German organ of theoretical Marxism since 1848.[11] Kautsky quickly became the

[7] Marks, *Reform and Revolution*, 23–31.

[8] *Ibid.*, 16, 33–36.

[9] *Ibid.*, 3, 32.

[10] *Ibid.*, 63.

[11] Karl Renner, *Karl Kautsky. Skizze zur Geschichte der geistigen und politischen Entwicklung der deutschen Arbeiterklasse* (Berlin, 1929), 9–25.

party's quasi-official intellectual leader, a position for which his universality of interests, his mastery of dialectical thinking, and his cautious, deliberative temperament admirably suited him. The drafting of the new program was a congenial task for Kautsky, the first of a kind he repeatedly performed as long as it was humanly possible: the reconciliation of antagonistic tendencies in Social Democracy by means of theoretical concepts.

The Erfurt program was divided into two parts, the first outlining a theory of social development and long-run objectives, the second laying down a series of immediate aims which the Social Democratic Party would try to realize within the framework of capitalist society.

The first part, obviously inspired by the *Communist Manifesto,* drew a sombre picture of the evolution of capitalist society. While the workers' productivity would increase, the growth of monopoly would rob the people of the fruits of their labor. The proletariat and the sinking middle class could expect only "mounting insecurity, misery, pressure, subordination, debasement and exploitation."[12] The program predicted economic crises of increasing severity and an "ever more bitter" class struggle between bourgeoisie and proletariat. To these problems there was only one solution: "the transformation of capitalist private property in the means of production — land, mines, raw materials, machines, transportation — into social ownership." This transformation could be "the work of the working class alone, for all other classes, despite the conflicts of interests among them, are bound to private property, and have a common goal in the maintenance of the present social order." The fight would be a political one, for the goal could be achieved only through the acquisition of political power.[13]

The second part of the program enumerated a series of immediate objectives to be pursued within the framework of capitalist society. The political aims differed little from those of the Gotha program: universal suffrage for all citizens over twenty years of age, including women; proportional representation; referendum and recall; "self-determination" in Reich, state, and community; direct election of officials; direct, graduated income tax, and other democratic reforms.

[12] Salomon, *Parteiprogramme,* II, 83.
[13] *Ibid.,* II, 84.

An economic section called for the eight-hour day, extension of the social insurance system with working-class representatives in its administration, guarantees of the right to organize, prohibition of child labor up to fourteen years, etc.

The Erfurt program was designed for a non-revolutionary period, one in which the working class was growing in numbers and political self-awareness, but was still too weak to make a serious bid for power. Part I of the program expressed the socialist ideal of a complete transformation of society; Part II, the political and economic interest of the worker within the existing order. The ideal could be realized only by a social revolution, a change in the locus of economic and political power — whether by violent or by peaceful means was not specified in the program. The worker's immediate interest could be pursued within capitalist society by organizing the economic and political power of labor. The tie that would bind these two aims together, according to the Marxian theory and the Erfurt program, was the development of capitalism itself, which, while isolating and depressing the workers, would develop in them the consciousness of the need for socialism and the strength and will to realize it.

In terms of the actual composition of the labor movement, in which both elements, ideal and material, revolutionary and reformist, were represented, if not yet clearly differentiated, the Marxism of the Erfurt program provided a basis of compromise. To the revolutionaries, the idealists, it said in effect, "Patience! The time is not yet. Remember, history is on your side." To the reformists, those interested in the immediate welfare of the workers, it said, "Reforms are the first task. Pursue them. But remember, you must fight for them. And the faith in the bright new society is a weapon in your struggle. Do not ignore it."

So long as the German state kept the working class in a pariah status, and so long as the working class, able to extract a share of the material blessings of a vigorous expanding capitalism, was not driven to revolt, the Erfurt synthesis would hold. Our study will be concerned with the dissolution of the Erfurt union of revolutionary and reformist forces under the pressures of a changing world.

ii. The Forces of Reform: The Southern Wing

Under the Erfurt program, the party launched its campaign of agitation and organization. The party's aim was to carry the socialist message to the people; its means, the unsparing criticism of the iniquities of the *Klassenstaat* and the capitalist order. Bereft of allies in the Reichstag, unrepresented in the Prussian Landtag, the party in the nineties made a fetish of its distance from the ruling powers. In the Reichstag the Social Democrats developed a tactic of "pure opposition," which found its symbolic expression in the refusal to vote for a national budget, or to participate in the *Hoch* to the Kaiser.[14] The Social Democrats used parliament more as a platform of agitation than as a legislative organ.

To the success of the tactic of pure opposition the electoral statistics bear witness. In 1887, Social Democracy polled 10.1 per cent of the vote in the Reichstag elections; in 1890, 19.7 per cent; in 1893, 23.3 per cent; in 1898, 27.2 per cent; and in 1903, 31.7 per cent. In numerical terms, the party's voters increased from 763,128 in 1887 to 3,010,771 in 1903.[15] Is it to be wondered that Social Democracy became attached to its "tried and true (*altbewährte*) tactic"?

In South Germany, the tactic of pure opposition was pursued with less rigor. Class lines were not so sharply drawn in the south, where industrialization had developed more slowly than in central and northern Germany. Moreover, the tradition of liberalism had a firmer hold on the middle classes. Where great urban agglomerations were few, any long-run success of Social Democracy was felt to depend on making some inroads into the independent peasantry and the peasant-artisan class. It was here that reformism first appeared in strength.[16] The southern Social Democratic leaders were inclined from the outset to tone down the revolutionary aspects of the party's ideology. The effort of party agitators to work among the peasants led to the first attempt to revise the Erfurt program's Marxian thesis that the independent peasantry was doomed to be crushed by large-scale agriculture. To tell a prosperous peasant that

[14] Marks, *Reform and Revolution*, 160–162.

[15] Hirsch and Borchardt, *Sozialdemokratie und Wahlen*, 24–26.

[16] Cf. Paul Frölich's survey of southern party development in Rosa Luxemburg, *Gesammelte Werke*, ed. Paul Frölich (Berlin, 1925–1928), III, 399ff.

he was fated to lose his holding, and that nothing could be done about it, was not the way to convert him to Social Democracy. Bavarian party leaders raised the demand for a policy designed to protect and defend the interest of the peasant, while southern theorists developed an analysis showing that small holdings, far from being doomed, were more efficient than large ones for certain types of agriculture.[17]

As early as 1891, Georg von Vollmar, an ex-army officer, led the Bavarian party in its unsuccessful opposition to the adoption of the Erfurt statement of Marxist principles.[18] In 1894, the Bavarian Landtag delegation voted for a state budget which contained certain provisions favoring the interests of the working class and peasantry. This action aroused the fury of the national party congress. Vollmar showed how the effort to win a following could react upon party principles. He pointed out to the Frankfurt congress (1894) that the Social Democrats had acquired an influence in Bavaria which went far beyond their numbers, but only because "we tore ourselves away from all mechanical forms of agitation, studied the country and the people, and accommodated our agitation accordingly. If we were to change our tactic . . . our successes would disappear."[19] For the northern radical majority, Vollmar's argument carried no weight. Budget approval was condemned by the congress, and a precedent was set which — in a party which increasingly lived by precedent as its inner cleavages became sharper — sustained the orthodox view of the budget question until 1913.[20] But southern reformism could not be extirpated by the condemnation of its parliamentary policy. When it acquired support from the growing trade-unions, it came to play an important role in the development of the party schism.

iii. The Forces of Reform: The Trade-Unions

In contrast to England, the trade-unions in Germany played a negligible part in the foundation of the working class movement.

---

[17] Erika Rikli, *Der Revisionismus. Ein Revisionsversuch der deutschen marxistischen Theorie (1890–1914)*, in Zürcher Volkswirtschaftliche Forschungen, XXV: 25, 45 (Zürich, 1936); Marks, *Reform and Revolution*, 237–282.

[18] Marks, *Reform and Revolution*, 53ff.

[19] Wilhelm Schröder, ed., *Handbuch der sozialdemokratischen Parteitage, 1863–1913* (Munich, 1910–1915), I, 100.

[20] *Ibid.*, 100–101.

The so-called "Free" trade-unions had been established by the social-ist parties in the 1860's primarily as recruiting agencies for the po-litical labor movement. Organized on a local rather than a national basis, they were numerically weak until the period of the Anti-Socialist Laws, when their membership increased more than five-fold.[21] Only after 1890 did the unions acquire an important role in the development of Social Democracy.

No sooner had the Anti-Socialist Laws been lifted than the unions were confronted with a crisis which pointed up the need to cen-tralize their organizational structure. In Hamburg a demonstration strike on May Day 1890 was answered by the Employers' League for Hamburg-Altona with a lockout embracing numerous branches of industry. The employers demanded that the workers withdraw from their unions as a condition for resuming employment. The Metalworkers' Unions in the leading centers of industry took the initiative in calling a general conference to lay the foundations for a nation-wide organization which could throw the combined weight of all Social Democratic labor into struggles such as that in Ham-burg. This conference set up a national central committee for the Free Trade-Unions. The general commission, as the central com-mittee was called, was charged with gathering statistics concerning the financial and numerical strength of the trade-unions, and with issuing a bulletin on their status and progress. It was to be an agency for the coördination of union activity on a national scale. The trade-unionists who composed it were Social Democrats, though the organization was not erected by the party itself.[22]

The unions which came under the roof of the general commission were of the most varied structure. The strongest were the so-called central leagues (*Zentralverbände*), organized partly on craft, partly on industrial lines. In structure they corresponded roughly to Amer-ican amalgamated unions. The Metalworkers, Woodworkers, Con-struction Workers and Mineworkers were the "big four" but there were also numerous small unions not affiliated with a central league. These "localist" unions reflected the local origins of the trade-union

---

[21] Otto Heilborn, *Die "Freien" Gewerkschaften seit 1890* (Jena, 1907), 2–4; Paul Umbreit, *25 Jahre deutscher Gewerkschaftsbewegung, 1890–1915* (Berlin, 1915), 1–2.

[22] *Ibid.*, 6–16.

movement and the enforced decentralization of the persecution period. Finally, there were the so-called "cartels" at the municipal level, which embraced the local unions of various branches of trade and industry, whether centralist or localist. They corresponded roughly to the American municipal trade-union councils. The cartels were more powerful than their American counterparts in that they generally controlled strike funds and therefore strike policy. When the general commission was established, then, there was a multitude of organizations already at hand, and a welter of organizational principles of a conflicting character.[23]

The same trade-union conference which established the general commission recommended a centralistic form of organization as best suited to modern conditions of production.[24] There ensued a six-year battle between centralists and localists in which the stronger central leagues emerged triumphant. This intra-union strife of the nineties had its political aspect. In the great cities, the local unions, the cartels, and even the branches of the central leagues were largely in radical control. The urban locals resisted the establishment of a paid bureaucracy, an integral part of trade-union growth, as tending to create vested interests which would militate against vigorous prosecution of the class struggle. For the same reason, the radicals opposed the conclusion of labor contracts with employers' associations. In 1896, when the conservative Book Printers' Union concluded a labor contract with an employers' association, the Leipzig cartel expelled the local of the Printers' Union. The fight was carried to the general trade-union congress of 1896, where it was decided in favor of the advocates of labor contracts. The Leipzig cartel was expelled from the national trade-union organization.[25] At the same time the central league representatives who controlled the general congress deprived all the cartels of separate representation at subsequent congresses, and took away their control over strike policy and strike funds.[26] These measures indirectly weakened the remaining localist unions, which had depended in strike actions on the financial strength of the cartels.

[23] Heilborn, Die "Freien" Gewerkschaften, 5-34.
[24] Umbreit, 25 Jahre, 10-11.
[25] Ibid., 54.
[26] Ibid., 56.

In the conflict between centralists and localists, the former rode the wave of the future. The concentration of industry, which was proceeding swiftly in the nineties, made the centralization of labor organization imperative.[27] It was likewise sound strategy to consolidate gains in labor contracts, so that the unions would not be compelled to expend their resources in sudden, unexpected struggles. The radicals combating both these policies in the interest of the revolutionary *élan* of the labor movement, took refuge in the outdated localist form of organization which doomed their cause to failure.

The centralists, while proceeding creatively to construct organizations capable of advancing the workers' interest under the new conditions of industrial organization, began to draw away from the Social Democratic Party. At the trade-union congress of 1892, Carl Legien, the chairman of the general commission and master builder of the centralized organization, enunciated the principle, hotly contested by the localists, that the trade-unions must be neutral in party politics.[28] The trade-unions depended for their success on the organization of the maximum number of workers. That the workers were not yet "ripe" for the reception of socialist ideas should be no bar to their becoming good trade-unionists. A sympathetic party leader described the trade-unionists' position as follows:

We must turn to the most indifferent of the indifferent workers, who are politically still under the spell of our enemies. For this purpose we must be free [of the Social Democratic Party] in our actions. Our enemies must not be able to say to us, 'You trade-unionists only pretend to pursue trade-union objectives, to agitate for the elimination of bad conditions in industry, for the improvement of wages and hours, but at bottom you are nothing but Social Democrats who have put on a trade-union mask . . . You are merely propagandizing for Social Democracy, and you have to do what the Social Democratic Party congress tells you to do' . . . One must know the prejudices of these politically unenlightened and economically inexperienced workers.[29]

[27] Alexander Wende, *Die Konzentrationsbewegung bei den deutschen Gewerkschaften* (Berlin, 1913), 4–42.
[28] Paul Barthel, ed., *Handbuch der deutschen Gewerkschaftskongresse* (Dresden, 1916), 375; Marks, *Reform and Revolution,* 405.
[29] *Protokoll über die Verhandlungen des Parteitages der Sozialdemokratischen Partei Deutschlands, 1906* (Berlin, 1906), 290. Hereafter cited as *Prot. S. P., 1906.*

The trade-unionists, like the southern Social Democrats, were finding the revolutionary character of the party a handicap in recruitment. Their natural tendency was, therefore, to emphasize only the pursuit of the workers' material interest, and to leave the propagation of the socialist gospel to the party.

In the early nineties, the tendency of the trade-unions to draw away from the party occasioned some alarm. It was felt in the party that the general commission was trying to set up a rival organization. At the Köln party congress (1893) this suspicion was voiced openly. Carl Legien defended his unions as "recruiting schools of the party." The trade-union leaders, he said, never thought of their movement as "anything but a palliative within present-day bourgeois society." Legien insisted that there was no danger of the trade-unions' winning the upper hand over the party.[30] At the time such a danger did indeed seem remote. The first trade-union resurgence of 1890–1891 had been halted by depression. Union membership fell from 277,659 in 1890 to 223,530 in 1893.[31] The number of party supporters at the polls — the only index of party strength — rose while trade-union membership declined. Where the ratio of Social Democratic votes to Free Trade Union members in 1890 was approximately six to one, in 1893 it rose to eight to one.[32] The party congress of 1893, feeling that the trade-union movement though useful had little future, allowed the question of competition between the two arms of the labor movement to drop, and adopted a conciliatory resolution urging its members to join the unions.[33] How great was the indifference of even the party theorists to trade-union affairs is shown by the fact that *Neue Zeit*'s semi-annual subject index contained no section on trade-unions until the last half of 1897.[34]

As the depression gave way in 1895 to a half-decade of prosperity, the trade-union movement began a tremendous expansion which continued almost unbroken until 1914. Between 1896 and 1900, the membership doubled and passed the 600,000 mark; by 1904, it had

---

[30] Richard Calwer, *Das Sozialdemokratische Programm* (Jena, 1914), 5.

[31] Umbreit, *25 Jahre*, 176.

[32] Calculated from Hirsch and Borchardt, *Sozialdemokratie und Wahlen*, 24–25; Umbreit, *25 Jahre*, 176.

[33] Adolf Braun, *Die Gewerkschaften, ihre Entwicklung und Kämpfe* (Nürnberg, 1914), 40–41; Marks, *Reform and Revolution*, 406–411.

[34] *Ibid.*, 406.

reached a million. The ratio between Social Democratic voters and trade-union members changed in favor of the latter. Eight to one in 1893, it reached almost four to one in 1898, three to one in 1903. By the time of the elections of 1907, the ratio was about two to one and one quarter; it remained the same in the elections of 1912, where the party had 4,250,000 voters, the trade-unions 2,530,000 members.[35] Trade-union members constituted an ever-increasing proportion of the party's voters.

Figures on the party's membership, which would offer a more secure basis of comparison between party and trade-unions, are not available for the early years. As late as 1898, Carl Legien stated that "the members . . . of the German trade-unions are for the most part members of the Social Democratic Party." [36] We cannot know whether this estimate was correct. By 1906, however, when the party took its first census, it emerged that its membership was 384,327 as against 1,689,709 for the trade-unions. During the recession of 1907–09, the party closed the gap somewhat. But even in 1913 the ratio was two and one-half to one in favor of the trade-unions.[37]

In the years 1895–1906, the trade-unions thus outran the party in securing the active allegiance of the working class. The trade-unions provided what the party could not directly give: a measure of economic security in the here and now. Tangible benefits exerted a more immediate attraction on the working man than the more rarefied ideas of socialism, especially after the end of Bismarck's overt persecution. Thanks to the vigor of capitalist development, and to the skill of the unions in exploiting the possibilities it offered, trade-unionism acquired a momentum and a *raison d'etre* of its own.

In the period of neutrality (1893–1906), the trade-unionists concentrated their energy on what they called "positive work" and "practical little tasks." In so doing they built a veritable state within

---

[35] Calculated from Hirsch and Borchardt, *Sozialdemokratie und Wahlen,* 24–25, and Umbreit, *25 Jahre,* 176.

[36] Barthel, *Gewerkschaftskongresse,* 376.

[37] Cf. *Prot. S. P., 1913,* 10, and Umbreit, *25 Jahre,* 176. For some interesting but fragmentary statistics on the local variations of the ratio of party members to trade-union members and voters in 1903–1905, see Robert Michels, "Die deutsche Sozialdemokratie. Parteimitgliedschaft und Zusammensetzung," *Archiv für Sozialwissenschaft und Sozialpolitik,* XXIII: 476–501 (1906).

a state. At the turn of the century they expanded the range of their social service activities to make the workers' life under capitalism more bearable. In 1899 the Frankfurt trade-union congress dropped its hostility to municipal labor exchanges, and encouraged its officials to enter them on a parity basis with the employers. The congress recommended the establishment of plant grievance committees to cooperate with state factory inspectors. It urged local cartels to establish "labor secretaries" to assist unions and workers in legal matters and in dealings with state insurance officials.[38] In 1903 the labor secretariats were organized on a national scale under the control of the general commission. The Stuttgart congress of 1902 empowered the general commission to organize the election of trade-union representatives to public bodies dealing with matters of social policy. An insurance company for the employees of both party and trade-union was established in the same year.[39] The central leagues rapidly developed their insurance systems to cover not only strike pay, but moving bills, sickness, accidents and unemployment.[40] Thus the Free Trade Unions became great and wealthy organizations, offering services in the field of social security which the state was unwilling to provide. Inevitably, the interest of the unions and their members became more and more closely identified with the existing economic system.

Under the impact of new functions, the character of the union leadership rapidly changed. Robert Michels has well described the contrast between the old and new union official:

The qualities of leadership required by an organization which, still financially weak, is devoted to the spread of ideas and leadership in strikes are of a different sort from those needed by a trade-union richly blessed with insurance establishments and seeking peace treaties [wage contracts]. The former requires enthusiasm and rhetorical ability . . . Even the crassest ignorance is no handicap. The nature of the propaganda is sentimental and romantic, its objective is rather moral than material in nature. All that changes in the later period. The complex of tasks — and the financial and technical [requirements of] the structure which the trade-unions create as they grow out of their idealistic swad-

[38] Umbreit, 25 Jahre, 55–56; Heilborn, Die "Freien" Gewerkschaften, 34–41.
[39] Umbreit, 25 Jahre, 72, 96.
[40] Heilborn, Die "Freien" Gewerkschaften, 66–80.

dling clothes — demand the replacement of the agitator by the schooled official with specialized knowledge. The merchant adventurer who deals in class struggle yields his place to the dry and unimaginative account-ant, the glowing idealist to the luke-warm materialist, the democrat, firm at least in theory, to the conscious autocrat.[41]

The new bureaucracy viewed its successes not, like the party radicals, as part of the process of the organization of the proletariat for revolution, but as triumphs in and for themselves, to be further expanded within the framework of the capitalist order. The old intransigent hostility toward both the entrepreneur and the state yielded to a willingness to compromise differences.

What a change in our judgment of tactical questions [a trade union leader wrote in 1903] has been produced by the continued practical and economic activity of the laboring masses! Who has not lived through the times when trade-union struggles . . . were fought to the death. No concessions! Either triumph or honorable defeat! No negotiations with the entrepreneur, no contact with the bourgeois! That was the old slo-gan and the old tactic. Meanwhile we've gotten away from it. The stead-ily increasing responsibility of the trade-union leaders has forced [them to] a new tactic. One negotiates with the entrepreneur, utilizes the state conciliation apparatus and — oh, horror! — tries to awaken understand-ing in the ministries for the demands of the workers. Not in order to practice lick-splitting, but to advance the workers' cause.[42]

By 1900, the trade-unions had ceased to justify their existence as recruiting stations for the political party. Political neutrality was generally held as an absolute necessity in trade-union circles, both for recruitment of non-socialists and for cooperation with the non-socialist unions. The party theoreticians, Kautsky in the van, assailed the neutrality principle, arguing that the party, as the representative of labor's total interest, must govern all aspects of the labor movement. The issue was not joined at the time (1900), and the neutrality of the union and its equal status with the party won *de facto,* if not *de jure* recognition.[43] Under the so-called "two pillars theory," the unions were to discharge the economic functions

[41] Robert Michels, *Zur Soziologie des Parteiwesens in der modernen Demokratie* (Leipzig, 1910), 288–289.

[42] *Sozialistische Monatshefte,* VII (IX), ii, 573. Hereafter cited as *S.M.*

[43] Marks, *Reform and Revolution,* 412–420.

of the labor movement; the party, the political ones. As long as no basic conflict of interest and tactic existed, the "two pillars theory" and its corollary, trade-union neutrality, were viable. Only when the party showed signs of developing a revolutionary tactic in 1905 would the trade-unionists emerge from their neutrality to reveal themselves as the most aggressive and powerful of the reformist forces.

iv. Bernstein's Revisionism

The conditions under which the vast expansion of Social Democracy and the trade-unions took place gave rise to doubts as to the validity of the social theory to which the party had committed itself at Erfurt. Social Democracy was expanding not in an atmosphere of increasing misery and unemployment, but in one of unprecedented prosperity. During the late nineties, gross real wages increased as industrial concentration proceeded.[44] Where the Erfurt program had prophesied an "ever more bitter class struggle between bourgeoisie and proletariat," a large sector of the bourgeoisie was swept up in what Werner Sombart called the "socialist epidemic" of the nineties, characterized by sympathy for the working class and interventionist economics.[45] Such was the atmosphere in which Bernstein introduced his "revision" of Marxist theory.

Eduard Bernstein (1850–1932), a man of unimpeachable intellectual integrity, had the particular kind of fortitude appropriate to his role: the courage of a conscientious objector in a militant society. Falling under the influence of the English Fabians during his years of exile in London, this cautious, self-made scholar came to the conclusion that the orthodox Marxism to which he had adhered was no longer adequate to the facts of contemporary history. During the 1890's he subjected Marxist theory to a series of criticisms out of which his own "revisionist" theory emerged.[46]

Bernstein provided a new conceptual scheme in which contem-

[44] Jürgen Kuczynski, A Short History of Labour Conditions under Industrial Capitalism, III, i, "Germany, 1800 to the Present Day" (London, 1945), 117, 129–130.
[45] Rikli, Revisionismus, 10–11.
[46] For Bernstein's intellectual development, see the excellent work of Peter Gay, The Dilemma of Democratic Socialism. Eduard Bernstein's Challenge to Marx (New York, 1952), passim.

porary development might be comprehended by socialists. Its tactical implications at the time of the great revisionist controversy (1898–1903) were minor, for all Social Democrats were agreed on the absence of any immediate revolutionary possibilities. Its long-run implications, at once grasped by friend and foe, were major: to deny that revolution would occur, and to enlist the power of the party to forestall it. In offering an alternative to the Marxian system, a second social philosophy through which the party members and leaders could evaluate their position and determine their role in history, Bernstein made a major contribution to the development of the schism.

Bernstein launched his attack against the most fundamental of Marx's propositions concerning capitalist development: that the incompatibility of the system of production and the forms of exchange produced growing anarchy in the capitalist economy. Where Marx saw growing anarchy Bernstein saw growing order. Extrapolating from the absence of any world economic crisis for the two decades since 1873, Bernstein advanced the theory that capitalism had developed a capacity for adjustment which would rule out major economic crises in the future. New credit mechanisms, rational market controls through cartels, and intensive exploitation of the world market were the principal factors making for a more or less indefinite expansion of the capitalist economy.[47] At the same time, Bernstein observed a trend toward the more equitable distribution of wealth.[48]

Having substituted an optimistic for a "breakdown" theory of capitalist development, Bernstein was impelled to draw the philosophic consequence; namely, the renunciation of dialectical materialism. Believing Marx's "abstractions" to be disproved by subsequent economic development, he could no longer regard socialism as resulting of necessity from capitalist development. Socialism could only come about as the result of a free, rational decision. As the "elemental sway of economic forces" was weakened by the progress of capitalism, individuals and whole nations would free themselves

[47] Eduard Bernstein, *Die Voraussetzungen des Sozialismus und die Aufgaben der Sozialdemokratie* (Stuttgart, 1906), 66–81.
[48] *Ibid.*, 46–66.

from "the influence of necessity compelling them without or against their will." Ideological and ethical factors would acquire "greater scope for independent activity than was formerly the case." [49]

To achieve a socialist society, Bernstein and the revisionists thus relied primarily upon the developing ethical sense of man.[50] The ethical sense was not, however, forced to the fore dialectically by conflicting interests, as with Hegel and Marx, but liberated by material progress to take flight out of its own inherent energies. The revisionists shifted the basis of the drive toward socialism from objective interest to subjective ideal. In so doing, they substituted Kant for Hegel as their philosophical guide.[51]

Since, in Bernstein's theory, reason and the ethical sense acquired greater freedom and power as the economic process eliminated conflicts of social interest, the exclusive role of the proletariat in "leading man from the kingdom of necessity to the kingdom of freedom" [52] was destroyed. Idealism and the sense of justice could flourish in all classes as "the common interest gains in power to an increasing extent as opposed to private interest." [53]

Thus socialism, seen by Marx as fostered by a negative proletarian reaction to capitalist development, was viewed by Bernstein as its idealistic offshoot. Progress toward socialism was brought into a positive dependency on capitalist prosperity. The enemy of the working class was then not capitalism itself, not the capitalist state, but the small group of private interests which stubbornly refused to see the light of reason and social justice. The institutional weapon to break the power of this little band of willful men was political democracy, through which men of good will of all classes could arrange the social order in the majority interest.

In this conceptual framework, revolution was unnecessary. It was also impossible — impossible because a revolution could neither do without capitalism "nor assure that certainty" which capitalism requires to operate effectively. The revolution "would ruin itself

[49] *Ibid.,* 10–11.
[50] Cf. Rikli, *Revisionismus,* 38–43.
[51] Cf. Karl Vorländer, *Kant und Marx* (2nd revised edition, Tübingen, 1926), 154–212.
[52] Friedrich Engels, *Socialism Utopian and Scientific,* trans. Edward Aveling (New York, 1935), 73.
[53] Bernstein, *Voraussetzungen,* 10.

on this contradiction beyond all salvation." [54] Having set out to
liberate the free will of man from the economic determinism of
Marx — "Calvinism without God," as he called it[55] — Bernstein
reintroduced one fundamental limitation on free will: a dependence
of the proletariat upon the capitalist economy so complete as to
preclude any major action to upset it.

The very teleology of Marxism now fell to the ground:

> Unable to believe in finalities at all, I cannot believe in a final aim of
> socialism. But I strongly believe in the socialist movement, in the march
> forward of the working classes, who step by step must work out their
> emancipation by changing society from the domain of a commercial,
> landholding oligarchy to a real democracy which in all its departments
> is guided by the interests of those who work and create.[56]

Bernstein urged the Social Democratic Party to direct all its attention toward its proximate aims: the acquisition of responsible parliamentary government, the development of the Free Trade Unions
and the coöperatives, and the enlargement of "municipal socialism." [57] In the pursuit of these aims, Bernstein promised Social
Democracy the support of a large sector of the bourgeoisie — but
to win that support the party "must find the courage to emancipate
itself from a revolutionary phraseology which is in fact out of date,
and be willing to appear as what it really is: a democratic-socialist
party of reform." [58] Thus Bernstein's revisionism provided an
alternative theoretical base for the reformism enshrined in the
Erfurt program. Thereafter the two terms, "revisionism" and "reformism," though not strictly synonymous, tended to be inter-
changeable in the language of the party.

"The first sensational piece of writing produced in the literature
of German Social Democracy," said Karl Kautsky of Bernstein's
Die Voraussetzungen des Sozialismus.[59] And rightly so: its author
had overthrown every tenet of the Marxist philosophy. He had

[54] Eduard Bernstein, quoted in Rikli, *Revisionismus,* 103, n. 3.

[55] Bernstein, *Voraussetzungen,* 4.

[56] *Idem, Evolutionary Socialism,* trans. Edith Harvey (New York, 1909), author's
preface to English edition, xxii–xxiii.

[57] *Idem, Voraussetzungen,* 140–167.

[58] *Ibid.,* 165.

[59] Karl Kautsky, *Bernstein und das sozialdemokratische Programm. Eine Antikritik* (Stuttgart, 1899), 1.

replaced a capitalism proceeding through contradiction to its own destruction with a capitalism moving through prosperity to a higher form of social organization. He had supplanted dialectic materialism with progressive idealism. He had destroyed both the necessity and the possibility of revolution, and had raised political and social reform from the level of means to the level of ends. Bernstein's optimistic philosophy of social development at once reflected and justified the feelings of security and accomplishment which had begun to prevail in the labor movement in the late nineties. In revisionism, the growing reformist forces acquired theoretical expression.[60]

The orthodox Marxists — or "radicals," as they came to be called — labored under real difficulties in defending their creed against Bernstein's attack. They themselves recognized the non-revolutionary character of the period, and accepted the necessity of a reformist tactic. They had now to establish some clearer relationship between that tactic and the party's revolutionary principles than was vouchsafed in the Erfurt program. In an optimistic era, the burden of proof that prosperity could not last fell upon the radicals.

In a comprehensive critique of Bernstein's economics, Karl Kautsky tried to demonstrate that the contradictory tendencies in capitalism, far from disappearing, were in fact sharpening. He restated the theory of "immiseration (*Verelendung*)," impossible to maintain on an absolute basis, to show that the proletariat as a whole was receiving a smaller share of its gross product than was formerly the case.[61] He rehabilitated the theory of crisis and surplus value, refuting Bernstein's idea of mounting equity in the distribution of wealth.[62] Kautsky made the implications of his counterattack in the warfare of statistics no less plain than had Bernstein. He wished the party to reckon "with crisis as with prosperity, with reaction as with revolution, with catastrophes as with slow peaceful development."[63] His objective was to keep the party "armed for every eventuality," to maintain a flexible tactic.[64]

[60] Cf. Gay, *Dilemma*, 256–258.
[61] Kautsky, *Bernstein*, 114–128.
[62] *Ibid.*, 42–104.
[63] *Ibid.*, 166.
[64] Cf. Paul Sweezy, *The Theory of Capitalist Development* (New York, 1942), 194–195.

The task of clarifying the relationship between the reformist tactic and the revolutionary goal of the party fell to a newcomer to German Social Democracy: Rosa Luxemburg (1871–1919). This extraordinary young woman was destined to play a leading role in the revitalization of the revolutionary tradition in Social Democracy. She combined one of the most penetrating analytical minds of her age with an imaginative warmth which make her writings unique in Marxist literature. A passionate fighter for her ideas, Luxemburg used only the sharp rapier of her wit in intellectual combat, never the bludgeon of character-defamation so favored by Marx and Lenin. Her revolutionary attitude expressed itself not merely in the cold hatred of injustice and oppression so common to revolutionary leaders but in a genuine love of humanity in the concrete as well as in the abstract. In a little note which she once wrote to herself, she revealed her almost sentimental revolutionary ethic:

Determined revolutionary activity coupled with a deep feeling for humanity, that alone is the essence of socialism. A world must be overturned, but every tear that flows and might have been stanched is an accusation. . . .[65]

From her Polish homeland, Luxemburg carried into German Social Democracy a passionate and activistic revolutionary spirit not common to Germany during the nineties. When the German revolutionary movement began to get under way in the new century, Luxemburg was in the van, giving it theoretical structure and tactical leadership, and spurring it on with her eloquence.[66]

In the Bernstein debate, Luxemburg devoted herself to the problem of interpreting the reformist tactic in the light of the party's revolutionary goal.[67] The function of trade-union and parliamentary activity, she said, was to prepare the subjective factor of the socialist revolution, that is, the proletariat itself. Reformist activities would perform this revolutionary function not through their successes,

[65] Paul Frölich, *Rosa Luxemburg,* trans. Edward Fitzgerald (London, 1940), 216–217.
[66] The best published biographies, both partisan, are: Frölich, *Luxemburg,* and Henriette Roland-Holst, *Rosa Luxemburg. Ihr Leben und Wirken* (Zürich, 1937).
[67] Rosa Luxemburg, *Sozialreform oder Revolution* (1900), reprinted in *idem, Werke,* III, 35–100.

but through their failures. Because the very nature of capitalist society would make impossible any fundamental alteration in the social position of the proletariat by reformist means, the necessity for the seizure of political power would be borne in upon the proletariat.[68] Where Bernstein had maintained that the trade-unions were extracting increased wages from the profits of the entrepreneurs, and thus enlarging the workers' share in the social product, Luxemburg argued that the functions of the unions were purely defensive. The increase in the labor force, resulting from the proletarization of the middle classes and the increase of the workers' productivity were two fundamental tendencies in capitalism which would always operate to reduce the workers' share in the gross social product. The unions could do no more than exploit the labor market within its natural limits, in order to counteract the depressive tendencies inherent in capitalism. Luxemburg called their work a "labor of Sisyphus" — a phrase which the trade-unionists could neither forget nor forgive.[69] She argued that the question "Reform *or* revolution?" was meaningless.[70] The pursuit of reforms could lead only to a revolutionary end, and should be carried on with that objective in mind.

Luxemburg's arguments did not extricate the radicals from their difficulty. They were forced by historical circumstances to agree with the revisionists on basic tactic. The distinction between the contenders remained largely a subjective one, a difference of ideas in the evaluation of reality, rather than a difference in the realm of action. Bernstein's rosy view of current economic trends was more in tune with the times than Luxemburg's black one. Fundamentally, Luxemburg demanded the maintenance of an attitude of frustration in the face of concrete achievements and material progress. This sense of frustration could be engendered only by establishing a radiant ideal of future social perfection against which the iniquities of the present social order could be measured, and in terms of which the small advances in material comfort would seem as nought.

[68] *Ibid.*, III, 61–62.
[69] *Ibid.*, III, 77–78.
[70] *Ibid.*, III, 35–36.

The paradox of Social Democracy at the turn of the century was that its materialistic philosophy had to be sustained largely by an idealistic attitude, while the new idealistic heresy battened on labor's material gains. The orthodox Marxists saw as their chief function the infusion of the *"sozialistischer Geist"* into the proletariat and the labor movement.[71] Until the opportunity for a radical tactic should present itself in 1905, the champions of orthodoxy had to rely on propagandistic and educational methods alone to stem the rising reformist tide.

Despite their handicaps, the radicals succeeded in preventing the recognition of Bernstein's doctrine by the party. They were favored by party tradition and by the social and political disabilities which, despite prosperity, the working class of Germany had to endure. In 1899 the party congress reaffirmed the Erfurt statement of principles and the idea of class struggle, and rejected "any attempt . . . to alter or obscure . . . the party's antagonistic attitude toward the existing state and social order and toward the bourgeois parties." [72] But neither this resolution nor a subsequent one against Bernstein in 1901[73] checked the spread of revisionist ideas. The party valued its numbers and its unity too highly to expel the minority. For the most part it was after all only a battle of ideas.

With the great electoral success of 1903, when the Social Democrats won eighty-one seats in the Reichstag, the controversy entered a broader, tactical phase. The reformists argued that the party had won its victory not as a mere proletarian party but as a representative of the liberal sector of the middle class as well. Social Democratic policy, they said, should be adjusted accordingly. The revisionist theorists, with Bernstein taking the lead, recommended that the Social Democratic deputies coöperate more fully with the Liberal parties in the Reichstag in work for practical reforms. As a first step they urged that the party accept a position in the Reichstag praesidium, even though this meant "going to court," that is, paying an official visit to the Kaiser, which was against Social

---

[71] Cf., e.g., *Prot. S. P., 1905*, 325; *1906*, 249.
[72] Luxemburg, *Werke*, III, 19–20.
[73] *Ibid.*, III, 20.

Democratic tradition.[74] Reinvigorated by two years of economic recession and by the electoral triumph, the left threw back the revisionist offensive at the Dresden congress. The famous Dresden resolution, which issued from the bitter debate of 1903, was the broadest condemnation of revisionism ever promulgated by the party. It denounced "revisionist efforts . . . to supplant the policy of a conquest of power by overcoming our enemies with a policy of accommodation to the existing order." It reasserted the idea that class antagonisms were increasing, and rejected in principle any participation by Social Democracy in bourgeois government.[75]

The left enjoyed the full support of the party leadership at Dresden. Party Chairman Bebel used all his influence to line up delegates in support of the grand condemnation before the congress convened.[76] The issue which held the executive and the radicals together was the defense of traditional principles and practice. Little more than two years later, when the leftists began to move in earnest toward radical action, they would find the party executive on the other side.

v. Party Discipline and Revisionist Federalism

In the long struggle against revisionism and the southerners' crime of approving state budgets, the radicals became firmly wedded to the idea of party discipline and a strong central authority. In order to preserve the possibility of dissent, the revisionists became the natural defenders of intra-party democracy and a loose form of organization. This relationship between political ideology and institutional forms was to have grave consequences for the later history of the party.

In their effort to withdraw from majority control, the revisionist parliamentary delegates put forward the idea of responsibility to their local constituency rather than to the party. The Social Democratic voters were, of course, less organized than the party mem-

[74] Cf. Eduard Bernstein, "Was folgt aus dem Ergebnis der Reichstagswahlen?" *S.M.*, VII (IX), ii, 478–486; *idem*, "Der neue Reichstag und die Aufgaben der Sozialdemokratie," *ibid.*, 641–649; Wolfgang Heine, "Der 16. Juni," *ibid.*, 475–478; Johannes Timm, "Sozialdemokratie, Politik und Wissenschaft," *ibid.*, 572–577.

[75] Schröder, *Handbuch,* I, 503–504.

[76] Wilhelm Keil, *Erlebnisse eines Sozialdemokraten* (Stuttgart, 1947), I, 247ff.

bers, and more indifferent to the principles of socialism.[77] The revisionists emphasized the incompatibility of broad popular support
with the maintenance of strict party discipline. They argued that the
party should limit its insistence on unity to those aspects of party
life where unity was called for, that is, to electoral activity and social
policy. Here all the wings of the party could work fruitfully together, as the 1903 elections had shown. But to achieve this fruitful
collaboration "there must be no unbrotherly compulsion which kills
the joy in our cause." A party of three million could not be
narrow-minded, said the revisionists; it must recognize variety in
principles while maintaining unity in action.[78]

Where in North Germany the revisionists could defend themselves only by democratic theory, the stronger revisionists of the
South sought to safeguard their position by establishing an intermediate authority at the *Land* (state) level, to serve as a buffer
between the central executive and the locals. Where the dominant
majority pressed for centralization, the minority espoused federalism. By 1903, Hessen, Baden, Württemberg and Bavaria had *Land*
executives. A *Land* party congress of Baden in 1903 discussed the
appointment of a permanent paid secretary for its organization.[79]
The *Land* executive committee in Baden already controlled the
policy of the party press which, in most Social Democratic organizations, was controlled by locally elected press commissions. Control over the local organizations, however, was still imperfect. In
1904, the Baden party congress discussed a new organization statute
which would oblige all Social Democratic locals to affiliate with the
Land organization and to pay regular dues.[80] In Hessen, too, the
construction of a *Land* organization was going forward in the first
years of the century.[81]

The national leadership was not entirely happy over these developments. When the party was to be given a new statute in

[77] Michels, *Zur Soziologie*, 189. Cf. also R. Blank, "Die soziale Zusammensetzung
der socialdemokratischen Wählerschaft Deutschlands," *Archiv für Sozialwissenschaft
und Sozialpolitik*, XX: ii, 507–550 (1905).
[78] *S.M.*, VII (IX), ii, 477–478.
[79] *S.M.*, VII (IX), i, 301.
[80] *Ibid.*, VIII (X), i, 327.
[81] *Ibid.*, IX (XI), ii, 906.

1905, the executive's draft proposals envisaged a minimum of financial autonomy for the *Land* organization. Regional organizations were to be recognized, but rather as arms of the central authority than as federal units with broad powers.[82]

To these proposals, the southerners opposed their doctrine of states' rights. They argued against the "unhealthy omnipotence of the executive committee, which is not consonant with the democratic sentiment of the party comrades."[83] Hugo Lindemann of Württemberg, one of the leading southern politicians, objected that the new statute would give the central executive the same position in the party which the bureaucracy had in the state, that Social Democracy was in danger of imitating the autocratic state which it opposed.[84] Lindemann exalted the federal states of South Germany as "cases of political progress," the value of which Social Democracy did not appreciate. The party should give up its attacks on particularism, and turn to the real danger: "Borussification." In order to strengthen the *Länder* against Prussian influence, the party should devote more attention to *Land* affairs; to do so, Lindemann urged, it must build up the state organizations and jettison its centralistic outlook.[85] The party did not abandon its centralism, but it left the *Land* organizations enough autonomy so that some years later, when the national executive and the radicals had parted company, the southern bastions of reformism could throw their weight into the scales against the left opposition.[86]

That the reformists had to defend themselves by means of federal institutions was a sign of their weakness within the party. Radicalism was still in the ascendant, and celebrated its greatest triumph at the Dresden congress of 1903. But the nineties had brought the forces of reform much strength. They had established themselves firmly in the South where they had violated the party's canons of parliamentary behavior with impunity. The trade-unions, borne aloft by the great economic expansion, had marshaled thousands of workers in the pursuit of purely reformist aims. With-

---

[82] *Prot. S. P., 1905,* 19–20. See below, Ch. V, n. 17 and text.

[83] Julius Bruhns, "Zur Neuorganisation der Partei," *S.M.,* IX (XI), ii, 482.

[84] Hugo Lindemann, "Zentralismus und Föderalismus in der Sozialdemokratie," *S.M.,* IX (XI), ii, 767.

[85] *Ibid.,* 769–770.

[86] See below, Ch. VIII, sec. iv–v.

drawing from the party under the mantle of neutrality, the unions developed into an independent center of power. In revisionism, the reformists acquired a doctrine suited to their needs. The radicals, powerless to pursue a revolutionary tactic, were largely confined to evangelical activity. Only at the level of ideas could the issue between radicals and revisionists be fully joined, and here the radicals successfully maintained the principles of Erfurt.

Chapter II

THE IMPACT OF THE RUSSIAN REVOLUTION OF 1905

The year 1905 was a turning point in European history. In the Morocco crisis of that year, the fluidity in diplomatic alignments which had accompanied the overseas expansion of the nineties came to an end. Germany found herself unexpectedly confronted by a phalanx of powers determined to block her further expansion. At the same time, the relationship of Russia to Western European political life was altered by her defeat at the hands of Japan. Almost overnight the ideological significance of Russia for Europe was transformed. The bastion of nineteenth-century reaction became the vanguard of twentieth-century revolution.

Repercussions of the Russian Revolution were felt throughout the European labor movement, but above all in Germany, where indigenous sources of class antagonism were strengthened by the Russian example. Labor conflict of unprecedented scope dominated the economic scene in 1905–06. In politics there began a mass movement to democratize the discriminatory suffrage systems in the federal states, a movement which was to harry the Imperial Government periodically from 1905 until its collapse.

These developments had a profound effect on German Social Democracy. With the Russian Revolution, the issue of revolution versus reform acquired a new concreteness. During the nineties, the reformists had developed their attack upon the Erfurt synthesis; in 1905 it was the orthodox Marxists who challenged the party's traditional tactic, who pushed forward to radicalize the labor movement and to prepare it for eventual revolutionary action through a new weapon, the political mass strike. Under this radical pressure, labor's conservative elements revealed for the first time their real power. Disputations over theory gave place to a struggle over party tactic. Trade-unions and party confronted each other in a conflict which could only be won, not compromised. This con-

flict, its background, course and outcome, will be our concern in
the present chapter.

i. The Intensification of Labor's Economic Struggles

Just as the international alignment which confronted Germany
in the Morocco crisis gradually took shape in the previous years,
so too capital and labor grouped and developed their forces during
the decade which preceded the greatly intensified labor struggles
of 1905 and 1906.

Thanks to their nation-wide organization, the unions had the
initial edge in the techniques of economic struggle. During the
boom years, 1895–1900, they developed a technique of labor struggle
known as *"Einzelabschlachtung"* — literally, "knocking them off
singly." The organized workers did not tackle an industry on a
broad front but plant by plant. While the workers of one plant
were on strike, their fellow-workers in other plants of the same
industry would continue work and provide funds for the strikers.
When the first establishment was conquered, the same procedure
was applied to the next, until the whole industry had granted the
union's demands.[1] The single employers, especially the financially
weaker ones, were more or less powerless against this strategy. They
could discharge the individual organizers, the agitators; they could,
if their resources permitted, import strike-breakers; but such measures only made the labor force more sympathetic to unionism. It
soon became apparent that organized labor could be fought only
by an organization of employers which corresponded in scale and
financial resources to the unions. The technique of *Einzelabschlachtung* would have to be broken by engaging the unions on a broad
front. To meet this need the German employers' associations were
formed. Few in number before the end of the nineties, these mutual
aid associations to combat strikes and unions sprang up rapidly
at the turn of the century. In 1898, nineteen were established; in
1899, forty-five; in 1900, fifty.[2] There followed a lull in the recession
years of 1900–1902, which gave place to a final process of concentration and proliferation of branches in the boom years 1903–1906.

---

[1] *S.M.*, XI (XIII), i, 424.
[2] Gerhard Kessler, *Die deutschen Arbeitgeberverbände*, Schriften des Vereins für
Sozialpolitik, CXXIV (Leipzig, 1907), 37.

In their formative years, the employers' associations experimented with many techniques of labor warfare.[3] Failing to halt the spread of unionism as such, their main efforts were devoted to breaking the unions' power through exhaustion of their treasuries. For this purpose, the most effective weapon developed by the associations was the mass lockout. The first great experiment in lockout technique was conducted in the Crimmitschau-Zwickau textile industry where over 7000 textile workers were shut out for five months in the fall and winter of 1903–04. The Central League of German Industrialists started a nationwide campaign of support for the Crimmitschau employers. Entrepreneurs in industries ranging from steel to shoes pledged one-half to one mark for every worker in his employ, and further promised a weekly contribution of two per cent of their payrolls until the Crimmitschau lockout was concluded. Gigantic sums were thus collected. The unions took fright at the power arrayed against them; before their funds should be exhausted in a hopeless struggle, they capitulated.[4]

As the Hamburg May Day lockout of 1890 had been the occasion for the consolidation of the Free Trade Unions on a national scale, so the Crimmitschau strike in 1903 brought together the employers into two great organizations: the *Hauptstelle deutscher Arbeitgeberverbände* and the *Verein deutscher Arbeitgeberverbände,* the first for heavy industry and textiles, the second for light industry. These performed for the member leagues the same functions of statistical research and overall coördination that the general commission provided for the central leagues of the Free Trade Unions. In December 1904, they agreed on mutual aid in actual labor struggles.[5] At the end of 1905 the two groups embraced the employers of roughly 1,500,000 workers. The membership of all unions at the close of 1905 was 1,822,343, of which 1,344,803 were in the Social Democratic unions.[6] Thus unionization had produced its counterpart — a powerful enemy, armed with equal or superior weapons.

[3] These are fully described in *ibid.,* 139–307.
[4] *Ibid.,* 47–48.
[5] *Ibid.,* 45, 48–52.
[6] *Ibid.,* 56–57; Internationaler Sekretär der gewerkschaftlichen Landeszentralen, *Internationaler Bericht über die Gewerkschaftsbewegung, 1905* (Berlin, 1907), 78. Hereafter cited as Internationaler Sekretär, *Bericht, 1905.*

Labor conflict under these circumstances became more widespread and more bitter, reaching an unheard-of breadth and intensity in 1905. From 1890 to 1899, the total number of workers engaged in strikes or lockouts was 425,142. From 1900 to 1904, the number rose to 477,516, thus exceeding in five years the number engaged in the previous ten. In 1905 alone, 507,964 workers were engaged in work stoppages,[7] more than the total for all of the nineties, more than the total for the previous five years, or for that of any other year between 1848 and 1917.

Half a million workers! This is not a mere statistic. It is a psychological fact of the first importance. More than one-third of the workers led by the Free Trade Unions participated directly in open labor warfare during 1905, and felt its consequences in their daily lives and households. In strikes and lockouts 7,362,802 man-days were lost.[8] No less than 66 per cent of the membership participated in wage movements, peaceful or with work stoppages; in this respect too, 1905 was a record year.[9] This was an atmosphere in which political radicalism could easily spread.

In the face of a rapidly rising cost of living, labor had to win increased wages to hold its own. The cost of food rose almost five per cent from 1904 to 1905, that of rent, three per cent. In 1906, food costs and rent rose again at about the same rate, so that the wage movements of that year were only slightly smaller than those of 1905.[10] Rising living costs and a contracted labor market produced new aggressiveness in the unions.

The entrepreneurs, fortified in their employers' associations, were fully prepared to resist labor's onslaught and, indeed, to take the offensive to reduce wages and lengthen hours. Thirty-four per cent of the workers who participated in work stoppages did so because the employer had taken the initiative, either through lockouts or the provocation of a defensive strike. It was clearly the larger enterprises that were the most aggressive: the average number of workers per struck enterprise, where the workers took the initiative, was

---

[7] *Ibid.*, 73.

[8] *Ibid.*, 76.

[9] Calculated from *ibid.*, *1912*, 108, 124, 126.

[10] Jürgen Kuczynski, *A Short History of Labour Conditions under Capitalism*, III, Part i, "Germany, 1800 to the Present Day" (London, 1945), 202.

264; per locked-out enterprise, it was twice that figure: 532.[11]

The employers' offensive was, of course, extremely costly, and, whatever its local successes, failed either to break the unions as a whole or to stem their growth. Membership of the Free Trade Unions increased from 1,052,108 in 1904 to 1,344,803; union income, from M. 20 to 27 million.[12] At the same time, 1905 was an exceedingly costly year for the unions. They spent in that single year 29 per cent of the total amount expended on strikes in the sixteen-year history of the Free Trade Unions.[13] The experience of labor warfare in 1905 tended to imbue the union leaders with even greater concern than before for their treasuries and organizational integrity. It confirmed and strengthened their cautiousness and political conservatism.

The same socio-economic situation which made the union leaders conservative had the opposite effect on the rank and file. The rising cost of living, the intense and widely shared experience of strike and lockout, and the unprecedented aggressiveness of the employers generated in the workers a new militancy and a receptiveness to radical political ideas. In this tense social situation, German Social Democracy received and reacted to the challenging tidings of the revolution in Russia.

ii. Restlessness in the Radical Camp

While the lines drew tighter on labor's economic front in the years 1903–1904, a mounting impatience with the pure parliamentary tactic appeared in the party. True, the "objective situation," so deeply respected by the orthodox Marxists, still offered no opportunity for radical action. But the interminable defensive battles against revisionism were no longer enough to engage the energies of the party radicals. Even Rosa Luxemburg, who played such a prominent part in the revisionist controversy, found the "pursuit of particular opportunistic boners" no longer satisfying.

I . . . marvel [she wrote to a friend] at the certainty with which some of our radical friends maintain that it is only necessary to lead the erring sheep — the party — back to the homely stall of 'steadfastness of princi-

---

[11] Calculations based on statistics in Internationaler Sekretär, *Bericht, 1905,* 72–75.
[12] *Ibid.,* 66.
[13] *Ibid.,* 68.

ple.' . . . They don't perceive that in this purely negative manner we move no step forward. For a revolutionary movement not to go forward means to go backward. The only means to combat opportunism radically is to move forward ourselves, to develop the tactic, to intensify the revolutionary aspect of the movement. Opportunism is in any case a swamp plant, which develops rapidly and luxuriously in the stagnant waters of the movement; in a swift running stream it will die of itself. Here in Germany a forward motion is an urgent, burning need! And only the fewest realize it. Some fritter away their energy in petty disputes with the opportunists, others believe that the automatic, mechanical increase in numbers (at elections and in the organizations) is progress in itself! [14]

Where was the "forward motion" to come from? How could the tactic be developed? It was while such questions were being posed in Germany that the general strike (the Germans called it the "political mass strike") began to be used elsewhere in Western Europe. In 1902, the Belgian working class launched a general strike in an effort to win equal suffrage. In 1903, the Dutch labor movement utilized the same weapon to combat an anti-strike law, while the Swedish Social Democrats initiated a great demonstration strike in order to force a general suffrage bill through the Riksdag.[15]

In German Social Democratic circles, the general strike suffered from the hereditary taint of its anarchist origins. The Germans had repeatedly rejected it at the congresses of the International as an anti-parliamentarian, syndicalist substitute for political action. Now the Socialist parties of other European countries were using the general strike as a supplement to and in reinforcement of parliamentary action for the attainment of specific political objectives. German Marxist theorists began to see the general strike in a new light.

Rosa Luxemburg, who studied the Belgian strike, was particularly impressed with its success in activating the political consciousness of the backward portions of the population. She was not yet, however, prepared to give it European-wide significance. Luxem-

---

[14] Letter to Roland-Holst, 17 Dec. 1904, in Henriette Roland-Holst, *Rosa Luxemburg. Ihr Leben und Wirken* (Zürich, 1937), 215–216.

[15] Henriette Roland-Holst, *Generalstreik und Sozialdemokratie* (Dresden, 1906), 53–69; Elsbeth Georgi, "Theorie und Praxis des Generalstreiks in der modernen Arbeiterbewegung" (Diss. Zürich, 1908), 41–55, 90–95.

burg felt it to be appropriate only in countries in which industry was geographically concentrated. For Germany, with its widely separated industrial regions and its enormous labor force, the mass strike would be a most difficult undertaking.[16] In October 1903, Rudolf Hilferding, a young Austrian on the editorial board of *Neue Zeit,* published an article designed to stimulate a discussion on the general strike.[17] Basking in the sun of the Socialists' electoral victory of 1903, Hilferding argued that the colossal increases in labor strength at every election would sooner or later impel the ruling classes to abolish or restrict universal suffrage lest it lead to the introduction of socialism by a Social Democratic-controlled parliament. In order to fend off such a catastrophe, the working class must prepare to use its economic power: "Behind universal suffrage must stand the will to the general strike." [18] Hilferding commended the general strike not as a weapon of "latin . . . pseudo-revolutionary putsches" but as "a means to . . . protect the forward march of the proletariat from forcible disturbances." [19] He was, in effect, absorbing the general strike into the parliamentary tactic of the Erfurt program. Even at the opposite end of the party's spectrum, Eduard Bernstein advocated consideration of the mass strike to defend or acquire universal, equal suffrage.[20]

Hostile critics could point out that, when the proletariat would not even come out to cast its votes in the Prussian Landtag elections, it was unlikely to jeopardize its daily bread for the sake of the suffrage,[21] but this did not put an end to the discussion. Nevertheless, the general consensus among the party pundits was that the mass strike would provoke the ruling class into the use of force, and that it was therefore a weapon of last resort. Behind it, as Hilferding had said, must stand "the will to the decisive battle." [22]

Meanwhile, from two other quarters the idea of the mass strike

[16] Luxemburg, *Werke,* III, 356–357.

[17] *Neue Zeit,* XXII, i, 134, n. 1. Hereafter cited as *N.Z.*

[18] *Ibid.,* 137–141.

[19] *Ibid.,* 141.

[20] Georgi, *Theorie und Praxis,* 61; Peter Gay, *The Dilemma of Democratic Socialism* (New York, 1952), 234–235.

[21] *N.Z.,* XXII, i, 446.

[22] *Ibid.,* XXIII, i, 142; cf. also articles by Eckstein, *ibid.,* 357–363; and Kautsky, *ibid.,* 685–695, 732–740.

received impetus. It appeared on the agenda of the Amsterdam congress of the International (August 1904). The congress rejected the position of the syndicalist-inclined Allemanists of France, that the general strike was "the most effective means to achieve the triumph of labor," and warned the socialist world against being "taken in by the anarchists." Yet the congress recognized that "a strike which spreads over a few economically important trades, or over a large number of branches of a trade, may be a means of bringing about important social changes, or of opposing reactionary designs on the rights of workers." [23] The Amsterdam resolution represented a considerable change in attitude on the part of the Second International, which in all previous congresses had declared, under German leadership, that the general strike was "indiscussible." [24]

At the same time (1903–1904), the gospel of the general strike in the syndicalist sense began to be preached in Germany itself. The chief apostle of the new faith was Dr. Raphael Friedeberg, the intellectual leader of the localist trade-unions. All the resentment of the localists against the central trade unions and the party's pure parliamentary tactic found expression in Friedeberg's "anarcho-socialism." Friedeberg saw in the general strike the key to the regeneration of the labor movement. It would liberate the worker's "free personality" from the crushing effect of the dull routine involved in the reformist tactic. Through the strike the worker could again win an active role in determining the destiny of his class.[25]

Friedeberg carried his battle for the general strike to the party congresses. In 1903, his proposal was thoroughly defeated. In 1904, however, some of the most prominent party intellectuals — Eduard Bernstein, Karl Liebknecht, Klara Zetkin — supported Friedeberg to the extent of urging the party executive to place the mass strike on the agenda of the 1905 congress.[26]

If the mass strike held little attraction for the party as a whole,

[23] Daniel De Leon, *Flashlights of the Amsterdam Congress* (new edition, New York, 1929), 155–156, 158–159.

[24] *N.Z.*, XXIII, ii, 17.

[25] Paul Umbreit, *25 Jahre deutscher Gewerkschaftsbewegung, 1890–1915* (Berlin, 1915), 73–74; *N.Z.*, XXIII, i, 7–8; Georgi, *Theorie und Praxis*, 62–63.

[26] Karl Kautsky, *Der politische Massenstreik* (Berlin, 1914), 108–109; Georgi, *Theorie und Praxis*, 63–64.

its application as a political weapon in other Western countries in 1903 and 1904 had made an impression on the party's intellectuals, particularly on those who were restless after the long years of pure reformist activity. Kautsky, who agreed with the opponents of the mass strike that "the whole character of our system of government" made an uncritical adoption of western methods undesirable, nevertheless urged that the study of the mass strike be carried forward. In October 1904, he observed "a general feeling in the party that great political changes are in the making; they can come sooner than we suspect, and they can confront us with new situations which we never anticipated. The proletariat would be well-advised to test in time all the weapons which are at its disposal." [27]

Three months later the party heard that the revolution in Russia had begun.

iii. The Russian Revolution, the Mass Strike, and the Trade Unions

The news of Bloody Sunday in St. Petersburg (22 January 1905) shook the socialist world of Germany. For a whole year thereafter, the Russian Revolution held the attention of the Social Democrats. *Vorwärts* instituted a daily front-page column giving a blow by blow account of the revolution's progress. The party locals held numerous sympathy meetings where the revolution was discussed and funds were collected for the eastern comrades.[28] To the Marxist intellectuals, the fresh wind from the East gave a new lease on life. Revolution — "the event which many of us had come to believe impossible after waiting so long in vain" — had come to pass.[29] New political vistas opened before the eyes of the long-frustrated revolutionary activists as the international class struggle seemed "to want to emerge from stagnation, from the long phase of parliamentary sniping, and to enter a period of elemental mass struggles." [30]

In Germany too, the masses seemed to be stirring. When the

---

[27] *N.Z.*, XXIII, i, 9.
[28] *Vorwärts*, 1905, *passim;* Paul Frölich, *Rosa Luxemburg. Her Life and Work,* trans. Edward Fitzgerald (London, 1940), 117–118; *Prot. S. P., 1906,* 20.
[29] Kautsky, *Massenstreik,* 109.
[30] Rosa Luxemburg, "Die Revolution in Russland," *N.Z.*, XXIII, i, 572.

news of the Russian Revolution reached that country, it was already in the grip of the first and greatest of the intense labor struggles of 1905, the coal strike in the Ruhr basin. This strike was distinguished from its predecessors both by its scale and by its wholly spontaneous character. Although the leaders of the four mine workers' unions tried in vain to prevent the spread of the conflict, the pent-up resentment of the miners against their arduous working conditions was no longer to be held in check. The strike fever, carried by the unorganized as well as the organized workers, traveled swiftly, and the unions had no choice but to accept the situation.[31] After a month, the strike was called off (9 February 1905), having achieved no tangible concessions from the employers, and leaving dissatisfaction smouldering in the rank and file.

The strike had developed in its course a political aspect which survived it. The strikers' demands included a call for the expansion of state supervision over labor conditions in the mines, for which there was considerable public sympathy. The Prussian Government responded to this appeal, and introduced reform proposals which were subsequently (January 1906) rejected by the propertied elements which controlled the Prussian Landtag.[32] In this setting the question of the political mass strike acquired a new concreteness and actuality. While the Russian Revolution took the form of mass strikes, Germany's greatest strike, started spontaneously by the rank and file for economic reasons, rapidly acquired political objectives. The radical theorists were quick to connect the two events and to herald the political mass strike as the weapon of the new era of revolution. Thus the Russian Revolution, the intensified labor struggle, and the Western-inspired interest in the general strike flowed together to revitalize the dormant radicalism in German Social Democracy.

Luxemburg felt that in Germany as in Russia the masses themselves were now in motion regardless of their leaders' attitudes. Pointing to the spontaneous character of the coal strike, she emphasized the role of the unorganized workers as the dynamic element in the labor movement. The action of the unorganized proletariat in the Ruhr had left to the trade-unions and the party

[31] *S.M.*, IX (XI), i, 201–210.
[32] *Ibid.*, 208–209; cf. also *N.Z.*, XXIV, i, 605ff.

only a choice between "placing itself at the head of the flood or being swept aside by it." Luxemburg viewed the strike as typical of the proletarian insurrections of the future. Its example revealed "the ridiculousness of the literary disputations as to whether we should 'make' a social revolution or cast this 'antiquated' and 'uncivilized' method into the discard and diligently have ourselves elected to parliament instead."[33] The events of 1905, as Luxemburg interpreted them, should have put an end to the debates of the previous decade concerning the possibility and desirability of revolutionary mass actions. The only remaining question was how the party and trade-unions should lead such actions successfully.

Kautsky too drew radical conclusions from the Ruhr strike, notably with respect to trade-union policy. The failure of the strike showed that "the position of the employers is so strong that it can no longer be assailed by pure trade-union means."[34] From now on, the tactic of the mine workers must be oriented entirely in a political direction, said Kautsky. The trade-unions must prepare their strikes not only by collecting funds and organizing new members but by giving the workers a political schooling.[35] More and more, the decisive strike actions of the proletariat — even the economic ones — would assume a political character. Since pure economic struggles perforce were turning into political actions, the political and economic organizations must draw together again, with the political aspect of trade-union struggle given greater attention — as in Russia.[36] Kautsky's argument was a thinly veiled attack on the neutrality of the trade-unions.

Sparked by the radical intellectuals, the idea of the political mass strike spread like wild-fire. The radical localist unions were of course hotbeds of mass strike sentiment. But now the idea took root in the large left wing of the party and thence began to be propagated even in the centralist trade union leagues.[37]

For the union leaders, carrying on extensive economic struggles in which the employers were all too often calling the tune, the sudden rise of the political mass strike question represented a triple

[33] N.Z., XXIII, i, 573.
[34] Ibid., 773.
[35] Ibid., 780.
[36] Ibid., 781–782.
[37] Umbreit, 25 Jahre, 74; S.M., IX (XI), i, 378.

threat. If the party should adopt a mass strike tactic, the principle of gradual gains by centrally controlled but localized strikes would be jeopardized; the organizations and their treasuries might be wiped out in a revolutionary adventure for political ends which the trade-union officials felt to be none of their concern; and the localists might gain strength among a rank and file infected with mass strike propaganda. For the union leaders, the mass strike question was dynamite.

Aware that the Social Democratic party congress might support the idea of a mass strike, the union leaders tackled the question openly at their triennial congress held at Köln in May 1905. They wished to make their position clear before the party congress met, so that they would not "run the risk of having to submit to resolutions taken in another quarter." [38]

The general commission chose as its spokesman on the issue Theodor Bömelburg, chief of the mason's union, a hard-headed, two-fisted labor leader with little sympathy for the intellectuals. "Our literati," who had "no notion of the practical labor movement," were Bömelburg's target.[39] With their agitation for the mass strike, they would destroy the concrete achievements of today for the dubious speculations of tomorrow. Bömelburg's image of a general strike was drawn neither from Sorelian theory nor from Russian actuality but from German trade-union practice in wage disputes. There must be financial resources to prevent the strikers from going hungry, and "such means are not presently available." Even if the unions should one day have "means so enormous as to conduct such great political struggles, we should completely exhaust ourselves during the fight," enabling the entrepreneurs to impose their terms on the separate fragments of the movement. For Bömelburg and most of the other union leaders, the whole future of the labor movement lay in organization. The mass strike, however, would surely shatter the organizations. "To develop our organizations further, we need peace in the labor movement," Bömelburg declared. "We must see to it that the discussion of the mass strike disappears, and that the solutions of [the problems

[38] Quoted in Kautsky, *Massenstreik*, 116.
[39] *Ibid.*, 118; Otto Heilborn, *Die "Freien" Gewerkschaften seit 1890* (Jena, 1907), 125.

of] the future are left open until the appropriate time arrives." [40]

This was strong language, language behind which lurked a real fear that the lively discussion in press and assemblies would draw the rank and file away from the practical work of trade-unionism. Accordingly, the general commission's resolution branded the idea of the general strike as "indiscussible," and warned the workers "not to let themselves be distracted by the reception and propagation of such ideas from the small day-to-day tasks of building up the organization of labor." It further recommended that the workers energetically oppose the "destructive . . . attempts to lay down a definite tactic through the propagation of the mass strike." [41]

Despite some opposition from the floor, an overwhelming majority of the congress supported the general commission's resolution.[42] The trade-unions thus declared war on the party radicals, and warned the party not to embark on a course which endangered the unions and their hard-won gains.

The action of the Köln congress on the mass strike brought to a focus the critically divergent development of trade-union practice and party theory which, for over a decade, had been proceeding unobtrusively within the framework of the Erfurt program and the "two pillars" theory of party-trade-union parity. No sooner had the spectre of revolution appeared on the eastern horizon, no sooner had the party theorists begun to consider a leftward revision of the Social Democratic tactic, than the trade-unions revealed in full force their essential political conservatism. Indeed, the very intensity of labor conflict in Germany, which encouraged radicalism in the radicals, produced a more-than-normal caution in the trade-union leaders.

The Köln decision on the mass strike unleashed a battle royal between the party and trade-union press. The radical *Reussische Tribüne* characterized the congress as "a triumph of the crassest ignorance," while the *Hamburger Echo* called for a curb on the "super-neutrality" of the trade-unions and on "the poisonous and crippling expressions of contempt for the 'sterile' theoreticians and

---

[40] Kautsky, *Massenstreik*, 117–118.

[41] *Ibid.*, 115.

[42] Paul Barthel, *Handbuch der deutschen Gewerkschaftskongresse* (Dresden, 1916), 132–134.

the superstitious encomia of practical work as the only road to salvation." [43] From the trade-union side, Otto Hué, editor of the *Bergarbeiter-Zeitung,* appealed to xenophobia in the fight against the radicals. He urged that "those who have such a surplus of 'revolutionary' energy" go back to Russia to participate in the fight for freedom "instead of propagating general strike discussion from their summer resorts." [44]

Theoreticians of the most varied persuasions agreed that the unity of the labor movement was in danger. Bernstein pointed out that the objectives of party and trade-unions had led to a basic divergence: The dominant theory of the party was politically pessimistic; that is, it reckoned with a sharpening of class antagonisms, and regarded the deterioration of conditions as the normal, their improvements as the abnormal development. Bernstein correctly observed that this pessimistic view of political reality was incompatible with the trade-union movement. The trade-unions must justify their existence through the improvements which they achieve. To impose on the trade-unions a tactic based on the "pessimistic" and revolutionary view would reduce them "to a political mass movement in trade-union dress." Where the party necessarily viewed struggle as the normal condition, the trade-union would always "regard a struggle as an exception, and peace — or a truce extended to a peace — as the rule, since otherwise it would undermine the conditions of its existence and the foundations of its successes." The conflict between these views, Bernstein thought, was unavoidable.[45]

The party radicals regarded the Köln decision as the logical outcome of the trade-unionists' neglect of theory as such. In their concern with the successes of the moment, it was said, the unionists had forced into the background the analysis of the capitalist economy and the class state. This development had now reached a point where it "must necessarily lead to conflict and clarification between party and trade-unions." [46]

Even within the trade-union movement, the Russian Revolution

[43] Quoted in *Prot. S. P., 1905,* 246, 344.
[44] Quoted in *ibid.,* 269.
[45] *S.M.,* IX (XI), ii, 579–581.
[46] Hermann Fleissner, "Partei und Gewerkschaft," *N.Z.,* XXIII, ii, 699–700. Cf. also Karl Kautsky, "Der Kongress von Köln," *ibid.,* 309–316.

and the radicalization of the German atmosphere in 1905 showed their effects. In Stuttgart, seat of the conservative Metal Workers' League, a great demonstration protested the Köln resolution.[47] At the congress of the Mine Workers' League, there was strong protest from the floor against the condemnation of the mass strike. The Leipzig local of the Metal Workers' League (later a stronghold of Independent Social Democracy) condemned the Köln decision, as did other assemblies of unionists throughout the country.[48] These differences between leadership and rank and file within the trade-unions only aggravated the basic conflict between the party radicals and the union leaders.

iv. The Battle of Jena and the Radical Victory

With tension at a peak, the annual party congress convened at Jena on 17 September 1905. The political mass strike was the principal item on the agenda. Trade-unionists and politicos alike seemed determined to force a decision on the crucial issue of trade-union-party relations. It was clear that the skill of that master tactician, Party Chairman August Bebel, would be taxed to its utmost to preserve the unity of the labor movement.

Bebel had not expressed himself on the question before the congress met; there was the greatest suspense as to which side he would support.[49] His three-and-one-half hour address took full account of the radicalization of the political atmosphere.[50] Bebel's keynote was the absolute irreconcilability of labor with the ruling classes. The broad coalition with the liberals, which some sanguine reformists had expected to follow the party's electoral victory of 1903, had not come to pass, he said; the Social Democratic Party remained isolated in state and nation. Bebel welcomed the sharpening of class antagonisms since it created a "clear situation" in which compromise with the ruling class was proved to be useless.[51]

Bebel's analysis was conceived in the Social Democratic tradition of "pure opposition." Its tactical implications, however, were less

[47] *Prot. S. P., 1905,* 254.
[48] *Ibid.,* 236, 250.
[49] *S.M.,* IX (XI), ii, 841.
[50] *Prot. S. P., 1905,* 285–313, 335.
[51] *Ibid.,* 288, 291.

aggressive than its tone. The course of political development, he said, would depend not upon Social Democratic initiative but rather on the attitude of labor's enemies. "Their actions prescribe our tactic; it is up to them alone whether things will develop peacefully, i.e., naturally, or whether catastrophes will occur." [52] Bebel made explicit the widely held assumptions of his fellow-socialists that the working class would continue to grow and that the party would one day embrace a majority of the population. The party would then press on to realize what he vaguely designated as the "rights of man"; a revolution would occur only if the bourgeoisie sought to prevent the realization of these rights. [53] Revolution was a purely defensive measure designed to safeguard the exercise of power legitimately acquired through the ballot. Bebel thus united a dialectic concept of social evolution with a linear concept of the acquisition of political power through the legal construction of a majority under a parliamentary constitutional system.

Within this conceptual framework, Bebel advanced his resolution on the political mass strike. As he saw revolution as a defensive act, so he recommended the mass strike primarily as a defensive weapon. The party executive's resolution declared it a duty of the working class to employ every appropriate means of defense against an attack on either universal suffrage or the right of association — the two prerequisites for the pursuit of the Erfurt tactic. "The party congress," the resolution continued, "considers the broadest utilization of mass work stoppage under certain circumstances one of the most effective weapons to defend itself against such a criminal political act against the working class, or to acquire an important basic right for its liberation." [54] The last phrase opened the possibility of an offensive employment of the mass strike, but Bebel did not elaborate on this aspect in his address. His view, like that of Hilferding in 1903, rested on the distinction between a mass strike and a revolutionary act. Bebel emphasized that the mass strike had nothing to do with the setting up of a socialist state

[52] *Ibid.*, 297.
[53] *Ibid.*, 291–297, 301.
[54] *Ibid.*, 143.

(*Zukunftsstaat*); it was useful only to defend "rights which are indispensable to the life and breath of the working class." [55] Moreover, he distinguished its application in Germany from its utilization in Russia. Russian conditions, he said, were "so abnormal that they cannot be adduced as an example for us." The key to the use of the mass strike in Germany lay, said Bebel, in the expansion of the organizations, both party and trade-union. He compared the Social Democratic Party to the other great achievement of the Prussian-German genius for organization — the German Army. Any use of the mass strike would be carefully planned and undertaken only when the means for an assured success were at hand.[56] His resolution therefore provided that "the greatest expansion of the political and trade-union organizations is necessary to make possible the utilization of this weapon." [57]

Despite these qualifications, Bebel's mass strike resolution and its adoption by the Jena congress were generally regarded as a victory for the left, and a major change in Social Democratic tactical conceptions. For the first time since the adoption of the Erfurt program, the party declared itself ready "under certain circumstances" to resort to general strike action in pursuit of its aims. Rosa Luxemburg interpreted the Jena resolution as a sign of the German party's capacity for revolutionary development.[58] Certainly the party leadership had responded to the radical pressure generated by the Russian Revolution. Yet, so far as the leaders were concerned, the Jena resolution was not the earnest of revolutionary intentions which Luxemburg and her colleagues sought to make of it. In Bebel's address, as in the resolution itself, the mass strike was recommended primarily as a weapon to keep open the possibility of a continued gradualist tactic. It was thus subordinated to parliamentary and trade-union activity. Now as before, the development of the organizations and the winning of a majority at the polls were recognized as the chief avenues to power. The function of the mass strike, according to the Jena resolution, was to keep these avenues clear of obstructions.

[55] *Ibid.*, 308. The revisionist Eduard David laid great stress on the defensive aspect of Bebel's position. Cf. *S.M.*, IX (XI), ii, 841ff.

[56] *Prot. S. P., 1905*, 306–308.

[57] *Ibid.*, 143.

[58] Luxemburg, *Werke*, IV, 417.

While the left claimed a victory in obtaining recognition of the new revolutionary weapon, the right stressed the limitations on its use.[59] Whatever interpretation one put upon the Jena resolution, it was clear that the party had rejected flatly the position taken by the trade-unions at their Köln congress. The Ruhr strike and Russian Revolution had left their mark.

v. The Suffrage Crisis

When the mass strike resolution was adopted by the party in September 1905, few could have expected that within a short time there would be a serious occasion to carry it into practice. Yet within a few months, the mass strike became a historical possibility.

The crisis was precipitated by new efforts to curb the Social Democrats at the polls by suffrage restrictions in certain states where the labor party was strong. Since the mid-nineties, the suffrage systems of the federal states had been undergoing changes. South of the Main, where the Social Democratic population was small, there had been a liberalization of the suffrage laws. In the Center and North, the tendency had been toward further restrictions. In 1896 Saxony abolished its comparatively liberal suffrage in favor of the Prussian three-class system. Here the lower middle class, as well as the working class, had resented the curtailment of its political rights. It had expressed its dissatisfaction in 1903 by helping to elect Social Democratic candidates in twenty-two of Saxony's twenty-three Reichstag districts. In the lower house of the Saxon chamber, by contrast, the Social Democrats had not a single seat until the election of 1905, which was held a few days before the Jena congress. Conducting a vigorous campaign on the issue of suffrage reform, the Social Democrats elected one Landtag member.[60] The Liberals, who likewise suffered from the suffrage law, wished some modification in the electoral system, and in the autumn of 1905, the Conservative government, fearing further radicalization, began to consider changes in the suffrage structure.[61]

[59] For left views see *Prot. S. P., 1905*, 320–321, 324–327 (Luxemburg, Zetkin, Zietz, Stadthagen and Liebknecht); for right views, 329–330, 332–334 (Südekum, Schmidt, and Bömelburg).
[60] *N.Z.*, XXIV, i, 97ff.
[61] *Ibid.*, 583–584.

In the free city of Lübeck, equal suffrage had been jettisoned in 1903–04, in another back-handed tribute to the success of Social Democracy.[62] Bremen boasted an eight-class voting system, which admitted no further improvement from the conservative point of view. In Hamburg, however, there was a three-class system, with the third class electing half the city council. In the summer of 1905, Hamburg's governing body decided to subdivide the third class into two classes, with the lower income group permitted to elect only twenty-four of 160 councilmen.[63] In Alsace and in Hessen, there were also conflicts over the inequitable suffrage systems in 1905.[64]

While in various portions of Germany the suffrage question was being thus agitated either by the right or left, new stimulus to the radicals was given from outside the country. In the last weeks of October, Russia was swept once more by a series of mass strikes which shook the Tsar into granting a constitution in his October Manifesto. The Austrian Socialists, at their congress of the same month, adopted in principle the weapon of the mass strike in order to extract universal suffrage from their government. In response to suffrage demonstrations which became general throughout the Austrian cities, the government promised to introduce a bill for suffrage reform.[65]

In Germany, the Saxon suffrage movement now began to assume serious proportions. Minister President von Metzsch's proposal for a corporative electoral system (27 November 1905) was answered by a series of protest meetings in the major cities.[66] In Dresden, resolutions were taken by the suffrage meetings stating that the participants would not rest with "paper protests, which have heretofore remained unrespected." [67] The meetings were followed by street demonstrations and clashes with the police. A second series of meetings on 16 December terminated, despite the opposition of the party leaders, in an attempt to march on the Minister President's

---

[62] S.M., X (XII), i, 204–205.

[63] Ernst Baasch, *Geschichte Hamburgs, 1814–1918* (Stuttgart, 1924–25), II, 109–122; S.M., X (XII), i, 205.

[64] *Vorwärts*, 12, 20 Dec. 1905.

[65] S.M., IX (XI), ii, 1055.

[66] *Vorwärts*, 29 Nov., 5 Dec. 1905; S.M., X (XII), i, 83–84.

[67] *Vorwärts*, 5 Dec. 1905.

residence, with the police inflicting saber wounds on the unruly mob.[68]

With the Saxon population growing more restive, talk of mass demonstration strikes, of a real offensive to win the suffrage began to course through the party.[69] The Saxon government in its nervousness forbade public meetings in Leipzig and other cities, while the local party leaders, equally nervous about the monster they had conjured up, began to apply the brakes.[70]

From Saxony, the movement spread to Hamburg, Alsace, Brunswick, Hessen, and Prussia.[71] In Hamburg, when the city council opened its deliberations on the new restrictive suffrage bill, the Social Democrats held their first political demonstration strike with thousands of workers milling around the Rathaus.[72] The movement reached its height on Sunday, 21 January 1906, the anniversary of Bloody Sunday, when there were protest meetings throughout Germany for universal suffrage in the *Länder*. In Saxony, most of the demonstrations were forbidden by the police; elsewhere in Germany, according to Social Democratic sources, troops were held in readiness against any eventuality.[73]

The popular unrest at the turn of the year was perhaps greater than at any time between 1890 and 1914, but it is unlikely that the suffrage movement could have gone much farther. Insofar as the radical wave received its impetus from abroad, it was certain to recede. For even as the movement in Germany was reaching its peak, reaction was on the march in Russia. The St. Petersburg Soviet was arrested on 16 December, the Moscow insurrection was suppressed in January, and throughout the winter punitive expeditions were quelling the insurrections in the provinces. Even the optimistic *Vorwärts* had to admit on 28 January that the Russian Revolution, though sure to revive, had received crushing blows.[74]

Of at least equal importance to the reverses of the Russian revo-

[68] *Ibid.*, 19 Dec. 1905.
[69] *Leipziger Volkszeitung,* No. 292, cited in *Vorwärts,* 20 Dec. 1905; *Dresdner Arbeiterzeitung,* n. d., cited in *Vorwärts,* 7 Dec. 1905.
[70] *Vorwärts,* 20 Dec. 1905.
[71] *Prot. S. P., 1906,* 28–31.
[72] *Vorwärts,* 18, 19 Jan. 1905; *N.Z.,* XXIV, i, 618–621.
[73] *Vorwärts,* 21, 22, 23, 25 Jan. 1906.
[74] *Ibid.,* 28 Jan. 1906.

lutionaries was the coolness of the German party executive to the whole precipitate drive toward action. As early as November 1905, the party executive had publicly rejected a proposal by the Breslau organization that the executive plan demonstration strikes for the suffrage on the occasion of the opening of the Prussian Landtag.[75]

Now that the movement had assumed really large dimensions, the executive became uneasy. Would the wave of electoral reform agitation carry the party into a mass strike in which the organizations would be endangered, as the trade-union leaders had predicted? And what would the powerful trade-unions do in such a case? In February 1906, the executive decided on consultation with the trade-union general commission to work out a joint position. The fact of the meeting was necessarily held secret, lest the radicals raise a hue and cry.

The secret conference, held on 16 February, adopted a series of six propositions as a tentative basis of party-trade-union coöperation in the mass strike question. The main points of the agreement represented a victory for the trade-union attitude. In them the party executive not only disclaimed any intention of propagating the mass strike, but pledged itself to "try to prevent one as much as possible." If a mass strike should nevertheless break out, the party would assume the sole burden of leadership. While the trade-unions would not participate in it officially, they agreed "not to stab it in the back." The costs of a general strike would have to be raised by the party alone. Only if lockouts and strikes should continue after the mass strike was called off would the trade-unions contribute to their support.[76]

The content of the secret agreement soon leaked out through the localist trade-union press. Its very publication put a damper on the continuation of the suffrage movement, since it revealed that the party executive had no enthusiasm for fulfilling the promise of the Jena resolution. As the suffrage movement itself died down, the energy of the party was diverted into internal conflict over the great issues raised by the events of 1905: the mass strike and the relationship of party and trade-union. In these issues was in-

[75] Prot. S. P., 1906, 28–29.
[76] Umbreit, 25 Jahre, 78; Prot. S. P., 1906, 244–245, 293–295; Luxemburg, Werke, IV, 70–71.

volved the question of the nature and function of the Social Democratic movement. On their solution at the coming party congress, the future of the party, reformist or revolutionary, largely depended.

vi. Mannheim: The Trade-Unions Strike Back

The chief task of the party congress which met at Mannheim on 23 September 1906, was to determine a lasting basis for unity between the political and economic wings of the labor movement, whose relations had become so seriously impaired during the years of renascent radicalism. Two theoretical possibilities were open: (1) to recognize the factual independence of the trade-unions from the party and to achieve the desired unity by mutual agreement of the leadership on common problems as they arose; or (2) to subordinate the trade-unions clearly to the party.

The executive's proposal, made by Bebel, followed the first course. It recognized the complete parity of the trade-unions with the party, and provided instrumentation for the parity principle. "In actions which affect equally the interest of trade-unions and party," the resolution declared, "the central leadership of both organizations should seek a mutual understanding in order to achieve a unified procedure." [77]

The political implications of this concept of organization were immediately apparent in the portion of the resolution dealing with the mass strike. Here it was stated that the Jena resolution on the mass strike (which advocated the use of the strike under certain circumstances) was "not in contradiction" with the resolution of the Köln trade-union congress (which forbade even the discussion of the mass strike). This masterpiece of logic was coupled with an injunction to the party executive to consult with the trade-unions "as soon as it considers that the necessity for a mass strike is at hand." [78]

The attitude of the trade-unions over the last two years had shown that the party would be powerless to engage in revolutionary activity if it could act only with the consent of the trade-union leadership. The radicals therefore pressed vigorously for the second solution. Kautsky offered to the congress an amendment to

[77] *Prot. S. P., 1906,* 131–132.
[78] *Ibid.*

Bebel's resolution which, without quite saying so, would have subordinated the trade-unions to the party. Kautsky's amendment declared it an "absolute necessity" that the trade-unions be "ruled by the spirit of Social Democracy." Social Democracy, that is, the party and its doctrine, was designated as "the highest and most catholic form of the proletarian class struggle." Kautsky and his friends clearly did not consider it politically practical to insist, in the face of the executive's attitude, upon the line authority of the party over the trade-unions. They sought to achieve the same end by establishing the primacy of the party's decrees in the conscience of the individual party member. The resolution proclaimed "the duty of every party comrade . . . to feel bound by the decisions of the party congresses in his trade-union activity." [79]

Kautsky explained the conceptions on which his resolution was based. Fundamental was the idea that the party had, by its very nature, the higher authority. The life of the trade-unions was limited only to the capitalist era, its purpose transient: to defend and improve the lot of the workers until the advent of socialism. The party was something broader, said Kautsky; it was "the representative of the total struggle for the liberation of the proletariat, . . . the representative of the program aspiring to renovate society." In the narrow sense of the term, the party was the political representative of the proletariat in the parliamentary struggle under capitalism, and in so far the trade-unions were its equal. But the party's constant concern for the achievement of the final goal, socialism, placed it above the trade-unions, which were limited both in function and in time.[80] Hence the trade-unions must subordinate themselves to the decisions of the party and be bound by them.

The very radicals who were later to lead the break-off from the party insisted at Mannheim on an absolutely rigid discipline as the only way to achieve proletarian unity.[81] Given the independence of the trade-unions as institutions, the will of the party could be exercised over them only if their members could be bound, through discipline and a higher loyalty, to the decisions of the party. Only thus could the final aim of socialism, the teleological element in

---

[79] *Ibid.*, 143.
[80] *Ibid.*, 257–258.
[81] *Ibid.*, 258, 287.

Marxist thought and action, be made the reference point in terms of which the practical daily work of the trade-unionists would be carried on.

Any reader of the Mannheim debates must agree that the sentiment of the congress was with Kautsky rather than Bebel. Even an opponent of Kautsky's amendment conceded that it would pass, though by a close margin.[82] There were no less than fourteen motions reaffirming the Jena position or calling for a more vigorous mass strike agitation.[83] Speakers from the Social Democratic urban strongholds generally supported the Kautsky view.[84] The party executive, however, made up through skill for its lack of initial support. At the last moment it added to its motion the first portion of the Kautsky resolution, which dealt with the need for the infusion of the Social Democratic spirit into the trade-unions, omitting the essential clause for its enforcement through moral discipline. This proposal was no sooner made than the debate was closed. The speed with which the executive managed this maneuver completely overwhelmed the left. One of the radical delegates protested in vain that the new proposal altered the picture, and that debate could not now be closed. Kautsky tried to indicate that Bebel's previous acceptance of the remainder of his resolution as "self-understood" would be a guide to the interpretation of the whole, but was ruled out of order by the chairman. To the less sophisticated majority of the delegates, of course, the adoption of part of Kautsky's resolution by the executive seemed an acceptable compromise. The Bebel resolution as amended became party law.[85]

The Mannheim resolution was a landmark in the history of German Social Democracy. It represented a kind of counter-revolution in the party, a reversal of the radical victory at the battle of Jena in the previous year. The trade-unions had demonstrated their power in bringing the party back to the traditional reformist tactic. But Mannheim was more than a mere return to the *status quo ante*. The trade-unions had emerged from their withdrawal, they had abandoned their neutrality to cast their weight into the scales of

[82] *Ibid.*, 288.
[83] *Ibid.*, 115–119, 128.
[84] *Ibid.*, 255–302, *passim.*
[85] *Ibid.*, 289–305.

the party's destiny. Kautsky, in an effort to console his wing in defeat, presented the end of neutrality as a "decided shift to the left" in trade-union policy.[86] The wails of the *Leipziger Volkszeitung* were nearer the truth: ten years of campaigning against revisionism had been in vain, "for the revisionism we have killed in the party rises again in greater strength in the trade-unions."[87] More than that, the trade-unions had passed from a position of independence of the party to one of effective control over it. The party's recognition of parity in principle meant the recognition of control by the trade-unions in practice. Whenever the party wished to move in a direction which threatened what Bömelburg had called the trade-unions' need for peace, the unions could legally withhold their sanction, and thus act as a brake on any overt attacks on the existing order. The relationship of parity between trade-unions and party was, as Luxemburg observed, like the arrangement by which a peasant woman sought to regulate her life with her spouse: "On matters of question between us, when we agree, you will decide; when we disagree, I shall decide."[88]

The Mannheim resolution on parity also affected the relationship of the party executive to its following. In theory, the executive remained responsible to the will of the majority of the membership, insofar as this was represented at the party congress. But since the executive could undertake no action which the trade-unions would not approve, it came almost imperceptibly to be responsible more to the general commission than to the party itself. To be sure, in decisions which would depend for their execution on the trade-unions, the party leaders were given a powerful weapon against recalcitrants in their own ranks. Thus, in arguing against the Kautsky resolution at Mannheim, a member of the executive said: "Do we wish the trade-union movement to break off from the political one? . . . Of what use would be a resolution adopted against the will of those whom it concerns [the trade-unionists], if they can say, 'Even the party leadership opposed this decision'?"[89]

[86] *N.Z.*, XXV, i, 10.
[87] *Leipziger Volkszeitung*, n. d., quoted in *S.M.*, X (XII), ii, 907.
[88] *Prot. S. P., 1906*, 315.
[89] *Ibid.*, 290–291.

By the same token, the internal cleavages in the party increased, and, with them, the difficulty of the executive's position. The reformists became emboldened to violate the decisions of the party congresses, knowing that the leadership was too committed to the trade-unions to risk drastic action against them. The radicals suffered from increasing frustration, and turned more vigorously against the leadership. The executive, having lost the aura of impartiality, was in a few years driven to the creation of a tighter organization to hold the radicals in check.

Even from the point of view of that labor unity which it was designed to serve, the Mannheim resolution was dearly bought. The line of division in the labor movement which, in the radical years 1905 and 1906, had run between the party and the trade-unions, was now shifted back into the party itself. The real locus of power, on the other hand, shifted outside the political movement to the unions, which in turn strengthened the reformist wing within the party, and laid the groundwork for the ultimate break-off of the isolated radicals. Though the fact was not openly recognized, the Mannheim congress accorded institutional recognition to the primacy of the material interest of German labor in the existing order, represented by the trade-unions, over the "ideal" interest of the working class, heretofore represented by the party, in the overthrow of capitalism.

vii. The Radical Legacy of 1905

"The brief May flowering of the new revolutionism is happily over," observed the revisionist Eduard David after the Mannheim congress. "The party will again devote itself with undivided heart to the positive exploitation and expansion of its parliamentary power." [90] With respect to the party's tactic, David was correct, for the labor movement was entering a period of three years in which not even the most militant revolutionary could discover a concrete opportunity for radical action. With respect to the attitudes and ideas of the radicals, however, David was wrong. The experience of 1905–06, both in the broad arena of politics and in the narrower

[90] *S.M.*, X (XII), ii, 914.

confines of party life, left an indelible impression on a portion of the radical wing. "Revisionism of the left" remained as a permanent challenge to the Erfurt synthesis.

The secret agreement with the trade-unions in February 1906 and, above all, the executive's position at Mannheim undermined the radicals' confidence in the party fathers. No longer could the leaders be regarded as partisans of the radical wing. Luxemburg suggested that the alliance between the orthodox Marxists and the executive was purely defensive, against the party revisionists. When the radicals tried to develop the offensive, the party leaders sided with the reformists. "The plain truth," Luxemburg concluded, "is that August [Bebel], and still more the others, have pledged themselves to . . . parliamentarism, and wherever anything happens which transcends the limits of parliamentary action, they are hopeless — no, worse than hopeless, because then they do their utmost to force the movement back into parliamentary channels." [91] Under the pressure of events, the radicals' lack of confidence in the leadership was destined to grow and spread until it resulted in a major revolt against the executive in 1911–12.

The second and more significant legacy of the years of the Russian Revolution was in the field of ideas. The notion of the political mass strike as the revolutionary weapon of the twentieth century was never to be expunged from the minds of the radical Social Democrats in our period. The mass strikes of Russia had proved that, if the days of barricade fighting were over, as Engels had said, this did not rule out revolutionary action until the armies of the ruling class should disintegrate.

Rosa Luxemburg gave to the "new revolutionism" its conceptual formulation in the one significant theoretical work of the years 1905–1906: *Mass Strike, Party and Trade-Unions*. The author drew not only upon her experiences in the fight for a radicalization of the Erfurt tactic in Germany, but also upon her participation in the Polish Revolution in the winter of 1905–06.[92] She attempted to integrate these two experiences into a new conception of revolutionary tactic for the German party. Her pamphlet, written at the request

---

[91] Letter to Clara Zetkin, n. d. [early 1907], quoted in Frölich, *Luxemburg*, 148–149.

[92] Frölich, *Luxemburg*, 122.

of the Social Democratic organizations of Hamburg to influence the delegates to the Mannheim congress, failed abysmally of its immediate purpose.[93] Like Bernstein's *Voraussetzungen,* Luxemburg's attempt at redefining the nature and function of Social Democracy was a pioneering work, the influence of which made itself felt only gradually. *Mass Strike, Party and Trade-Unions* laid the basis for the intellectual structure of the group which after 1910 emerged as the "left radical" wing of the German party that later provided the connecting link to Russian Bolshevism.

The central problem of the pamphlet was to define the relationship between the mass strike and revolution. Luxemburg's concept of the mass strike was not, like Hilferding's or Bebel's, one of a planned action executed on command from the leadership. No resolutions of party congresses, she said, could determine the conditions under which mass strikes would appear. History — "in which Social Democracy with its resolutions is, to be sure, an important factor, but only *one* among many" — would decide the outbreak of the mass strike.[94] The mass strike was neither a weapon to be used for a planned, limited purpose nor a single act performed at a given signal from the party authorities. It was rather "the form of movement of the proletarian mass, the form of proletarian struggle in the revolution itself." [95]

Luxemburg thus sharply distinguished the mass strike as a modern social revolutionary form from a political demonstration strike such as the traditional May Day strike. A short, planned mass strike was possible, but this would bear the same relationship to revolutionary mass strikes as sending a cruiser to a foreign port does to war: it would be an earnest of the willingness to fight. When the revolutionary *period* set in, the workers would start mass strikes themselves.[96]

Luxemburg's criticism of the German discussions of the mass strike was thus directed at what she considered a confusion of the demonstration strike with social revolution. She saw the broad interest in the mass strike as "a symptom of the deep internal change

[93] Luxemburg, *Werke,* IV, 389.
[94] *Ibid.,* 418.
[95] *Ibid.,* 438.
[96] *Ibid.,* 439, 443–444.

in class relationships," and as a sign of the lively intelligence and "revolutionary instinct" of the German masses.[97] But the interpretation of the Jena resolution by the "practical politicians" as a defensive weapon, as a mere appendage of parliamentarism, Luxemburg dismissed as illusionistic. An attack on universal suffrage might indeed unleash a political storm, in which the mass strike would probably be used. But in that case, all the weighty discussions between the leaders of party and trade-unions concerning coverage of expenses, provisioning, etc., would prove entirely beside the point. To plan on financing a revolution, on maintaining the usual insurance coverage of a trade-union strike, would be "like trying to measure the ocean with a tumbler." [98]

She thus applied her distinction between revolutionary mass strike and demonstration strike in Germany to draw a contrast between the "healthy revolutionary instinct" of the rank and file, and the narrow "parade-ground mentality" of the leadership, which, in her view, confused the demands of peacetime organization for legal parliamentary and union activity with the forms demanded by revolution itself. What she emphasized was the spontaneous character of the revolutionary process. The wellspring of action in a revolutionary period, she insisted, lay in the masses themselves, through whom that mystical force, history, operated. The function of leadership and of the party as a whole was to give them guidance and direction, not to command them like an army.[99]

Her "spontaneity theory" served her as a weapon to attack the idea of the leaders that they could control the actions of the masses through disciplined organizations. Indeed, Luxemburg moved toward a real contempt for organization. With her unbounded faith in the revolutionary will of the people, she pooh-poohed the shallow concern of the trade-union leaders who saw their organizations threatened by mass actions. She pointed out that the German trade-unions had emerged from the period of the Anti-Socialist Laws with five times the membership they had had in 1878. "This is the specific method of growth peculiar to proletarian class organizations: to test themselves in combat, and to emerge from combat

[97] Ibid., 416–417.
[98] Ibid., 417, 444–445.
[99] Ibid., 445.

revitalized." [100] She criticized similarly the party's view of the relationship between the number of votes it received and the size of the party organization. Where the party assumed that the development of its organization accounted for its electoral success, she maintained that the growth of the organization, as well as the increase in Social Democratic votes, developed from the electoral struggle itself.[101] In combating the leadership's position that a tremendous development of the organizations was the prerequisite to any radical action, Luxemburg now swung to the other extreme: she posited an intensification of the struggle as the prerequisite for the development of the organizations.

As part of the same shift in emphasis from leadership to mass, from organization to action, Luxemburg urged the party to pay more attention to the unorganized masses. The class struggle could not be waged with a strategy which took into account only the organized proletariat, she said. The problem which confronted the party was not the "schooling" and "disciplining" of the organized minority but the development of a strategy which would win the support of the unorganized majority, especially in a moment of historical crisis.

Drawing the conclusion from her arguments, Luxemburg wrote:

Let us leave the pedantic schema of a demonstrational mass strike of the organized minority artificially commandeered by party and trade union. Let us turn [instead] to the living picture of a genuine movement of the people, rising with elemental might out of the political situation and the extreme sharpening of class antagonisms, and unleashing itself in tempestuous mass struggles and mass strikes, political as well as economic. Then it becomes obvious that the task of Social Democracy lies not in the technical preparation and leadership of the mass strike, but in the political direction of the movement as a whole.[102]

In *Mass Strike, Party and Trade-Unions*, Luxemburg formulated what was to be the basic position of the revolutionary left. If it was the peculiar product of Luxemburg's personal experience of the contrast between the unorganized energy of the Russian Revolution and the organized caution of the German party and

[100] *Ibid.*, 453–454.
[101] *Ibid.*, 454.
[102] *Ibid.*, 456–457.

trade-unions, it was also the first major assault from the left on the premises on which the German party, including its radicals, had operated.

While her optimistic views of the creative revolutionary energy of the masses were partly Russian-inspired, her ideas of organization were German-inspired, at least in a negative sense. She feared deeply the power of bureaucracy as a dangerous substitute for the expression of the popular will, and had, as early as 1904, bitterly opposed Lenin's idea that a cadristic party structure with an omnipotent central executive could serve as a defense against opportunism.[103] Her unbounded faith in the masses, coupled with her experience of a reformist bureaucracy in the German trade-unions, found its expression in a kind of revolt against organization as such. *Mass Strike, Party and Trade-Unions* was the first full expression of this attitude. As the political consequences of the trade-union conquest of the party at Mannheim became apparent over the following years, Luxemburg's combination of revolutionary and anti-bureaucratic attitudes would become the hallmark of the German left. It was a legacy of 1905 with consequences no less grave than those of the Mannheim congress for the Erfurt synthesis of revolutionary theory and gradualist tactic.

[103] Rosa Luxemburg, "Organisationsfragen in der russischen Sozialdemokratie," *N.Z.*, XXII, ii, 484–492, 529–535.

Chapter III

THE ELECTIONS OF 1907 AND THE
"NATIONAL QUESTION"

i. The Elections of 1907: The Victory of the "World-political Idea"

While Social Democracy was passing through the internal crisis described in the last chapter, the government and the Reichstag were increasingly occupied with Germany's position as a world power. The maladroit handling of the Moroccan episode in 1905, Germany's Pyrrhic victory in the Algeciras Conference of the following year, the collapse of the Kaiser's dream of a continental alliance — all these developments contributed to Germany's growing isolation on the diplomatic scene without bringing any compensating increase in international power. Even those who supported Germany's quest for a place in the sun became uneasy over the "zig-zag course" of German foreign policy.[1]

Native revolts in Southwest Africa brought the opposition to a head in the parliamentary arena. In a faint adumbration of the later Weimar Coalition, Centrists, Progressives, and Social Democrats pressed the chancellor into reforming the colonial administration (1906). When, despite the reforms, the Centrists continued their attacks upon the colonial office, Chancellor von Bülow resolved to take the issue to the country.

With consummate political skill Bülow transformed the failures of his foreign and colonial policies into a domestic triumph in the elections of 1907. The government interpreted the election as "a great test of whether Germany is capable of developing from a European into a world power or not."[2] The dissolved Reichstag,

[1] Otto Hammann, *The World Policy of Germany, 1890–1912*, trans. Maude A. Huttman (London, 1927), 149–171.
[2] *Norddeutsche Allgemeine Zeitung*, 13 Dec. 1906. Quoted in George D. Crothers, *The German Elections of 1907* (New York, 1941), 105.

which had challenged Germany's honor and threatened her colonial empire, was pictured in the campaign as the non- and anti-national element of the state. Bülow explained that his call to the polls was motivated by the need "to protect the government's authority and its position *above* the parties." [3] Thus foreign-political and constitutional issues were blended into one. The election was a plebiscite both on the content of Germany's world policy and on the autonomy of the chancellor in pursuing it without "unendurable meddling" from the Reichstag. Not only the Conservatives and National Liberals supported the government's cause. In a spectacular about-face, the Progressives jettisoned their traditional oppositional attitude to join the government bloc against the "ultra-montanists" and "revolutionaries." [4] The Centrists were subjected to a propaganda barrage reminiscent of the Kulturkampf. The Social Democrats, however, remained public enemy number one in Bülow's "struggle for the honor and welfare of the nation." The chancellor put them first, he said, "because every set-back of the Social Democrats will be a reprimand for their blind over-confidence, a strengthening of a faith in the orderly progress of our inner development, and a strengthening of our position abroad; and because the likelihood would therefore be less that a bourgeois party [that is, the Center], with the help of the Social Democrats, should ever occupy a dominant position above the other bourgeois parties again." [5]

The Social Democrats entered the "Hottentot campaign" in a spirit of high optimism. With their organization strong, their treasuries full, and an increase in the working-class electorate apparently assured, the theoreticians and party leaders agreed that new mandates would be added to the eighty-one seats captured in 1903. [6]

The Social Democrats reckoned without the host. In the political arena, just as in the field of labor conflict, the upper classes had adapted to their own ends the techniques of mass agitation used with such singular success by the Social Democrats in the election

[3] Crothers, *Elections*, 250.

[4] For the Progressives' shift, see Theodor Heuss, *Friedrich Naumann* (Stuttgart, 1937), 238–243, 320–323; and Crothers, *Elections*, 45–55.

[5] Crothers, *Elections*, 253. For the chancellor's attitude toward Social Democracy, cf. Prince Bernhard von Bülow, *Imperial Germany*, trans. Marie A. Lewenz (New York, 1914), 208–247.

[6] *N.Z.*, XXV, i, 437, 507–509; *Vorwärts*, 1 Jan. 1907.

of 1903. A formidable battery of non-party organizations of the German middle and upper class — the Navy League (with government funds), the Pan-German League, various colonial societies and veterans' groups — made the campaign one of broad public education for imperialism.[7] The Reich League against Social Democracy concentrated on the main enemy, contributing funds and technical advice on electioneering to the "parties of order," and providing trained speakers, newspaper columns, and over ten million pamphlets to the campaign.[8]

The vigor and unity of the government forces achieved results. The campaign brought out the vote, as the Social Democrats had anticipated, but the proletarian party did not profit by the increase.[9] The politically indifferent citizens who were galvanized into voting by chauvinistic slogans and the fear of the anti-national and subversive Social Democrats threw their weight in the balance to produce a resounding defeat for the S.P.D. Though it held its own in the proportion of votes cast, the party lost almost half its Reichstag seats. Its mandates fell from eighty-one to forty-three.

The extent to which the nationalist campaign crystallized sentiment against the Social Democrats was strikingly manifested in the behavior of the Progressive voters in the run-off elections. The Progressives, representing the left wing of the middle classes, had in the past given their support to Social Democratic candidates where the alternative was to vote for an outspoken reactionary. In 1907, the Progressives voted against the Social Democrats in thirty-seven run-off contests. In thirty-five their vote was decisive. In four cases they supported candidates of the Anti-Semitic Party, although the Progressives were supposed to be committed against anti-semitism in principle, and received much of their support from Jewish banking and commercial circles.[10] All concern for liberalism and

---

[7] Crothers, *Elections*, 103–109.

[8] *Ibid.*, 144–145; Philipp Scheidemann, *Memoiren eines Sozialdemokraten* (Dresden, 1928), I, 93ff.; *Prot. S. P., 1907*, 26; *N.Z.*, XXV, i, 747.

[9] Cf. Friedrich Naumann, *Die politischen Parteien* (Berlin, 1913), Appendix, Table 3.

[10] Crothers, *Elections*, 173–174. The shift of the Progressives was perhaps most strikingly illustrated in Württemberg. Allies of the Social Democrats in the *Landtag* elections in early December 1906, they reversed field in the Reichstag elections a few weeks later to join forces with the rightist parties against the Social Democrats. Cf. Wilhelm Keil, *Erlebnisse eines Sozialdemokraten* (Stuttgart, 1947), I, 248ff.

constitutionalism, even in the most liberal sector of the German middle classes, vanished where a "national" issue was involved, and Social Democracy was the victim of the process.

The Center did not share the fate of Social Democracy in the elections. Secure in the Catholic districts, it not only maintained its proportion of the popular vote (slightly over 19 per cent), but through the benevolent neutrality of the Conservatives and the assistance of the Social Democrats in certain run-off contests, it captured five additional seats.[11] It remained the strongest party in the Reichstag. The fact that the Center could point to a twenty-year record of support for the government's foreign policy in general, and for armaments and colonial expansion in particular, no doubt contributed to its success.[12] The Social Democratic Party, committed to the pure opposition expressed in the slogan *"Diesem System keinen Mann und keinen Groschen,"* neither would nor could escape the consequences of its opposition to the government's foreign and colonial policy.

Out of the elections of 1907 the imperial system of government emerged with a new lease on life. The electorate had granted *carte blanche* to the regime for the pursuit of its world policy. In jubilation, the *Norddeutsche Allgemeine Zeitung* wrote on 26 January:

When national questions are involved, the German people can ride down everything that stands in the way of the nation. They will not tolerate the slightest weakening of their national strength, even when only an African colony and a couple of thousand men are concerned . . . The national, imperial, and world-political idea has won a brilliant victory . . .[13]

In terms of the issue out of which the election arose, it was not only the "world-political idea" which won a brilliant victory. The government won public sanction for its right to unhindered control over foreign policy; its parliamentary critics were rejected. Henceforth, the government could proceed with little fear that any bourgeois party would risk the danger of provoking it to a point where it would carry an issue of foreign policy to the people. The

[11] The adherence of four former Alsatians to the Center accounted in part for the increase in seats.

[12] Crothers, *Elections,* 129–140, 180–181.

[13] Quoted in *ibid.,* 167.

Social Democrats were not merely defeated but condemned to conduct their opposition to the government's *Weltpolitik* in total isolation.

ii. Disunity in Defeat

To the ruling groups the elections of 1907 brought a new unity; to the Social Democrats, increased dissension. The battle between radicals and revisionists, suspended during the campaign itself, broke out anew over the meaning of the campaign for the tactic of the party. The elections raised a crucial issue which the party had previously been able to ignore: its relationship to state and nation in the era of imperialism. The "national question," as this issue was called, became a central problem in the internal development of the party. In the Reichstag, in the congress of the Socialist International, and in the Essen party congress, factional alignments on the national question began in 1907 to assume definite form.

In their post-mortem analyses of the elections, the party pundits of right and left could agree on one fundamental feature of their defeat: the fellow travelers from the middle class, who had helped the party to victory in 1903, had deserted it in 1907. Social Democracy had retained only the districts of overwhelming labor concentration. Its signal failure in the run-off elections was a sure sign that the middle classes were behaving as a "reactionary mass." Why had the professional men deserted? Why the shopkeepers, the salaried employees — all those who, though not workers, lived in dependence on capitalism and who had identified themselves with Social Democracy four years before? On one answer the analysts could agree again: that the government's national appeal had been effective. Kautsky felt that the ruling class had found the political answer to the vision of socialism in "the fascinating effect of the colonial state of the future." Social Democracy, said Kautsky, had underestimated the attractive power of imperialism, which was growing symbiotically with the increasing fear of socialism.[14] The revisionists too saw the national and colonial appeal as a factor in the defeat, though they assigned it a secondary position.[15]

But neither radicals nor revisionists saw in the power of chau-

[14] *N.Z.*, XXV, i, 588–590.
[15] *S.M.*, XI (XIII), i, 104–106, 111–112, 245.

vinism a sufficient cause for the loss of the election. In their further analyses, and in the consequences they drew for the party tactic, their paths sharply diverged. So bitter did the war of words between the factions become that, only two weeks after the first election returns were in, the executive had to issue an appeal to the party reminding its members "that we are party comrades," and that the elections should be discussed "in a strictly factual manner." [16]

The core of the revisionist analysis was that the party had brought on its own defeat by its excessive radicalism. Social Democracy had lost its nimbus, the revisionists argued, by its illusionistic dedication to revolutionary phraseology which alienated the middle-class fellow travelers. The existence of the "reactionary mass" could not be denied, said the Baden revisionist leader, Wilhelm Kolb, but it was a creation of the Social Democratic Party. Revolutionary theory was hamstringing reformist practice. Social Democracy could "no longer transgress against the evolutionary idea." [17] Thus the revisionists used the defeat of 1907 to justify a new assault on the party's radicalism.

The radicals, who began with the premise that the party program and tactic were correct, could see in the election only a confirmation of their own thesis: that the class struggle was sharpening. The party's errors were errors not of basic policy, but of agitational technique.

In the desertion of the middle-class fellow travelers the radicals found proof of the fundamental unreliability of that sector of society as supports of a socialist party. Here, according to Kautsky, was the unstable social element *par excellence*. The middle-class fellow travelers gave the party its victory in 1903 and deprived them of it in 1907. Why? In 1903, said Kautsky, a large sector of the middle classes feared the rising cost of living which the tariff of 1902 might bring. They supported the Social Democratic Party in an electoral campaign against the tariffs. Since that time, the cost of living had indeed risen in the midst of a wave of prosperity, but this had brought a great intensification of labor struggles and strikes in 1905 and 1906. The middle-class voter held labor responsible for his ris-

---

[16] *Ibid.*, 247.
[17] *Ibid.*, ii, 702ff. For variations on the same theme, see also *ibid.*, i, 265–271, 451–459; ii, 693–702.

ing cost of living. The swift development of consumer coöperatives — another product of the workers' effort to keep pace with the cost of living — alienated the small tradesman from the S.P.D. The peasant profited from the high meat prices, which Social Democracy had to combat, while he suffered from the high price of consumers' goods, fixed by cartels but blamed on labor. These were the economic and psychological factors which Kautsky used to explain the susceptibility of the former fellow travelers to the anti-Social Democratic, nationalistic appeal.

With his customary subtlety, Kautsky thus advanced his counterargument to the revisionist thesis: not revolutionary agitation drove the lower middle classes into the arms of the enemy, but rather the "practical daily work" of the labor movement which every reformist accepted — the unions' fight for higher wages and the expansion of the coöperatives.[18]

Kautsky's analysis was supplemented during February and March by a series of articles in *Neue Zeit* which examined the election results in specific regions.[19] These only confirmed the hypothesis that, when the chips were down, the peasant and lower middle classes arrayed themselves against Social Democracy. Far from concluding that a change in party line was called for, the radicals would generally have agreed with Franz Mehring that the party must adhere to its "true course": The cloak which "the flattering sunshine" of electoral victory in 1903 could not tempt the party to discard "can still less be torn off by a raw wind."[20]

For all their fondness for their old cloak, the radicals felt the lash of the raw wind. They too sought for ways in which the party could strengthen itself against future storms. The politically indifferent and the middle classes had given reaction a free hand. The consequences would be increased armaments and taxes, greater suspicion of Germany abroad, growing isolation, and the danger of international crises and of a world war. This, according to Kautsky and his friends, was the dark future which the party must prepare to face.

Where the revisionist commentators drew as the principal lesson

---

[18] N.Z., XXV, i, 590–595.
[19] Cf. *ibid.*, 668–682, 706–708.
[20] *Ibid.*, 619.

of the election the need to drop the radical tactic, Kautsky called upon the party to dedicate its full energy to a hitherto neglected task: the fight against chauvinism and war. With their opponents prepared to dig their own graves through their world policy, Kautsky observed, the Social Democrats could give only one answer to the nationalist challenge: "Social Democracy is Peace!" [21] *Vorwärts* moved the problem of militarism into the center of discussion, not without a pessimistic twist: the political pressure on the exploited class would grow with the state's military might, and as this pressure increased, "the weakening of the state through a war" would become "the precondition for its development toward freedom." [22] Karl Liebknecht, who had been trying since 1904 to focus the party's attention on the growing importance of the problem of war, could now use the election results to hammer home his views:

The elections . . . showed how shamefully slight was the German people's capacity to resist the pseudo-patriotic catchwords of the contemptible professional patriots . . . For the proletariat, the elections [should bring] necessary clarification, self-examination, a lesson on the social and political alignment of forces, . . . liberation from the unfortunate 'habit of victory,' and a welcome compulsion to deepen the proletarian movement and its understanding of the psychology of the masses with respect to the national question.[23]

The radicals' response to the electoral defeat was thus to demand a sharper attack on that nationalism which had been the party's undoing at the polls.

iii. The Status of the National Question before 1907

The rapid development of fundamental divisions within the party on the issues of foreign policy and war was favored by the absence of a firm line on such questions in previous party history. During the long period of peace after 1871, Social Democracy neglected international questions for problems of general theory, organization, and domestic political action. The party had, to be sure, a legacy

---

[21] *Ibid.*, 596.

[22] *Vorwärts*, 8 Apr. 1907.

[23] Karl Liebknecht, *Militarismus und Antimilitarismus unter besonderer Berücksichtigung der internationalen Jugendbewegung* (Berlin, n. d. [1919?]). Preface (11 Feb. 1907), vi.

of judgments by Marx and Engels on war and diplomacy, based on
the criterion of the revolutionary struggle of the European working
class against reaction. From their masters, the German Social Democrats took over two ideas: Russophobia and the idea of the citizen
army or militia. Both these standards of judgment were based on
conditions prevailing in mid-nineteenth-century Europe: Russia as
the "bastion of reaction," great-power alignments roughly following
institutional differences among the major European states, a living
democratic tradition in the middle classes, and the absence of an
organized proletariat as an independent political force. All these
factors (except the third in Western Europe) tended to disappear
as the nineteenth century drew to a close. In the nineties, with the
conclusion of the Franco-Russian alliance, it became difficult for
German Social Democracy to oppose both Tsar and Kaiser. The
party began to lay greater stress on the principle of national defense,
which was added to Russophobia and militia as a third criterion for
the party's judgments on foreign policy.

With the turn of the century and the alignment of powers according to no recognizable constitutional principle, the connection
of these criteria with the revolutionary interest of the European
proletariat became tenuous indeed. After the Tsar's sponsorship of
the first Hague Peace Conference in 1899 and, above all, after the
Revolution of 1905, it became clear that Russia was no longer able
to serve as the "bastion of reaction" for all Europe. Meanwhile,
"world politics" — what we now call imperialism — began to occupy
the center of the stage.

Under these circumstances, the traditions of Russophobia, national defense, and the citizens' militia became detached from Social
Democracy's internal doctrine of revolution. While emphasizing the
latter and turning its primary attention to domestic affairs, the Social Democratic delegation in the Reichstag sought simply to freeze
the international *status quo* against the unsettling dynamic of world
imperialism.

Emphasis on the defensive criterion led the Social Democrats to
replace the problem of the relationship between the sovereign bourgeois state and the international revolution by a different problem:
that of international ethics among the bourgeois states. The vital
question was no longer: "Which state is the greatest enemy of the

revolution?" but rather, "Which is the aggressor?" The interest of
the proletariat was assumed to be that of the attacked nation. While
the maintenance of peace and "saturation" became the ends of their
peacetime foreign policy, the principle of national defense prepared
a justification for Social Democratic support of the state in the event
of war. Similarly, the demand for a militia lost its revolutionary
flavor in the era of imperialism when more stress was placed on the
militia's relationship to the principle of national defense than on its
revolutionary implications. The party in parliament could advance
the non-fulfillment of its demand for a militia system as a reason
for voting against military budgets. It would thus not be too national. But, on the same basis, it could indicate its readiness to support the nation in the event of attack. It would thus be national
enough. Such was the position which the Social Democratic Reichstag deputation slowly evolved during the first fifteen years of William II's reign.[24]

Outside the Reichstag, the party's interest in foreign affairs and
the great problems of war and peace remained surprisingly slight
before 1907. Between 1900 and 1907, only one congress saw a full-
fledged discussion on foreign policy: that of 1900 at Mainz, where
world and colonial policy was debated.[25] If the revisionist theorists
from the late 90's onward pressed for a more positive orientation
toward national issues,[26] their views were treated not as part of
the "national question," but as just another aspect of the revisionist
heresy.[27] The serious application of Marxian economic theory to
the problem of imperialism — the work of Luxemburg, Kautsky,
Hilferding et al. — was not begun until after 1907. Social Democ-

[24] Hans Rothfels, "Marxismus und auswärtige Politik," in Deutscher Staat und
deutsche Parteien, ed. Paul Wentzcke (Munich and Berlin, 1922), 308–341. Sinclair
W. Armstrong, "The Internationalism of the Early Social Democrats of Germany,"
American Historical Review, XLVII: 245–258 (1942); Carlton J. H. Hayes, "German
Socialism Reconsidered," ibid., XXIII: 62–101 (1917); Max Victor, "Die Stellung
der deutschen Sozialdemokratie zu den Fragen der auswärtigen Politik (1869–1914),"
Archiv für Sozialwissenschaft und Sozialpolitik, LX, i: 147–179 (1928); Arthur
Rosenberg, Democracy and Socialism (New York and London, 1939), passim.

[25] Prot. S. P., 1900, 154–170; for resolution adopted, see ibid., 245.

[26] Cf. Erwin Dörzbacher, Die deutsche Sozialdemokratie und die nationale Machtpolitik bis 1914 (Gotha, 1920), 109ff.

[27] See, for example, Rosa Luxemburg, "Miliz und Militarismus" (1899), reprinted
as an annex to Sozialreform oder Revolution (Leipzig, 1908), 53–64.

racy organized occasional demonstrations against the government's foreign policy, such as those held during the Morocco crisis of 1905,[28] and the party press continually fulminated against armament bills and colonial expenditures which weighed upon the proletarian taxpayers. But the basic fact remains: until 1907 the problems of foreign policy, war, and peace occupied a secondary position. The party left the determination of policy on these issues largely to its parliamentary delegates.

Yet here too, the years 1904–1906 brought signs of change. As usual, the intellectuals responded first to the increasingly threatening international atmosphere and began to point out the inadequacy of party doctrine on militarism and foreign policy. Two stormy petrels of Social Democracy, Karl Liebknecht and Kurt Eisner, both destined for leading roles in the German Revolution, began to press for a more vigorous tactic against war.

Karl Liebknecht (1871–1919), the mercurial son of Wilhelm Liebknecht, who had been co-chairman of the party until his death in 1900, first began to concentrate on the problem of militarism in 1904. He saw in militarism the basic and ultimate weapon of capitalism against the upsurge of Social Democracy. Building upon Engels' idea that the success of a modern revolution was contingent on the conversion of the soldiers, he called upon the party to lift the fight against militarism out of the general agitation of Social Democracy for special, intensified treatment.[29] Liebknecht felt that the place to begin the fight against militarism was among the youth before they were conscripted and subjected to militarist indoctrination. He urged the Bremen congress (1904) to authorize the development of an extensive anti-militarist propaganda among potential recruits.[30] Liebknecht's proposal was rejected by the party leaders as both impractical and unnecessary. The German courts, they said, would never tolerate anti-militarist agitation among the youth.[31] The fight against militarism was being conducted indirectly through the propagation of socialism. Before the victory of socialism, the executive's spokesman said, militarism could not be

[28] Prot. S. P., 1905, 35–38.
[29] Ibid., 1904, 178–179. His ideas achieved maturity in the pamphlet, Militarismus und Antimilitarismus, published in 1907.
[30] Prot. S. P., 1904, 131 (motion no. 105).
[31] Ibid., 179.

overthrown.[32] While Liebknecht's motion received a little support from the floor, his later recollection of its fate was essentially correct: it was "rejected with a certain amount of scornful laughter." [33]

The radical upsurge of 1905, taken together with the Moroccan crisis, created a somewhat more favorable atmosphere for Liebknecht. At the Jena congress, he introduced a much sharper resolution than that of 1904, designating militarism and navalism as "the strongest pillars of the present ruling classes," and calling for "a regular, well-planned and well-executed agitation." As a "first step," public meetings were to be held before the day of induction to inform future soldiers of their rights under military law. Thus enlightened, the recruits would "see for the first time how the service regulations are violated by their superiors" and would "acquire a repugnance for militarism." [34] Bebel rejected the first part of the motion which sought to give new primacy to anti-militarist activity. He was prepared to accept Liebknecht's concrete proposal for pre-induction meetings — deleting, to be sure, the ominous designation of the action as a "first step." So it was voted.[35]

Meanwhile, Kurt Eisner (1867–1919) opened up the struggle for a reorientation of Social Democratic policy at another level, that of foreign affairs proper. A gifted literary critic of middle-class origin, Eisner was one of the outstanding revisionist intellectuals.[36] No believer in dialectical materialism, he was drawn to Social Democracy by his burning democratic idealism which could find no home in the other parties of the time. Eisner accepted nothing in life that did not conform to his high, Condorcet-like conception of the human potential for good. He shared neither Bernstein's idea that a just social order would emerge from the linear progress of the economy, nor the Marxist view that it would be produced by a dialectic process. A voluntaristic humanist, Eisner believed that "the task of all human activity is not to make necessary what is possible, but to make possible what is necessary." [37] "Necessity" was for him

[32] *Ibid.*, 185.
[33] *Ibid., 1905*, 284.
[34] *Ibid.*, 99 (motion no. 19).
[35] *Ibid.*, 283–285.
[36] See the appreciation by Robert Michels, "Kurt Eisner," *Archiv für die Geschichte des Sozialismus und der Arbeiterbewegung*, XIV, iii: 364–391 (1929).
[37] Kurt Eisner, *Gesammelte Schriften* (Berlin, 1919), I, 267.

a kind of categorical imperative which was applied to history through the will of man. His philosophy of socialism bears more kinship to that of Jean Jaurès than to that of any German.[38]

As early as 1900, Eisner had concerned himself with the problems of militarism and imperialism. He had then advanced the thesis that Social Democracy was distinguished from all other parties not by advocacy of socialism, which he saw spreading throughout society, but by its opposition to war and *Weltpolitik* through its refusal to countenance "the plunge into the abyss." [39] The Morocco crisis came to him as a tremendous shock, making him realize "that German world policy was no mere rhetorical romanticism, no mere . . . dilettantish Niebelungen aesthetics." He saw the world war approaching "like an ineluctable fate." [40]

Eisner thenceforth devoted his energy to spur on the Social Democratic fight against war. Although forty years old when the Morocco crisis broke, he embarked for the first time in his life on a speech-making campaign. His Social Democratic audiences responded to his ideas with passive resistance. Eisner was made to feel that matters of foreign policy lay far outside their interest. "War belonged to the many articles of faith in which one did *not* believe, or perhaps more correctly: to which one had become so accustomed as a phrase [used] in meetings and the newspapers that it had lost its content." [41]

Eisner tried to fill the empty phrase, to make the party aware of the concrete content of German foreign policy. Thus in the beginning of 1906, he wrote an extensive pamphlet analyzing the Moroccan affair, drawing on the French yellow book for material.[42] His claim that his was the first effort in recent Social Democratic history to present the detailed facts of international life is, as nearly as I have been able to discover, justified. As editor of the Nürnberg party organ, he continued his campaign, often to the irritation of the local party brethren.[43]

[38] Eisner's philosophy was not systematic. It is to be gathered in his plays, literary criticism, and political essays collected in the *Gesammelte Schriften,* 2 vols.
[39] Cf. "Der goldene Magnetberg," *ibid.,* I, 264–284.
[40] *Ibid.,* I, 326–327.
[41] *Ibid.,* I, 329.
[42] Eisner, "Der Sultan des Weltkriegs," *ibid.,* I, 326ff.
[43] *Ibid.,* I, 330.

Eisner's efforts were always handicapped by the fact that he was a revisionist, though his ideas on foreign policy were the opposite of those generally prevailing in the revisionist camp. The Berlin radicals forced his resignation from the staff of *Vorwärts* in November 1905 because he opposed the mass strike. Partly because of his position on domestic and theoretical questions, a deaf ear was turned to his valuable contributions in the field of foreign affairs. His pamphlet on Morocco was not even distributed.[44] The revisionists who honored Eisner for his anti-radicalism on domestic questions had no sympathy for his "anti-national" views.

At the Mannheim congress in 1906, Liebknecht again tried to get the party to embark on a more determined anti-militarist agitation. He now had an added counter to play: a newly organized Social Democratic youth movement which placed great emphasis on the fight against militarism.[45] Liebknecht could point to a resolution of the International of 1900, which imposed the duty of anti-militarist agitation among the youth.[46] Where the French and Belgian Socialists had achieved much in carrying out the International's resolution, the German party had done "as good as nothing." Even the Jena resolution on pre-induction propaganda had remained a dead letter. Liebknecht proposed that the party institute a special central commission for anti-militarist agitation, a kind of "general staff" to lead the attack against this "last . . . and strongest bulwark of the ruling class." [47]

This was the Mannheim congress, not Jena. Bebel came down on Liebknecht like a ton of bricks. His unparalleled heat indicated that this was an issue on which he would brook no opposition — and no change. The comparison with the French and Belgian parties particularly nettled Bebel and brought out all his innate nationalism.

It is incomprehensible to me how he can hold up to us the example of Belgium. A country which signifies nothing, and whose army cannot be

[44] *Ibid.*, I, 328–329.
[45] See below, Ch. IV, sec. iii.
[46] For the text of the International's resolution, see Carl Grünberg, *Die Internationale und der Weltkrieg*. Part I, "Vor dem Kriege und während der ersten Kriegswochen" (Leipzig, 1916), 9–10.
[47] *Prot. S. P., 1906*, 383–384.

compared to Prussian military organization. In France it's the same.
There anti-militaristic agitation has been carried on only in the last two
years. (Liebknecht: And excellently!) No! in such a one-sided and exaggerated fashion! (Lively approval) If it were done in like manner in
Germany — no, thank you! I should decline.[48]

Bebel raised the Liebknecht proposal at once to an issue of confidence. He accused Liebknecht of trying, through his proposed committee, to undermine the authority of the executive. The only function of the executive under Liebknecht's plan, he said, would be to
do the bidding of his anti-militarist commission. Bebel paid no attention to Liebknecht's denials. If the party congress accepted the
motion, he said, it would also have to "choose appropriate authorities to execute it." [49] Liebknecht's supporters did not feel strong
enough to show themselves in the face of Bebel's wrath. The motion was buried.

The changed status of the Russian question was likewise touched
upon briefly at the Mannheim congress. Here again nothing was
settled, but the later divergence of view between the radicals and
the executive was adumbrated. The Mülhausen (Alsace) delegation
introduced a resolution pointing to the fulminations of the rightist
press against the Russian Revolution as an indication that the German government might intervene against the revolutionaries. It
asked that the party executive consult with the general commission
of the trade-unions concerning the use of the mass strike against
a German war of intervention in Russia.[50]

Bebel's initial rejection of this proposal was based on two arguments: first, that Germany would not intervene lest she unleash a
European war; second, that when war came the military would
take over law and order, and any resistance would be folly. He
described the conditions which would prevail on the outbreak of
war: the chauvinistic atmosphere, "the fever which will grip the
masses," the workers called to the colors, the powerlessness of the
party, the ruthlessness of military courts, etc. The description, as
the event proved, was accurate enough; to his listeners, however,
it was a sign that Bebel had no will to prepare the party for such

[48] Ibid., 386–387.
[49] Ibid., 385.
[50] Ibid., 117.

an eventuality, that he saw the situation as hopeless from the start.[51]

The radicals were indeed shocked by his position. Their statements make it clear that they were not aware how far the executive had departed from the revolutionary criteria of international politics. Indeed they tended to regard Bebel's utterance as a slip of the tongue rather than a serious statement of policy.[52] Luxemburg expressed her surprise with her accustomed wit:

I wanted to say a few words on the address of Bebel, but I am not sure that I correctly grasped his words, for I was sitting on the left side of the house while he was speaking today toward the right.[53]

Luxemburg focused her criticism upon the crucial difference in Bebel's attitude toward reaction in domestic matters and in foreign affairs: Bebel had asserted that the proletariat would have to fend off an attack on universal suffrage by every means — including the mass strike — even at the risk of defeat. But in the case of a war — even a war of counter-revolutionary intervention — he was not prepared to take such a risk. Luxemburg contrasted his speech with the statement of the French Socialist leader Vaillant, who had declared, with respect to a war of intervention in Russia, *"Plutôt l'insurrection que la guerre."* [54]

Whatever the sentiments of the delegates at the Mannheim congress, only the future Spartacists felt moved to speak against Bebel on the intervention question. Mülhausen in Alsace, which offered the resolution on the question, was the bailiwick of Ludwig Emmel who was later to be among the first to join Liebknecht in voting against the war credits. The speakers against Bebel were Liebknecht, Luxemburg, and Hermann Duncker of Dresden — all later Spartacists. Although they had not yet formed a separate wing in the party, their behavior at the Mannheim congress was a portent of the future role they were to play as gadflies of the party on the war issue.

Bebel gave some ground before the attacks of the radicals. In his closing words he returned to his customary posture of oratorical

[51] *Ibid.*, 240–241.
[52] *Ibid.*, 261–262, 274, 282.
[53] *Ibid.*, 261.
[54] *Ibid.*, 261–262.

defiance of war and reaction, alleging that his words had been mis-
understood.[55] His reversal did not quiet the misgivings he had
raised in the breasts of the radicals. Kautsky wrote that Bebel's
assurances in his closing words "could not remove the impression
which his first speech had made." [56] Anti-tsarism, the principal nineteenth-century criterion of international Socialist and, indeed, democratic behavior, was for the most part an anachronism. But in
1906, when it attained a brief moment of at least hypothetical ap-
plicability, the executive made it clear that it had abandoned the
old standard. Bebel showed that he looked upon action against the
government on the outbreak of war — even an overtly counter-
revolutionary war — as a futile procedure. He likewise opposed
with the greatest vigor Liebknecht's effort to persuade the party to
pursue a more active anti-militarist agitation. Thus the same congress of Mannheim which brought the conservative reversal on the
mass strike question revealed that a new divergence was arising
between the more extreme radicals and the party leadership on the
question of war and peace.

iv. The Party Practitioners: Compromise
with Nationalism?

If division on the national question was foreshadowed before
1907, it was not until that year that its importance became generally recognized. The electoral defeat brought home to the party as
no international crisis had the fact that problems of foreign policy
and war could no longer be ignored. Not because they were recognized as vital in themselves, but because they had affected the
progress of the party on the domestic front, the party was impelled
to face up to them in one way or another. We have already considered the broader role assigned to the national question by the
radical theorists in their analysis of the elections. We must now
turn to the impact of the defeat on the behavior of the party prac-
titioners.

The party leadership in the Reichstag — which, on this problem,
meant Bebel — was more determined than ever to clear Social Democracy of the "slanderous" campaign charges that it was anti-

[55] *Ibid.*, 300–301.
[56] *N.Z.*, XXV, i, 9.

national. The Reichstag debates on the military budget in April 1907 gave Bebel his opportunity. With the assistance of a freshman deputy, Gustav Noske, he showed how the old concepts of militia and a people's army could be turned to support the idea of national interest.

Bebel attacked the abuses of German militarism with the usual examples of brutal treatment of soldiers and of harsh military justice. But his humanitarian critique of the army flowed into a more prominent argument: that militarism and its abuses impaired the fighting quality of the German army. Endless drill took valuable time away from real war training while low pay for soldiers and the unnecessarily long term of service (two years) made military life unattractive to youth. Bebel held up as an ideal the *"Scharnhorstgedanke"* of a citizen army. He cited long commentaries from German generals and military writers extolling the morale and efficiency of armies based on the militia system, such as Switzerland's and Sweden's. Perhaps most striking was Bebel's advocacy of compulsory pre-military training for youth. He held before the Reichstag the example of Japan's fencing schools, where " 'little tykes go at each other with such a fiery zeal . . . that any European must recognize [the high value of] this gymnastic training for the future defenders of the realm.' " [57]

Bebel rejected charges that Social Democracy was dishonest in advocating any reforms. [58] Proletarians made up the bulk of the army, Bebel replied; almost all party members went through it. As the consistent defender of its followers' material interest, the party was only true to itself when it fought for improvements in the army. It voted against the military budgets only because the financial burden fell upon the people. Were the funds provided by direct Reich taxes rather than by indirect taxes, Social Democracy would vote the funds for the military establishment.

[57] Cited by Bebel from *Leipziger Neueste Nachrichten,* 1906, No. 138, in *Stenographische Berichte der Verhandlungen des deutschen Reichstages,* CCXXVIII, 1062. Hereafter cited as *Reichstag Debates.* It was not the first time that Bebel recommended compulsory training for youth. Cf. Victor, "Stellung der Sozialdemokratie," *Archiv für Sozialwissenschaft,* LX, i, 155, n. 38.

[58] Made by the National Liberal, Count von Oriola, *Reichstag Debates,* CCXXVIII, 1049.

The burden of Bebel's address was thus to justify the militia system on grounds of military efficiency and of national interest and to indicate that Social Democracy had both a material stake and an ideal interest in a powerful, reformed army. His party wished only that, through democratic reforms, the German army regain its lost position of primacy among the armies of Europe.[59]

The premises for Bebel's position were expounded by Gustav Noske. It was Noske's first major speech in the Reichstag: a fitting start for his later career as political chief of the counter-revolutionary armies in the first stormy year of the Republic.[60] Denying the persistent representations of Social Democrats as "vagabonds without a fatherland," Noske stated that the party's stand on militarism was "conditioned by our acceptance of the principle of nationality." Advocating the independence of every nation, the Social Democrats would of course fend off attacks on Germany "with as much determination as any gentleman on the right side of the House." They wished that Germany be "as well armed [*wehrhaft*] as possible" and that "the whole people have an interest in the military establishment which is necessary to the defense of our fatherland." But these goals could be achieved only if the government and the other parties would "work with Social Democracy to make Germany as liveable, as free and as culturally great as can be imagined."[61] Where the party traditionally advocated military reform as part of the struggle for a free society, Noske called for a freer society in order to produce a stronger state.

The government, in the person of Prussian War Minister Count von Einem, was quick to seize upon these protestations of patriotism. The count accepted Noske's statement "that his party is determined to defend the German Empire against an aggressive war

---

[59] *Ibid.*, 1058ff.

[60] Noske sat for the 16th Saxon district, the center of which was Chemnitz. Although Chemnitz was a large industrial city and a later Communist stronghold, the Social Democratic machine had for years been in control of the right wing. Noske inherited the seat of the pioneer revisionist, Max Schippel, who was pressed into resigning his mandate because he favored a high tariff policy, which the national party opposed. Cf. Ernst Heilmann, *Geschichte der Arbeiterbewegung in Chemnitz und dem Erzgebirge* (Chemnitz, 1912[?]), 295–300; also Gustav Noske, *Erlebtes aus Aufstieg und Niedergang einer Demokratie* (Offenbach, 1947), 20–21.

[61] *Reichstag Debates*, CCXXVIII, 1098–1101.

in the same manner and with the same devotion as the other parties." [62] While thus welcoming the Social Democrats into the national camp, von Einem took occasion to point out that the professions of their Reichstag deputies did not coincide with the views of the party agitators. Von Einem quoted editorials from *Vorwärts* and the Erfurt *Tribüne* denigrating the heroism of the soldiers in the Franco-Prussian war and extolling striking workers as the real heroes of Germany.[63] He touched Bebel in a sensitive spot — no doubt unwittingly — by quoting a flaming passage from Liebknecht's newly published *Militarism and Anti-militarism,* showing how the persistent mishandling of German soldiers in the army could serve as "a splendid means to combat militarism from the ground up and with success, to whip up ever broader masses of the people against it, to carry class-consciousness into . . . otherwise inaccessible sectors of the population." The minister drew the conclusions for his Social Democratic hearers: if this passage was true, then the deputies were making their complaints concerning the maltreatment of soldiers "less to combat them than to make propaganda." If the party leaders had no such motives, they should combat such books as Liebknecht's.[64] Von Einem drew the same lesson from his newspaper quotations: "If you don't want the editors to write that way, . . . then throw these editors out of the window, take another set . . ." So too the party leaders should liquidate the Social Democratic youth organization whose propaganda was inconsistent with national defense.[65]

The minister's quotations had their due effect. Bebel, obviously annoyed and embarrassed at the citations from Liebknecht, declared in answer to von Einem that the party's position was as he had stated it. He added — and it was a bold statement for a Social Democratic leader to make — that comments made or written by persons outside the house "are not and cannot be representative of the party in any way." [66]

The minister of war had played his hand well. Mingling his

[62] *Ibid.,* 1101.
[63] *Ibid.,* 1102.
[64] *Ibid.,* 1081–1082.
[65] *Ibid.,* 1102.
[66] *Ibid.,* 1089.

gratification at the Social Democrats' professions of patriotism with Homeric taunts, he pointed out to Bebel and his co-believers that their next task was to carry their good fight into the party. If they meant what they said, let them clean house! Thus the government took advantage of the atmosphere created by the recent elections to force the national issue forward within the Social Democratic camp.

Where the government had reason to be gratified, the radicals were quick to blame. While the nationalist papers echoed von Einem's pleasure at Noske's stand, the left-wing *Leipziger Volkszeitung* went over to the offensive.[67] Its attack on Noske unleashed a general hue and cry in the radical party press against compromise on the war question and an almost unanimous protest against Noske's excessive stress on Social Democracy's willingness to fight for the Kaiser. The revisionists leapt to Noske's defense. Deep into the summer raged the "Noske debate," in which, for the first time, the national question was broadly discussed in the party.[68]

v. The International Congress; the National Question Begged

The "Noske debate" blended into a discussion of the policy which the German party should pursue at the congress of the Socialist International scheduled to meet in Stuttgart in August 1907. The agenda was to include militarism and colonialism. The revisionists, evidently fearing that the International would take a doctrinaire line on these problems, advocated limitations on the competence of the congress. The International was not the authority "to regulate the policies of the separate countries," let alone to impose "binding obligations to undertake any sort of specific action." [69] The International was to be left only enough authority to "decisively disavow anti-militarism," to "compel" the French party "to proceed more strongly against the mischief [of the extreme anti-militarists] in its own ranks," and to emphasize that

[67] *Prot. S. P., 1907*, 260. The *Berliner Tageblatt* on 26 April 1907 paraphrased Lord Byron's remark on Grillparzer: "Noske is not a melodious name, but posterity will have to pay heed to it." Quoted in *N.Z.*, XXV, ii, 178; cf. also Noske, *Erlebtes*, 29.

[68] *Prot. S. P., 1907*, 282; *N.Z.*, XXV, ii, 177–178, 855–856; *S.M.*, XI (XIII), i, 434–440; Noske, *Erlebtes*, 30.

[69] *S.M.*, XI (XIII), ii, 675–67

socialism is not against colonies in principle.[70] The *Sozialistische Monatshefte* published an article by Ramsay MacDonald demonstrating that "everything tends to drive international socialism into national channels," and that therefore the national sections must be accorded maximum freedom of action.[71]

The radicals in *Neue Zeit* argued that where the bourgeoisie was dividing into mutually antagonistic states the proletarian interest in a stronger International necessarily increased. The organization must widen its competence, lay down firm lines on all problems of international import. The effort of doubters who wished to reduce the International to the level of a tea party for the exchange of views, Mehring said, would have to be firmly resisted.[72]

Within the German delegation to the Stuttgart International congress the possibilities of resistance to the conservative current were small indeed. The system of selection was worked out by party executive and general commission before the Mannheim congress, and bore the stamp of their 1906 conservatism. Half the delegates were to be provided by the trade-unions. The other half were to be selected not by the party congress, but by the state or provincial organizations — a system which assured strong representation to the revisionist machines of Bavaria, Baden, Württemberg, Hessen, and Hanover.[73] Thus the radicals were hopelessly outnumbered. German policy at the congress faithfully reflected the composition of the delegation. It followed the line not of the official *Neue Zeit,* but of the unofficial *Sozialistische Monatshefte:* maximum autonomy to the national sections, minimum authority to the International on all major questions.

The most important task facing the Stuttgart congress was to hammer out a position on militarism and war. Under the impact of the international crises of 1905–06, voices had been raised in the socialist parties of all countries for a more precise definition of the obligation to combat militarism and war, and of the methods whereby this might be done. The French party at its Limoges congress in 1906 had taken a position which confirmed the principle of

[70] *Ibid.,* 676–677.
[71] James Ramsay MacDonald, "Der internationale sozialistische Kongress und die nationalen sozialistischen Parteien," *S.M.,* XI (XIII), ii, 589–594.
[72] *N.Z.,* XXV, ii, 620; cf. also 660–667.
[73] *Prot. S. P., 1906,* 133 (motion no. 144), 222.

national defense against an aggressor, but which also called upon the international proletariat to join their efforts "to prevent and forestall the outbreak of war by all means, from parliamentary action, public propaganda and popular demonstrations, to general strike and insurrection." [74] This resolution, reaffirmed at the congress of Nancy in 1907, became the basis of the French majority position at Stuttgart.[75] Gustave Hervé, of the quasi-syndicalist wing of the party, submitted to Stuttgart a separate resolution denying that a defensive war could be consistent with the proletarian interest and imposing upon all countries the duty to "answer any declaration of war, from whatever side it might come, with a military [soldiers' and reservists'] strike and insurrection." [76]

At the International Bureau meeting in March 1906, the Germans had opposed in vain the French effort to include anti-militarism on the coming congress' agenda.[77] Succumbing to international pressure to go beyond the previous decisions, Bebel submitted to the Stuttgart congress' committee on militarism a lengthy resolution against war. The resolution emphasized the duty of "the workers and especially their representatives in parliament . . . to combat land and sea armaments and to refuse the funds therefore"; recommended the militia system "as an essential guarantee against aggressive wars"; and urged that, if war should threaten, each country's working class use the means most likely to prevent it or, "if it should break out, intervene for its speedy termination." [78] The resolution contained no hint of joint international action by the Socialist parties, nor were any actions beyond moral protest indicated.

Bebel and the ex-army officer, Georg von Vollmar took the most intransigent position with respect to the French majority resolution which they attacked as syndicalism and "Hervéism." Arguing now the unreality of any threat of war and the pacific intentions of the German government, now the impossibility of full-fledged anti-military agitation in autocratic Germany, Bebel and Vollmar resisted

[74] Jean Jaurès, *Oeuvres*, V, *Pour la Paix*, iii (Paris, 1933), 101ff.

[75] *Internationaler Sozialisten-Kongress zu Stuttgart, 1907* (Berlin, 1907), 86. Hereafter cited as *Int. Kong., 1907*.

[76] *Ibid.*, 87.

[77] Robert Michels, "Die deutsche Sozialdemokratie im internationalen Verbande," *Archiv für Sozialwissenschaft und Sozialpolitik*, XXV, 227–228 (July 1907).

[78] *Int. Kong., 1907*, 85–86.

any "method of struggle which might harm the party or, under certain circumstances, become fatal to its existence." [79] What the Germans most feared, of course, was any mention of — let alone a commitment to — the use of the mass strike. Hence their attack on the French centered in an assault on Hervéism. Bebel and the trade-unionists could not win as easy a victory at the International congress as they had in reversing the commitment to the mass strike at home. Neither Belgians nor French, Poles nor Russians wished to exclude the mass strike from the possible forms of action against war. In vain did Vollmar argue that the French offered "nothing but an old recipe, a warming over of the suggestions of Nieuwenhuis" whose anarchistic proposals on the general strike had been repeatedly rejected at earlier International congresses.[80] The concept of the mass strike was too firmly established in twentieth-century left-wing socialism to be rejected with nineteenth-century precedents. Lenin, who was a member of the committee, probably reflected the views of a substantial segment of radical opinion when he wrote in his diary:

Even though Hervé did show that he was lightminded, superficial . . . , it would be extreme short-sightedness to reply to him by a mere dogmatic exposition of the general truths of socialism. Vollmar particularly dropped into this error, and Bebel and Guesde were not entirely free of it. With the extraordinary conceit of a man infatuated with stereotyped parliamentarism, Vollmar attacked Hervé without noticing that his own narrow-mindedness and hardened opportunism *compel* one to recognize the living stream in Hervéism *in spite* of the theoretical absurdity and folly of the manner in which Hervé himself presents the question. It sometimes happens that at a new turning point of a movement, theoretical absurdities cover up some practical truth . . .[81]

The "practical truth" which Lenin saw in Hervéism was that the working class could not identify itself with the interest of any

[79] *Ibid.*, 81–83, 91–93, 98–101.

[80] *Ibid.*, 92. Domela Nieuwenhuis of Holland had tried to win acceptance of the mass strike as an anti-war tactic at the Brussels and Zürich congresses (1891 and 1893). Until the congress of 1907, the method had been viewed as an anarchist or syndicalist heresy. Cf. William English Walling, *The Socialists and the War* (New York, 1915), 42–48.

[81] Quoted in Bertram D. Wolfe, *Three Who Made a Revolution* (New York, 1948), 599.

one of the belligerents in a coming conflict but that it could "take advantage of the crisis created by the war for hastening the downfall of the bourgeoisie." [82] The revolutionary socialists' new policy toward war was taking form: unable to find its advantage in the cause of any given belligerent, the proletariat must now oppose war, as well as might be, with revolution. Believing that a revolutionary era was again at hand, the radicals could not follow Bebel in adhering rigidly to previous methods of struggle; but as Marxists who believed that mass strikes and insurrections could arise only under certain historical conditions they could not follow Hervé in fixing in advance the specific type of action to be taken on the outbreak of war.

Their intermediate theoretical position made it possible for the Eastern European members, under Rosa Luxemburg's leadership,[83] to propose an amendment which synthesized Bebel's passive Marxism with the French demand for mass action in case of war. The amendment read as follows:

If the outbreak of war threatens, it is the duty of the workers and their parliamentary representatives in the countries involved, with the aid of the International Bureau, to exert all their efforts to prevent the war by means of coordinated action. They shall use the means which appear the most appropriate to them, and which will necessarily vary according to the sharpness of the class struggle and the general political situation. If war should nevertheless break out, they have the duty to work for its speedy termination, and to exploit with all their might the economic and political crisis created by the war to arouse the population and to hasten the overthrow of capitalist rule.[84]

The Luxemburg amendment thus turned Bebel's resolution in a revolutionary direction. Since it imposed no obligation for a specified type of direct action, however, it was finally acceptable to the Germans. The principal French demand was met by including the mass strike in a long list of actual actions which had been taken against war in various countries. Thus the deadlock was compro-

[82] *Ibid.*, 600.
[83] Luxemburg represented Poland at the congress.
[84] There is slight variation between the official French text, which is used here, and the German text. The French text is given in Carl Grünberg, *Die Internationale und der Weltkrieg*, I, 12–13; the German, in *Int. Kong.*, *1907*, 102.

mised, with the revolutionary Marxists of the East serving as brokers.

In the Stuttgart resolution on war we see again the unresolved dynamic character of the period after 1905 reflected in socialist thought. Morocco and the Russian Revolution were felt as harbingers of an era of war and social upheaval. The challenge was at hand: one had either to prepare for the crisis or abandon the attempt to meet it. But the crisis itself had not yet assumed concrete form. Most of those who wished to prepare for it could not yet, like Hervé, specify with precision the means with which to face it; while those who would abandon the attempt to revolutionize society were still able to accept a further verbal commitment to follow the revolutionary road as long as the question of specific action was left open.

If a European war was a probability to the Socialists of 1907, colonies were an actuality. Here the Socialist world was therefore more sharply divided. One could accept or reject colonialism; one could not hedge, one could not answer, as to the question of a future war, "Let's see when it comes." The reformists of the colonial powers, led by David of Germany and van Kol of Holland, controlled the committee on colonialism. They introduced into their resolution a passage which, departing from the position taken by the International in 1900 and 1904, stated (1) that the benefits of colonies for the working class "are exaggerated"; and (2) that "the congress does not reject colonial policy in principle and for all time, since it could operate as a civilizing factor under a socialist regime." [85] Both points represented a weakening of the International's previous intransigent opposition to colonialism. On the war question, the left had sought to radicalize the International's tactic; on the colonial issue, the right pressed to alter the International's principles.

The defense of the traditional position on colonies was led by two veteran German parliamentarians, Georg Ledebour and Emanuel Wurm. On behalf of the minority of the colonial committee, they submitted a resolution reaffirming the absolute hostility of the International to colonialism. Thanks to the votes of the delegates from non-colonial countries this minority resolution carried the

[85] *Int. Kong.*, *1907*, 24

congress, 127 to 108.[86] The French, British, and Italians split in the voting. The Germans, however, governed by the unanimity rule, cast their entire block of votes against the minority resolution.

The debates on this issue in the German delegation were particularly bitter since the German party was supposed to be governed by the anti-colonial resolution of the Mainz congress (1900) which the majority, led by Bernstein and David, was now prepared to jettison.[87] The radical minority, "in the face of the compact mass of trade-unionists who control half the votes," was powerless.[88] It had to rely on the votes of the other national sections to rescue its position.

The Stuttgart congress marked a milestone in the evolution of German Social Democracy. The party had revealed itself as the leader of the conservative forces in the International. On the one hand, it had resisted the formulation of a more radical policy against militarism and war in the face of growing international tension; on the other — and this was a really significant change in policy — it had pressed for a fuller acceptance of colonialism. At Stuttgart it became clear in whose favor the post-election debate on these issues was being resolved in the high councils of the German labor movement. Bülow's national election crusade of 1907 here showed, even more strongly than in Bebel's and Noske's Reichstag speeches, its impact on the foreign policy of the party. And if the elections provided the external impetus for the accommodation of Social Democracy to the facts of life in the era of imperialism, the trade-unionists were the primary agency in bringing about that accommodation. Behind Stuttgart stood the victorious coalition of Mannheim: the triple alliance of trade-unionists, party revisionists, and party executive who pushed back the German radicals on the questions of war and colonialism as they had earlier defeated them on domestic tactic.

The party leaders could not, of course, take a step toward the right without provoking thunder on the left. Three weeks after the

[86] *Ibid.*, 24–25, 38–39.

[87] The debate within the German delegation was repeated at the Essen party congress, q.v. in *Prot. S. P., 1907*, 269–292. For the German fight as it appeared in the plenary session at Stuttgart, see *Int. Kong., 1907*, 28–40.

[88] Hugo Haase, Letter to his wife, 22 Aug. 1907, in Ernst Haase, ed., *Hugo Haase, sein Leben und Wirken* (Berlin-Frohnau, n. d. [1929?]), 96.

Stuttgart congress closed, the storm broke at the Essen party convention. In the gloomy, smoky atmosphere of Germany's Pittsburg the controversies on militarism and colonialism were enacted once more.

A whole day of the congress was devoted to the "Noske debate," in which the radicals raked Noske and Bebel over the coals for their support of national defense in the Reichstag. Noske insisted that he had said nothing which had not been said by others before him. He read numerous patriotic citations from the party's "Handbooks for Social Democratic Voters" of 1898, 1903, and 1906, which, though differing little from his own statements, had passed unchallenged in the party. Noske charged that the criticism against him was made "not . . . in order to maintain old party attitudes, but to break ground for new ideas, . . . to push the party further left." [89]

Noske's words contained more than a grain of truth. The same socio-political pressures which made him and Bebel emphasize the aspects of the Social Democratic tradition consistent with patriotism stimulated the radicals to jettison these in favor of a more vigorous anti-military policy. That was the task to which Liebknecht and Eisner were wholeheartedly devoting themselves. The new radical attitude was summed up in a phrase of the *Dortmunder Arbeiterzeitung:* "Rather ten Hervés than a single Vollmar." [90]

Through the debates at Essen ran the dolorous memory of the election defeat. The party realized now that electoral successes on the one hand, and a hostile attitude toward the imperial nation-state and its foreign policy on the other, were increasingly incompatible. Noske was praised or damned according to whether one placed higher value on winning votes or on combating imperialism.[91] The party would one day have to choose between the requirements of a pure parliamentary tactic and its fight against war; that day was not yet, but it had been brought nearer by the events of 1907.

[89] *Prot. S. P., 1907,* 230–231. In his autobiography, by contrast, Noske claimed to be a pioneer in revising the party's position. "The speech, in form and content, went far beyond the previously customary framework," he wrote in 1933. Cf. Noske, *Erlebtes,* 28.

[90] *Prot. S. P., 1907,* 232.

[91] *Ibid.,* 232, 235, 237, 242–243, 246, 249–250.

Acrimonious though they were, the debates led to no test of strength on either the colonial or the military questions.[92] The Stuttgart congress had not only revealed the conservatism of the German delegation, but had also outvoted it. The resolutions of the International which lay before the congress of Essen for ratification were entirely satisfactory to the radicals and were now supported, as compromise decisions of the International, by the executive and most of the right wing. Vollmar, to be sure, said that the party would stand by the resolutions "as we . . . construe them" [93] — a phrase later to become famous when spoken by Chancellor Michaelis with respect to the futile Reichstag peace resolution of 1917. Thus the radicals of France, Russia, and the other countries had saved the German party from more serious division. The resolutions of the International covered the conflict on the national question until the hard facts of the second Moroccan crisis broke the skein of verbiage. Meanwhile the issue took its place beside the mass strike question as a major source of factional cleavage in the German labor movement.

Before the year closed there was yet one more portent of the future. The Imperial Government intervened directly in the affairs of Social Democracy to help Bebel carry out War Minister von Einem's injunction to clean house. On 12 October 1907, the Imperial High Court condemned Karl Liebknecht to one and one-half years in prison for the treasonable statements contained in his pamphlet, *Militarism and Anti-militarism*. Liebknecht made the fullest use of the trial to propagate his views.[94] For his co-believers his trial was a clarion call to even greater exertions against the hated system; for his opponents, a stimulus to greater caution and better party discipline; and for Liebknecht himself, the beginning of a long career of politically explosive martyrdom.

[92] For the colonial debate, see *ibid.*, 269–292.
[93] *Ibid.*, 256.
[94] Karl Liebknecht, *Militarism*, trans. anon. (New York, 1917), i–iv; Richard Calwer, "Der Hochverratsprozess Liebknechts," *S.M.*, XI (XIII), ii, 956.

PART II

THE CONSOLIDATION OF THE RIGHT
1906–1909

Chapter IV

THE EXTENSION OF TRADE-UNION INFLUENCE

i. The Fallow Years

In the two foregoing chapters we have been concerned with the reaction of Social Democracy to the external events which crystallized differences in social theory into conflicts over party practice. The impact of the first of these, the Russian Revolution, had been sufficiently strong to galvanize the party into action. Though brief and abortive, the mass movement for suffrage left an indelible double legacy: the idea of the mass strike as the weapon of the twentieth-century revolution; and the trade-unionists' extension of their power over the party to forestall any further experimentation with such dynamite. The second event, the election of 1907, brought home to the party the power of the imperialist ideology, the state's principal weapon against the socialist threat. The electoral defeat swept the questions of colonialism and war into the arena of factional conflict and deepened the intra-party cleavage. Were it not for the radicalism of the International at Stuttgart, the election experience might have brought the German party even closer to an accommodation to militarism and, therefore, to a split. Thanks largely to the Socialist parties of other nations, German Social Democracy could beg the question at its Essen congress. The period of renascent revolutionism which had opened with a bang in 1905 had ended with a whimper.

With the autumn of 1907 we enter an undramatic period in the party's history. Until mid-1909 the national political scene was dominated by the Bülow Bloc, an alliance of Progressives, National Liberals, and Conservatives which closed off all possibility for Social Democracy to pursue a reformist tactic in the Reichstag. The intra-party conflict over tactic, though it continued at the theoretical level, lost the flavor of actuality. The revisionists ruefully recognized that "positive collaboration" was made impossible by the united front of the ruling parties and the hostility of the state to the labor movement. They agreed with the radicals that, under such circumstances, the party had no choice but to "sharpen its oppositional attitude" and to confine itself to extraparliamentary agitation.[1]

If the historical milieu of the Bülow Bloc was uncongenial to a reformist policy, it was no more favorable to a radical tactic. In the autumn of 1907 the American business depression began to have its repercussions in Germany. The German economic slump was not severe by modern standards. Only in the winter of 1908–09 did unemployment among trade-union members exceed 3 per cent.[2] Nevertheless, the slump was sufficient to sap the vitality of the labor movement as a whole. For the first time since the depression of 1891–1893 the Social Democratic trade-unions lost members.[3] With a contracting labor market, wage movements were inaugurated only under exceptional circumstances. The employers took advantage of the unemployment to cut wages, lengthen hours, and impose lockouts. Three-fourths of the workers involved in work stoppages were forced out on the initiative of entrepreneurs.[4] The unions lost all aggressiveness. In 1909 the numbers involved in work stoppages showed little increase as the depression continued: from 126,883 to 131,244. These figures are slight compared to 507,960 for 1905, 316,042 for 1906 — or 369,011 in the stormy year

[1] Robert Schmidt, "Positive Arbeit," *S.M.*, XI (XIII), ii, 733ff. Cf. also Wilhelm Schroeder, "Vereinsgesetz und positive Tätigkeit," *ibid.*, 516; Eduard Bernstein, "Die Aussichten der Wahlreform in Preussen," *ibid.*, 826; *idem*, "Der Block, der Freisinn und das Landtagswahlrecht," *ibid.*, 906–907.

[2] In the fourth quarter of 1908, unemployment reached its peak of 4.83 per cent. Cf. Internationaler Sekretär, *Bericht, 1909*, 119.

[3] Of 1,865,506 members in 1907, 33,775 were lost in 1908. Less than 1000 were added in 1909. Cf. *ibid.*, *1908*, 126; and *1909*, 120.

[4] Calculated from *ibid.*, *1908*, 139–140.

1910 which was to bring the period of economic depression and political quiescence to a close.[5]

Throughout the years of our study there is a high correlation between the intensity of labor struggle and political radicalism. The years 1903, 1905–06, 1910, and 1913 were all marked by aggressive radicalism within the Social Democratic Party. Only the last was a depression year; but unlike previous depressions, it was characterized by labor unrest and wildcat strikes.[6] In the age of unionism labor militance tends to be highest when the labor market is tight and the cost of living rising; the former factor is the condition of successful union struggle, the second the spur to it. In the years 1907–1909, when the unions could not activate their following, political radicalism was dormant.

Its aggressiveness thus weakened in the years of the Bülow Bloc, Social Democracy returned of necessity to the Erfurt policy of pure but actionless opposition. The internal development of the party during the fallow years, however, was of the greatest consequence for the party's future. In a series of steps hardly perceived by the external world the reformist forces firmly established their control over the party.

The most important aspect of this development, the construction of a mighty party apparatus manned by a reformist bureaucracy, will be reserved for the next chapter. The present chapter will deal with a process which paralleled the building of the party machine: the extension of trade-union power over the party on the basis of the Mannheim "parity" agreement. Having observed in passing how the trade-unions exercised their influence in the framing of party policy toward colonialism and war, we must now analyze the process by which they neutralized two institutions of party life which were significant sources of radical strength: the May Day strike and the youth movement. These case studies will enable us to reconstruct the pattern of trade-union conquest of the party. We shall then examine the beginnings of confusion and division in the radical camp in the face of the alliance between the trade-union general commission and the party executive. Finally, we shall show

[5] *Ibid., 1912*, 124.
[6] See below, Ch. X, sec. ii.

how the external and internal conditions of party life~affected radical theory in the Bülow Bloc period.

ii. The Destruction of a Symbol

May Day was labor's high holiday of defiance. According to international socialist tradition it could be properly celebrated only by a one-day strike. The German radicals adhered with great tenacity to this annual ritual sacrifice in which the workers risked real economic privation to demonstrate their loyalty to their faith. For them May Day was an important factor in strengthening class consciousness: through a symbolic act of defiance of the employer, the workers' sense both of alienation from the capitalist world and of solidarity with their fellow-workers was believed to be heightened. The workers risk the sacrifice of their immediate material interest for an idea? So much the better, the radicals would say. The May Day strike was psychologically useful precisely because it hurt. It bound the proletarians to the greater rather than the lesser cause.

The leaders of the trade-unions, whose political thought centered upon the immediate material interest of the workers, had long rankled under the sacrifices which the May Day strike had often cost the unions. Increasingly, employers exploited the May Day strikes as an occasion for counterattacks on the unions. In 1905 the number of workers locked out after May Day was 6,404; in 1906 a minimum of 32,000 suffered that fate in four cities alone.[7] At the Amsterdam congress of the International in 1904, the German trade-union representatives had tried in vain to have the May Day observance changed from a strike to an evening demonstration.[8] At the Köln trade-union congress of 1905 there were again bitter attacks against the May Day strike, but the top leadership counselled patience. With the concurrence of the general commission, the

[7] Berlin, Hamburg, Leipzig, and Breslau. Cf. Gerhard Kessler, *Die deutschen Arbeitgeberverbände.* Schriften des Vereins für Sozialpolitik, CXXIV (Leipzig, 1907), 245–246. For May Day strike participation and employer counteraction in 1906, see *S.M.*, XI (XIII), ii, 646–648.

[8] Otto Heilborn, *Die "Freien" Gewerkschaften seit 1890* (Jena, 1907), 116–117; Paul Barthel, ed., *Handbuch der deutschen Gewerkschaftskongresse* (Dresden, 1916), 286.

party executive offered a resolution on May Day at the Jena Congress (1905) which re-enunciated the desirability of the demonstration strike "wherever the possibility for it exists." [9]

In 1905 and 1906 the union leaders had not seriously pressed the party for a change in May Day policy. More important issues — the mass strike and the general relationship of party and trade-unions — demanded their full combative energies. With the major battle decided in their favor, however, the trade-unionists proceeded to tackle the May Day question in earnest in 1907.

The problem was not an easy one for the union leadership. The May Day strike enjoyed broad support in the party — and, indeed, in the trade-union rank and file. It was a tradition which, far from losing popularity, had won new vitality with the recent radical wave. Both the number of resolutions offered at the Jena party congress (1905) in favor of strict observance of May Day and the number and vigor of the speakers who opposed the watering-down of May Day action attest to the lively hold which this tradition had on the mind of the party.[10] Any frontal attack on May Day at a party congress would almost certainly have failed. As in the case of the mass strike in 1906 the union leaders had to find some less direct approach.

Their first attack was through the party executive in April 1907. The general commission could present a sound case to the executive. With numerous unions already engaged in strikes and lockouts, and other wage pushes scheduled for the near future, a too rigid observance of May Day might play into the hands of the employers. Sensitive to this appeal, the executive issued on 15 April a release to the party advising against a May Day strike wherever the threat of lockout existed.[11] The release was entirely "legal" for the Jena resolution on May Day had specified only that "work should be stopped wherever the possibility to do so is at hand." [12] The executive simply interpreted this clause in a conservative sense; that is, where employer countermeasures threatened, the "possibility to do

[9] Barthel, *Gewerkschaftskongresse*, 286–288; *Prot. S. P., 1905*, 141 (resolution no. 147).

[10] Cf. *ibid.*, 123, 232–279.

[11] "Vorstandsbericht," *ibid., 1907*, 46–47.

[12] *Ibid., 1905*, 141

so" was not "at hand." Its order became known as the "braking decree (*Bremserlass*)."

The decree introduced great confusion into May Day observance in 1907. Employers took advantage of it to threaten retaliation while the opponents of strike action in local party and trade-union organizations were given new authority for their position. Although the executive reported after the event that the May Day celebration of 1907 "went off as brilliantly as in any previous year," the delegates to the Essen party congress presented strong evidence to the contrary.[13]

The "braking decree," for all its effectiveness in weakening the May Day observance, was no permanent solution for the trade-union leaders. Seeking a new expedient for getting around the party's opposition, they decided to utilize the occasion of the International congress at Stuttgart in August 1907 for a reopening of the question.

The union leaders summoned their delegates to the congress one day before the party delegates were scheduled to arrive. Without the knowledge of the party delegates, they drafted a resolution on May Day. The question was not, as it happened, on the agenda of the congress, although party and trade-union had agreed in 1905 to settle it there. When the party delegates arrived they were presented with the trade-union resolution on the question. The latter affirmed the continuation of May Day observance by strike, but proposed that where it resulted in punitive action by the employers the workers should receive monetary support. The funds were to be provided in equal parts by party and trade-unions. The officials of both groups were to agree on methods for raising them.[14]

The party delegates were swept off their feet by these proposals which would have meant the end of May Day as they had known it. The party income for the fiscal year 1906–07 was M. 1,191,819; that of the trade-unions, M. 51,396,784 — about fifty times as great! [15]

[13] Compare "Vorstandsbericht," *ibid., 1907*, 46–47, with the congress debates, 295ff. For a brief summary of party press reaction, see *N.Z.*, XXV, ii, 106–107. Radical editors used such phrases as: "the horrendous decree"; "the reduction of May Day to a farce"; "the greatest service of all time to the entrepreneurs."

[14] *Prot. S. P., 1907*, 293; *1908*, 277.

[15] *Ibid., 1907*, 66; Paul Umbreit, *25 Jahre deutscher Gewerkschaftsbewegung, 1890–1915* (Berlin, 1915), 172.

Yet the party and trade-unions were to share the cost of support on a parity basis. Even more surprising was the support principle itself. Certain unions, such as the Shoemakers' and the Metal Workers', had granted strike pay for workers penalized for May Day observance.[16] But support in principle had never had a place in any resolutions of the party. If assurance of support should become the prerequisite for engaging in a May Day strike, the whole symbolism of the demonstration as a kind of sacrificial offering would be lost.[17]

The party delegates were outnumbered by 150 to about 115, but they put up a strong fight. They denied that the delegation to Stuttgart had any competence to decide a question which was the prerogative of the national party congress, and they rejected the crippling provision that party and trade-unions should bear the cost of support equally. The trade-unionists, in order to secure some declaration which could serve as a basis for further negotiation, sacrificed the clauses of their resolution covering these two points. The compromise resolution provided that the next party congress should decide the question of support, and that meanwhile the party executive and general commission should draft a plan for the distribution of the burden between party and trade-unions.[18]

If the trade-unions did not win their full demands they nevertheless scored a signal victory. The principle of support to victims of the May Day strike was accepted as crucial to the May Day question, and the center of discussion from that time forward shifted to the modalities of support. Therewith the immediate material interest of the worker was given precedence over the sacrificial element.

The general commission and the party executive were unable to agree on a plan for the distribution of the financial burden before the Essen congress met on 15 September 1907. The executive, however, brushed aside all motions from the larger urban locals demanding stricter observance.[19] It presented a resolution again

[16] *Prot. S. P., 1907,* 404–405, 408.
[17] Cf. *ibid.,* 298; *1908,* 267–269.
[18] *Ibid., 1907,* 293–294.
[19] *Ibid.,* 166–167, 175. Bremen, Frankfurt-am-Main, Magdeburg, Berlin V., Bunzlau-Lübben, and Ottensen (an industrial suburb of Hamburg) submitted resolutions.

reaffirming the Jena declaration, and giving itself the power to continue negotiations on the support problem. Its proposal was put to a vote and carried before the other motions, thus killing off the latter.[20] The question was thus committed once more to high officialdom for solution.

There followed two years of endless negotiations. On one point the general commission remained adamant throughout: the funds of the central trade-union leagues were not to be utilized, except on a voluntary basis, for the support of the victims of May Day. This was the second arm of the pincers in which the union leaders squeezed the party, the first being the principle of support to which the party had agreed. The party executive finally accepted a plan whereby the administration of May Day was to be placed in the hands of local committees composed of an equal number of trade-union and party officers. All funds for the support of locked-out workers were to be raised solely on a local basis with the cost prorated to party and trade-unions according to the number of members.[21] This scheme would, of course, have been a death warrant to May Day strikes, and was indubitably intended as such. The very history of the trade-unions was a monument to the superiority of central over local administration of resources. To turn the clock back to "localism" for the administration of May Day funds was a cure designed to kill.[22]

With the party executive's blessing the Hamburg trade-union congress of 1908, not without some protest from left-wing unionists, ratified the plan. The executive for once, however, reckoned without the host. The party, more radical than its top leadership, rejected the local financing plan at its Nürnberg congress (1908) and recommitted the question for further negotiation. At long last a formula was found in the creation of May Day funds on a regional rather than a local basis. On trade-union insistence the funds had to be collected separately for this purpose; general funds were to remain untouched. This agreement, with more protest than approval from the floor, was accepted by the party congress of Leipzig in 1909. Under the new plan, the May Day celebra-

[20] Ibid., 294–295, 306.
[21] Barthel, Gewerkschaftskongresse, 292–293.
[22] Cf. Wilhelm Dittman, "Die Maifeiervereinbarung," N.Z., XXVI, ii, 115–118.

tion, made safe and sane, could limp along until the outbreak of the war.[23]

It is one of the more significant features of the period that the party congress was more radical than the party executive on the May Day issue. That was why the trade-unions had to operate *outside* the congress, first through the spurious institutional device of the Stuttgart delegation, later through negotiations with the party executive. But the party congress weakened in its attitude just enough to permit the support question to become central. Thereafter, the May Day strike was doomed. Concern for the immediate material interest of the working class was the weak point in the armor of the party's idealism. With the settlement of 1909 the form of May Day was preserved, but its revolutionary significance was drained from it.

The radicals were fully aware of the meaning of the compromise. But in the face of the sustained trade-union offensive they divided in their attitudes. The extreme leftists fought against the principle of support until the end. They used the opposite logic from that of the trade-unionists: the way to make May Day safe was not to knuckle under to employers' threats but to expand the May Day strike to such gigantic dimensions that the employers would not dare to act. Safety for them lay in mass solidarity and determined action.[24] This line of thought was partly traditional, but it was reenforced by the radical ideas and experiences of 1905–06. Many of its proponents viewed the May Day demonstration strike as a means "to educate the comrades to be able eventually to execute a mass strike with the necessary force." [25]

Another tendency in the radical camp, perceptible in 1907, became increasingly evident as the controversy dragged on: to give up the May Day strike entirely. The radicals who advocated this course were themselves adherents of the strike, and bitterly opposed to the trade-union position. But they saw the demonstration losing all significance as the attitude of national union and party leaders created doubt, hesitation, and confusion on the local level. Rather

[23] Barthel, *Gewerkschaftskongresse*, 292ff.; *Prot. S. P., 1908*, 48–50, 262–284; *1909*, 39–41, 401–428, 511–512.

[24] *Prot. S. P., 1908*, 267–269, 273, 275–276.

[25] *Ibid., 1907*, 298–299.

than see the purity of the ritual sullied in half-hearted observance they preferred its total abolition.[26] By 1909, this attitude of purist resignation had made wider inroads in the party. It resulted in the same practical proposal as that of the most conservative of the trade-unionists: celebration of May Day in the evening or on the first Sunday after May first.[27] The emergence of this attitude was, so to speak, a repercussion at the party level of the employers' pressure on the trade-unionists on the class level. Rather than fight the confusion to re-establish the revolutionary content of May Day, this group of radicals bowed to the pressure of the trade-unions. So, indeed, did the radicals as a whole in accepting the final agreement in 1909.

The settlement made clear that the equality of the two powers, theoretically established at Mannheim, had rapidly shifted, as must all such arrangements, in favor of the stronger. With persistent pressure and with the help of the party executive, the union leaders had succeeded in undermining May Day as a symbol of the revolutionary will to sacrifice. The struggle over symbols was later to repeat itself in actual event, where the alignment would be the same but the stakes of a different order of magnitude.

iii. Curbing the Youth Movement

Where the pressure of the employers drove the trade-union leaders into their war of attrition against the May Day strike, the pressure of the state proved helpful to them in curbing another institution whence the radicals drew strength: the youth movement.

The youth movement of Social Democracy was no official creation of the party. Sometimes with the assistance of sympathetic party members, more often purely spontaneously, youth groups suddenly mushroomed in the fertile political climate of 1904–1906. A group of Berlin apprentices, banding together for mutual protection against their masters, created the nucleus of the North German movement in 1904. Their example spread rapidly to other cities and in December 1906 the various local organizations of the North

---

[26] Cf., e.g., *ibid.*, 295.

[27] Three motions were submitted to this effect at the Leipzig congress. One of these, however, was that of a trade-unionist stronghold (Bielefeld), which was not motivated by "purism." Cf. *Prot. S. P., 1909*, 196, 410, 413–414.

formed a "Union of Free Youth Organizations of Germany," with the economic defense of young workers as their primary, and cultural advancement as their secondary aim. The leaders of the Union were socialistic in outlook, but the rigors of Prussian law forbade youth from political activity.[28] Despite police persecution the Union had gained almost 4,000 members by 1907.[29]

The conditions under which the northern youth groups lived at once made them hotbeds of radicalism. The organization of artisan apprentices was forbidden by many of the guild corporation charters. The need for secrecy concerning membership imparted a conspiratorial flavor to the enterprise. To the best of my knowledge, the youth of the North were the first German Social Democrats to engage in quasi-underground activity in the twentieth century. In Königsberg, after the youth local was broken up and its leader imprisoned in February 1906, the organization was continued by means of cells romantically called *"Tirailleurketten,"* sharpshooter cells.[30] Thus the northern youth movement recapitulated in a small way the early history of the socialist movement. It was born under adverse social and legal conditions which left no place for conservatism.

In the cities of the South, where freer conditions prevailed, the youth organizations were openly political from the outset. The southern "League of Young Workers of Germany," founded in 1906, enjoyed the advice and counsel of one of the few outstanding personalities in the Social Democratic movement: the gifted young lawyer, Dr. Ludwig Frank (1874–1914). Despite his youth — he was in his early thirties — Frank had already made a name for himself as a brilliant orator and parliamentarian.[31] He was a revisionist of a radical variety; that is, his chief aim was not a

[28] Under section 8 of the Law of 11 March 1850 "Concerning the Prevention of Abuse of the Right of Association and Assembly Endangering Freedom and Order under the Law." Sachse-Weimar, Brunswick, and Saxony had similar legislation. Württemberg, Baden, and the three Hanseatic republics had no such restrictions. Hessen and Bavaria had certain legal curbs, but they were dead letters. Cf. Karl Korn, *Die Arbeiterjugendbewegung* (2nd edition, Berlin, 1923), 103–104.

[29] *Ibid.*, 62–63.

[30] *Ibid.*, 48–50.

[31] *Ibid.*, 68–69; S. Grünebaum, *Ludwig Frank. Ein Beitrag zur Entwicklung der deutschen Sozialdemokratie* (Heidelberg, 1924), *passim.*

socialist revolution but the establishment of democratic institutions; to accomplish this objective, however, he was prepared to resort to radical action.

Under Frank's guidance the southern movement set out to do consciously and deliberately what the northern movement had forced upon it by its composition and its environment: to recapitulate the early history of the party. Deploring the necessary division of function in the complex modern labor movement, Frank wished every young person to pass through an organization in which political, educational, and trade-union aspects were united as in the beginnings of the party.[32]

When the adult movement was already sharply divided into economic and political sectors, the youth movement thus set out somewhat quixotically to recreate a sense of unity from below with Marxian theoretical knowledge as the fluxing substance. Add to these elements of the program the ingredient of youth's inevitable idealism and you have a sure formula for the cultivation of a radical outlook.

The southern League showed its radicalism chiefly in vigorous anti-militarist agitation.[33] Here the example of the Belgian youth movement, which from its origin in 1894 had concentrated primarily upon agitation among potential conscripts and in the barracks, was a decisive influence.[34] Frank became familiar with the Belgian "Young Guards," from which the South German League's journal took its name, at the Amsterdam congress of the International in 1904, and encouraged the adaptation of its anti-militarist agitation to the German scene. Liebknecht saw in the youth movement the key to an effective fight against militarism, "the chief prop of capitalism." Both men made efforts at the party congresses of

[32] *Prot. S. P., 1906*, 380; cf. also Korn, *Arbeiterjugendbewegung*, 89.

[33] Korn, *Arbeiterjugendbewegung*, 79–81. Almost every issue of the *Junge Garde* contained information on and propaganda against the abuses and injustices prevailing in the army.

[34] Like so many other radical elements of European socialism, the "Young Guards" of Belgium underwent a rapid expansion in 1905. The fact that the army in Belgium was frequently used against strikes gave a particular sharpness to anti-militarist agitation there, which dated back to the 1880's. Cf. Karl Liebknecht, *Militarismus und Antimilitarismus, mit besonderer Berücksichtigung der internationalen Jugendbewegung* (Berlin, n. d. [1919?]), 51–52, 73–77.

1904, 1905, and 1906 to enlist the support of the party for the youth organizations in general and their anti-militarist activity in particular.[35]

It was perhaps out of a sense of the weakness of their own cause that some of the extreme radical leaders, such as Liebknecht and Klara Zetkin, turned hopefully toward the new movement. Zetkin, herself a school teacher, developed a theory of youth training which was an interesting composite of revolutionary Marxism and the ideas of progressive education. Through simultaneous encouragement of individual and group initiative, she thought, the youth movement could provide a needed dynamic in party life. Youth was "the most reliable force to keep us in continuous intellectual and moral development, to prevent [us from] resting or rusting . . . At the side of the adult fighters, whose duty it is to weigh and consider, there must be younger elements who have the will to risk, to dare." [36] Of those who wished to steer a more revolutionary course, Zetkin was among the first to recognize in the youth movement a significant asset.

It should not surprise us to find the party fathers taking a different view. Richard Fischer, Hermann Molkenbuhr, Georg von Vollmar, and Bebel saw no reason why there should be special organizations for youth, which they regarded as "dangerous playing around." They were particularly opposed, as we have seen in the preceding chapter, to any intensification of anti-militarist agitation.[37] They did not, however, throw their full weight into the balance to prevent a vague endorsement of the youth movement by the Jena and Mannheim congresses.[38] They were no doubt moved

---

[35] *Prot. S. P., 1904,* 178–179, 188–189; *1905,* 279, 283–284, 362–363; *1906,* 380–381.

[36] *Ibid., 1908,* 540. Zetkin addressed a full statement of her position to the Social Democratic Womens' conference at Nürnberg. Cf. *ibid.,* 521–543.

[37] See above, Ch. III, sec. iii; also *Prot. S. P., 1904,* 179–180, 185–187.

[38] The Jena congress turned over to the executive the following proposals for its consideration: 1. "In future, the party is to inaugurate a broad agitation, oral and written, among the proletarian youth, and, wherever feasible, to found a youth organization." 2. "May the party congress resolve to empower the executive to support the organizations of young workers as strongly as possible, and to publish a paper at least once a month for the enlightenment of the young workers, and, further, to accomplish centralization of the youth organization." (*Prot. S. P., 1905,* 99, 283.) The executive did nothing about these suggestions during the succeeding year, when the youth of North and South founded their leagues and journals on

by Frank's argument that the party must choose between a youth
movement regulated to suit its needs and one which would "grow
wild." [39]

Shortly after receiving the half-hearted endorsement of the
Mannheim congress, the southern League held a convention in
Stuttgart, where the Belgian Young Guard was represented and
where Liebknecht, with the warm support of the delegates, presented his views on the need for more intensive anti-militarist
activity among the young. This awakened the concern of the
conservatives of the labor movement. *Sozialistische Monatshefte*
warned against the support of any youth organization which followed the Belgian kind of anti-militarism, "which we in Germany
neither can nor should imitate." [40] More serious for the future of
the youth movement was the sudden interest of the trade-union
leaders. At a conference of the central trade-union league executives in November 1906, Carl Legien, chairman of the general
commission, made it clear that the policy of the party executive —
to ignore the youth organizations — no longer satisfied the union
leadership. An independent youth movement, said Legien, could
harm both the youth themselves and the labor movement as a whole.
He asked the executives of the central leagues to lay the basis for
a definite, uniform, trade-union program to organize the youth
from above. The unions took their first step toward bringing the
youth movement under adult control by adopting Legien's proposal without discussion. [41]

With the elections of 1907 and the extensive controversy over the
national question, the party leadership had little time to concern
itself with the youth problem. On the last day of the Essen congress

their own. The executive's report for the year 1905–1906 contained only a brief
word on the youth movement: "We take it that agitation and organization among
young workers has been carried on in sufficient measure by the local party organizations." (*Ibid.*, *1906*, 22.) At the next congress, the executive had prepared no
resolution on the problem. The congress then adopted the following resolution
proposed by Liebknecht: "We welcome the ubiquitous awakening of proletarian
youth to independent organizational activity. Wherever the laws of association permit
it, the party comrades are urged to encourage the founding and further development of youth organizations." (*Ibid.*, 145, 381.)

[39] *Ibid.*, *1906*, 380.
[40] *S.M.*, X (XII), 972.
[41] Korn, *Arbeiterjugendbewegung*, 120–121

Karl Liebknecht again berated the party for its "passive resistance," its "coldness and indifference" toward the youth movement.[42] The congress, which had been unable to record its disapproval of Noske's concessions to militarism, was sensitive to Liebknecht's appeal that the party and trade-unions were committed by the Stuttgart International congress' anti-militarist resolution to "rear the youth in the spirit of socialism." A motion pledging the party to assist more intensively than previously in the creation of youth organizations was uncontested from the floor and easily carried.[43]

The Essen resolution might well have remained a dead letter like its predecessor of Mannheim had the state not then taken a hand in the youth question. Bülow had promised the Progressives of his bloc the satisfaction of one of their oldest demands: a uniform law of association and assembly for the whole Reich. The bill which the government submitted to the Reichstag in November 1907 was a product of what Bülow called "the mating of the conservative and liberal spirit." In some instances it provided for the removal of Prussian and other federal state curbs on freedom; in others, for the extension of Prussian restrictions to the freer south German states.[44]

The principal liberal features of the government's draft law were the abolition of restrictions on the participation of women and youth in political assemblies and organizations. These represented a real advance over regulations prevailing in all but a few states. They undoubtedly took the Social Democrats, who generally expected the worst, by surprise.[45] The youth movement and its sponsors were delighted with the new turn of events.[46] It would now be possible for the northern youth to engage in overt political activity and for youth throughout the nation to organize on a uniform basis.

For the trade-union leaders, the liberal youth provisions of the

[42] *Prot. S. P., 1907*, 390.

[43] *Ibid.*, 391, 408–409.

[44] Fritz Hartung, *Deutsche Geschichte von 1871 bis 1914* (Bonn and Leipzig, 1920), 222–223; Hans Block, "Vereins- und Versammlungsrecht in Deutschland," *N.Z.*, XXVI, i, 288–295.

[45] Cf., e.g., the predictions of Liebknecht, *Prot. S. P., 1907*, 391.

[46] Korn, *Arbeiterjugendbewegung*, 105.

bill opened unpleasant vistas of intensified radical youth activity. A
conference of trade-union executives of 16–17 December 1907 began
formal discussion of the issue. Robert Schmidt, who had led
the trade-union campaign on the May Day question, assumed the
leadership in the youth problem. He told the conference that the
youth organizations had failed in what should be their main aim:
to educate the youth "in our attitudes and ideas," to make them
good members of trade-union and party. Instead, they had tackled
political questions of concern only to the parent organizations, and
had engaged in what Schmidt called, untranslatably, *"internationale
Phantastereien."* The only solution to overcome the dangers of an
irresponsible movement was to take the movement out of the hands
of youth entirely. Schmidt urged that the trade-unions and party
take over jointly the "cultivation" of the young. The conference
empowered the general commission to enter into negotiations with
the party executive to find an appropriate solution.[47] The familiar
pattern which we have observed for the accomplishment of the
union leaders' will on the mass strike and the May Day issues was
beginning to repeat itself.

It would have been difficult indeed for the party executive to
win approval for curbing the youth organizations at the moment
when the state was about to give them freedom. Fortunately for
the trade-union leaders, however, Bülow's plan miscarried. The
Conservative Party, in which, *mutatis mutandis,* the Social Democratic youth movement inspired the same fears as in the trade-
unions, refused to surrender Prussian restrictive legislation against
the young.[48] The draft bill was revised to include restrictions on
youth which in some respects went beyond those of Prussia. It
forbade not only membership in political organizations to persons
under eighteen years of age, but even attendance at political gather-
ings.[49] The revised bill passed the Reichstag on 8 April 1908, and

[47] *Ibid.*, 121–122.
[48] Bethmann-Hollweg, Secretary of State for the Interior, was well aware of the
Conservative attitude, and had tried to make the liberal provisions on youth palatable. The government had avoided any restrictions on youth's right of association,
he explained to the Reichstag, "in order not to prejudice the institutions which the
bourgeois parties and the friends of mankind had established to fight against Social
Democratic influence over the youth." Quoted in *ibid.*, 107.
[49] The provisions are quoted in *ibid.*, 110. Cf. also *S.M.*, XII (XIV), i, 536–537.

the liberal regulations for youth activity in southern Germany were superseded by Prussian restrictions.

Now that the state had spoken there was a new and more cogent justification for adult control over the youth movement. Should the youth organizations flout the law they could seriously embarrass the whole labor movement. Certainly the southern League could no longer be permitted to continue as a political organization. The general commission took up the problem with the party executive. On 24 April joint principles were formulated for presentation to the youth organizations of the South.[50]

The southern League held an emergency conference at Darmstadt on 3 May 1908 to decide on a course of action to meet the situation created by the new law.[51] Robert Schmidt for the trade-unions and Hermann Müller for the party executive told the delegates that the adults were now prepared to "parry the blow" against youth. Schmidt, who had fulminated against the youth organizations only five months before, promised that the appropriate authorities would devote themselves "with zeal and affection" to the work which the youth had begun. Secretary Müller promised that the next party congress would take up the problem for it was now "a matter of honor and duty for the adults to carry out what the youth can no longer execute." [52] In accordance with the principles agreed to by the general commission and the executive it was proposed that the League dissolve. Pending a decision by the party congress, the possibility was left open that the youth locals turn themselves into "cultural societies" without centralization, and that a central "agitation committee for youth" be established by those over eighteen years. Meanwhile, the central committee of the League was empowered to turn over its funds and its organ, the *Young Guard,* to the party executive. After a heated floor fight, with Ludwig Frank urging acceptance, the proposals of the adults were adopted.[53]

The northern Youth Union condemned the southern League's decision to disband as a surrender without a fight. The Union had fully expected that the southern organization would now adopt the

[50] *Prot. S. P., 1908,* 211.
[51] The law was to take effect on 15 May 1908.
[52] Korn, *Arbeiterjugendbewegung,* 112–113.
[53] *Ibid.,* 113–116; *Prot. S. P., 1908,* 24–25.

traditional tactics of the northern youth and that in the face of uniform conditions, bad though they were, a unification of the two organizations could be put through. The *Arbeitende Jugend* warned party and trade-union authorities that the northern Union would, for its part, maintain its independence.[54]

During the month of June the plans of the party and trade-union authorities took a turn even more threatening to the youth organizations. To the triennial trade-union congress at Hamburg in June 1908, Robert Schmidt submitted a plan for the eradication of an independent youth movement, a plan which, like its predecessor, was the fruit of negotiations between party executive and general commission. Schmidt's proposal provided that (1) the cultivation of youth was a responsibility of the adult labor movement; (2) this task could be accomplished by lectures on natural science, law, history, art, etc., and by instituting social and sport activities; (3) "for these purposes a special youth organization is not required"; (4) to carry through this program joint committees were to be established locally by the trade-union cartels and the party organizations "which should coöpt a few representatives of the youth." Under this program "the representation of economic interests and the decision of political party questions shall always remain the task[s] of the trade-unions and the political organizations respectively." [55]

Forgetting the honeyed words he had addressed to the Youth League at Darmstadt, Schmidt launched an all-out attack against the idea of any independent youth organizations and their "unclear, youthful leaders." [56] His resolution passed with little opposition. As one trade-unionist observed, it would assure that "the youth be not conceded an active influence on party policy or trade-union affairs." [57] The Hamburg resolution marked the second step in choking off the independent youth movement and the renascent radicalism which it represented.

The northern and southern youth organizations which had been

[54] Korn, *Arbeiterjugendbewegung,* 116–118.
[55] Barthel, *Gewerkschaftskongresse,* 247.
[56] *Ibid.,* 248.
[57] *S.M.,* XII (XIV), ii, 909. For representative views of the trade-union position at this stage, see Carl Legien, "Zum Gewerkschaftskongress in Hamburg," *ibid.,* ii, 712; and Robert Schmidt, "Jugendbildung," *ibid.,* 732–735.

divided since the Darmstadt youth congress in May were reunited in opposition to this "betrayal." The southerners were particularly outraged at Schmidt's insistence that there be no autonomous youth organizations whatever, since he had at Darmstadt supported the decision that "the previous local organizations [of the League] are to be converted into non-political cultural societies wherever possible." [58] In southern Germany the Hamburg resolution precipitated not only protest against the latest action of the trade-unions, but also against the Darmstadt decision to disband the League, which in retrospect seemed no more than a maneuver preparatory to the destruction of any independent youth activity. At the end of August a youth conference representing all branches of the movement met in Leipzig and decided to establish a national organization for economic and cultural activity on the northern pattern.[59] The *coup de main* of general commission and party executive seemed to be producing the opposite of what was intended.

Meanwhile, the radicals awoke to the fact that they had a stake in the youth issue. Quite suddenly after the Hamburg congress, the party press took up the cudgels for an independent youth organization. In almost all places where a youth group existed the party local rallied to its defense.[60] The radicals particularly condemned the executive's agreement with the general commission, the content of which was in contradiction to the Essen congress resolution. The *Leipziger Volkszeitung* branded the agreement a "secret conventicle," and the term quickly spread through the party press.[61]

By the time the party congress met at Nürnberg in September 1908, sentiment ran strongly in favor of independent youth organizations: there were no less than twenty-four motions on the question.[62] Hermann Müller, for the executive, held the now familiar

---

[58] Korn, *Arbeiterjugendbewegung*, 124–125, 130–131.

[59] *Ibid.*, 130–133.

[60] *Ibid.*, 131. Korn takes the position (124) that the youth question became a political football between revisionists and radicals. He fails to grasp that the political coloration of the youth movement made politics the essence of the question. For the press discussion, cf. *N.Z.*, XXVI, ii, 465ff., 557ff., 561ff., 602–603, 612ff., 642ff., 714ff., 765ff., 798ff., 842ff.

[61] Korn, *Arbeiterjugendbewegung*, 124; *Prot. S. P., 1908*, 210–211.

[62] Korn, *Arbeiterjugendbewegung*, 136.

threat over the heads of the recalcitrant delegates: if the congress did not "seal the agreement" of executive and general commission, the trade-unions would say, " 'That doesn't suit us; we shall withdraw and not bother about the whole matter.' " Such an outcome, said Müller, would only play into the hands of the confessional youth organizations. The Reich Law of Association served him as a cogent argument for bringing the young under the parental wing where they could be protected from exposing themselves to the rigors of state persecution.[63]

The executive had, however, rephrased the Hamburg resolution to make it less offensive to the party. Thus it added a reference to educating the youth "for class struggle in the sense of our socialist outlook." The flat statement of the trade-unions' Hamburg resolution that "special youth organizations are not required for these purposes" was modified to read: "In order to serve these purposes even without special youth organization . . ." [64] The sugar-coating was still insufficient to make the pill palatable to the congress. A committee was set up under Hugo Haase to work out an acceptable compromise.[65] The committee's proposal maintained the principle that the youth movement should have no independent central organization. Party and trade-union were to establish local youth committees to care for the needs of the young. But the Nürnberg congress, on the committee's recommendation, restored to the youth the right to separate local organizations which could manage their own affairs "with the agreement of the adults." [66]

Speaking for the committee in terms reminiscent of Klara Zetkin's, Haase warmly recommended to the party that it grant the maximum freedom to youth in the pursuit of its activity.[67] It is conceivable that the problem might have been overcome had the spirit of the committee's report guided the execution of the party's new youth policy. But the devolution of authority to the local youth

[63] *Prot. S. P., 1908,* 211–212, 214.

[64] *Ibid.,* 171–172.

[65] The radicals were strongly represented on the committee. Of fourteen members, at least seven were of the radical wing (Haase, Zietz, Zetkin, Westmeyer, Heinrich Schulz, Brandler, and Rudolf). Only three were prominent antagonists of separate youth organizations (Müller, Schmidt and Sänger). *Ibid.,* 226.

[66] *Ibid.,* 450–451, 551.

[67] *Ibid.,* 450–452.

committees of adults meant that the degree of freedom and initiative left to the young varied with the local conditions. Where the trade-union and party secretaries were sympathetic, the youth retained a large measure of autonomy; where their seniors were too patronizing, the youth grew impatient. The party youth central, headed by the cool and determined Friedrich Ebert, operated as a brake to keep the young from kicking over the traces.[68]

The future would show that the Nürnberg decisions on youth were an untenable compromise, like so many other compromises of Social Democracy in this period. Outwardly, the trade-unions had their way: youth "movement" was transformed into youth "cultivation." But under the aegis of parental "protection" the radicalism of youth smouldered on, fanned after 1911 by increasing state persecution, until it burst into flame during the war. Only then did it become clear that the effort of the trade-union and party authorities to extinguish the dangerous spark in the younger generation had failed.

iv. The Pattern of Trade-Union Conquest and its Significance

If we look back over the great issues on which the Socialist movement divided in the years 1906–1909, we discover that in all those in which the trade-unions threw their weight into the scales the reformist attitude was the one to prevail. Three major advances of the radicals were thus hurled back: the mass strike commitment of 1905, the intensified anti-militarism of 1906–07, and the youth movement of 1905–1908. On two other issues earlier radical policies were modified in a conservative direction: colonialism (insofar as the German stand at Stuttgart was concerned) and the May Day strike.

We are now in a position to discern in all these episodes a common pattern of trade-union conquest, which may be roughly summarized as a series of three steps:

1. The division of Social Democracy into two camps on each issue was generally crystallized by a specific economic or political action of the ruling groups against labor or the party, an action

---

[68] Paul Kampffmeyer, "Friedrich Ebert, ein Lebensbild," in *Friedrich Ebert, Schriften, Aufzeichnungen, Reden* (Dresden, 1926), I, 72.

which evoked in the radicals the will to a counteroffensive and in the trade-unionists the desire to adjust to the new situation.[69]

2. The conservative position, except in the military and colonial issues, was first put forward by the trade-unions. In no case could the trade-unions secure ratification for their views by a direct appeal to the party congress. They therefore found it necessary to present the congress with *faits accomplis* to which the party executive sooner or later lent its coöperation and support.[70]

3. The party congress, softened up and confused by the process indicated in step two, ended by accepting a compromise. The content of the compromise was normally the attachment of a radical statement of principle to a program of action containing the essence of the trade-union position.[71]

[69] (a) Mass strike: Extensive application of the lockout and changes in the state electoral systems unfavorable to labor. The Russian Revolution, of course, played a decisive role here.

(b) Military and colonial questions: The campaign for imperialism and the government's electoral victory on that issue in January 1907.

(c) May Day: The intensified use of May Day as an occasion for lockouts.

(d) Youth movement: Intensified police persecution in Prussia. The Reich Law of Association.

[70] (a) Mass strike: The trade-union position at its Köln congress overridden by the Jena party congress. Secret agreement between general commission and party executive, February 1906, as prelude to victory at Mannheim.

(b) Military question: Strong position favoring national defense taken by Bebel and Noske in the Reichstag. More radical stand forced on German delegation by other nations at the Stuttgart meeting of the International.

(c) Colonial question: Revisionists and trade-unionists together outvote the radicals of the German delegation at Stuttgart in effort to reverse Social Democratic tradition. Same outcome as in military question.

(d) May Day: Surprise resolution put through the union-controlled Stuttgart delegation, establishing support principle. Hamburg trade-union congress decision (1908), sanctioned by party executive, rejected by Nürnberg party congress.

(e) Youth movement: general commission and party executive draft Darmstadt principles. Again with the executive's consent, the Hamburg trade-union congress goes beyond these to propose exclusion of youth from the administration of local youth committees.

[71] (a) Mass strike: Jena resolution declared to be the same as Köln resolution. On party-trade-union relations, the first half of the Kautsky resolution, dealing with principle, was attached to the Mannheim agreement, which negated the Kautsky position in practice.

(b) Military and colonial issues: Settlement rendered unnecessary by action of International.

In this process the differentiation between the politically conscious party members and the politically unorganized trade-unionists was crucial. The ratio of trade-union to party members in 1906 was approximately four to one.[72] Not every member of the party was a radical Social Democrat; but the party members as a whole were surely more radical than the trade-union members as a whole. The attractive power of the party lay in its political idea; that of the trade-unions, in their advancement of the worker's material interest. Yet it was precisely this distinction which gave the trade-unionists their power over the party executive. As long as the power of the party could be measured only at the polls, its leaders were compelled to rely on masses of fellow-travelers, a large proportion of whom were politically indifferent trade-unionists. The fear that the trade-union leaders might withhold electoral support from the party made the executive acutely sensitive to the trade-unionists' demands. The unionists, with their anti-revolutionary attitude, may be presumed to have represented more accurately than the Social Democratic Party the mass of German workers in our period. By organizing these masses where the party could not, the union leaders were able to transmit the subjective attitudes of the politically passive workers into the Social Democratic Party itself, with the party executive as their agent. In this sense the trade-union conquest made the party more representative of German labor than it had been before 1906. Yet herein lay a fatal difficulty: the trade-union bureaucracy was anti-revolutionary *in Permanenz,* by virtue of its corporate interest in the existing order. The working class was not similarly committed, and the party had heretofore represented the proletariat's revolutionary potential as well as its reformist actuality. By capitulating before the trade-unions in our period, the party surrendered its political flexibility, and thus prepared the ground for its subsequent dissolution.

(c) May Day: Machinery for support established, but at the regional rather than the local level. Principle of the strike as the proper form of May Day observance reasserted.

(d) Youth movement: Youth deprived of the right to independent national organizations; latitude for independent self-administration of youth at local level recommended, with decision on its scope falling to local committees set up by adults.

[72] See above Ch. I, n. 37 and text.

*v. The Radical Position in the Bloc Period; Kautsky's
"Road to Power"*

Although the radicals lost certain critical intra-party battles between 1906 and 1909, they were not stripped of all influence by the
reformist onslaught. They maintained control of the women's organization though the women's "cultural societies," which were
really Marxist study groups, were threatened like the youth movement by the intra-party repercussions of the Reich Law of Association.[73] The radicals also maintained a firm grip on the party school
established in 1905 to train party and trade-union functionaries.
Mehring, Luxemburg, and other radical luminaries composed the
teaching staff.[74] In 1908 the revisionists, led by Bernstein, Eisner,
and Maurenbrecher, launched a concerted attack on the doctrinaire character of the school's instruction.[75] The trade-unions did
not enter this battle, however. They solved their relationship to
the party school by leaving their student quotas unfilled.[76] With no
trade-union support the revisionist campaign failed. Marxist theory,
after all, was still revered by the party; it was quite proper that the
radicals should be the keepers of the keys to this area of party life.

The most celebrated success of the radicals in the Bloc period was
the renewed condemnation of the southern Landtag delegates for
voting for *Land* budgets. Yet the event itself showed that the
radicals were on the defensive. If one compares the outcome of the
bitter three-day debate on budget-voting at the Nürnberg congress
in 1908 with that of Dresden in 1903, the only striking difference
is the greater degree of defiance in the revisionist camp. In 1903
the revisionists voted for the resolution which had condemned
them; in 1908 they answered the congress' reaffirmation of its
Dresden position with a declaration denying the national party
congress' competence to lay down a line on affairs of concern only

[73] *Prot. S. P., 1908*, 208; "Bericht über die 5. sozialdemokratische Frauenkonfer-
enz," *ibid.*, 482–506; *S.M.*, XII (XIV), ii, 1218–1220, 1372.
[74] For an account of the school and its activity, see *Prot. S. P., 1907*, 90–94.
[75] Eduard Bernstein, "Bildung, Wissenschaft und Partei," *S.M.*, XI (XIII), ii, 708–
709; *idem*, "Parteischule und Wissenschaft," *ibid.*, XII (XIV), ii, 1263–1270; *Prot.
S. P., 1908*, 227–240.
[76] *Prot. S. P., 1911*, 47.

to the *Länder*.[77] They also did the unthinkable by voting against the re-election to the executive of Co-chairman Paul Singer and Secretary Wilhelm Pfannkuch, who had opposed them in the debate.[78] The revisionists were well aware that despite the congress' action they had won a moral victory by standing their ground. Ludwig Frank confidently predicted after the congress that "the transformation of the party" in a reformist direction would "proceed surely and swiftly in the next years." [79]

The position of the radicals in the Bloc period found its expression in the one comprehensive theoretical treatise of that era: Karl Kautsky's *The Road to Power*.[80] In it Kautsky kept alive the hope that the revolution was not far off, but drew consequences for party tactic which contrasted sharply with the position which Luxemburg had set forth three years before in *Mass Strike, Party and Trade Unions*.

Where Luxemburg had seen a series of mass upheavals as the form of the twentieth-century revolution, Kautsky denied that it was possible to "know the form and character of the revolution." [81] One could not foresee whether the decisive battles of the social war would be bloody or whether they would be "fought exclusively by means of economic, legislative and moral pressure." [82] The revolution was to be an inevitable product of capitalist development, but it could no more be stimulated or prepared by the Social Democrats than it could be prevented by the ruling class.[83]

Kautsky saw four conditions as necessary to a successful revolution:

1. Confidence in the ruling regime, both in its power and in its stability, must have been destroyed by its own tools, by the bureaucracy and the army.

[77] *Ibid.*, *1908*, 426.
[78] *Ibid.*, 460.
[79] Letter to Leonie Meyerhof-Hildeck, 21 Sept., 1908, in Ludwig Frank, *Reden, Aufsätze und Briefe*, ed. Hedwig Wachenheim (Berlin, n. d.), 125.
[80] Karl Kautsky, *The Road to Power*, trans. A. M. Simons (Chicago, 1909). All quoted passages have been checked against the original, *Der Weg zur Macht* (2nd edition, Berlin, 1910).
[81] *Ibid.*, 10.
[82] *Ibid.*, 50.
[83] *Ibid.*

2. The great mass of the people must be decisively hostile to the regime.

3. There must be an organized party in irreconcilable opposition.

4. The party must represent the interests of the people and possess their confidence.[84]

Contemporary developments, Kautsky said, pointed toward the fulfillment of all these conditions. With respect to the first, he singled out three factors: (1) increased armament expenditures, which heightened international tension and brought nearer the threat of war; (2) national revolutions in backward areas as they became modernized; and (3) the moral decay of the ruling class.[85]

Kautsky gave particular weight to the factor of moral decay. While the Socialists had grown not only in numbers and organization, but in moral conviction, he said, the prestige and sense of assurance of the ruling class had been "scattered to the winds" since the unification of Germany. "Petty intrigue and unprincipledness" pushed to the front as the ruling class passed from the revolutionary to the conservative stage in its development.[86] The idea of corruption in the ruling groups was no mere invention of Kautsky's. It filled the air during 1907 and 1908 as the inevitable accompaniment of Harden's and Holstein's defamation campaign against Philipp Eulenburg. The conviction grew in the population at large that their Kaiser had for years been under the influence of psychologically unbalanced and intellectually incompetent court advisers.[87] In Kautsky's view this element of corruption would raise the revolutionary potential of the peasantry and lower middle class, and thus fulfill the second condition of the revolution by making the mass of the people decisively hostile to the regime. The more these two classes relied on the government for economic assistance, the stronger would be their reaction against it when its prestige was shattered in war or catastrophe.

What should the Social Democratic Party do to exploit the situation? Moral integrity must be its response to increasing corruption.

[84] *Ibid.*, 64.
[85] *Ibid.*, 107–117.
[86] *Ibid.*, 118–119.
[87] Johannes Ziekursch, *Politische Geschichte des neuen deutschen Kaiserreiches* (Frankfurt-a.-M., 1930), III, 191.

The Socialists, said Kautsky, must remain true to themselves; they must increase their authority by maintaining "an indestructible power in the midst of the destruction of all authority." Only thus could they fulfill the fourth condition of the revolution: that the opposition party possess the people's confidence. It followed too that any participation in the ruling corruption, any "ministerialism" (or budget-voting), could only be moral and political suicide.[88] The proletariat had the opportunity to progress and grow strong "through strictly legal methods alone." [89] Through them it could extract concessions from the ruling class. It could also, by participation in elections, obtain a good index of its own power, and thus avoid revolutionary adventurism and premature trials of strength.[90] But here again Social Democracy could take advantage of its legal opportunities only if it maintained its pure oppositional attitude and its revolutionary goal. In effect, Kautsky argued to the reformists that the working class would remain loyal to the party and its reformist tactic only so long as it retained its revolutionary theory: "We may say that there is today one force that would cause the workers to turn of their own accord from the 'peaceful' methods of struggle . . . the loss of faith in the revolutionary character of our party." [91] Kautsky thus tended to harness revolutionary theory into the service of reformist practice.

In its essentials *The Road to Power* represented a return to the Erfurt synthesis which the radicals had abandoned during the stormy days of 1905–06. In his prognosis of the future Kautsky affirmed more clearly than before the revolutionary implications of imperialism. Yet his analysis of the future revolutionary process was remarkable for the passive role which he assigned to the working class and its party. While pointing to an intensification of class struggle as characteristic of the era,[92] he assigned only two clear functions to the proletarian party: agitation and organization. Even if the revolution should be violent, which Kautsky left uncertain, the dynamic element in it would be the ruling class which, through its inner contradictions, corruption, and loss of self-assurance, would

[88] Kautsky, *Road to Power*, 124–126.
[89] *Ibid.*, 54–55.
[90] *Ibid.*, 52.
[91] *Ibid.*, 60.
[92] *Ibid.*, chapters vi and vii, *passim.*

hurtle the existing order to destruction. The proletariat would be the passive beneficiary of the process thanks to having maintained its oppositional integrity. Where Luxemburg viewed the proletariat as an irresistible force, Kautsky seemed to see it as an immovable object. In the revolution itself Social Democracy would stand as an island of morality in a turbulent sea of iniquity; when the storm had exhausted itself, its surviving victims would take refuge on the island.

Although Kautsky's descriptions of the objective development pointed toward revolution more surely than his earlier writings, his conception of the role of the proletariat and the party showed an evolution toward passivity and away from the position he had held in the mass-strike discussions of 1905–1906. In part, the passive element may be accounted for by the actual paralysis of Social Democracy under the political and economic conditions of the time. It was due perhaps in even larger measure to the situation which prevailed in the party. In terms of the divergent groups composing Social Democracy, Kautsky's theory may be viewed as a proposal for a truce under which the trade-unionists and revisionists would give up their attack on revolutionary theory and their effort to come to terms with the ruling class, while the ultraradicals would cease their drive for a revolutionary tactic. The theoretical concept with which the truce was to be sealed was that of the passive revolution. Under it Social Democracy would move neither toward further acceptance of the existing order, nor toward action to hasten its collapse. It would organize and agitate, and maintain its moral integrity while waiting for the ruling class to destroy itself. Thus the effort to reconcile antagonistic political and intellectual tendencies led Kautsky not so much to a synthesis as to a stalemate.

Chapter V

PARTY STRUCTURE AND FACTIONAL POWER

Our history thus far has been concerned with the struggle over the political content and direction of the labor movement as manifested first in ideas, then in tactical decisions. The subsequent development of the inner-party conflict cannot be understood without considering the development of the party's institutions. No one of the political factions could convert its ideas into reality without gaining control over institutions through which its power could be exercised. The factional conflict acted in turn upon the party institutions, reshaping them to meet the purposes of the dominant political forces. As internal tension mounted the party organization became the captive of the dominant group, and thus progressively less able to satisfy the demands of the substantial oppositional tendencies, until it was burst asunder during the First World War. The foundations of this development were laid in the period 1905–1909. The advances of the reformists in the field of organization in those years were less obvious than their victories in certain tactical questions but more significant for the future of the party.

Bureaucracy has long been singled out as a leading characteristic of German Social Democracy. The party won the reputation of being managed by a neatly structured hierarchy of professional politicians, by a huge apparatus extending from the party executive at the top to the shop leaders and block leaders at the bottom. The reputation is essentially correct. The German Social Democratic Party was the first to devise the great bureaucratic institutions for mass control which were subsequently adapted to their own purposes by the Communists, Fascists, and National Socialists.

The bureaucratization of Social Democracy has been regarded as one of the principal factors making for conservatism in the party. Robert Michels, whose pioneering work remains the most penetrating study of the structure of Social Democracy, advanced the thesis that the need for organization inevitably dooms any democratic movement. Because the working class is completely at the mercy of economic forces, because, as individuals, the workers are the weakest members of society, Michels argued, their only strength lies in numbers. These numbers must be given structure, they must be organized. Organization, the *sine qua non* to democratic action, is also "the spring from which conservative waters flow into the democratic stream."[1] Michels maintained that organization meant a "tendency to oligarchy": "The power of the leaders grows directly in proportion to the expansion of the organization."[2]

Michels marshaled the evidence to show that the bureaucratization of Social Democracy led to an identification of the interest of its functionaries with the status quo. The labor bureaucracy opened a career to talent; it did for the worker what the Church had traditionally done for the peasant. It not only offered the self-made man of labor comparative economic security, but also raised his social status. Soon the working-class functionary passed psychically as well as economically into the *petite bourgeoisie.*[3]

Max Weber, Michels' teacher, pointed out as early as 1907 that the ruling classes were making a serious mistake in not granting full freedom (particularly universal suffrage) to Social Democracy, since they were thus sustaining the revolutionary forces in the movement at the expense of the bureaucratic element, which had acquired a strong material interest in the existing order. Describing how the party was becoming a state within a state with an "increasing army of persons who have an interest in advancement, . . . [and] material benefits," Weber said:

One must ask who has more to fear from this, bourgeois society or Social Democracy? Personally, I believe the latter; i.e., those elements within it which are the bearers of the revolutionary ideology . . . And if the contradictions between the material interests of the professional politicians on the one hand and the revolutionary ideology on the other could develop freely, if one would no longer throw the Social Democrats out of veterans' associations, if one would admit them into church administrations, from which one expels them nowadays, *then* for the

---

[1] Robert Michels, *Zur Soziologie des Parteiwesens in der modernen Demokratie* (Leipzig, 1910), 22–23.

[2] *Ibid.,* 32–33.

[3] Michels, "Die deutsche Sozialdemokratie," *Archiv für Sozialwissenschaft und Sozialpolitik,* XXIII: 541–543 (1906).

first time serious internal problems would arise for the party. Then . . . it would be shown not that Social Democracy is conquering city and state, but, on the contrary, that the state is conquering Social Democracy.[4]

Both Weber and Michels perceived the conservative implications of the bureaucracy for the Social Democratic Party; we have no wish here to review their contributions or to rehearse the well-known analysis of Social Democracy as a state within a state. Our problem is rather to understand the relationship between the bureaucratization of the party and the split in Social Democracy. The Weber-Michels sociological analysis of bureaucracy does not adequately illuminate this political problem. The Communist parties too have built centralized, hierarchical, paid bureaucracies; but in non-Communist countries these have not been a conservative force, nor have their functionaries been tied by material interests to the *status quo*. In order to understand the political coloration and influence of a bureaucracy it is necessary to examine it genetically. A bureaucracy is constructed for the purposes of those who build it. Political and social aims enter into its fiber at its birth, while the mentality and outlook of its framers are reflected and perpetuated in its lower echelons. If we are to discern the factors — political as well as sociological — which made the Social Democratic party apparatus a conservative force, we must examine its genesis and historical development.

i. Toward a Uniform Party Structure

Before 1905 the rational, hierarchical organization for which German Social Democracy became famous existed only in embryo. Whether at the central, regional, or local levels the party was loosely organized and the functions of its officers were uncoördinated and ill-defined.

The national leadership rested, since Bismarckian times, in the

---

[4] Address to the Verein für Sozialpolitik, in *Schriften des Vereins für Sozialpolitik*, CXXV: 296–297 (1908). For other descriptions of the conservative impact of bureaucracy on the party, see Harry Marks, "The Sources of Reformism in the Social Democratic Party of Germany, 1890–1914," *Journal of Modern History*, XI: 347ff. (1939); Gustav Schmoller, "Der Weltkrieg und die deutsche Sozialdemokratie," *Schmollers Jahrbuch*, XXXIX: 1103ff. (1915).

hands of Reichstag deputies — the only Social Democrats who, under the Anti-Socialist Laws, enjoyed some measure of immunity.[5] The executive, though elected by the congress to carry on the business of the party, rarely took a major decision without consulting the whole Reichstag delegation. As late as 1900 this practice continued even with respect to purely organizational matters.[6] The chief concern of the executive before the turn of the century was political agitation, conducted primarily through the medium of the Reichstag and the party press. Accordingly, political rather than administrative personnel predominated in the executive. In the twelve-member executive of the 1890's only three persons held administrative offices (two secretaries and a treasurer).[7] Until 1906 the party leaders, unlike their colleagues in the trade-unions, did not even know the size of their organization. There was no regular system of reporting from the local units. The financial structure of the party was likewise shaky.[8]

With the expansion of the party in the late 1890's the need for more systematic management made itself felt. The increasing burden of work could no longer be properly handled by an undifferentiated body of political leaders. In 1900 the leadership was divided into the party executive proper, composed of two chairmen, two secretaries, a treasurer and two associates (*Beisitzer*), and a nine-man control commission with powers of review over all actions of the executive.[9] While this new arrangement permitted the control commission to continue for some years to participate in major policy decisions, it nevertheless marked the beginning of the separation of administrative and political powers which would later result in

---

[5] Robert Michels, "Die deutsche Sozialdemokratie," *Archiv für Sozialwissenschaft und Sozialpolitik*, XXIII: 477 (1906).

[6] Thus a revision of the party's organization statute in 1900 was considered by the Reichstag delegation. *Prot. S. P., 1900*, 16, 132.

[7] Wilhelm Schröder, *Geschichte der sozialdemokratischen Parteiorganisation in Deutschland*, in Abhandlungen und Vorträge zur sozialistischen Bildung, Max Grunwald, ed., Heft 4 and 5 (Dresden, 1912), 75.

[8] In 1900, the party's income was M. 249,582 (for 11 months); in 1906, M. 810,917; in 1912, M. 1,697,630. Cf. "Kassenberichte" in *Prot. S. P., 1900, 1906, 1912*.

[9] Schröder, *Parteiorganisation*, 79–80; cf. also *Prot. S. P., 1900*, 7, 149, 185–186; *ibid., 1907*, 383.

the ascendency of the former over the latter. Within the executive itself the addition of three more secretaries in the years 1904–1906 gave the bureaucratic element a clear majority.

Below the central level the organizational apparatus was a patchwork of different forms varying with local and regional conditions. Until 1899 the party was forbidden by law to organize across the borders of the federal states. The conditions of political association also varied from one state to another.[10] Throughout the nineties the party feared a revival of anti-socialist legislation. These conditions dictated the loosest possible form of party structure. Each local group was left free to organize in the manner best suited to its conditions. The only uniform institution was that of the *Vertrauensmann* — a locally elected agent who maintained contact between the local organization and the party executive.[11] After the repeal of the prohibition on interstate organization in 1899 there was some pressure to establish uniformity among the local units, but the statute of 1900 still left open the local form of organization and reaffirmed the centrality of the *Vertrauensmann*. It was now possible, however, for the *Vertrauensmann* to be a local officer of the party.[12] At the same time, because of the growing importance of electoral activity in the life of the party, there was a tendency to fuse local organizations (*Ortsvereine*) into organizations corresponding to the Reichstag electoral districts (*Wahlkreisvereine*).

At the *Land* (state) level, too, organizations slowly emerged. The *Land* organization was particularly characteristic of southern Germany where the laws were more liberal and Social Democratic participation in state elections well established.[13] The parties of Württemberg and the Grand Duchy of Hessen both had *Land* or-

---

[10] *Ibid., 1900,* 16.

[11] Fritz Bieligk, "Die Entwicklung der sozialdemokratischen Organisation in Deutschland," *Die Organisation im Klassenkampf.* Rote Bücher der "Marxistischen Büchergemeinde," II (Berlin, n. d. [1931?]), 31–32.

[12] See "Organisationsstatut," *Prot. S. P., 1900,* 6; also *ibid.,* 137.

[13] Participation in Prussian elections was the subject of a great party controversy in the nineties. The Köln congress of 1893 maintained the principle of boycott as a protest against the three-class voting system. The boycott was lifted in 1897, and the Mainz congress (1900) agreed that the Social Democrats should run candidates in the next election. Not until 1903 did the party launch a full-fledged electoral campaign. Cf. Paul Hirsch, *Der Weg der Sozialdemokratie zur Macht in Preussen* (Berlin, 1929), 26.

ganizations before 1900, the latter run by one of the first regional bosses of Social Democracy, Karl Ulrich of Offenbach, who was known as the "Red Duke." [14] By 1905 Bavaria, Oldenburg, Mecklenburg, Schleswig-Holstein, and Alsace-Lorraine had also developed permanent *Land* organizations.[15] In Prussia and Saxony, where the main strength of the party was located, there was no comparable development before 1905.[16]

After 1903 the question of reorganization was much discussed in the party. The electoral success of that year, when the Social Democrats won eighty-one seats in the Reichstag, stimulated the demand for even more effective organization of the electorate. At the same time the revisionist controversy, which reached its height at the Dresden congress of 1903, gave rise to a radical pressure for a tighter organization in which party discipline could not be so lightly broken. Both these factors contributed to produce a revision of the party organization statute during 1904 and 1905. The new statute, adopted at the Jena congress, laid the basis for the centralized, bureaucratic organization which rapidly became the hallmark of German Social Democracy.

Under the new statute the electoral district organization (*Wahlkreisverein*) became the basic unit of the party. Its officers were directly responsible to the party executive and were to report to it annually on membership, financial condition, expenditure of funds, activity, etc. At the same time provision was made for the establishment of a uniform organization at the regional level. All electoral district associations were to band together into *Land,* provincial, or agitational district organizations. Their officers were likewise to be responsible for a full annual report to the party executive, and were to be under the latter's control.[17]

We have already seen how the southern reformists had developed the *Land* organizations to give them some immunity against the radical majority of the party.[18] Taking a federalist position on party

[14] Philipp Scheidemann, *Memoiren eines Sozialdemokraten* (Dresden, 1928), I, 85.
[15] *Prot. S. P., 1905,* 348–349.
[16] Although Saxony had a state organization, the more active regional units were the four "agitational districts," dominated by the great cities: Leipzig, Dresden, Chemnitz and Zwickau. In Prussia, certain provinces were organized as agitational districts, but this was not uniformly the case. Cf. *Prot. S. P., 1904,* 30.
[17] *Ibid., 1905,* 6–7.
[18] See Ch. I, sec. v.

organization, they had little sympathy with the centralism of the new party statute. They particularly protested against the limitations on the financial liberties of the state organizations though their real concern was no doubt for their political independence of national party policy on such questions as budget-voting and electoral alliances with bourgeois parties.[19] Federalism in German Social Democracy was at that time an institutional mechanism for the preservation of conservative dissent from the majority. Hence the adoption of the new party statute seemed to represent a radical victory.

The intermediate, regional organizations were not, however, eliminated. On the contrary they were encouraged to develop as instruments under the executive's control. Under its new statute Social Democracy was to become not a federal state, as the reformists wished, but a centralistic one. The radicals, who in 1905 still looked upon the executive as their champion, raised no objection to the new centralism.

ii. The New Bureaucracy

In order to strengthen the executive itself for the management of the larger administrative tasks which now fell to it, the section of the party statute dealing with the composition of the executive was altered in 1905 to leave open the number of paid secretaries to be elected in any given year, while the "political" membership was fixed at four.[20] Thus the way was paved for the creation of a permanent bureaucratic majority in the executive.

The radicals, who later developed passionate hostility to the professional bureaucracy, were at this time entirely indifferent to it.[21] In 1905 the radicals felt confident. They could scarcely realize that the centralized organization and the bureaucratic executive which they now sanctioned — partly as a weapon against revisionist federalism — would soon turn against them. The revisionists were as a rule no more anti-bureaucratic than the radicals in this period. Thus the clause fixing the number of "political" members of the

[19] See Hugo Lindemann, who spoke for 80 federalist opponents of the new statute at Jena, *Prot. S. P., 1905*, 348–349. Cf. also *ibid.*, 177, 189.

[20] The four were the two chairmen and two members elected by the control commission. See section 18 of the new statute, *Prot. S. P., 1905*, 8.

[21] Cf. e.g., *ibid.*, 361.

executive but giving elasticity to the number of paid secretaries was proposed by the revisionist-controlled Munich delegation.[22] Not bureaucratization as such but whether it should take place in a centralist or federalist framework was the political issue at the Jena congress, where the centralists carried the day.

One further act of the Jena congress was to have a profound effect on the future of the Social Democratic Party: the election of Friedrich Ebert to the executive. The new paid secretary, then almost unknown, was destined to play a leading role in transforming the party into a bureaucratic machine.

Friedrich Ebert (1871–1925) was the archetype of the new Social Democratic functionary. A saddler by trade, he had participated in organizing activity as a journeyman, and had more than once lost his employment on this account.[23] In the late eighties Ebert settled in Bremen where for over fifteen years he participated energetically in every aspect of the labor movement — party, trade-union, and coöperative. His outstanding qualities were his business flair and his tireless attention to administrative detail. In 1890, in order to devote himself more fully to labor work, he became a saloon-keeper. In those days, when Social Democrats and trade-unions had few halls of their own, the *"Parteikneipe"* was a vital institution and its owners frequently exercised considerable influence in the party.[24] A cheerless, prosaic soul, Ebert was not happy in his employment as a host. His wife is said to have told him, "As a host you should not look like a vinegar merchant who has had to drink his own vinegar." [25] Uncongenial though the work was, Ebert the saloon-keeper became known to a wide circle of Bremen workers and acquired a reputation for his solidity and sound judgment.[26]

Ebert seems always to have been in the van of the new, practical activities which slowly sapped the revolutionary *élan* of the German labor movement. It was he who in 1892 presented the general commission's case for a strong centralized trade-union structure and overcame the opposition of the Bremen localists.[27] It was he who

[22] *Ibid.*, 132.
[23] Friedrich Ebert, *Kämpfe und Ziele* (Dresden, n. d.), 329ff.
[24] Michels, *Zur Soziologie*, 272–275.
[25] Ebert, *Kämpfe und Ziele*, 337–338.
[26] *Ibid.*, 339–341, 344.
[27] *Idem, Schriften, Aufzeichnungen, Reden* (Dresden, 1926), I, 155.

in 1900 became Bremen's first paid labor secretary — advisor to the
workers on their rights under existing law.[28] The labor secretary,
as one of Ebert's biographers tells us, saw the proletariat not as a
theoretical construct, but as it really was. He met the worker in his
moments of trouble and need and dedicated himself to solving the
individual's daily, practical problems on a short-run basis.[29] Such
activities brought out the talent of Ebert, the gift of the patient organizer and administrator. "He was rooted in the existing," wrote
Paul Kampffmeyer. "Never did he seek his next objective beyond
the limits of the attainable," said Otto Landsberg. And Konrad
Haenisch wrote of him that "he always knew very clearly what he
wanted, and because he always kept the goal clearly in mind . . .
he could keep the strings in his hands even in the most difficult
situation." [30] Colorless, cool, determined, industrious, and intensely
practical, Ebert had all those characteristics which were to make
of him, *mutatis mutandis,* the Stalin of Social Democracy.

When Ebert came to Berlin in 1906 to take up his new duties in
the executive he was shocked by the unbusiness-like conditions of
the office. The little establishment boasted neither telephone nor
typewriter. The old comrades, still living in the memories of Bismarckian days, burned all incoming letters and made no copies of
outgoing ones. Ebert slowly persuaded the old gentlemen to permit
the adoption of more modern methods. Before his first year was
out the office boasted not only typewriter and telephone, but also
a stenographer.[31]

Ebert was assigned three initial tasks: assisting the aging and
sickly treasurer, Gerisch; keeping an eye on the party press; and
creating the party statistics from the reports made obligatory by the
1905 organizational statute.[32] The first and third of these assign-
ments brought Ebert at once into contact with the local and regional party officials. They gave him his opportunity to become the
business manager of the Social Democratic bureaucracy.

The new statute had said nothing concerning the functionaries
who were to man the new institutions, yet through them a uniform

[28] *Idem, Kämpfe und Ziele,* 344.
[29] *Idem, Schriften,* I, 61–62.
[30] *Ibid.,* 36; *idem, Kämpfe und Ziele,* 389, 30.
[31] *Ibid.,* 348–350.
[32] *Ibid.,* 348.

machine was to be built. According to a decision of the Bremen congress of 1904, the executive had the right to appoint paid secretaries at all levels of the organization. The local or regional organizations could make nominations, but final authority rested with the executive which was to pay the salaries.[33] This arrangement did not prevent the subordinate organizations from appointing their own secretaries without the approval of the executive if they would bear the expense themselves.[34] Only a few organizations, however, availed themselves of this luxury.[35] For the most part they were happy to have a full-time functionary appointed from above.

Within two years of Ebert's advent the establishment of the intermediate regional echelon in the party structure was very nearly complete. Ebert could announce in 1907 that a skeletal organization existed in every region but one. Functionaries appeared only slightly more slowly. By 1906 the executive had appointed sixteen regional secretaries; another eight more were added in 1907, four more in 1908. Seven regions had named and supported their own secretaries. By 1909 the secretarial structure was complete except for a few small districts among the forty-three regional organizations.[36]

The reorganization of the locals into electoral district associations proceeded somewhat more slowly than the construction of the regional hierarchy. Treasurer Gerisch complained in 1906 that the great mass of party comrades were loath to break away from the loose, informal *Vertrauensmann* system in favor of the more impersonal electoral district organization.[37] Yet the executive had every reason to be pleased with its progress: 278 of the 397 electoral districts of Germany had Socal Democratic organizations tailored to them by 1906. In 1907 forty-six more followed; in 1908, another thirty-one. Thus by 1908 only twenty-two electoral districts were without formal uniform organization.[38]

[33] The beginning salary was fixed at M. 2000 per year, with M. 200 increases promised for every three years of service. Cf. *Prot. S. P., 1904*, 134 (motion no. 127).

[34] *Ibid.*, 176.

[35] Of the regional organizations with paid secretaries in 1907, only seven had appointed their own (Greater Berlin, Brandenburg, Schleswig-Holstein, South Bavaria, Pfalz, Anhalt, and Hamburg). Cf. executive's report, *Prot. S. P., 1907*, 19–20.

[36] Executive's reports, in *ibid., 1905*, 15; *1906*, 22–25; *1907*, 19–20, 189; *1908*, 20; *1909*, 20.

[37] *Ibid., 1906*, 173.

[38] *Ibid., 1908*, 20. In ten of these there seems to have been a party agent of some sort; in only twelve does the party report having no contact.

As the electoral district organizations spread, the professional party secretaries began to proliferate at the local level. In 1907 twenty-seven secretaries were reported; in 1908, forty-one; in 1909, sixty-two; and in 1912, eighty-four, "with the number," according to Otto Braun of the executive, "happily growing almost weekly."[39]

Professionalization was stimulated by the new demands of the executive on the locals. In 1907 Ebert began to send out questionnaires for his annual report. At the due date 150 of the electoral districts had not yet replied. At the Essen congress Ebert excoriated the locals for their sloppy methods. He called for a "uniform management of our administrative affairs" and promised to send out instructions accordingly.[40] Paper work was henceforth to be an important ingredient in the life of the local party officer. It quite naturally sped the transition from voluntary to paid, full-time officials.

The election defeat in 1907 contributed further to the intensification of the bureaucratic demands. The one failure of Social Democracy which the executive explicitly recognized was the inadequate organization of the electoral campaign. The executive's report for the year cited with admiration the technical methods of the Reich League against Social Democracy, which had used voting lists and a door-to-door canvass so that it might identify and give special attention to potential converts to its cause. The executive recommended the Reich League's technique for "the mobilization of the indifferent mass."[41] Ebert urged the organizations to devote themselves to building up their electoral machine between elections. He called for "an exact survey of the social position of the inhabitants" in every district, and for "experienced comrades with whose help we should be in a position to establish personal contact with the social strata of the population standing closest to us."[42] The construction of the next electoral victory was to be prepared well in advance of the day — which was five years off.

To increase the number of members, the intake in dues, and the dissemination of the press,[43] and to prepare a smoothly operating electoral machine: these were the demands which the executive

[39] *Ibid., 1907*, 20; *1909*, 20; *1912*, 286.
[40] *Ibid., 1907*, 190.
[41] *Ibid.*, 33–34.
[42] *Ibid.*, 189–190.
[43] *Ibid.*, 194.

posed to the local organizations. Their fulfillment required the use of paid secretaries in the larger districts. Volunteers could not keep up with the burden of administration and paper work. They were only too happy for the opportunity to turn over the task to a career man. Thus bureaucracy above tended to breed its likeness in the lower echelons of the party.

The purposes for which — and the circumstances under which — the bureaucracy was constructed were far stronger forces for conservatism than the mere fact that the functionaries were salaried. Unlike Lenin's corps of professionals, Ebert's was built primarily to compete with other political parties, to get members and voters, not to shatter the existing order. It was constructed almost entirely in the years 1906–1909 when the radical wave had temporarily receded, when the trade-unions were consolidating their hold on the party, and when the executive itself was tending in a more conservative direction. Moreover, the fact that the cleavages within the party were widening had to be taken into account in appointing new functionaries. The men who were selected to serve as secretaries would have to enjoy a reputation for neutrality, for being above the intra-party struggles. This qualification could only reinforce the "unpolitical" character which the secretary's regular tasks might impose in the first instance. When almost every new issue in political life unleashed a factional struggle within the party, the bureaucracy tended to recoil from "politics." The principle positive task of the bureaucracy, to build up the party for electoral victories, necessarily involved a negative attitude toward any pressure for a change in tactic which would either divide the party or alienate the nonsocialist voter.[44] What the party functionary wanted above all else was peace and unity in the organization. In the riven condition of the party this made him a natural opponent of both criticism and change. And as the pressure for change came increasingly from the left, the functionary identified himself increasingly with the right.

iii. Regional Organizations: The New Centers of Power

The creation of the regional organizations and the proliferation of an administrative officialdom slowly produced a change in the relationship between the party executive and the locals. Decisions

[44] Michels, Zur Soziologie, 352–353.

tended more and more to be made at the national and regional level rather than by the local organizations whose role was reduced to that of executors of policy made at the higher echelons. The paid local officials, selected not so much for political talent as for their attentiveness to administrative detail, did not, like the old part-time officials, share directly in the workers' life in the shop. The regional secretaries in turn had even less contact with the rank and file than the local secretaries. The line of political responsibility, like the line of personal advancement, tended to be upward to the executive rather than downward to the rank and file.[45]

The loss of contact between top and bottom was soon felt. Hermann Müller, a member of the executive, stated in 1908 that since the creation of the regional organizations "the tie between party executive and the separate electoral districts is no longer as close as it was when each separate electoral district dealt with us directly." [46] A Hamburg delegate proposed that the executive meet directly with the local organizations on important questions, or at least send representatives to regional conferences to learn more about local sentiment and thus to avoid friction.[47] In 1912 it was suggested that the executive hold conferences of all electoral district (local) secretaries to re-establish the lost connection.[48] By that time, however, the number of conferences, exclusive of the annual congress, had swelled to such dimensions that Ebert could correctly reject the proposal as impractical:

I must declare that we have almost reached the point of having too many conferences. We have business managers' conferences, editors' conferences, regional conferences, secretaries' conferences; librarians' conferences have been suggested, and goodness knows what others may yet be before us. If we should hold electoral district secretaries' conferences besides all the others, we should have a continual [round of] little party congresses.[49]

---

[45] Cf. Kurt Laumann, "Organisation und Apparat," *Die Organisation im Klassenkampf*, Rote Bücher der "Marxistischen Büchergemeinde," II, 135–138, for an excellent discussion of the problem. Laumann deals with the Weimar era, but the same tendencies were present in the period under consideration here.

[46] *Prot. S. P., 1908*, 251.

[47] *Ibid.*, 229–230.

[48] *Ibid., 1912*, 153.

[49] *Ibid.*, 286.

The regional organizations — variously organized by *Land*, province, or agitation district — tended to produce machines which gave a clear preponderance to one or another faction in a given area. Where the district was a geographically concentrated industrial area dominated by a single city, the regional organization was often radical. Such was the case in Bremen, Brunswick, Gotha, and, to a lesser extent, East Prussia. The Lower Rhine district, the seventh largest in the party in 1913, was likewise in radical control.[50] Here the conservative elements in the party probably found less expression than their numbers warranted.

Radical regional organizations, however, were the exception. As a rule the regional organizations were a conservative force and operated to dampen the radicalism of the cities. Here it must be remembered that among the chief purposes of the new regional bureaucracy was the building up of the weak Social Democratic districts where a small-town and rural electorate predominated.[51] The temptation was strong for the district leader to accommodate to the small-town outlook, which meant moderating the radicalism of the party. The conservative pressures in the provinces were so great as to affect even the Progressive Party. One of its leaders described the difficulties of working with the small bourgeois and conservative working classes, which, he said,

are not the strongest elements of the population. Practically all of them must have due regard for themselves, their families and their business. If the state throws its full power . . . against them, they don't stand up. They bear up as little if fanatical individuals use their social superiority against them. Our friends in the countryside have already had to reckon with such dangers even if they only come forward as liberal individuals. If they are then branded as allies of the most radical, and the red feather is stuck into their hats, then the personal disadvantages and economic damage become endless. . . . It is easy for the *literatus* in the metrop-

---

[50] It included the industrial centers of Düsseldorf, Essen, Solingen, Duisburg, Elberfeld-Barmen, Remscheid, *et al*. Cf. *ibid.*, *1913*, 13, 63. In June 1913 the Lower Rhine regional conference called upon the executive and general commission to prepare for the propagation of the mass strike — a sure sign of radicalism. This is, to my knowledge, the only regional organization — as opposed to many locals — which advocated such a measure. Cf. *ibid.*, 321.

[51] In 1909 sixteen agitation districts issued special periodicals for the country population. *Ibid.*, *1909*, 27. See also reports on the *Volkskalender*, an agitational medium for backward areas, *1906*, 24; *1909*, 27.

olis to hand out bold suggestions. The man in the provinces who follows them can pay with his whole civic existence.[52]

If the Progressives suffered from such social pressure, how much harder must have been the lot of the Social Democrats? In the small town, to be a party member at all was a bold undertaking.[53] Radicalism was little likely to flourish in such an atmosphere. It was easy enough to defy the social order in the great industrial center where one was part of a crowd and where one did not risk ostracism, family tension, etc., for one's political views. In the small towns the old loyalties, reinforced by social pressure, had greater vitality.

The regional bureaucracy not only sought to win the weak and conservative areas to Social Democracy, but also tended to base its power upon them. The less radical Social Democrat outside the metropolis became a prop of bureaucratic conservatism in the party. This factor did not, of course, operate uniformly in all districts: the urban regional organizations, like Bremen, Hamburg, and Berlin, were, by their very structure, not susceptible to it. But in the larger provincial areas it played an increasing role as the purely electoral aims of the party occupied a larger share of its attention.

The *Land* organization of Württemberg provides an extreme example of how the regional leadership built its organization on the small-town membership as a weapon against urban radicalism. The instrument of conservative control was the Württemberg party congress. Let us examine its structure and operation.

In 1911 the Württemberg party had a membership of 27,776. Of this membership, 8659 — a little under one-third — were concentrated in Stuttgart. At the *Land* congress of the party in 1911, Stuttgart's 8659 members were represented by forty-three delegates. Seven hundred and twenty-three members who lived in rural communities with from six to twenty members were represented at the same congress by forty-nine delegates.[54] In 1912 it was reported that 17,000 city voters elected ninety delegates to the *Land* congress of

[52] Cited from Hermann Pachnicke, *Liberalismus als Kulturpolitik* (Berlin, 1907), in *S.M.*, XI (XIII), ii, 960–961.
[53] Cf. the rural campaign experiences described in Scheidemann, *Memoiren*, I, 68ff.; Wilhelm Keil, *Erlebnisse eines Sozialdemokraten* (Stuttgart, 1947), I, 147.
[54] *Prot. S. P., 1911*, 314.

Württemberg, while 5000 members in smaller places elected 224.[55]
I have been unable to find a complete description of the system for
electing delegates. But it is a fact that the organizations having up
to 100 members had one delegate, those from 101 to 499 had only
two.[56] The effect of this delegation system was to create an overwhelming rural and small-town majority in the congress although
the membership was in its majority urban.[57] The rural and small-
town delegates gave the revisionist *Land* officers their "mass" basis
— and a free hand in the pursuit of those revisionist policies for
which they had so often been censured by the national party congress.

By 1907 the first signs of serious difference between the Stuttgart
organization and the *Land* party leaders had appeared. The city
organization held meetings to discuss the Social Democratic Landtag representatives' vote for the state budget. The *Land* leaders ur-
gently requested that no vote be taken on the issue, and their wish
was respected; the tension had not yet reached the boiling point. At
the same time the *Land* party congress supported the Landtag delegation's action.[58] In the following year the Stuttgart organization
went into open opposition on the budget question.[59] Thenceforth,
the cleavage between the Stuttgart city organization and the *Land*
leadership became ever wider and began to spread to other cities in
Württemberg. With the nation-wide radical wave in 1910[60] the
conflict passed from the realm of policy debate to a struggle for the
instruments of power.

The struggle began over the control of the *Schwäbische Tagwacht,* a newspaper serving as joint organ of city and *Land* organizations.[61] The city local in 1911 sought to institute a press
commission in which it would be the controlling element. On the

[55] According to Stadthagen, a leftist sympathizer. The cities to which he refers are
presumably Stuttgart (11,900) and Cannstadt (6,418). Cf. *ibid., 1912,* 308, and
membership chart, 66–67.

[56] *Ibid., 1911,* 312.

[57] *Ibid.,* 77, 313.

[58] *S.M.,* XI (XIII), ii, 883, 946–947; Keil, *Erlebnisse,* I, 241.

[59] *Prot. S. P., 1908,* 480; Keil, *Erlebnisse,* I, 216.

[60] See below, Ch. VII, *passim.*

[61] Its chief editor was Wilhelm Keil, who had drifted steadily toward the revisionist camp after 1906; the second editor, Friedrich Westmeyer, now took the
lead of the radical wing. Cf. Keil, *Erlebnisse,* I, 243.

mediation of Ebert, the city leaders agreed to a press commission in which the Stuttgart and *Land* organizations would receive equal representation. The *Land* leadership, however, utilized its control over the state party congress to have the compromise proposal rejected. The forty-three Stuttgart delegates walked out of the state congress. Adding insult to injury, the *Land* executive dismissed the radical members of the *Tagwacht* editorial staff.[62] Subsequently, through the intervention of the national executive, an agreement was reached in which a new radical editorial board was installed.[63]

The press conflict was but one of a series of struggles in Württemberg which continued until the outbreak of the war.[64] Both Stuttgart and Cannstatt, though radical, were represented in the Reichstag by conservatives. Karl Hildenbrand, who sat for Stuttgart, was among the most outspokenly nationalistic revisionists; Wilhelm Keil believed in the revisionists' ideas, but did not believe they should be expressed lest the mass of party comrades take umbrage.[65] Both men were at odds after 1910 with the party organizations in their respective districts. "Personal quarrels," Keil tells us, made his life in the Württemberg party unbearable. He resigned his editorship of the *Tagwacht* and confined his Württemberg activities to

[62] *Prot. S. P., 1911,* 312–319. Keil writes that he resigned from the *Tagwacht* editorship over the protest of the *Land* executive, and that the other editors resigned thereafter. He makes no mention of the dismissal of the radicals, especially of Fritz Westmeyer, who, according to Keil, "left" the paper at the same time. Keil, *Erlebnisse,* I, 261.

[63] The new dispensation provided, however, that when the press commission, in which the city organization and the *Land* executive had equal representation, should disagree, the *Land* committee should have a deciding vote. The latter body did not exercise its power until the war when it expelled the radical editors who refused to support the vote for the war credits. Cf. Keil, *Erlebnisse,* 306ff.; also Karl Weller, *Die Staatsumwälzung in Württemberg, 1918–1920* (Stuttgart, 1930), 24.

[64] For other instances, see *Prot. S. P., 1911,* 299–312, 332; *ibid., 1912,* 209–215, 225–240; and Ch. IX, sec. iv, below. The tension was augmented by the fact that the urban majority grew as the years went on; i.e., the cities, where the radicals operated, recruited the most new members. Thus Stuttgart accounted for 25 per cent of the Württemberg membership in 1907; 31 per cent in 1911; and 33 per cent in 1912 and 1913. The five city districts with a membership of over 2000 included 72 per cent of the state membership in 1911, 75 per cent in 1912, and 76 per cent in 1913. Of these all but one (Brackenheim-Heilbronn, membership 3288 in 1913) were in radical hands. [Computed from tables given in *Prot. S. P., 1911,* 77, and *1913,* 66–67. The executive's annual report did not include a breakdown by city until 1911. The figure for Stuttgart in 1907 is taken from *1911,* 313.]

[65] Keil, *Erlebnisse,* I, 242.

his duties as a member of the *Land* executive.[66] Once in 1911, when Hildenbrand was called before a mass meeting in Stuttgart to justify his defiance of Social Democratic etiquette by attendance at an official state banquet, he was greeted by vociferous protests from the assembled membership. He called to the crowd: "Get as mad as you please, I'm not talking for you, I'm talking for my own peace of mind." [67] Despite his defiance of his constituency, Hildenbrand was nominated and elected again to the Reichstag in 1912 to represent the radical city of Stuttgart. The control of the nomination was vested not in his electoral district organization, but in the *Land* committee.

Thus thwarted by a revisionist bureaucracy basing its power on the minority country locals, the Social Democrats of Württemberg's cities became increasingly revolutionary. Württemberg was one of the greatest breeding grounds of future Communist leadership: Zetkin, Walcher, Hörnle, Westmeyer, Thalheimer, and Käthe Duncker all "went to school" there. Arthur Crispien, later Independent Social Democratic leader, likewise gained part of his political training in Stuttgart. When the Social Democratic Reichstag deputies voted the war credits in 1914, the Stuttgart organization led certain other Württemberg locals in the first significant break from the mother party.[68]

In the Württemberg example we see at its most striking the dialectic relationship of revisionism and radicalism. The revisionist policy of political compromise in the interest of democratic reform was maintained at the expense of democracy within the party and was imposed on an urban majority by the leadership through the overrepresentation of a small town, conservative minority in the congress. Reformism and undemocratic party structure helped to breed in the cities their opposite: a revolutionary attitude toward the state and, as we shall see, an ultra-democratic concept of party organization.

The kind of individual psychological frustration which could be generated by the conflict between a conservative regional bureauc-

[66] *Ibid.*, I, 262.
[67] *Prot. S. P., 1911,* 314.
[68] Eugen Prager, *Geschichte der U.S.P.D.* (Berlin, 1922), 39–40; Keil, *Erlebnisse,* I, 306ff.

racy and a radical urban local is illuminated by the letters of Konrad Haenisch, editor of the *Dortmunder Arbeiterzeitung*. In 1910 the extreme left controlled the local organization in Dortmund. The *Arbeiterzeitung* was one of the most radical Social Democratic papers in Germany. The regional authority, the central commission for Rhineland-Westphalia, also had a voice in the policy of the *Arbeiterzeitung*. Left-wing editor Haenisch was regularly at odds with this body of whose eleven members only one was radical.

They constantly have me . . . on the ropes [Haenisch wrote in 1910] because of my 'unilateral exercise of authority' (without which *absolutely nothing* would come to anything!). Think of it, the commission is divided over six cities of Rhineland and Westphalia, and is supposed to meet only *once a quarter!* . . . [Yet] nothing should be done without an official decision of the commission. Nothing at all! [69]

Haenisch's letters are pervaded with his running battle against the regional bureaucracy.[70] At least once he turned his resignation in only to reconsider and stay on. On this occasion he wrote,

Although I receive one unanimous vote of confidence after another in the mining communities, the conditions in the party have become so unbearable under the top bureaucrats [*"Oberbonzen"*] that I can no longer remain under any circumstances.[71]

The officials were occasionally willing to use a radical for special problems requiring skill in winning mass support. Thus a functionaries' conference for Rhineland-Westphalia designated Haenisch as chief of a special "anti-Centrist" office to combat the hold of the Catholic party on the workers. But Haenisch's appointment did not stand:

Yesterday the party executive, which had been represented at the conference and had favored my election, refused its official sanction, since in the meantime the executive of the Mine Workers' Union . . . lodged a full-dress protest against my appointment with the party executive, the general commission [of the trade unions] and the conference of

[69] Letter to Rudolf Franz, 11 Dec. **1910**; in Rudolf Franz, "Aus Briefen Konrad Haenischs," *Archiv für die Geschichte des Sozialismus und der Arbeiterbewegung*, XIV: 462 (1929).

[70] *Ibid.*, 448–484, *passim*.

[71] Letter to Rudolf Franz, 20 Oct. 1910, *ibid.*, 460.

trade union executives. The party executive will certainly not admit pub-
lically that the *post hoc* is also a *propter hoc*. But no man here doubts
the connection. And this in spite of the fact that the second-in-command
was to be Pokorny of the *Bergarbeiter Zeitung* [organ of the Mine
Workers' Union]; that is to say, an entirely 'reliable' man.[72]

Thus the unions could step in to block a radical from above when
the regional bureaucracy grew too lenient.

Haenisch was not the only radical who suffered in Dortmund.
Power over the Dortmund local was shortly taken out of radical
hands entirely. In 1913 the Dortmund delegation to the party congress voted solidly conservative on the two issues on which a roll-
call vote was taken.[73] It was a great change from 1910 when the
Dortmund delegates had all signed a radical resolution on the mass
strike question.[74] The transfer of power seems to have taken place
in a series of explosions in 1911.[75] Available sources throw no light
on the details of the operation but the outcome was clear: the radicals were thoroughly beaten by 1913.

The examples of Württemberg and Dortmund cast only a dim
light on a problem which requires study on a local and regional
basis. Both examples suggest that radicalism received less than its
share of influence in the party councils by virtue of the connection
between the regional functionaries and the more conservative social
strata: in Württemberg, the small-town worker; in Rhineland-
Westphalia, the politically unorganized trade-unionist. Only a series
of intensive regional studies could illuminate some of the crucial
questions arising out of the above examples: What was the constitutional structure of each regional organization? What was the
social basis of the bureaucracy and its policy in each area? Of radicalism? One can come to no firm conclusions without detailed in-
vestigations, but there is enough evidence to suggest that the defeat
of radicalism within the party was aided by the establishment of
the regional bureaucracy and regional institutions which based their
power on the small-town worker and/or on the non-party trade-

---

[72] *Ibid.*

[73] On Luxemburg's mass strike resolution and the question of support for liberal
tax bills to cover military expenditures. Cf. *Prot. S. P., 1913*, 337, 516.

[74] Haenisch, Lex and Schöbel, *ibid., 1910*, 182.

[75] Franz, "Aus Briefen Konrad Haenischs," *Archiv für die Geschichte des Sozialismus*, XIV, 464, 469.

union member whose political attitudes toward the social order were not nearly so negative as those of the urban party member.

iv. The Party Congress: Structure and Politics

The party congress was the central institution in the party's constitutional structure. Here basic party policies were, if not made, then at least sanctioned. Here also the resistance to the extension of trade-union influence over the party and to the executive's conservative tendencies came to a focus. Sometimes, as in the case of the form of the May Day observance, the party congress' resistance to rightist innovation lasted over years. Yet the resistance of the congress to the executive's policies was not effective in the long run. Why not?

The power of the executive over the congress was, as we have seen, in part established between congress sessions by the creation of *faits accomplis* to which the congress had to reconcile itself.[76] The executive's control over the procedure of the congress was, as in any parliamentary body, a powerful weapon. Thus the right of the executive to designate a rapporteur, the *Referent,* to present each issue at length, and its even more important privilege of the *Schlusswort,* the "last word" of summary and plea before the vote was taken, were strong instruments for influencing the balloting. Moreover, the question of confidence, seldom posed but always an imminent threat, had the nature of an ultimate sanction which few delegates would have dared to face. The members tended to identify the party with the persons of its leaders, thus strengthening a well-established tradition of continuity in the leadership which enhanced the executive's position.[77] Then too the very split in the party placed the executive in a powerful position as the guardian of unity. As long as unity was valued above the nature of the party's policy by all concerned, the executive drew strength from the party's factional strife.

Above and beyond all these factors, however, was the structure

---

[76] Cf. Ch. IV, *passim.*

[77] Robert Michels attributes this phenomenon to the psychological "need to worship" (*Anbetungsbedürfnis*) on the part of the masses. He cites the replacement of Luther's picture in the homes of Saxon workers by that of Bebel. Cf. *Zur Soziologie,* 48–60, 68.

of the congress itself. The nature of its representative system not only strengthened the executive's power, but also favored the conservative forces in the party over the radical.

The basic unit of representation at the party congress was the electoral district organization. Before the Anti-Socialist Laws, when the party was small, every local organization could send as many delegates as it wished. In 1891, after the Anti-Socialist Laws were lifted, and when the party had begun to increase greatly in numbers, it was agreed to fix the number of delegates arbitrarily at three per electoral district. As the party organized locals in the smaller cities and towns, the fixed delegation system strengthened the representation of the smaller districts at the expense — in terms of members per delegate — of the larger ones.[78]

Over the course of years the cities made sporadic attempts to win the larger representation to which they felt their huge membership entitled them.[79] In this question, as in so many others, 1905 energized the urban radicals. There was a flood of proposals from the strong city districts to introduce some form of proportional representation.[80] But the executive, which so ardently advocated proportional representation for the Reichstag elections, had no desire to see it in the party. Speaking for the leadership at the Jena congress, von Vollmar argued that it was easier to recruit members in the great industrial centers. If representation were proportional to membership, the industrial centers would be "always predominant" at the congresses. Moreover, one could then tell beforehand how the congress would vote on any issue after the strong locals, in their membership meetings, had instructed their delegates. Vollmar said that proportional representation would "create class differences among the delegates."[81] This was a curious argument since "class differences" in representation were already at hand, but the weak districts were the privileged class.

The reform effort of 1905 failed. The executive postponed bring-

---

[78] *Prot. S. P., 1905,* 169–170.
[79] *Ibid.*
[80] Such proposals were submitted by five of Berlin's six districts, all three of Hamburg's, Bremen, Erfurt, Königsberg, Niederbarnim (an industrial district outside Berlin), two Saxon districts, Merseburg-Querfurt, Brunswick, and Schleswig-Holstein VI. Cf. *ibid.,* 104–123.
[81] *Ibid.,* 169–171.

ing in its proposals for organizational reform until the sixth day when the left had already won its victory in the mass strike question, and when the delegates were too weary to raise any more problems. The old form of representation stood.

In 1909, again under pressure from the cities, the executive gave way: the form of representation was modified to introduce a certain degree of proportionality. Electoral districts with less than 1500 members were entitled to one delegate, those with up to 3000, two; 6000, 3; 12,000, four; 18,000, five; and over 18,000, six.[82] This system still left the centers of Socialist strength under-represented. But it was a great improvement from the point of view of democratic structure. Why was the executive now willing to make such a broad concession to the demands which it had resisted in 1905? We have no direct evidence on the point, but would suggest that the year — 1909 — is not without significance. In that year the bureaucratic structure of the party was virtually completed.[83] It also marked the close of the fundamental steps in the extension of trade-union influence over the party.[84] The executive perhaps felt safe, in view of these two developments, to introduce greater representation for the party's urban strongholds.

The operation of the new proportional representation system may be illustrated by the composition of the congress of 1911. At that congress, 778,308 members were represented. Of these, 400,518 or 52 per cent, belonged to electoral districts having 8000 members or more. This metropolitan 52 per cent of the membership was represented at the congress by ninety-four of 349 delegates, or 27 per cent of the delegates. The organizations of less than 4000 members which embraced in all 245,457 persons, or 31 per cent of those represented, had 183 delegates present, a clear majority.[85] The ratio of represen-

---

[82] "Organisationsstatut," sec. 7, *ibid., 1909,* 7.

[83] See above, Ch. V, n. 36, 38 and text.

[84] See above, Ch. IV, *passim.*

[85] Of the 397 organized electoral districts 173 had no representation at the 1911 congress. These embraced approximately 50,000 members; 119 of them had less than 300 members. On the other hand, there was a total of 57,671 members in districts of over 18,000 who had no representation. Thus the unrepresented from city and country roughly cancel each other out, and our calculations of the representative system as revealed in the 1911 congress remain valid. Cf. R. Lipinski, "Das Delegationsrecht zum Parteitag," *N.Z.,* XXX, ii, 858, table, and statistics on the unrepresented, 857, 861–862.

tation at the 1911 congress ranged from one delegate for fifty-seven members in the smallest district to one for 5700 in the largest.[86] But these extremes are of less political importance than the block of votes which the overrepresented small districts would reliably deliver to the executive.

The representatives of the smaller places were the strong silent men at the congresses. They were the back-benchers of Social Democracy — inarticulate and prepared to vote as the leaders wished. At the congress of 1911, where the representatives of the organizations under 4000 had the majority of delegates, only thirteen of their number spoke at all, out of a speakers' list of 114.[87] Their performance as voters, however, was clearly conservative, as we shall see.

A further reform of the representation system in 1912 gave to the largest districts an additional congress delegate for every 6000 members above 18,000. Here again the executive moved when it had become safe to do so. An analysis of voting at the Jena congress of 1913 reveals that the delegates of the larger centers were, on the whole, more loyal to the executive than those of the medium-sized districts (3000–6000 members) where the contact between rank and file and leadership was more direct and intimate. At two extremes lay the centers of executive support: in the smallest districts, where conservative control was the natural reflection of the attitude of the party members themselves, and in the majority of the largest cities where radical and conservative attitudes were both present but where the large, impersonal machines seem to have worked more strongly in favor of the conservative than of the radical forces.

To analyze the voting pattern at congresses is made difficult by the peculiar voting tradition of the party. It was customary to avoid roll-call votes wherever possible. This was due in part to the desire to maintain the myth of unity against the hostile outside world; in part, no doubt, to the reluctance of the potentially losing side to measure its defeat in public. The executive's opponents would nor-

---

[86] *Prot. S. P., 1912*, 301.

[87] Foreign delegates are not included. Of the thirteen from the smaller organizations, two were Reichstag members, a third was Rosa Luxemburg, who sat for the district of Lennep-Mettmann, which had 3,950 members. These statistics are derived from *Prot. S. P., 1911*, by comparing the list of speakers, p. 483, with the list of delegates, pp. 476–482, and the list of local membership strength, pp. 69–80.

mally accept a slight concession so that without losing too much face they could rally behind the executive's position at the balloting.

In 1913, however, when the party was nearing its dissolution roll-call votes were taken on two issues in which the line between conservative and radical was sharply drawn, with the executive supporting the conservative side:[88] (1) a resolution to abandon the reformist course for an offensive tactic of mass actions; and (2) a resolution sanctioning the parliamentary delegation's support of a government tax bill to cover arms increases. The divisions on these questions give us an opportunity to observe the machinery in action. Voting at the congresses was theoretically not by unit, but by individual, and the votes are so recorded. These votes can be regrouped to ascertain the political complexion of the local and regional organizations.[89] On this basis one can establish certain correlations between political behavior and institutional structure.

The electoral district organizations having under 1500 members were represented at the congress of 1913 by ninety-six delegates, only sixteen of whom voted radical on both issues. The proportion of radical votes from the small organizations was thus about 11 per cent as compared to 30 per cent for the congress as a whole.

The importance of the regional machinery is revealed in this vote. Every one of the ten radical votes cast by the smallest districts came from areas in which the radicals controlled the regional machine.[90] Yet it is clear that the radicals did not have the same appeal in the weak districts as the conservatives. Thus the radical region of Frankfurt-am-Main managed to have only three of its seven small locals represented. In the Lower Rhine one of the securely radical

[88] For a discussion of the issues themselves, see below, Ch. X, sec. vi

[89] The delegates' names appear with their records on the two issues in *Prot. S. P., 1913*, 337–338 and 515–516. These were then traced to their constituencies through the "Präsenzliste," 560–569. The constituencies, with the voting records of their delegates, were catalogued by membership size and by regional organization, 54–71. There is a small margin of error due to the discrepancies in the party records themselves and to the fact that I have combined the votes on two issues in the tables. Although in certain instances the delegates voted radical on one and conservative on the other, this occurred so rarely that it seemed wiser to spare the reader the greatly increased complexity of a double table, at the price of a negligible error.

[90] Frankfurt-am-Main, Lower Rhine, East Prussia, West Prussia, Thuringia, Pomerania and Brunswick.

regional organizations, only three of six small locals sent delegates and one of these voted conservative. In Halle, another radical region, the locals of less than 1500 members split from the regional leadership to cast three votes for the executive.

The conservative regional machines, where they really worked at it, had no comparable difficulties either in getting the small-towns to send delegates to the congress or in keeping such delegates in line. Brandenburg, commanded by that able organizer, Otto Wels, had all ten of its small organizations represented, and they voted solidly for the executive. Even South Bavaria, scarcely fertile soil for Social Democracy, mobilized fourteen of its eighteen small locals. In no case did the delegate of a small local in a region where the voting record of its city districts at the congress was unanimously conservative jump out of line in the balloting. The radicals had no comparable record. The natural conservatism of the smallest organizations was thus a real help to the national party leaders.

We should expect the number of radical-controlled delegations to increase as we move from the rural or semi-rural into the urban industrial areas, and so indeed it does — up to a point. Table I shows the peculiar nature of the correlation between size of organization and political complexion.

As indicated in Table I, column V, unanimity in voting tended to decline as size increased. This is not, however, an entirely reliable guide to political attitude for the possibility of registering dissent increased with the size of the organization. The striking characteristic of column V is that in the organizations of from 4000 to 18,000 members (D to H) the percentage of delegations voting unanimously was so high, averaging 62 per cent.

It will be observed that in the size classes 1500–3000 and 3000–4000 (B and C) the conservatives held two-thirds of the unanimously voting districts, the radicals one-third (columns VI and VII). In the twenty-five districts of between 4000 and 6000 (D and E) the radicals did quite as well as the conservatives, each winning control of eight delegations. That the contests were close in districts of this size is attested to by the fact that an unusually large number of delegations had an evenly divided vote (column XII). In the size classes over 6000, however, the radicals' fortunes went into a sharp decline. In the twenty-one districts of over 6000 mem-

TABLE I

Political Behavior of Delegations at the Congress of 1913, Classified by Size of Organization

	I	II	III	Delegations voting as a unit				Organizations with divided delegations				
				IV	V	VI	VII	VIII	IX	X	XI	XII
Class	Size of organization	No. of delegates each	No. of organizations	Total no.	% of size class	No. voting conservative	No. voting radical	Total no.	% of size class	Conservative majority	Radical majority	Evenly split
A	1– 1,500	1	96	96	100%	86	10	0	0	–	–	–
B	1,500– 3,000	2	51	51	100	34	17	0	0	–	–	–
C	3,000– 4,000	3	24	20	83	14	6	4	17	1	1	2
D	4,000– 5,000	3	16	11	69	5	6	5	31	0	0	5
E	5,000– 6,000	3	9	5	55	3	2	4	45	3	1	0
F	6,000– 8,000	4	15	10	66	9	1	5	33	2	2	1
G	8,000–12,000	4	10	5	50	4	1	5	50	3	1	1
H	12,000–18,000	5	8	5	62	5	0	3	38	1	1	1
I	over 18,000	6+	9	1	11	1	0	8	89	5	2	1

bers whose delegations voted as a block, nineteen were conservative. In other words, the correlation of increased radical control with the increasing size of the district, perceptible in the upper half of our chart, is reversed in the organizations of 6000 and over.

If we add together the unanimous delegations with those having a preponderance of the same political coloration (columns VI and X, VII and XI) we find the same resurgence of conservative strength in the giant districts. The results are indicated in Table II.

TABLE II

Political Dominance by Size Class, 1913

		No. of organizations				% of organizations		
Class	Size	Total no.	Con-serv.	Rad.	Evenly split	Con-serv.	Rad.	Evenly split
A	1– 1,500	96	86	10	–	89%	11%	0%
B–C	1,500– 4,000	75	49	24	2	65	33	2
D–E	4,000– 6,000	25	11	9	5	44	36	20
F–G	6,000–12,000	25	18	5	2	72	20	8
H–I	12,000 and over	17	12	3	2	71	18	11

From this table it may be seen that the executive won proportionately greater support from organizations of over 6000 members than from those of between 1500 and 4000.

In all the large organizations there were, as in the medium ones, "two souls in one breast" — one reformist, the other revolutionary. But that the reformist soul was so much stronger in the large than in the medium units as the voting record would suggest is doubtful. I have tried to find some sociological or regional basis for this difference, but without success. Why should Mannheim, with a liberal political tradition and an industrial character similar to that of Stuttgart, be conservative while Stuttgart was radical? Why should Königsberg be radical, Lübeck conservative? Why Hamburg, later a communist stronghold, be conservative while its sister city, Bremen, was radical?

It is clear that in the larger cities, as in the medium ones, a struggle for power was in progress between the factions, and that the conservatives were scoring most of the victories. We find that the following organizations of over 6000 members which were conservative on the mass strike question in 1913, had offered or underwritten radical resolutions on it in 1906 and/or 1910: Hamburg III, Elberfeld-Barmen, Dortmund, Schleswig 8 and 10 (Altona), Dresden Rechts der Elbe, Teltow-Beeskow-Storkow, Niederbarnim, and Berlin VI.[91] Since they took the initiative on the mass strike issue, these districts may be assumed to represent a minimum list of large organizations radical in the years 1906–1910 which subsequently underwent a change. Here again we are in no position to trace the development of conservative control in the large districts accurately without detailed studies of the party in each city. Inevitably, however, the conclusion suggests itself that in these giant districts, where the local leadership was necessarily separated from the mass by several echelons of functionaries, the impact of the rank and file upon policy was less direct and the leaders enjoyed greater autonomy than in the smaller organizations. Thus the difference between the political machines from one large organization to another was in considerable measure the product of the personal predilections of the leaders. And since the executive was the keeper of the keys to a party career it was natural enough that the urban leadership should be tempted to keep its organizations well in line with the executive's policies. This was easier to do in the large impersonal machines than in the smaller ones where the varied opinions of the rank and file would make themselves more directly felt.

Thus our analysis of the voting pattern would indicate that the executive enjoyed two sources of voting strength at the party congresses. One of these, the vote of the conservative small districts, may be called natural in that it rested on the convictions of the rank and file in the smaller areas. Through the overrepresentation of the rural districts at the congress, however, the weight of this

---

[91] Cf. *Prot. S. P., 1906*, 115–119; *ibid., 1910*, 181–182 (motion no. 100), and 491ff. ("Präsenzliste"). The 1906 instances were motions on the mass strike proposed directly by the organizations to the congress. In 1910, the resolution offered by Luxemburg was signed by 62 delegates among whom were those of Berlin VI (Dobrohlaw, Frank, Rosenfeld); Elberfeld-Barmen (Dröner, Gewehr); Dortmund-Hörde (Haenisch, Lex, Schöbel); Niederbarnim (Bühler, Muth, Witzke and Arendsee).

class was expanded beyond its true proportion. The other factor was at least partially factitious: the achievement of conservative predominance in the great cities in which, as the past had shown and the future would confirm, the radical current ran strong. Here, as on the regional level, the machines tended to act as a significant conservative force. The great apparatus of Social Democracy, which was in part a product of factional struggle, thus became a decisive instrument in shaping its course in the congresses as elsewhere in the party.

PART III

TWO TACTICS FOR CONSTITUTIONAL REFORM
1909–1910

Chapter VI

THE BREAK-UP OF THE BÜLOW BLOC:
REFORMIST POSSIBILITIES

The armaments race of the first decade of our century placed a severe strain on the fiscal structures of the European states. In England, France, Austria, Italy — even in Holland — there were crises in state financing. In England and Germany the issue of the distribution of the tax burden developed into a major constitutional crisis. But where in England the struggle over Lloyd George's budget terminated in a Liberal victory and the Parliament Act of 1911, in Germany the Junkers succeeded in maintaining both their privileged position as taxpayers and their constitutional ascendancy.

The first phase of the financial-constitutional struggle in Germany opened in 1909, and with it came a realignment of political parties which had a profound influence on the schism in Social Democracy. The break-up of Bülow's "Conservative-Liberal mating" activated the reformist forces in the party as the Russian Revolution had breathed new life into the radicals four years before. Only if we grasp the complex nature of the political opportunities which after years of frustration seemed now to open for the Social Democrats, can we understand their effect on the party's internal dialectic and on the radical wing which divided in the aftermath of crisis.

i. The Reich Financial Crisis and the
Dissolution of the Bülow Bloc

The German Empire's tax structure still bore the strong stamp of the state's federal origins. In 1867, when the North German Federation was organized, and in 1871, with the establishment of the Reich, the customs duties and other common income were assigned to the Reich government. These sources of revenue were supplemented with *Matricularbeiträge,* contributions of the federal states. In 1879, with the revenue from Bismarck's new tariffs, the Reich income became sufficient to make the *Matricularbeiträge* unnecessary, and indeed to provide a surplus which was distributed to the federal governments. At the end of the century the surpluses began to give way to deficits and the states again had to make contributions. By 1904 the Reich grants to the states had to be largely abolished.[1]

The abolition of the grants was not sufficient to stem the downward trend in the Reich's financial condition. The Conservative Party, defending its economic interest under the doctrine of states' rights, saw to it that the Reich raised its additional revenues only by indirect taxes. The funds for fleet construction were obtained largely from loans. A financial "reform" of 1906 which imposed a new burden of indirect taxes proved insufficient to cover even half of the increased needs.[2]

By 1909 — with substantial increases in the army and navy budgets of 1908 — the Reich debt had mounted to 5 billions. The value of imperial bonds had been falling steadily with the growing debt. A broad class of affected investors was thereby inclined toward a fundamental reform of the state finances. Business interests as well as public corporations favored raising the income of the Reich in order to reduce the inroads by the state in the always restricted German capital market. The Bülow Government also wished to increase its revenues sufficiently to cover current expenditures and to begin the retirement of the Reich debt.[3]

[1] Edwin R. A. Seligman, *Essays in Taxation* (8th edition, New York, 1919), 496–499.

[2] Johannes Ziekursch, *Politische Geschichte des neuen deutschen Kaiserreiches* (Frankfurt a. M., 1930), III, 181–183.

[3] *Ibid.,* III, 213.

How were the funds to be raised? The National Liberals and Progressives made it clear that the burden of indirect taxes could not be increased indefinitely, and that some direct taxes would have to be imposed. The government likewise inclined to this view and was prepared to apply the unused power of the Reich to levy direct taxes.[4] The government's bill was drafted cautiously with a weather eye to the Conservative partners in the Bülow Bloc. Four-fifths of the needed M. 500 million were to be raised through indirect taxes, one-fifth through an imperial inheritance tax. The proposal was far from radical: no effort was made to levy either income or personal property taxes lest the states represented in the Bundesrat make difficulties. The overwhelming burden fell directly on the shoulders of the propertyless class through taxes on beer, tobacco, spirits, gas, and electricity.[5] The Bundesrat approved the bill in the autumn of 1908. In November it was introduced into the Reichstag.

In the seven months of debate and negotiation which followed, the Conservative-Liberal alliance fell completely apart. The National Liberals and Progressives generally supported the government proposals because they introduced the principle of direct taxation in such a form as to affect the wealthy agrarians equally with the industrial and commercial class. The Conservatives were absolutely adamant against any direct taxation and refused to accept the inheritance tax feature of the Bülow bill. With the support of the Center the Conservatives condemned the inheritance tax for "striking [a blow at] the family at the worst possible moment" though the tax was to be levied only on fortunes over M. 10,000 with rates graduated from 1 to 4 per cent.[6] The Conservatives also saw a threat to their economic interest in the position taken by the government on the spirits tax. As one of the fruits of their power, the agrarians had enjoyed a lucrative bounty designed to compensate them for the rise in liquor prices which was expected to ensue from the spir-

[4] In the finance reform of 1906 the Reich had levied one direct tax: an inheritance tax. In order to maintain traditional practice, however, it was collected not by the Reich but by the state governments, which turned over two-thirds of the proceeds to the Reich. This tax did not apply to direct descendants. Cf. Seligman, *Essays*, 499.

[5] Erich Eyck, *Das persönliche Regiment Wilhelms II* (Erlenbach-Zürich, 1948), 528–529. For a breakdown of the tax, see "Bericht der Reichstagsfraktion," *Prot. S. P.,* 1909, 110, 113–114.

[6] *Schulthess' Europäischer Geschichtskalender, 1909* (Munich, 1910), 689; Eyck, *Wilhelm II,* 529.

its tax.[7] The parties of business and labor had long pressed for the removal of this indirect subvention to the agrarians, popularly known as the "gift of love [*Liebesgabe*]." The state secretary for the treasury did not remove the bounty in the new bill, but pointed out that it "was no longer to be regarded as consonant with the times [*zeitgemäss*] . . . since . . . the prices of spirits had not risen unduly."[8] The Conservatives, not without reason, felt that the admission of direct taxes would provide an opening for the ultimate destruction of the lucrative bounty.

Quite beyond the threat to their economic privileges, the Conservatives saw in the bill a menace to the constitution; that is, to their political power. The "organic development" of the Prussian suffrage system, promised by Bülow in 1908, was still on the books. The suffrage question, which had been reactivated by the Prussian elections of 1908 and the *Daily Telegraph* affair, was made even more pressing by the recalcitrance of the Conservatives on the tax question itself. In January 1909 the National Liberals, Centrists, Poles, Progressives, and Social Democrats introduced reform proposals into the Prussian House of Representatives while the Social Democrats were again holding great street demonstrations for equal suffrage.[9] The Conservative leader in the Reichstag, Dr. von Heydebrand und der Lasa, stated that his party's refusal to vote for the financial reform was determined "in the last analysis" by its unwillingness "to vest [the power of] such general taxation of property . . . in the hands of a parliamentary body resting on equal suffrage."[10]

Thus the tax issue brought to the surface the economic and political conflicts of interest between the agrarian party on the one hand and the parties of industry and commerce on the other. What the "world-political idea" had joined together against Social Democracy and the Center, the tax bill rent asunder. The Conservatives showed — if more evidence were needed — that they were the real power in the Bülow Bloc and that they could live without it.

The Center, eager to regain its lost position, combined with the

---

[7] Seligman, *Essays*, 502–503 and note.
[8] Quoted in "Bericht der Reichstagsfraktion," *Prot. S. P., 1909*, 113.
[9] *Schulthess, 1909*, 30–45.
[10] *Reichstag Debates*, CCXXXVII, 9323.

Conservatives to draft a finance bill composed entirely of indirect taxes and including the indefinite perpetuation of the "gift of love." For the portion of the revenue requirements which Bülow and the Liberals had wished to raise through the inheritance tax, they introduced taxes on tea, coffee, matches, and other consumer items. Of more significance as a spur to the opposition of the business community were the indirect taxes on commercial papers and credit instruments included in the Conservative-Center draft. The agrarians thus prepared to cast virtually the entire increased tax burden on the other classes of society. Since the Conservative tax plan promised to provide the needed M. 500 million, it was accepted by the Bundesrat. The new Reichstag majority of Conservatives, Centrists and Poles completed passage of the revised program on 10 July 1909. Four days later Chancellor Bülow carried out his previously stated resolve to resign if his tax plans were defeated.[11] The era of the Bülow Bloc was at an end.

The tax crisis and the dissolution of the bloc seemed to open new possibilities for a broad assault on the Conservative hegemony over Germany. The Liberal parties, as well as the Social Democrats, were now clearly the victims of the flaws in the German constitutional system. Thanks to the outmoded delineation of the electoral districts, the Reichstag representatives of the right with only 3,992,-734 voters behind them were able to outvote those of the left whose electors numbered almost twice as many (6,984,552).[12] The Bundesrat, controlled by the Junkers through the preponderance of Prussian representation, had, in the end, thrown its weight behind the Conservative program. With no recognized principle of parliamentary responsibility, the chancellor had no obligation to take the issue to the country. Less than a year before there had been, in the *Daily Telegraph* affair, a crisis which lay bare the dangers in the "personal regime" of the emperor, but the opportunity thus offered for constitutional reform had passed unexploited. Now the taxation issue struck the middle classes where it hurt, and where previously the Conservatives had generally protected them; namely, in their pocketbooks. Would they be galvanized into a real opposition movement for constitutional change?

[11] Ziekursch, *Politische Geschichte*, III, 215–216.
[12] *Schulthess, 1909,* 245–246.

The government, to be sure, would not help the parties thus forced into opposition, though its interest too had been affected by the refusal of direct taxes. Bülow had no will — and perhaps no way — to take the issue to the country.[13] As a chancellor above party he said that he "could not wax enthusiastic for an election campaign which would have had to be conducted against the right, and which would necessarily have had as its consequence an incalculable strengthening of radicalism and particularly of Social Democracy."[14] Of course it is doubtful that the emperor, who hated his chancellor with a blind passion since the *Daily Telegraph* affair, would have pursued the course of dissolution which might have prolonged Bülow's political life.[15] Bülow's explanation must nevertheless be taken as an honest statement. Shifting and unreliable though he was in most matters, his deep animosity to Social Democracy was a sincere, lasting, and fundamental feature of his political character. Such liberalism as there was in Bülow's resignation lay not in the direction of constitutionalism, but in its admonitory character to the Conservatives: that they learn to give a little to middle-class opinion lest they lose their privileged position through their too great rigidity and selfishness, and thus jeopardize "the interests of the monarchy and the country."[16]

ii. A Coalition for Reform? — The Progressives and the National Liberals

With the Conservative victory recognized by Bülow's resignation and sanctioned by Bundesrat and Kaiser, the question now arose as to how the new opposition would deport itself. The "Conservative-Liberal mating" was at an end. Would a "Liberal-Socialist mating" take its place, a coalition from Bebel to Bassermann, which would work as a bloc for suffrage reform in Prussia, the key to constitutional reform in the Reich? Could National Liberals, Progressives, and Social Democrats overcome their traditional antagonisms to unite against the Conservative-controlled "personal regime"? In part the answer would depend on the Social Democrats,

---

[13] See the speeches of Bassermann (Nat. Lib.) in *Reichstag Debates*, CCXXXVII, 8605; and Singer (Soc. Dem.), *ibid.*, 8618.

[14] *Schulthess, 1909,* 285.

[15] Eyck, *Wilhelm II,* 535–536.

[16] *Schulthess, 1909,* 285–287.

and there were those among them, as we shall see, who pressed eagerly for a party tactic acceptable to the Liberals. But as much would depend upon the middle-class parties. To what extent did their development in the bloc period and during the tax crisis give grounds for hope in effective collaboration?

For the three Progressive parties, the experience of the Bülow Bloc had produced discord, but a discord out of which a new unity was born. The crisis of 1906 had permanently settled the attitude of the Progressives toward the "national" question. Thenceforth the three Progressive parties supported all naval and military expansion programs and Germany's struggle for a place in the sun, though they often criticized the abuses of militarism and — less frequently — the government's foreign policy. National power came to be regarded as a good in itself which deserved support regardless of the form of government. Entry into the Bülow Bloc on this premise, however, did not mean that the Progressives had abandoned all ideas of domestic political reform. A few of them had opposed the coalition with the Conservatives from the beginning, aware, as Theodor Barth put it, "where the journey would lead."[17] Those who entered the bloc tried earnestly to hold it leftward — in vain. Bülow's rejection of the Reichstag suffrage for Prussia on 10 January 1908 began a general process of disillusionment among the more determined Liberals.[18] As a result of the *Daily Telegraph* affair and the financial reform crisis, discontent with the bloc policy grew from the exception to the rule. From the start of the tax discussions, the Progressives sought to entwine the financial question with that of constitutional reform, to treat the levying of direct taxes as an aspect of widening the powers of the Reichstag over the federal states. When the Conservatives in March 1909 served notice that they valued their own views on taxes more highly than the continuation of the Bülow Bloc, the Progressives went into open opposition.[19]

Out of this situation there arose a general desire to consummate

[17] Oskar Stillich, *Die politischen Parteien in Deutschland, II.* "Der Liberalismus" (Leipzig, 1911), 323.

[18] For the crisis of Progressivism, *ibid.,* 322–323; Theodor Heuss, *Friedrich Naumann* (Stuttgart and Berlin, 1937), 328ff.

[19] See the crucial speeches of Otto Wiemer, Progressive floor leader, on 30 March and 18 June 1909, *Reichstag Debates,* CCXXXVI, 7844ff; CCXXXVII, 8648ff.

the unification of the three splinter parties into which the Progressives were still divided. This effort, begun in 1905–06, had been interrupted by the dissension unleashed within the fold during the bloc period. Negotiations among the three parties, resumed in June of 1909, were successfully concluded by December. On 5 March 1910 the establishment of the Progressive People's Party (*Fortschrittliche Volkspartei*) was formally completed.[20]

Though the unification of the Progressives represented increased strength at the organizational level, the question of the vigor with which the new party would develop its policies of constitutional and social reform remained open. The Progressive Party was but the fourth of the five major parties in size and its history at the polls since the 1880's had been one of almost steady decline.[21] Its greatest weakness was its lack of a mass base. Its former supporters — the liberal mechanic, the liberal peasant, and the liberal schoolteacher — had drifted off into other political parties where they felt their interests to be more effectively represented.[22]

At the height of the tax crisis, in the summer of 1909, the formation of a new politico-economic organization of the business classes gave the Progressives hope that the problem of its mass base might be solved. The new organization, designed to combat the agrarian-conservative *Bund der Landwirte* and its selfish tax policy, was called the *Hansabund*. It embraced representatives from chambers of commerce, stock and commodity exchanges, banks, large and small industry, artisan and merchant associations. The temper of its founding meeting bore eloquent testimony to the ire of the business community against the Conservatives.[23] Its program,

[20] *Schulthess, 1909*, 403; *ibid., 1910*, 163; Heuss, *Naumann*, 379–380. Cf. also, for the new program, Felix Salomon, *Die deutschen Parteiprogramme* (4th edition, Leipzig and Berlin, 1932), II, 77–80.

[21] In percentage of the total vote cast, the three Progressive parties' record was as follows:

1881	21.2%	1893	14.3%
1884	19.3%	1898	11.1%
1887	14.1%	1903	9.3%
1890	18.0%	1907	11.0%

Cf. Paul Hirsch and Bruno Borchardt, *Die Sozialdemokratie und die Wahlen* (Berlin, 1912), 26.

[22] Stillich, *Liberalismus*, 330–331.

[23] For an abridged version of its proceedings, see *Schulthess, 1909*, 198–201; cf. also Theodor Eschenburg, *Das Kaiserreich am Scheideweg* (Berlin, 1929), 241ff.

adopted on 4 October 1909, called for a position of equality for
trade, handicraft, and industry in the state administration and
legislation, and declared that the *Hansabund* would work toward
breaking "the unhealthy influence of the one-sided agrarian-dema-
gogical current on the healthy economic development of the nation." [24] There was, to be sure, some doubt from the outset as to
the political cohesiveness of the *Hansabund*. Its framers inserted in
their program a clause pledging that the organization would maintain "strict neutrality on questions of social policy where conflicting
interests are present among the organizations represented in it or
among their members." [25] But despite the known differences in the
Hansabund, it still seemed a powerful new force in support of the
reformist cause. Even the jaundiced eye of the Socialist Franz
Mehring saw in the *Hansabund*'s vigorous attack on the Junkers
"no lack of *nervus rerum, . . .* a refreshing and stimulating thing
for the Progressives." [26]

Whether or not they could strike new roots in the economically
organized sectors of the population, the Progressives could hope to
carry through political reforms only with political allies. It was no
accident that the idea of a bloc "from Bebel to Bassermann," originally put forward by Friedrich Naumann at the turn of the
century, should have taken stronger hold in the Progressive camp
in 1909–10. For only by exploiting their intermediate position between the larger National Liberal and Social Democratic parties
could the Progressives have a *raison d'être* as the party to bind
together big business and labor in a common democratic front.
If they could succeed in this in the relatively favorable atmosphere
of 1909–10, the Progressives could make a real contribution to the
democratization of the Empire.

As in their social position the members of the Progressive Party
stood between big business and labor, so in their political conceptions they had come to occupy a middle ground between National
Liberalism and Social Democracy. The ideas of Friedrich Naumann
and Theodor Barth, who saw in national military power and the
rise of labor the two dominant facts of the new age, seeped their

---

[24] Salomon, *Parteiprogramme,* II, 102–103.
[25] *Ibid.,* 105.
[26] *N.Z.,* XXVII, ii, 394.

way into the Progressive camp during the first decade of the century.[27] Where Eugen Richter had maintained doctrinaire Manchesterian opposition to both imperialism and social legislation, Naumann erected them both into pillars of his system. Germany's future lay in its development as an industrial state with a foreign market. And "whoever wants the new industrial market must want the fleet" and military power.[28] At the same time, the emperor's power abroad must be based on a democratic and social constitution at home. Naumann called upon the National Liberals to abandon their anti-labor attitudes, and upon the Social Democrats to give up their anti-imperialism in the interests of his higher synthesis.

Appropriate though these ideas were to the Progressive position in the political and social spectrum, they depended for their realization on forces external to the fold. As long as the fundamental antagonism between business and labor continued on the socioeconomic front, a National Liberal-Progressive-Social Democratic rapprochement at the political level would, to put it mildly, be difficult to realize. Yet, failing this, the Progressives would tend to divide over tactic. For the same ideological elements which could give them a crucial role as mediator and synthesizer could also, should that role be closed to them, operate as a disintegrating force on the Progressive Party. The conservative element generally stressed building the bridge to the National Liberals, while the more liberal group gave greater scope to the "Barthian tactic" of collaboration with Social Democracy. The former wing, representing the North German *petite bourgeoisie*, was the stronger and obtained a majority in the executive of the new united Progressive Party.[29] Nevertheless, the very fact that a united party was emerging from the wreckage of the bloc policy gave grounds for hope in 1909 that, through a

[27] The National Social Association, founded by Naumann in 1896, dissolved in 1903. One of its leaders, Max Maurenbrecher, went into Social Democracy while the remaining leaders joined the Liberal Union (*Freisinnige Vereinigung*). Within the latter group, the National Socials supported the "Barthian tactic" of collaboration with Social Democracy. Completely swamped by the bloc policy of 1907, some of the most important Barthians seceded in 1908. Though they did not join the united Progressive Party, their ideas gained new force there in view of the disillusionment with the bloc policy. Cf. Stillich, *Liberalismus*, 318–319; Heuss, *Naumann*, 230ff.

[28] Friedrich Naumann, *Demokratie und Kaisertum* (4th edition, Berlin-Schöneberg, 1905), 217.

[29] N.Z., XXVIII, i, 482–483.

synthesis of the two tactics along Naumann's lines, the Progressives might serve to bind together the disparate enemies of Conservatism.

. . . . .

Far less committed than the Progressives to the idea of reform were the National Liberals. For their leaders, liberal principles and constitutional reform were, since the time of Bismarck, well subordinated to the pursuit of economic advantage and of a vigorous, militaristic national policy. Again unlike the Progressives, they looked upon the "Conservative-Liberal mating" in the Bülow Bloc as a thoroughly satisfactory arrangement, and were content to let the Conservatives call the political tune as long as their economic interests were respected.[30]

Where as early as March 1909 the Progressives awaited the end of the bloc "with cool composure," [31] the National Liberal leader Bassermann feverishly worked to rescue it.[32] His Reichstag speeches were almost all directed toward persuading the Conservatives not to take the step which must destroy their fruitful alliance. He strove now to cajole with appeals to patriotism, now to frighten with the spectre of a Social Democratic tidal wave.[33] When the bloc finally dissolved, Bassermann lamented its passing as "a serious blow to governmental authority." [34] Small wonder that he brusquely rejected the "bold hopes" of "certain dreamers" in a bloc from Bebel to Bassermann! Liberalism, he insisted, would never conclude "this death-bringing alliance with Social Democracy." [35]

Within Bassermann's party, however, there were growing countercurrents against the Conservative orientation, and it is these which we must bear in mind in evaluating the burgeoning of reformist hopes in the Social Democratic fold. In Baden the National Liberal Party went through a crisis in 1909 from which the left wing emerged victorious. To the acute annoyance of the party's national

---

[30] For a National Liberal view of the bloc period, see Eschenburg, *Kaiserreich, passim*.

[31] *Reichstag Debates*, CCXXXVI, 7847.

[32] Eschenburg, *Kaiserreich*, 176–236.

[33] *Reichstag Debates*, CCXXXVI, 7841; CCXXXVII, 8602–8603, 8605.

[34] Address to a National Liberal conference, 4 July 1909, quoted in *Schulthess, 1909*, 251–252.

[35] *Reichstag Debates*, CCXXXVI, 7842.

leadership, the Baden section not only entered an electoral agreement with Progressives and Social Democrats, but after the election
formed with them a parliamentary bloc, the so-called Baden Great
Bloc against the Center and Conservatives in the Landtag.[36]

North of the Main, the Young National Liberals — an association
of party members under forty years of age — also exerted some
leftward pressure on the leadership. If they were unsympathetic
with Social Democracy and quite as imperialistic as their elders,
they were pioneers for the unification of liberalism of all shades,
and thus advocated accommodation to the outlook of the Progressives. As early as 1906 they had come out for the introduction of
the Reichstag suffrage into Prussia.[37] In 1909, when the exaspera-
tion with the ruling system became general, the Young National
Liberals' pressure was sufficient to extract from the leadership
modest proposals for ministerial responsibility and Prussian suffrage
reform.[38]

In the high councils of the party the battle now raged over the
direction in which the National Liberals, with the Bülow Bloc dissolved, should seek allies. The leader of the left wing, Dr. Junck,
sent a long memorial to Bassermann urging a rapprochement, if
not yet a coalition, with Social Democracy. Pointing to the growth
of revisionist influence and to the large vested interest which the
Social Democratic Party had acquired in the existing order, Junck
advocated that the National Liberals at least occasionally ally
themselves with the Social Democrats in order to draw them more
and more toward the state.[39]

On the right wing three of the most prominent National Liberal
leaders resigned from the party in protest against its tax policy.[40]
The rightists who remained launched a campaign for returning to
a coalition with the Conservatives. For a year after the breakup of
the Bülow Bloc, it was uncertain which of these internal forces

[36] *Schulthess, 1909*, 56; Wilhelm Kolb, "Nach den badischen Wahlen 1909," *S.M.*,
XIII (XV), iii, 1461–1466; Ludwig Frank, *Aufsätze, Reden und Briefe*, ed. Hedwig
Wachenheim (Berlin, n. d.), 145–146. For the regional differentiation of the National
Liberals, see Walter Koch, *Volk und Staatsführung vor dem Weltkriege* (Stuttgart,
1935), 21–22.

[37] Stillich, *Liberalismus*, 319–321.

[38] *Schulthess, 1909*, 694.

[39] Eschenburg, *Kaiserreich*, 268–269.

[40] *Ibid.*, 265–266.

would prevail.[41] The protracted troubles of Bassermann in plotting a new course for his party at least left open the possibility of a reformist coalition. Where there was no clarity there could be hope.

The tax crisis, shattering the Conservative-Liberal alliance, thus vitalized the leftist elements in both the Liberal parties. For the first time since the founding of the Reich there was a possibility that the Liberals, supported by an irate business class, might throw themselves into a real fight for a reform which would break the Junker stranglehold on German political life. The "ifs" were many, but not so many as to deprive of any rational and factual basis the optimistic temper which now developed in the Social Democratic Party.

iii. Social Democracy and the Financial Reform

Before we turn to the Social Democratic reaction to the possibilities of a reform coalition, we must give some attention to the party's position on Bülow's financial reform. For the first time there was an opportunity to realize a reform demanded in the Erfurt program: direct taxation. Yet the opportunity did not present itself in a form so clear and unalloyed as to be equally acceptable to all factions of the party. Three thorny questions were involved: (1) Should the party vote for a direct tax even though this would aid the government in burdening the people with four times as large a sum in indirect taxes? (2) Should the party support a direct tax designed to defray armaments costs? (3) Should the party support the tax in order to work toward a basis for collaboration with the Liberal parties and thus to exploit Conservative-Liberal antagonism? To these three questions the revisionist wing of the Social Democratic Reichstag delegation answered yes, the radical, no.[42]

Had the 100 million in direct taxes been wrapped into the same bill with the 400 million in indirect taxes, the Social Democratic delegation would have had to reject the whole. The government, however, in order to get its total program through, divided the financial reform program into separate bills in the hope that the

[41] Ibid., 272 Koch, Volk und Staatsführung, 50–54.
[42] For a detailed account of the Social Democratic delegation's behavior in the finance reform, see "Bericht der Reichstagsfraktion," Prot. S. P., 1909, 107–123, 167–184; for the division within the delegations, see ibid., 289–364.

indirect taxes might be passed by the non-socialist majority, while the inheritance tax might be carried separately with the help of Social Democratic votes. In this way the government gave the Social Democrats an opportunity to realize one of their programmatic demands without assuming the onus of the new indirect taxes.

It was a clear challenge to the party to contribute positively to legislation. The party conservatives were eager to seize it. The less sanguine radicals were trapped by the party's tradition of parliamentary procedure, of working to expand the party's influence on a bill until the final vote on the third reading.[43] Hence they too had to support the inheritance taxes on the first and second reading. That the inheritance taxes were killed on the second reading (24 June, 1909) did not eliminate the conflict in the party as to what would have been done if it had come to a third. It was no mere idle dispute about what might have been but was not. The party had to clarify its position in anticipation of the day when military necessity would drive the government to request direct taxes again. Thus the controversy continued through the autumn of 1909, terminating in a two-day debate at the Leipzig party congress in mid-September.

The reformists placed the immediate, material interest of the workers squarely in the forefront of the discussion. For them it was unthinkable that the party should reject an occasion to realize, even if only partially, one of its own demands. How could the people understand Social Democracy's taking the same position as the Junkers by voting against the inheritance tax?[44] It was the duty of the party to make taxes as little burdensome to the masses as possible — and this meant to vote the direct taxes even on the third reading if necessary. Only thus could the confidence of the people be retained.[45] The radicals, on the other hand, stressed the "fig-leaf" character of the direct taxes. Not the inheritance tax, but the indirect taxes were decisive for them. To support the direct taxes was simply to play into Bülow's hands, to abet a huge hoax against the people, and to "pull Bülow's cart out of the mud."[46]

[43] Ibid., 119–120.
[44] Cf. David in ibid., 313; also S.M., XIII (XV), ii, 1086.
[45] This point was repeatedly made in the review of the question at the Leipzig congress. Cf. Prot. S. P., 1909, 308ff.
[46] Ibid., 304–306, 310–311.

The second problem ran deeper: the relationship of tax reform to the arms race and to imperialism. The government and all the other parties were at one in justifying a financial reform, whatever its nature, in terms of sustaining Germany's military and naval power. The new taxes would be used to support that arms expansion which Social Democracy had consistently opposed. What then was to be decisive for the party, the type of tax, or the purpose for which the revenues were to be employed?

Here too the reformists had the stronger case in terms of precedent. The party was to some extent engaged by arguments which it had previously employed. Thus in 1898 its spokesmen had advocated that the cost of the fleet be covered by direct taxes; it was then only a rhetorical device to show the public the limitations of ruling-class patriotism.[47] In the navy bill debate of 1908 Bebel had based his attack against the proposed naval expansion in part on the mode of financing. Eduard David went beyond Bebel when he stated in the Reichstag that the Socialists would oppose the bill "on principle unless [N.B.] new sources of revenue were found." [48] The rhetoric employed at a time when direct taxes were not politically possible provided the basis for the reformist position when they moved into the realm of the realizable. The reformists argued the question on short-run, practical premises: Social Democracy was powerless to halt the armament expansion; therefore it must within the framework of the possible relieve the proletarian of the tax burdens resulting therefrom.[49] They also insisted that direct taxes were in themselves a means of combating the armaments race. If the tax burden for armaments were placed on the advocates of military expansion, David prophesied, "their enthusiasm for this sort of thing will cool off perceptibly." [50]

The radicals disagreed on both counts. "To this system, no man

[47] Ibid., 337.
[48] Quoted in George D. Crothers, The German Elections of 1907 (New York, 1941), 227.
[49] S.M., XIII (XV), ii, 769–770.
[50] Prot. S. P., 1909, 313. Cf. Eisner's similar stand, ibid., 322. In the Reichstag, David proposed in jest that a graduated tax be levied on property over M. 100,000 whenever a new ship went down the ways. His jest was, however, not far from his real view. Cf. Reichstag Debates, CCXXXVI, 7849.

and no penny" — the old slogan summed up their position on voting funds to the government. For the radical parliamentarians, the issues of armaments and imperialism had acquired such primacy that the short-run, material interest of the workers in direct taxes must be sacrificed to the long-run interest of the party in avoiding every indication of compromise with militarism. Hence the radicals — Singer, Kautsky, Karski, Hoch, Wurm, Parvus, Ledebour, and Stadthagen — took the position: "No new taxes, but reduction of armaments!" [51] They saw it as the duty of the party to carry this message to the people, to make them understand that the fight against imperialism came first and foremost. That direct taxes were in the program imposed no obligation upon the party to vote them under all circumstances, according to the radicals. What, asked Emanuel Wurm, if part of the direct taxes were to be used to hire Pinkerton men to combat the unions? Would the revisionists and union leaders still favor voting the taxes merely because they were direct? [52] Certainly not. Wurm's example throws light on the difference between the radical and reformist hierarchy of political values as applied to concrete problems of the day. The radicals were as devoted to the principle of opposition to armaments as to that of the right of coalition. With the Bosnian crisis fresh in their minds they were more chary than ever of granting any concessions on the tax question which might make the Naumann synthesis of imperialism with democracy and social reform palatable to the working class. In line with the ideas expressed in Kautsky's *Road to Power*, they strove to keep the clear oppositional position of Social Democracy intact.[53] Concessions in the matter of spurious reforms, they thought, would in the last analysis only weaken the party in a real crisis. Co-chairman Singer, who sided with the radicals against Bebel and the reformists, denied that the party would suffer in elections from opposition to the direct taxes.[54] He

[51] *S.M.*, XIII (XV), ii, 767–768; *N.Z.*, XXVII, ii, 838ff, 912–913; *ibid.*, XXVIII, i, 783ff; *Prot. S. P.*, *1909*, 289–364, *passim*.

[52] *Prot. S. P.*, *1909*, 338.

[53] See above, Ch. IV, sec. v.

[54] Bebel did not participate in the tax debate in the Reichstag for reasons of health. But he later let it be known that he would have sided with the reformists. *Prot. S. P.*, *1909*, 364.

sustained the old-fashioned, idealistic *Prinzipienfestigkeit:* the party had grown great and strong because it had stood for its principles "in battle against the whole world." [55]

The radicals rejected the idea that direct taxes would cool the ardor of the ruling class for military expansion. They understood better than the economic mechanists of the right wing that the upper-class taxpayers would sooner or later bear the cost of national power willingly. Kautsky called upon the party to prepare itself for the idea that one day 500 millions of new taxes — all direct — would be proposed by the government. What would the party do then? Vote the taxes merely because they were direct? [56] Kautsky, who in 1907 had explained that the ruling groups had found the answer to the socialist myth in the nationalist vision,[57] could not accept the idea that the upper classes would refuse to shoulder the cost. Wurm pointed to the British example where the ruling classes had long since assumed the burden of direct taxes to support armaments. Bülow, he said, had been brought to the verge of despair by the dull-wittedness of the Conservatives in this respect, but they would one day see the light. Social Democracy, according to Wurm and his friends, must see the light now and not confuse the greater with the lesser cause.[58]

The third level of considerations was the connection between the tax crisis and the possibility of a new era of reform based on an oppositional alliance of Social Democracy with the National Liberals and the Progressives. To support the direct taxes was, for the revisionists, the least that Social Democracy could do to promote and exploit the Liberal-Conservative antagonism, and thus perhaps to produce a dissolution of the Reichstag.[59] Viewed thus as an opportunity to help create the conditions for a Social Democratic-Liberal partnership, the tax issue itself was dwarfed by the broader possibilities of a peaceful revolution in German politics, whose effect on the party we must now consider.

[55] *Ibid.,* 332; cf. also Ledebour, *ibid.,* 298.
[56] *N.Z.,* XXVII, ii, 912.
[57] See above, Ch. III, sec. ii.
[58] *Prot. S. P., 1909,* 338.
[59] *Ibid.,* 307–308.

iv. Reformist Opportunity and the Vacillation of the Radicals

The dissolution of the Bülow Bloc was good news to any Social Democrat. To the revisionists, however, it gave the same kind of spiritual lift as the Russian Revolution of 1905 had given to the radicals. The "reactionary mass" against Social Democracy, which had barred the door to all "positive collaboration" and to all parliamentary progress, was splitting wide open. Heretofore, the tide of political life had run in accordance with radical preconceptions; at long last it seemed to be turning.

The formation of the *Hansabund* showed, according to Richard Calwer, that the conflict between "mobile" and "immobile" capital was fundamental, while the "common interests [of the two types of capital] against the rising claims of labor" were now revealed as only "of a transient nature." The interest of the working class, the third entity in the social trinity, lay on the side of mobile capital which created the workers' prosperity. The workers, said Calwer, must exploit the cleavage by throwing their weight on the side of the business community.[60] Wolfgang Heine hailed the new "material basis for a policy against the bureaucracy, against the exaggerated claims of militarism, and against the dynastic system."[61] Max Maurenbrecher, writing on the political aspects, was most optimistic. He saw in the fact of Bülow's resignation a "mighty step forward" toward ministerial responsibility, though it had been taken "on quiet soles."[62] The usually cautious Bernstein, swept away by the ebullient mood of the moment, declared that "the days of the existing suffrage system in Prussia are numbered."[63]

The consequences for party policy were clear to the revisionists. The party must abandon its "revolutionary isolation" and build a broad coalition for reform which would embrace the majority of the people.[64] The Social Democratic Party must abandon its foolish hope that it would absorb the lower middle class, said Wolfgang

[60] *S.M.,* XIII (XV), ii, 875–878. Calwer was of the extreme right ("social imperialist") wing of the party.
[61] *Ibid.,* 776.
[62] *Ibid.,* 940–941.
[63] *Ibid.,* iii, 1661.
[64] *Ibid.,* ii, 943.

Heine. That hope was well and good for the nineties. Since then, the rise of the trade-unions had made the party the representative of the material interests of the industrial workers whose wage struggles particularly hit the little man of the middle class. The intellectuals too, who used to join the party out of democratic sentiment, were now kept away by "revolutionary saber-rattling — or, better — newspaper-rustling." Therefore Social Democracy must accept its minority role and seek to win the middle-class parties as allies.[65]

Radical commentators were of course more reserved than the revisionists in their judgment of the new situation. Their distrust of the bourgeoisie was too much a matter of dogma to allow them to hail the collapse of the Bülow Bloc as a golden dawn. Yet even that hard-bitten old radical, Franz Mehring, began to wonder if perhaps the bourgeoisie might not be awakening out of its years of slumber. His weekly political lead articles in *Neue Zeit* showed during 1909 a halting but nevertheless perceptible modification of his opinion of the Liberals. In May he castigated them for falling into the trap which Bülow set for them in the form of the inheritance tax in order to make them swallow the direct taxes.[66] In early June he argued that even if their leaders might be amenable to collaboration with Social Democracy their followers would not support them because of their deeply ingrained opposition to higher wages.[67] At the end of June and in early July, however, he welcomed the *Hansabund* and the Liberals' call for dissolution of the Reichstag as real signs of life.[68] Late in July when the revisionists began to press for collaboration, Mehring returned to issuing warnings. While recognizing that the middle classes were aroused, he cautioned against taking too seriously the "moral indignation of the sober philistine" which "usually fades out very soon." [69]

Against the revisionist view that there were three classes with conflicting interests — agrarian, business, and labor — Mehring in-

---

[65] *Ibid.*, 776–777. For other expressions of the revisionist view, see Eugen Dietzgen, "Isolierung oder Bündnispolitik," a review article on Kautsky's *Weg zur Macht*, stressing the revolutionary potential of the German middle class, *S.M.*, XIII (XV), ii, 1018ff.; Karl Leuthner, "Klassengegensätze und Parteibündnisse," *ibid.*, 1078ff.

[66] *N.Z.*, XXVII, ii, 258–259.

[67] *Ibid.*, 324.

[68] *Ibid.*, 394, 458–459.

[69] *Ibid.*, 593.

sisted that for all practical political purposes there were only two: workers and Junkers. The bourgeoisie was but the feeble accomplice of the Junkers, who in turn would never let go of any basic element of power unless, as Lassalle said, "a finger were in their eye and a knee on their chest." [70]

Yet even while casting cold water on the hopes placed in the Liberals, he followed the unification efforts of the Progressives with eager interest. Having attacked in August their incapacity to unite as a sign of weakness, in September he attributed the delay to the question of relations with Social Democracy, on which they would have to base any plans for domestic reform. If they should conquer this obstacle and unite for a fight against the Junkers, the Social Democrats should not hold their past sins against them.[71] When Progressive fusion finally was agreed upon, he was disappointed again because the conservative wing secured a majority in the new executive. However, he no longer closed doors as he had done a half-year earlier; he recommended an attitude of "watchful reserve" to see what liberalism would do.[72]

Mehring's vacillations sprang from the position in which the radicals now found themselves. On the one hand, they did not wish to ignore any opportunities for the long-overdue democratization of Germany; on the other, they had a real fear of embarking on a course which would lead them into what, in effect though not in intention, would be a revisionist snare. To embark on a course of collaboration with the Liberals meant, as the revisionists never tired in pointing out, to drop the revolutionary lingo, the vague threats of strike and insurrection, the time-honored language of intransigent class struggle.[73] The tactic of the party would have to emphasize the parliamentary arena at the expense of extra-parliamentary mass agitation *pour ne pas épater le bourgeois*. Such a tactic would lead the masses away from the idea of revolution and would at the same time mean a capitulation to the revisionists within the party. The whole revolutionary cause might be jeopardized for the sake of an alliance with a deeply suspect middle class.

[70] *Ibid.*, 595.
[71] *Ibid.*, 644, 833–835.
[72] *Ibid.*, XXVIII, i, 481–484, 546.
[73] E.g., *S.M.*, XIII (XV), iii, 1665; *ibid.*, XIV (XVI), i, 4–5.

Thus, where the revisionists tended to overestimate the anti-Junker aggressiveness of the opposition Liberals, the radicals feared to encourage what aggressiveness there was lest the experiment come to naught and they find themselves in the end with the revolutionary *élan* of the party dissipated.

Moreover, the program on which the collaboration with the Liberals would have to rest would have been Naumann's. The tax bill itself, as we have seen, offered the jewel of reform in a setting of military steel. For the Liberals there was no road back from the commitment to German world policy and armed might. If democracy were now achieved in Germany, would this strengthen the anti-imperialist forces? One must doubt, with the Social Democratic radicals, that such would have been the case. The elections of 1907 and the behavior of the mass of the German people in 1914 suggest that their commitment to German nationalism and military power was deep seated. The real grievances of the German common man, and especially of the worker, were domestic grievances: the lack of economic security and of political democracy. The struggle against the semi-autocratic constitution in 1909–10 could not be identified with the struggle against imperialism. If the former succeeded, the latter might well receive a serious setback. The radicals could not publicly express such a fear, but does it not emerge in their insistence that a vote for the direct taxes was inconsistent with the party's opposition to militarism? Is it not present in their expressed concern that the party, by voting for direct taxes, would contribute to making the worker satisfied with the armaments program because the rich would then be seen to share its burdens? [74] When the revisionists and trade-unionists, who had spearheaded the fight against strong resolutions opposing war and colonialism at Stuttgart, favored a policy of giving primacy to problems of domestic reform, the radicals could not but react negatively. The ominous international possibilities also made the radicals resistant to the temptation of reform, lest the proletariat thus disarm itself for the revolutionary opportunity which they thought a war might bring. Fearful of a final revisionist victory with all its consequences, they tended to maintain socialist isolation.

Kautsky revealed, if only indirectly, how large a role the fear

[74] *Prot. S. P., 1909,* 337–338.

of revisionism played in the radical attitude in the crisis. In marked contrast to his views after his break with Luxemburg six months later, he wrote in September 1909:

The smaller the real community of interest between the several bourgeois parties and Social Democracy in particular instances, and the smaller the number of these instances, the more important it seems to certain [revisionist] parliamentarians to stress most strongly those rare points of contact, to look around for new ones and, if possible, to create them through clever diplomacy; the more important, too, to let the existing antagonisms come out as little as possible, to behave as though we were not combatting the whole of bourgeois society, but for the moment only one particular class thereof, such as the Junkers in Prussia, the Ultramontanists in Baden.[75]

Kautsky's answer to the question as to how to exploit the reform possibilities was not coöperation with the bourgeois parties, but attack. The more the Social Democrats fought them and exposed them, he said, the more they would be forced to take the wind out of the Socialists' sails and to behave better toward the workers. To achieve coöperation with the Liberals, the Socialists must continue independent agitation against them. Thus Kautsky tried to bring Social Democratic isolation and anti-Junker collaboration into a dialectic unity.[76]

The tactical problem was simply not susceptible to any neat solution, given the depth of class antagonisms and the consequent hardiness of the German constitution. Certainly the revisionists made sense when they argued that the collaboration of the bourgeois parties was not to be won by saying, "Give us the suffrage, so that we may dispossess you." [77] To win the middle class required at the minimum a surrender of revolutionary socialist agitation by the Social Democrats. Even could such a *volte face* have been accomplished — and it was at that stage psychologically impossible for the party — there remained the economic struggles which necessarily alienated the middle class.

Let us assume that Social Democracy could have succeeded in reversing itself, in adjusting its behavior to the mentality of the

[75] *N.Z.*, XXVII, ii, 841.
[76] *Ibid.*, 841–843.
[77] *S.M.*, XIV (XVI), 4.

middle class, what would be the effect on the Junkers? Would they permit their power to be broken? We can only conjecture here, but it is almost inconceivable that this should have been the case. The Conservatives' refusal to give in even to an overwhelming public sentiment on the question of taxation was a sign of their extraordinary inflexibility. "Inflexibility" is a mild word for the mentality of a class whose parliamentary representatives rose in demonstrative applause to the ringing challenge of the Conservative Herr von Oldenburg auf Januschau: "The King of Prussia and the German Emperor must always be in a position to say to any lieutenant: 'Take ten men and shoot the Reichstag!'" [78] It is hard to escape the conclusion that purely parliamentary action would have been insufficient to induce the Conservatives to surrender their seats of power. They could understand only the threat of force, could respond in the last analysis only to fear.

Thus the dilemma of Social Democracy lay in the fact that the tactic required for winning middle-class support was in contradiction with the tactic required to extract concessions from the Conservatives. The demonstrations and mass actions of the Social Democrats would frighten the middle class back into the arms of the Junkers; but without strong action supported by the middle class as well as the workers the Junkers could not be moved to make concessions. In this socio-political *impasse,* the tragic legacy of Germany's incompleted bourgeois revolution came to the surface once again. There was in fact no right tactic for Social Democracy to pursue in terms of the constitutional issue alone. The constitutional issue was one which, in the long run, was solved only by revolution; and it is difficult to see how, whatever the tactic of Social Democracy, it could have been otherwise.

As it was, the possibilities of reform through coalition with the now oppositional bourgeoisie gave the revisionists greater confidence in their position, while the fear that the revisionists might lead the party astray, and the conviction that the Junkers would respond only to the threat of extreme measures, radicalized the radicals. The party could not take a firm line in either direction but like the National Liberals swung indecisively between two possible tactics while the factional strife grew worse.

[78] *Schulthess, 1910,* 88.

The Leipzig congress of September 1909 brought to an inconclusive close the first phase of devising a tactic to meet the new political situation. The party clarified its position on neither the future tax policy nor collaboration with the Liberal opposition.

Not only the congress, but also the party executive was divided on the tax issue. The co-chairmen, Singer and Bebel, took opposing sides, and the executive produced no resolutions to resolve the debates. The congress failed to decide whether the type of tax or the purposes for which it would be used should guide the party's parliamentary action. The congress, by default, delegated its power of decision to the parliamentary delegation, which would be free to act according to its own lights. The revisionist spokesman, Wilhelm Schröder, rightly interpreted this outcome as a partial victory for his wing of the party: "The very fact that the party does not bind itself through any particular dogma, that it reserves its decision [to be made] according to the coming situation, shows that it is willing to apply the methods of politics, not of doctrine."[79]

On the question of collaboration with the Liberals, the congress vacillated in the strangest fashion. At first it adopted a harshly worded Berlin resolution condemning any idea of collaboration with the Liberals as a "bloody insult to the party" because of the Liberals' "continuous chain of betrayals of the working class," their alliance with the Junkers in the 1907 elections, and their readiness to vote the 400 millions in indirect taxes.[80] On the morning after the passage of the resolution, a group of delegates petitioned for a revote on the grounds that they had voted for it in error believing that they were voting on a different motion. How this error could have been committed simultaneously by any large number of delegates remains unexplained in the protocols. One suspects rather that the leadership, which had failed to speak against the motion, canvassed a number of trusties to reopen the question. Whatever the origin of the petition for a revote, it was granted. The motion was defeated in the revote.[81]

So far as the public could tell, Social Democracy had thus com-

---

[79] *S.M.*, XIII (XV), iii, 1228. Cf. also Robert Schmidt, "Die Ergebnisse des Leipziger Parteitags," *ibid.*, 1226–1228.

[80] *Prot. S. P., 1909*, 193 (resolution no. 41); 364.

[81] *Ibid.*, 393.

pletely reversed itself on the vital question of collaboration with the bourgeois parties. Some of the non-socialist newspapers — especially those Liberal organs which favored alliance with Social Democracy — hailed the reversal as a great victory for revisionism and moderation, a proof of the "quiet but fundamental transformation" of the party since the Dresden congress, a turning point in Social Democratic history.[82] It was now the turn of the radical delegates at the congress to become alarmed. They introduced a resolution stating that the withdrawal of the motion on the party's relationship to Liberalism did not constitute a weakening of the Dresden resolution on tactics, in which the revisionist heresy of accommodation to the bourgeois parties had been condemned. The radical spokesman for this motion asserted that the only reason for the reversal had been that the party could not lay down in advance a hard line on its tactical relationships to other parties during elections. The motion was unanimously accepted,[83] but it constituted no return to the position of the retracted Berlin resolution. Thus, when all the seesawing was over, the party congress had affirmed the principle of collaboration with the Liberals in a clearer fashion than ever before. The reformists had won a narrow victory in the first phase of adjusting the party's policy to the new situation created by the break-up of the Bülow Bloc. Whether the opposing forces within the party and the political situation outside it would permit the successful pursuit of a reformist policy still remained to be determined.

[82] *Ibid.*, 498–499; N.Z., XXVII, ii, 905–908; Koch, *Volk und Staatsführung*, 28–30. Significantly, the *Freisinnige Zeitung*, like the Conservative press, denied any revisionist victory; this was the organ of the former Richter Progressives who, now in control of the new Progressive Party executive, were cool to collaboration with Social Democracy.

[83] *Prot. S. P., 1909*, 498–501. The revisionist contingent voted for the reaffirmation of the Dresden resolution after issuing a declaration that they regarded the motion as unnecessary, but that they did not wish to disturb the unity of the party which had been documented at the congress (presumably by the revocation of the original Berlin motion against Liberalism) by a divided vote on a resolution concluded so long ago.

Chapter VII

THE CONSTITUTIONAL CRISIS: THE SWING TO THE LEFT AND THE DIVISION OF THE RADICALS

i. The Tactic for Suffrage Reform

As the year 1909 drew to a close, it was clear that the issue of Prussian suffrage reform could no longer be put off by the government. The promises made by Bülow in 1908 as concessions to the Progressive partners in his bloc were still on the books. These were vague, to be sure, having been formulated to fit the disparate political components of the bloc. In January 1908 Bülow had recognized the need for reform in an address to the Prussian Landtag, but had rejected the introduction of the Reichstag suffrage and the secret ballot.[1] In the address of the crown in October 1908 he expressed his general willingness to work for "an organic development" of the electoral system to make it correspond "to economic evolution [and to] the spread of culture and patriotic understanding." [2] Still no concrete proposals were forthcoming. In January 1909 Progressive and Social Democratic pressure for the Prussian suffrage reform evoked from Bülow assurances that the preliminary work necessary for the preparation of a new bill was being pursued "with great zeal." [3] Throughout the year 1909 the government made no proposals while the demands for suffrage reform increased as the Conservative-Liberal alliance disintegrated over the tax issue.

Bülow's successor as chancellor, Theobald von Bethmann-Hollweg, was desirous of some reform. As a loyal Prussian civil servant, his first object was to strengthen the position of the crown. He had no liking for political parties as such, but he wished to tie as many of them to the crown as possible, and to bind up the wounds left

---

[1] Erich Eyck, *Das persönliche Regiment Wilhelms II* (Erlenbach-Zürich, 1948), 462.

[2] *Ibid.*, 463.

[3] *Schulthess, 1909,* 17.

by the warfare over taxation.[4] Obliged to rely on the newly constituted Blue-Black (Conservative-Center) Bloc in the Reichstag,
Bethmann nevertheless wished to do anything consistent with the
royal prerogative to bring the Liberals back into the government
camp. There was reason to expect some action from him, albeit of
a limited variety, on the Prussian suffrage question in the winter
session of the Prussian Landtag.

Even before the close of 1909 public agitation for reform began
outside Prussia in those federal states having inequitable electoral
systems. The first center of activity was the Grand Duchy of Hessen where in November a "reform" of the electoral system was
instituted which decreased rather than increased the political influence of the working class electorate.[5] Social Democratic agitation
against the Hessen bill was followed by a similar movement in
Brunswick which had an even worse electoral system than Prussia's.[6] In the succeeding months the Social Democrats in Prussia,
Bremen, Dessau, and Mecklenburg likewise organized demonstrations and inaugurated parliamentary actions for suffrage reform
where possible.[7] The greatest and most important of these was in
Prussia.

For the determination of the tactic to be employed in the struggle
for reform, a Prussian Social Democratic congress was summoned
for 3 January 1910. It was here that the party would decide whether
to continue in the direction of collaboration with the Liberals, to
which the Leipzig congress had tended, or to return to a tactic of
extra-parliamentary action and socialist isolation.

The revisionists prepared for the congress a special issue of the
Sozialistische Monatshefte to carry their views to the delegates.[8]
The articles all pointed in the same direction: to seize the oppor-

---

[4] For his position on the political parties, cf. Theobald von Bethmann-Hollweg,
Betrachtungen zum Weltkrieg (Berlin, 1919), I, 14–25, 98; and his address on inter-
nal policy, 9 Dec. 1909, quoted in *Schulthess, 1909,* 350–352. See also Walter Koch,
Volk und Staatsführung vor dem Weltkrieg (Stuttgart, 1935), 33–37.

[5] A description of the Hessen electoral system before and after the reform is given
in *N.Z.,* XXVIII, i, 523–529. Cf. also *Prot. S. P., 1910,* 34–35.

[6] The electoral system of Brunswick and the reform efforts of the Social Democrats
from 1908 to 1912 are discussed in *N.Z.,* XXX, i, 187–192, 739–743; cf. also *Prot.
S. P., 1910,* 32–33.

[7] *Prot. S. P., 1910,* 29–35.

[8] *S.M.,* XIII (XV), iii, 1655ff.

tunity for a joint parliamentary offensive with the Liberals in the Prussian House of Representatives. They warned against excessive street demonstrations or demonstration strikes which might weaken the united front. Maurenbrecher showed how, in a previous street demonstration where there had been collisions with the police the main issue — suffrage reform — had receded into the background; how the slogan, "The Reichstag electoral system for Prussia," had given way to "Fight for the right of the streets," which had nothing to do with the case. In the Reichstag the Social Democrats had found themselves defending clashes with the police instead of assailing Prussian suffrage.[9] The street demonstration could be used with effect, said Maurenbrecher, only when those beyond the party were already aroused; when, except for the small ruling group, "the whole nation participates in the movement." This unanimity could only be prevented, not created, by a premature tactic of demonstration.[10] The right way to begin to cultivate the proper atmosphere would be through a congress of intellectuals for universal suffrage. Maurenbrecher recommended that the Prussian party congress indicate its willingness to participate in such a gathering.[11]

Bernstein proposed a legislative strategy for the Social Democrats in the Prussian House. He laid out the power situation in the House: there were 445 delegates of which 104 were Centrists, 65 National Liberals, 37 Progressives, 15 Poles, 6 Social Democrats, 2 Danes. Taken together, these had a majority, and all wished *some* reform. But the Center opposed any redistricting which would reduce the overrepresentation of the rural population and cost it seats, while the National Liberals wanted plural voting, not equal suffrage. What hope was there then? It lay in the Progressives, said Bernstein. If they could persuade the National Liberals to give up their insistence on plural suffrage, then the Center would control the balance, and the fate of the reform would be in their hands. Bernstein hoped the Center would not risk the loss of the labor element in its electorate by sabotaging the whole reform, and therefore would drop its opposition to redistricting. Such was the delicately wrought chain of parliamentary ifs and buts on which the

[9] *Ibid.*, 1669.
[10] *Ibid.*, 1669–1670.
[11] *Ibid.*, 1670–1671.

passage of a reform bill would hang. Social Democracy's chief duty lay, then, in creating the right atmosphere so that the Progressives could persuade the National Liberals without undue disturbance.[12]

When the Prussian party congress convened on 3 January 1910 it quickly emerged that the revisionists' proposals had not the slightest chance of acceptance. The contrast between the temper of the Prussian congress and that of the national congress at Leipzig four months earlier was striking. At Leipzig, though the bitterness of the debates showed that both radicals and revisionists felt that the party was at the crossroads, the revisionists had won a victory, even if not a clear and decisive one. Not so in Prussia. The mood of the Prussian comrades was aggressively radical.

The position of the left was set forth by Heinrich Ströbel, an editor of *Vorwärts* and later one of the first to break from the old party. Ströbel advocated the utilization of "all means" in the fight for the suffrage. Ströbel's explanation of what he meant by "all means" showed the ear-marks of Luxemburg's conception of a graduated, intensified mass action. His resolution, he said, was intended to imply possible recourse to street demonstrations and the political mass strike, although these were not specifically mentioned. The time when such means would be utilized would depend "on the degree of ardor which will be aroused in the masses by our enlightenment and agitation. In the struggle for electoral reform, our principal emphasis must be placed on the job of arousing this ardor of the masses." [13] Ströbel wished not only to use radical means in fighting the issue of reform, but also to use the issue of reform to heighten the radicalism of the masses.

The whole tenor of the proceedings was to convert the congress itself into a demonstration against the ruling system. On the Prussian suffrage question there was a "voluntary" abandonment of debate in order to manifest the unity and determination of the party. That this was in the nature of a steam-roller against the revisionists is highly probable; had any substantial minority opposed it, however, it would not have been attempted. When even Breslau and Magdeburg, organizations not normally accounted as radical, submitted resolutions calling for the use of street demonstrations

[12] *Ibid.*, 1662–1665.
[13] *Vorwärts*, 5 Jan. 1910.

and the mass strike, it is safe to say that the rank and file were in no mood for compromise. What the Prussian congress called for was a "suffrage storm." [14]

Operating on the assumption that the parliamentary possibilities were extremely limited, the congress paid almost no attention to the prospects for an alliance with other parties. It was futile, Ströbel said, to take account of the feelings of Progressives and Centrists.[15] The fight for suffrage reform was but an aspect of the class struggle in which the workers must bear the principal burden. To make the line between Social Democrats and Progressives amply clear, the congress reaffirmed the party's demand for universal, equal, and direct suffrage for elections to municipal councils, which the Progressives opposed. The speaker on this issue was Julius Hirsch, one of the more moderate Social Democratic deputies in the Landtag.[16] His intransigence was another indication that the Prussian party would go into the reform movement united on the basis of splendid isolation.

That the Prussian wing of the party should have reversed the trend toward a reform coalition perceptible at the Leipzig congress was not unnatural. The Prussian comrades lived under the three-class suffrage system; they had had the spirit of compromise beaten out of them by years of petty persecution at the hands of the Prussian administration and the courts.[17] The ire of the rank and file against the behavior of the Conservatives in the tax reform question could not easily be converted into friendship for the Liberals. After all, both Progressives and National Liberals were prepared to vote the enormous increase in indirect taxes.

Even for those less swayed by habitual attitudes of hostility toward the Liberals, the fine-spun tactic of Eduard Bernstein gave little promise of success in the unreformed Landtag. The portents of the summer and fall of 1909, that the National Liberals might swing leftward, had come to nothing. Bassermann had given in no more to the pressure of his left wing than to that of his right—

---

[14] *S.M.*, XIV (XVI), i, 3; Luxemburg, *Werke*, IV, 544.
[15] *N.Z.*, XXVIII, i, 549.
[16] *Schulthess, 1910*, 1.
[17] Liebknecht delivered to the congress a lengthy indictment of Prussian judicial and bureaucratic discrimination against the labor movement. Cf. *Vorwärts*, 6 Jan. 1910; *N.Z.*, XXVIII, i, 551.

nor could he have if his party was to be held together. The National Liberals continued in their opposition to equal suffrage for
Prussia; plural voting, of little benefit to the workers, was as far
as they would go. The Progressives' reform program for Prussia
was entirely satisfactory, but they remained a weak reed on which
to lean. The *Hansabund* as a political force for reform scarcely survived the taxation crisis which gave it birth. The conflicts of interest and the differences in political outlook in the business community were too great to permit its developing any real striking power.
Within a short time of the *Hansabund's* founding, the heavy industrialists of the *Zentralverband deutscher Industrieller,* whom we
have encountered earlier as the architects of the national employers'
association, kicked over the traces. Fearful lest the Conservatives
avenge themselves in the field of tariff policy for industry's defiance
on the tax question, they began to mend their fences with the *Bund
der Landwirte,* and thus broke the united front of the business
world.[18] Even the Progressives had to give up their hopes that the
Hansabund would rally the business community behind a reform
movement.[19] As the leftward swing in the middle class was halted
and turned, the rightward tendency in Social Democracy was likewise reversed.

The Prussian party congress expressed the radical resurgence in
the sharpest possible form, more sharply than a national party congress would have done. For the structure of the Prussian *Land*
organization with its broader representation of the urban districts,
and with an overriding influence accorded to the Berlin organization in its standing committee, placed the radicals in a position to
dominate the proceedings.[20] The voices of those who shared the

[18] Rochus Freiherr v. Rheinbaben, *Stresemann, der Mensch und der Staatsmann*
(Dresden, 1928), 63–64.

[19] Theodor Heuss, *Friedrich Naumann* (Stuttgart and Berlin, 1937), 381.

[20] The Prussian *Land* organization was not established until November 1907. In
harmony with the anti-federalist attitudes of its radical framers, it did not have the
broad functions of the southern state organizations. Except during *Landtag* elections
and periods of agitation for suffrage reform, it was inactive. The organization was
so constructed as to maximize radical strength. A system of proportional representation, more equitable than that of the national party congress, was used in the election of delegates. Paid officials, advocated by the revisionists at three successive Prussian congresses — 1904, 1907, and 1910 — were always rejected by the majority.
Over revisionist opposition, the Prussian organization was closely geared to the na-

spirit of compromise of the party south of the Main were silenced by the dominant mood of radical intransigence. The suffrage movement which was soon unleashed carried the stamp not of the Leipzig congress, but of red Prussia.

ii. The "Suffrage Storm" and the Division of the Radicals

On 4 February 1910 the government released Bethmann-Hollweg's long-awaited draft bill for Prussian suffrage reform. Free, equal, and secret suffrage for all citizens over twenty years of age? — far from it. The bill provided only that the so-called *Kulturträger* — ministers, parliamentarians, higher officials, certain classes of well-educated persons, army officers, retired noncoms, etc. — should no longer be obliged to vote in the third class. The three-class voting system was to be left untouched. The only substantial improvement promised was the substitution of direct for indirect election.[21]

The proposed reforms were so inadequate that far from satisfying democratic opinion they only aroused it further. The press reaction on every hand was hostile but that of the Progressives and Social Democrats was wrathful in the extreme. "To those who cry for bread, it gives a stone," cried the *Vossische Zeitung* (Progressive). The *Berliner Tageblatt* said that the bill through which the chancellor " 'thought to educate the people' to 'political understanding' and 'a sense of political responsibility' " could evoke in the reader of its provisions only a "mixture of burning shame and seething indignation." *Vorwärts,* pointing to the fact that three-fourths of the population would remain in the third class, "the class of the right-less," condemned the bill as a "brutal and contemptuous declaration of war."[22]

Social Democracy declared war in turn and mobilized swiftly. On 6 February came the first of a series of street demonstrations in Halle, Bielefeld, Solingen, and elsewhere. When on 10 February

---

tional executive. It had no independent *Land* executive, but only a *Land* commission composed of provincial representatives, which rarely met. The Berlin organization exercised considerable power as the principal element in the standing business committee (*geschäftsführender Ausschuss*). For the long controversy over the form of the Prussian organization, see N.Z., XXV, i, 356–362; S.M., X (XII), ii, 996–997; *ibid.*, XI (XIII), ii, 898ff., 1038; *Prot. S. P., 1908,* 25.

[21] The draft is given in *Schulthess, 1910,* 99–102.

[22] For these and other comments, see the summary of press reaction, *ibid.*, 104–106.

Bethmann-Hollweg mounted the rostrum in the Prussian House of Representatives to explain the government's reform proposals, the Social Democratic delegates greeted him with calls of "Pfui!" and "Traitor." The rightist benches clamored for the eviction of the Social Democratic deputies.[23] It was a fitting opening for the rowdy debates of the succeeding three months.

In the consideration of the reform bill in the Prussian House all of Bernstein's calculations went awry. Social Democrats and Progressives stood together, but the National Liberals retained their independent line based on plural voting. The Center, desirous above all else to stay on the good side of the Conservatives, made a deal whereby they won Conservative backing for the secret suffrage in exchange for supporting the restoration of indirect election. Thus amended, the Conservative-Center majority passed the bill on 16 March 1910. The Prussian House of Lords introduced a few minor improvements in the bill, but these were rejected by the House of Representatives. Thereupon Bethmann-Hollweg withdrew the whole project.[24] All these negotiations were accompanied by the stormiest scenes in the Landtag. *Simplizissimus,* the liberally inclined humor magazine, kept up a stream of acid satirical comment on the proceedings which fed the resentment of the middle-class public.[25]

Social Democracy responded with one of the longest periods of active agitation the party had ever seen. From February to April there were meetings and street demonstrations not only in Prussia, but throughout Germany. On 13 February there were simultaneous demonstrations in almost every city in Prussia. Clashes with the police occurred in Frankfurt-am-Main, Halle, Duisburg, and the Berlin industrial suburb of Rixdorf. In Frankfurt the party launched a second demonstration on 27 February to protest against the action of the police as well as the inadequacies of the reform bill. The second Frankfurt demonstration was remarkable for the fact that Progressives participated in it. This time the police were more severe and numerous persons were injured in the clashes.[26]

---

[23] *Ibid.,* 110.

[24] *Ibid.,* 110–292 *passim.*

[25] *Simplizissimus,* XIV, No. 51 to XV, No. 3 inclusive, *passim.*

[26] *S.M.,* XIV (XVI), i, 284. The Liberals held meetings to press their suffrage demands, but these did not, as a rule, take the form of mass demonstrations, and

Perhaps the most striking demonstration was that held by the Berlin Social Democrats after the Conservative-Center alliance put through their revisions in the electoral reform commission of the Prussian House. Against this action the Berlin organization scheduled a mass rally for 6 March. The Berlin chief of police[27] forbade the demonstration. Thereupon, the Social Democratic leaders, not without a touch of Berlin humor, issued a call for a "suffrage promenade" (*Wahlrechtsspaziergang*) in Treptow Park. There was, after all, no legal prohibition against walking in a park. The police cut off the trolley and *S-Bahn* service to Treptow and stationed a strong force to block every approach to the park. While the police were thus engaged, the word was passed through the party cadres that the demonstration would be held instead in the Tiergarten. According to the perhaps enthusiastic estimates of the party at least 150,000 foregathered for the *Spaziergang*. The outwitted police arrived only near the end of the proceedings.[28]

The incident made a tremendous impression on the German right. "The deeply serious aspect of these events," wrote the Conservative *Reichsbote,* "is the insight [which they give] into the tight organization of Social Democracy, which consists of a network of secret threads, so that a confidential order can fly silently through a city of millions and direct a hundred thousand men [to gather] without a sound at a specific place and according to a fixed plan." [29] The Catholic *Märkischer Volksbote* declared that the Social Democrats were using the suffrage issue merely to train the masses for revolution. It was only "a short step" from the Tiergarten demonstration to "the revolutionary deed." [30]

These fears were of course vastly exaggerated, perhaps in some measure deliberately so to justify the Conservative-Centrist opposi-

---

were held separately from the Social Democratic rallies. A Liberal rally in Berlin, however, ended in a demonstrative march to the royal palace, where the crowds cried "Down with Bethmann! Down with the Junker Parliament!" This demonstration seems to have represented the high-water mark of the Liberal protest movement. *Schulthess, 1910,* 151.

[27] Traugott von Jagow, later a leader in the Kapp Putsch of 1920.

[28] For the Berlin episode and the movement as a whole, see Luxemburg, *Werke,* IV, 496–498; *Prot. S. P., 1910,* 30–32; *S.M.,* XIV (XVI), i, 499; *Schulthess, 1910,* 31, 80, 108, 128, 133, 137, 189, 208, 213; *Vorwärts,* 6–7–8 Mar. 1910.

[29] *Reichsbote,* 7 Mar. 1910, quoted in *Vorwärts,* 8 Mar. 1910.

[30] *Märkischer Volksbote,* n. d. (7 Mar. 1910?), quoted in *Vorwärts,* 8 Mar. 1910.

tion to suffrage reform. The demonstrations simply expressed the
frustration of Social Democracy's followers at the blighting of their
hopes for constitutional progress. Yet there was a kernel of truth
in the Conservatives' concern: the demonstrations undoubtedly contributed to an increasingly radical atmosphere.

The militant mood was further strengthened, as in 1905, by developments on the economic front. The year 1910 was one of serious
labor trouble. As the depression drew to a close in the last half of
1909, and the labor market contracted once more,[31] the unions began to push for wage increases. No year since 1905 had seen so
large a number of workers engaged in work stoppages as 1910:
369,011.[32] For an accurate grasp of the political atmosphere of 1910
it is significant to note that two-thirds of those engaged in work
stoppages were locked out by their employers. The total union expenditures for lockouts reached M. 11.9 million — almost double
the previous record established in 1906.[33]

Both workers and employers were thus aggressively disposed in
1910. In January strike-unrest in the Mansfeld coal fields reached
such proportions that the regular army was sent in to maintain
order.[34] The biggest single prewar union conflict was brewing during the first three months of the year: that in the building industry.
On 8 April the employers' association announced a lockout for the
whole building industry, affecting about 175,000 workers.[35] This
great conflict broke out within a few days of the second vote on
the reform bill in the Prussian House (12 April), when there was

[31] In the second quarter of 1909, the unions began to regain the 33,775 members
lost in 1908. By the close of 1909, they counted 936 more members than in 1908.
Cf. Internationaler Sekretär, *Bericht, 1908*, 126; *ibid., 1909*, 119.

[32] The number of workers engaged in work stoppages were as follows:

1905	507,960
1906	316,042
1907	281,030
1908	126,883
1909	131,244
1910	369,011

Internationaler Sekretär, *Bericht, 1910*, 125.

[33] *Ibid.*, 127.

[34] Cf. *Schulthess, 1910*, 36–43.

[35] August Winnig, *Der grosse Kampf im deutschen Baugewerbe, 1910* (Hamburg,
1911), 27–108 *passim*.

again a great wave of demonstrations throughout the country.[36]
Thus social and political unrest coincided once more, as they had
in 1905–06, to create an atmosphere of political radicalism in the
working class.

The mood of the Social Democratic rank and file waxed stormier
as the hopelessness of reform from the top grew more apparent from
week to week. Demands for the use of the mass strike began to be
heard. In Königsberg, Essen, Breslau, and Bremen the local organizations discussed it; in Kiel and Frankfurt half-day demonstration strikes were held. The organizations of Halle and Hessen-
Nassau formally petitioned the national executive to take up the
mass-strike problem.[37]

As was her wont, Luxemburg took the intellectual leadership of
the movement to drive on to more radical action. She embodied her
views in an article entitled "What Further?" which she dispatched
in March to *Vorwärts.* Here she argued that the movement could
not go on indefinitely at the present level of intensity. Either it
would have to be driven forward, assume the form of demonstration strikes and perhaps develop into a general strike, or the excitement and will to action of the masses would weaken and the movement collapse of its own weight. Everything now depended, she
said, on the determination of the party which led the movement.
She therefore urged official encouragement of demonstration strikes
and a general discussion of the mass strike to see how far the masses
would respond to the idea.[38] Luxemburg, with a considerable body
of party sentiment and the elastic resolution of the Prussian congress of January behind her, thus called for the application of the
doctrine she had laid down four years earlier. She wished the leadership to steer the aroused populace as near to revolution as possible.
History had caught up with her theory, she thought, and the time
for action was at hand.

It was an unpleasant situation for the party and trade-union leadership: the ghost of 1905 was abroad in the land. The organizations
would clearly be threatened by an intensification of the mass ac-

[36] *Schulthess, 1910,* 213.
[37] Luxemburg, *Werke,* IV, 527–528.
[38] *Ibid.,* 509–518.

tions. The Prussian police had shown no timidity in coping with
the demonstrators, the ruling groups no failure of nerve. Whether
from aversion to mass action as such, or from a sober evaluation of
the prospects — both undoubtedly played a role — the leadership
did not wish to go forward. But it could not, in view of the pressure from the lower echelons of the party, go backward by calling
off the whole suffrage campaign. It adopted a middle course: to let
the storm ride itself out while using its influence to keep the discussion of the mass strike at a minimum.[39]

Vorwärts, though it was the organ of the Berlin as well as of the
national party, followed the executive's line. It carried no reference
to discussions of the mass strike in its reports of Berlin meetings.
In printing the party news bureau's syndicated story of an address
by Luxemburg to a Frankfurt mass meeting, *Vorwärts* struck out
one sentence carried by the other papers: "The speaker evoked the
enthusiastic approval of the participants when she advocated propaganda for the mass strike." [40] The editors also returned Luxemburg's article, "What Further?", with a note that party instructions
forbade them from printing propaganda for the mass strike. After
accepting the article and actually setting it to type, Kautsky, as editor of *Neue Zeit,* decided that it was too dangerous and returned
it to its author. Kautsky subsequently gave as the primary reason
for rejecting this article that "the excitement of the masses was not
nearly sufficient for such a strenuous action . . . but it was great
enough so that the stimulus of Comrade Luxemburg could well
evoke isolated attempts, experiments in the direction of the mass
strike which would have failed . . ." [41] Thus in the face of radical
pressure the two chief organs of the party, *Vorwärts* and *Neue Zeit,*
embarked in a modest way upon a career of censorship which was

[39] I have found no evidence to support the statement of Paul Frölich that "the
executive, in a secret circular, forbade the continuation of the movement." (*Ibid.,*
498.) If such had been the case, it is odd that the fact was not mentioned by the
ardent advocates of intensified mass action at the Magdeburg congress of 1910, where
the whole course of events was reviewed.

[40] *Ibid.,* 528–529.

[41] *N.Z.,* XXVIII, ii, 336; cf. also Frölich, *Luxemburg,* 200–201. Frölich claims that
Kautsky succumbed to pressure from the party leaders, a charge also made by Luxemburg's partisans at the time, for which I have found no direct evidence. That
Kautsky shared the leaders' anxiety would have been sufficient motivation for his
behavior.

to be intensified during the succeeding years until it ended in a thorough purge of all left radical journalists during the First World War. New dangers justified new political methods of an authoritarian character. Kautsky felt that the party had "not only the right but the duty to utilize its organization to prevent all attempts at a premature mass strike, which must fail." [42]

To buttress the position of the leadership in its opposition to the growing pressure for more radical action, Kautsky wrote a serialized article entitled "What Now?" in which he advocated a return to the parliamentary tactic.[43] A polemic against the use of the demonstration strike and mass strike in the electoral reform movement, the article had Rosa Luxemburg as its particular target. "What Now?" marked not only the end of a long friendship, but, more importantly, the crystallization of latent theoretical differences in the radical camp into divergent tactical positions.

Following the tradition of Engels in his later years, Kautsky expressed the problem confronting the party in military terms. He saw two possible strategies open: a strategy of direct engagement to force a decision, and a strategy of attrition. Kautsky urged that as long as reaction sat strong in the saddle and the proletariat was not yet fully organized, the strategy of attrition was the only course.

The mass-strike advocates, he said — and not without reason — would only raise the hopes of the masses for reform and would lead them to expend their energies in a costly struggle from which defeat and discouragement alone could result.[44] In a long discourse on Fabius Cunctator, Kautsky recommended the emulation of his strategy.[45] He urged that the street demonstrations in Prussia be continued: "No rest in Prussia as long as equal, direct suffrage is not achieved." [46] But he rejected Luxemburg's idea that the movement must go forward at any cost. That he expected — indeed, hoped — that it would go backward was indicated by the conclusion of his article where he urged the party to turn its attention to

[42] N.Z., XXVIII, ii, 666.

[43] Karl Kautsky, "Was nun?", ibid., 33–40, 68–80. The article is reprinted in idem, Der politische Massenstreik (Berlin, 1914), 224–245, from which it is here cited.

[44] Kautsky, Massenstreik, 234–235.

[45] Ibid., 228–232.

[46] Ibid., 235.

the next tactical objective, the coming Reichstag elections. Kautsky offered his readers even higher hopes than those for which he criticized Luxemburg: if not at the next election, then within a few years, the Social Democrats could have an absolute majority. "Such a victory would signify nothing less than a catastrophe for the whole ruling system." [47]

Kautsky thus held out the possibility of an early, peaceful revolution by parliamentary means. If the ruling class should resort to force to maintain its power after the Social Democrats had achieved a Reichstag majority, the proletariat would then be in a position to fight its great decisive battles on a "new and far broader basis than today"; that is, it would have the majority of the people behind it.

It will be observed that the controversy between Kautsky and Luxemburg left the issue out of which it grew — electoral reform tactic — far behind. The real problem was that the population was aroused as it had not been since 1905–06. A mass movement of substantial proportions was at hand: What should be done with it?

Luxemburg and her allies wished to use the occasion to stimulate the revolutionary consciousness of the masses through action, to absorb the electoral reform agitation into a more general quasi-revolutionary movement. Thus she urged the party to advance the demand for a republic to broaden the goal of the movement. Where Kautsky treated the electoral reform agitation as a separate, transient undertaking, Luxemburg conceived it as a "partial manifestation of our general socialist class struggle." [48] She therefore advocated — against Kautsky — that the nation-wide construction workers' lockout be tied into the political struggle. She wished to harness for political action the general hostility to capitalism aroused by a great strike. [49] Kautsky's separation of the electoral reform movement from economic struggles in theory and practice, Luxemburg argued, made sense only if one was operating in alliance with bourgeois parties who would be put off by a general fight against capitalism. [50] For her the great problem was to build up the revolutionary spirit. Her wing was prepared to risk the organization in the

[47] Ibid., 241–242.
[48] Luxemburg, Werke, IV, 520–523, 537.
[49] Ibid., 536.
[50] Ibid., 536–537.

struggle because, even if it failed, the class consciousness of the proletariat and its hostility to the existing order would be greater than before. As Klara Zetkin expressed it, the real success of the suffrage fight lay "not in the positive result but rather in the ever greater unification of the laboring masses, a unification which prepares the ultimate victory." [51]

"Rebel's impatience" was the term which Kautsky later found to describe the new ultra-radicalism and its precipitous drive toward action. He saw it as a product of the sharpening of class antagonisms since 1907 which "again awaken mass instincts to which Marxism in its crassest, most absolute and simplest form is most congenial." [52] The characteristic of rebel's impatience, said Kautsky, was to drive toward socialist revolution as rapidly as possible without regard to the objective limitations of the political and social scene. Kautsky contrasted this tendency with its opposite, "statesman's impatience." This was the revisionist tendency to speed up the drive toward socialism by concluding deals with the ruling class and trying to avoid class struggle. Statesman's impatience was, said Kautsky, the product of a period of prosperity and lessened class tensions, that of 1895 to 1907.[53] What Kautsky asked in 1910 was that the party yield to neither, that it escape both premature revolutionary adventurism and the course of collaboration with the bourgeoisie advocated by the revisionists. In 1909, on the tax question, he had turned his guns against the revisionists. In the early spring of 1910 he fought Luxemburg and the mass strike advocates. Then, when the Baden Social Democratic deputies voted for the budget again in July 1910,[54] Kautsky's artillery was firing on two fronts simultaneously. This was the situation in which the so-called Marxist center took form. Kautsky heralded its birth with a figure of speech:

When we look at the Grand Duchies of Baden and Luxemburg on the map, we find that between them lies Trier, the city of Karl Marx. If

[51] *Prot. S. P., 1910*, 445.

[52] *N.Z.*, XXX, ii, 664. It was perhaps out of personal necessity that Kautsky chose 1907 rather than 1905 as the turning point in the history of the contemporary class struggle, since he himself was so closely identified with "rebel's impatience" in the radical revival of 1905–06.

[53] Kautsky, *Massenstreik*, 213–222.

[54] *Prot. S. P., 1910*, 15–16.

from there [Trier] you go left across the border, you come to Luxemburg. If you go sharp right to beyond the Rhine you reach Baden. The
situation on the map is a symbol for the situation of German Social
Democracy today.[55]

The very emergence of the center as a separate faction shows the
terrible strain to which the party had been subjected by the years
1909–10. The revisionists had drawn strength from the tax reform
crisis and from the possibility of a Liberal alliance which emerged
from it. The drive for suffrage reform and the frustration engendered by the attitude of government and the ruling parties, however,
had acted in the opposite direction: it rolled up the highest wave of
radicalism since 1905–06. Yet militant radicalism achieved no more
than had the parliamentary tactic of coöperation in the tax bill. Had
the radical tendency been driven further — surely Kautsky was
right in this — a major defeat would have been the consequence.
At the end of May, when the suffrage bill was withdrawn, the party
executive designated the next Reichstag elections as the appropriate
point to hit back at the government and the enemies of suffrage
reform.[56] Therewith the reformist tendency came to the fore again.
On 14 July 1910 the Social Democrats in the Baden "Great Bloc"
(National Liberals, Progressives, and Social Democrats) voted for
a state budget in the Landtag. Thus the frustration of Social Democracy at the hands of the government and the Blue-Black Bloc
in 1909–10 fed now the pure reformist, now the revolutionary tendencies, so that both gained strength at the expense of the Erfurt
synthesis.

Was there a middle position between the two? Theoretically,
there was. Social Democracy could keep its distance from the bourgeois parties, eschew the road to reform, yet keep its powder dry by
avoiding premature revolutionary engagements. That was the tactic
advocated by Kautsky in his six-month-long polemic against both
left and right.[57] But the party could not stand absolutely still. The

[55] Karl Kautsky, "Zwischen Baden und Luxemburg," N.Z., XXVIII, ii, 667.

[56] S.M., XIV (XVI), ii, 752.

[57] For Kautsky's articles against the left, see N.Z., XXVIII, ii: "Was nun?", 33–40,
68–80; "Eine neue Strategie," 332–341, 364–374, 412–421; "Zwischen Baden und
Luxemburg," 652–667; "Schlusswort," 760–765; against the revisionists, ibid., "Der
Aufstand in Baden," 612–625; and "Auch ein Arbeitswilliger," 689–700. For the
most succinct statement of the position of the Marxist center in 1910, see Rudolf
Hilferding, "Der Parteitag in Magdeburg," ibid., 892–900.

leaders — and with them the center — sought the solution by pressing to the fore the preparations for the next Reichstag elections. It was hoped that these would provide an outlet for the pent-up energy of the frustrated party members.

Yet planning the far-distant election campaign was not, and could not be, a pure middle ground between revisionism and left radicalism. Inevitably the campaign would be fought not against the bourgeoisie as a whole, but against those directly responsible for the failure of the financial and constitutional reforms. The slogan of the campaign, "Against the Blue-Black Bloc," inevitably implied not socialist isolation, for which the party center still stood, but alliance with the Liberals.[58] It implied not preparation for the revolutionary showdown, which the centrists, like the left radicals, insisted was coming, but a primary emphasis on parliamentary activity. Thus when the centrists shrank back from pushing the mass action further, when they espoused the tactic of devoting all energy to the next elections, they strengthened the other tendency which they abhorred: revisionism. At the very moment of its birth as a separate wing the center found itself unable to generate a political momentum of its own. It could be vital only insofar as it supported the dynamic factions to its right or left.

iii. The Revisionist Offensive and Radical Disunity

As a solid phalanx the revisionists supported the tactic of concentrating on the next Reichstag elections as the key to Prussian reform.[59] Before the Prussian "suffrage storm" the revisionists had drawn encouragement from the political realignment in the nation as a whole; after the failure of both Social Democratic tactics in the reform movement of 1910, they drew strength from the division of the radicals within the party. The perspicacious Wilhelm Kolb, Baden revisionist leader, celebrated the Kautsky-Luxemburg feud as representing the bankruptcy of radicalism. He skillfully concentrated his fire on Kautsky and the center. The question for the party, said Kolb, was "whether the party should pursue a serious revolutionary or a serious reformist policy." Bernstein had of course posed this question at the turn of the century, but at that time the

---

[58] For the application of the tactic, see below, Ch. IX, sec. i.

[59] See the numerous articles in *S.M.*, XIV (XVI), ii and iii, No. **9 to No. 19–20,** *passim.*

orthodox Marxists rejected it as unreal and had defended the Erfurt synthesis of revolutionary aims and reformist tactics. As the belief in proximate revolutionary opportunity increased, the left radicals came to accept the revisionist formulation of the problem though offering a different solution. Kolb exploited the attitude of the left radicals in his warfare against the ambivalent center:

[T]he attempt of the Marxists of . . . [Kautsky's] school to demonstrate the correctness of their teaching breaks down in the face of reality. K. Kautsky permits railroad workers, yes, even minor officials, to take part in a general strike — in theory. But as soon as Comrade Luxemburg comes along and wishes to make a practical test, Kautsky, the adamant man of principle, transforms himself with the turn of the hand into an *opportunist,* and the bankrupt *Klassenstaat* equally suddenly becomes a *rocher de bronze.* The breakdown of the breakdown theory has never been so clearly illuminated as in the controversy of Rosa Luxemburg vs. K. Kautsky in the matter of the mass strike.[60]

If the center understood that it must turn from the adventures of mass action to a sensible concentration on the next election, the revisionists argued, then it should go all the way to make the election politically useful; jettison its theory of proletarian isolation and ally itself with all forces opposed to the Conservative regime. For the center to say "A" and refuse to say "B" made no political sense.

With the moderate radicals returning to the parliamentary tactic, the revisionists resumed their offensive for a Social-Democratic-Liberal alliance. When they voted for a budget in Baden in 1910, their behavior had a significance different from that of previous similar actions. It was embarked upon not merely to accomplish "positive work" in Baden, but to create a *fait accompli* which would commit the party further to the policy of collaboration with the Liberals on a national scale. Two months before the Baden Landtag delegates made their decision, Wilhelm Kolb held up the Baden Great Bloc of Liberals and Social Democrats as a shining example for the national party to follow.[61] The decision to vote for the budget was taken in the certain knowledge that the next party con-

[60] Wilhelm Kolb, "Das Problem der Taktik," *ibid.,* XIV (XVI), iii, 1184–1186.
[61] *Ibid.,* i, 551ff. Cf. also Ludwig Frank's address to the Baden party congress, 20 August 1910, in his *Aufsätze, Reden und Briefe,* ed. Hedwig Wachenheim (Berlin, n. d.), 183–186.

gress would condemn it. Still, the Baden leaders calculated that it would be worthwhile from the point of view of its long-run influence on party policy. Ludwig Frank, now one of the three outstanding leaders of the Baden party, wrote to a friend of his decision on the budget vote:

Wish me luck for the next months of struggle; it is a hard time for me. But I am not depressed, because I have a clear political conscience, and because one must follow the God in one rather than the decisions of a party congress. I will admit to you, however, that on the night before the decision, I had a long struggle with myself as to which direction I should steer the ship . . . [But] I knew that the time was right, and I had the power to put it through . . . The party as a whole will be helped by this episode. Even if not immediately, it will be pushed by my propaganda of the deed to apply its dormant . . . powers. . . . The policy which I pursue is a long-term investment.[62]

The revisionists saw that as long as the majority of the radicals accepted the parliamentary tactic no harm could come of their efforts to carry it to its logical conclusion. Even though the party congress would condemn the Baden action, "an internally disintegrating majority" would be "insufficient to struggle against reason and logic" in the long run.[63]

Thus the revisionists drew strength for an assault on the policy of pure opposition from the collapse of the suffrage movement, the return to the parliamentary tactic, and the division of the radicals. With a stout heart they prepared themselves for the blows they would receive at the party congress, knowing, as Frank said, that the national leadership would not dare go beyond "a word-rattling resolution which, naturally, will not make much of an impression on us."[64]

The radicals of all persuasions joined in condemning the budget-voters. In the press and in party meetings the hue and cry against the heretics was raised in chorus. There were, however, two distinct tones in the criticism of the revisionists: one sounded by the center, the other by the left radicals.

The center emphasized the breach of discipline. Seventeen Baden

[62] Letter to Leonie Meyerhof-Hildeck, 21 July 1910, *ibid.*, 170–171.
[63] *S.M.*, XIV (XVI), iii, 1189.
[64] Letter to Natalie Frank, 6 Aug. 1910, Frank, *Aufsätze*, 173.

Landtag delegates had violated a clear party policy. Kautsky called the erring parliamentarians "strike-breakers" against the solidarity of labor in the political struggle.[65] According to Hilferding, the party could not ignore the problem of discipline in the year of Our Lord 1910, for the political situation had led to strong centrifugal tendencies to left and to right. If the Landtag representatives were permitted to violate the party discipline with impunity, the same freedom could rightly be claimed by the leaders of other party factions. The organization, he said, had made the party great; the organization resolved the tension between revolutionary and reformist tendencies, inevitable under capitalism, into a working political synthesis. Its law must be maintained against both right and left now more than ever before.[66] The closer the party moved toward final schism, the greater became the need to hold it together by discipline.

What Kautsky and Hilferding implied, the less intellectual scribes and orators proclaimed more openly. They called now for the expulsion of the reformist offenders from the party, now for their resignations as Landtag deputies.[67]

The left radicals too called for vengeance against the treasonable Landtag members. Rosa Luxemburg, however, focussed attention on a different aspect of the problem: the Baden local organizations and the rank and file. The Baden leadership had carried the issue to local meetings all over the state for *ex post facto* approval and had won the support it sought. The "tragic significance" of the Baden incident lay in the approval of the locals which revealed "the lack of proper understanding for the politics of proletarian class struggle and for the basic demands of the revolutionary position of Social Democracy."[68] More than a question of discipline was involved, Luxemburg maintained: "We cannot expel the Landtag deputies and ignore the party organizations which stand behind them and give them full support."[69] Luxemburg placed the responsibility for the attitude of the Baden rank and file not merely on the Baden leadership, but on the national party as a

[65] *N.Z.*, XXVIII, ii, 689ff.
[66] *Ibid.*, 892ff.
[67] Cf. *S.M.*, XIV (XVI), iii, 1174.
[68] Luxemburg, *Werke*, III, 451.
[69] *Ibid.*, 452–453.

whole. Above all, an excessive emphasis on parliamentarism had led the Baden members astray.

Doesn't the party have on its conscience the sins that have reared parliamentary cretinism, except that its own [sins] pertain to the Reichstag elections? Are we not, at this very moment, experiencing a notable example of this parliamentary cretinism, when the events in Baden are greeted from every side with the indignant cry: 'You dare to do such a thing when we are approaching an election and have such brilliant prospects?' Think of it! . . . It's a matter of to be or not to be for Social Democracy — and the whole thing is handled as a question of competition in the next Reichstag elections! As though a hundred mandates could compensate us, when we are threatened with the loss of the foundation of our strength: irreconcilable class struggle.[70]

Luxemburg charged the party with ignoring the whole day-to-day development of the movement south of the Main. It behaved, she said, like a nightwatchman who only blows his horn when there's a public scandal on the streets. Revisionism could never be beaten by an occasional defensive action, by formalistic prohibitions or by discipline alone. It must be fought offensively, day in, day out, with the broadest possible development of mass actions whereever the situation would permit. The revisionist resurgence, Luxemburg maintained, was the product of party policy as a whole: the rejection of mass actions in the suffrage question, the "cult of Reichstag elections," and the watering down of May Day. It followed that the answer to Baden would have to be given on *all* questions of party policy, in a general radicalization of the tactic. Thus Luxemburg tried to turn the Baden crisis into another assault on general party policy.

iv. Aftermath at Magdeburg: The Triple Split

At the Magdeburg congress in September the three-way split in the party emerged in full clarity. On the question of the Prussian suffrage, revisionists and centrists were aligned against the left radicals. On the issue of budget-voting, centrists and left radicals stood together against the revisionist offenders.

The executive's report on the Prussian reform movement, sent

[70] *Ibid.*, 455.

out before the congress, showed how the leaders hoped to have that problem handled. Principal emphasis was placed on the orderly character of the demonstrations which had shown the "quiet determination" and "political ripeness" of the proletariat. The paragraph of the report dealing with the Prussian congress of January omitted any mention of the radical tone of the discussion or the resolution which emerged from it. The demonstration strikes were entirely ignored; likewise the lively discussion of more radical forms of action. The whole tenor of the report was designed to sustain the impression that the suffrage movement was in fact only what the leadership had wished it to be: a demonstration by an orderly, well-disciplined party for the rectification of a particular flaw in the political structure. Thus the executive tried to define as narrowly as possible the problem for discussion at the congress.[71]

The left radicals were not to be put off. Sixty-two delegates headed by Rosa Luxemburg submitted a resolution which declared, affirming the January decision of the Prussian party congress, "that the fight for the suffrage in Prussia can be waged to victory only through great, determined mass actions in which all means must be employed, including the political general strike if necessary." Accordingly the resolution stated that "the party congress declares it necessary to inaugurate the discussion of the mass strike in the party press and in party meetings in order to increase in the broadest sectors of the proletariat its feeling of power and political consciousness, so that the masses will be grown to the great task when the situation calls for it." [72] As the speeches in support of the resolution showed, its proponents insisted that the mood of the masses alone could determine when a mass strike could be made. The idea that revolutionary initiative lay with the masses had as its natural corollary the duty of the party to educate the masses in the means available to them.[73]

At the opposite extreme from this position stood the trade-unions. Thirty-four trade-unionists submitted a declaration of "most decisive protest" not merely against the content of the Luxemburg resolu-

[71] *Prot. S. P., 1910*, 30–31.

[72] *Ibid.*, 181–182 (motion no. 100).

[73] Cf. especially Klara Zetkin, *ibid.*, 444; also the general discussion, *ibid.*, 426–450.

tion, but against the very submission of it. Since matters affecting the interests of both branches of the labor movement could not be decided by one branch alone, the trade-unionists considered it "indispensable that the question of the discussion and propagation of the mass strike be considered by party executive and general commission before it reaches the party congress for a decision." [74] In short, the trade-unionists' declaration denied the party congress the right to take a position on the question on its own initiative. The Mannheim agreement again! Carl Severing, citing its establishment of parity between party and trade-union, presented the union position as follows:

You cannot even attempt this understanding [between party and trade unions] if, by accepting Comrade Luxemburg's motion, you present the general commission of the trade unions with a *fait accompli*. If you come to the general commission with this motion, there is no room for negotiation; you compel the trade unions to accept the content of the motion . . . That is a status of servility into which the trade unions cannot commit themselves. [75]

The alternative was of course that the party congress limit its competence, that it transfer its power to decide on any course of action to the party executive. In effect, it was this alternative which was being followed. The language of the trade-unionists' declaration reflected the fact when it designated the party executive as "the supreme representative organ (*oberste Vertretung*)" of the party. According to the party statute, not the executive, but the party congress was "the supreme representative organ." [76] So far had the concentration of power in the executive progressed that not even the left radicals observed the trade-unionists' misstatement of the constitution.

The party executive still managed to engineer a compromise on the mass strike question at Magdeburg. Luxemburg's resolution had somewhat the flavor of shutting the barn door after the horse was stolen; the suffrage movement was already dead. The executive resorted to the strategy which has become so familiar to us:

[74] *Ibid.*, 182 (motion no. 102).
[75] *Ibid.*, 446.
[76] "Der Parteitag bildet die oberste Vertretung der Partei." Cf. "Organisationsstatut," sec. 7, *Prot. S. P., 1910*, 7.

it recommended that the statement of principle in Luxemburg's motion be adopted, while the specific recommendation for encouragement of discussion of the mass strike be dropped.[77] The wind was taken out of the left radicals' sails by the maneuver.

It is unlikely that the Luxemburg resolution, if it had come to a vote, would have had the support of a majority at the congress. Only sixty-two delegates had signed her petition, though this is not an accurate gauge of the support it would have received.[78] Even the Prussian *Land* leaders, who had supported the calls for action and the radical threats at their January congress, were now split on the issue.[79] The dying down of the suffrage movement, taken together with the opposition of the national leadership to mass strike discussion, had broken the spell of radical unity.

On the Baden budget question, where defense of the traditional attitude of pure opposition to the existing order and loyalty to established party principles were at issue, the old radicals agreed with the new. Together they composed the majority of the party congress.[80] They supported a resolution, signed by 211 delegates, to the effect that another vote for a budget would automatically terminate the party membership of the offenders.

But let us observe that those who waged the floor fight against the southerners in 1910, prominent party men all, were, with rare exceptions, later of the Independent Social Democratic Party.[81] They were either left radicals or what we shall soon have to call, to complicate the picture further, "left centrists." The party executive now stood to the right of this group. Although Bebel fulminated against the Badeners, he rejected the resolution for their automatic

---

[77] *Ibid.*, 422, 450, 488–489.

[78] Klara Zetkin, who spoke for the resolution from the floor, did not sign the petition. Evidently the Leipzig and Hamburg delegations had not been approached for signatures, for there were among them radicals who would unquestionably have supported it.

[79] *Prot. S. P., 1910,* 440.

[80] See the voting on the resolutions concerning the budget issue, *ibid.*, 373–376, 383–385.

[81] Lipinski, Haase, Zubeil, Fleissner, Stadthagen, Dittmann, Ledebour, Vogtherr, Zetkin, Luxemburg, Liebknecht, Westmeyer, Dröner, and Emmel. There were also one or two obscure southerners who objected to the behavior of their leadership. The only prominent speaker on this occasion who remained in the party after the schism in 1917 was Gustav Hoch.

expulsion.[82] So strong was the sentiment in its favor, however, that he was obliged to threaten the southerners with expulsion proceedings (not automatic expulsion) should they vote for a budget again. This threat was made into a motion by the opposition and accepted by the congress.

The Magdeburg congress was the last in which the defense against revisionism was the central item on the agenda. Even as the party condemned the Baden revisionists in terms of the principles of intransigent class struggle and socialist isolation, it had returned to a reformist tactic. Theoretical differences between centrists and revisionists were bridged by a common defense of gradualist practice against left radical pressure.

The revolutionary hopes aroused in the left radicals and their followers in the spring of 1910 did not die. They were fed anew by the continued intransigence of the ruling groups and the failure of the parliamentary tactic to produce reform after 1910. "Rebel's impatience," which Rosa Luxemburg had first expressed in theoretical terms in 1906, had acquired factional form in 1910. Her group became henceforth the revolutionary goad of the party. Always precipitate in its tactical judgments, it was nevertheless to win allies among the old radicals, the centrists, whenever the leadership's rightward course seemed to endanger the sacred principles of the party.

To what unholy confusion had the party now arrived! On the right and left were the two dynamic factions whose divergent positions had been strengthened, respectively, by the hope of reform in 1909 and its collapse in 1910. On the one hand, the revisionists pressed for political and social reforms which would be achieved, thanks to the vitality of the Junkers and the political weakness of the middle classes, only by a social revolution. On the other hand, the left radicals demanded a tactic to prepare the masses for a social revolution which, when it came, would bring no more than the political reforms sought by the revisionists.

---

[82] For Bebel's speeches, see *Prot. S. P., 1910*, 238–259, 343–360; for his rejection of the majority resolution, *ibid.*, 359–360. Bebel's position was, as usual, governed by the problem of organizational unity. He therefore opposed both the budget-voters, who aroused the majority by their acts, and those who wished the expulsion of the offenders.

Between these two centrifugal forces stood the leadership and the center, trying to maintain a precarious balance. They could not desert the revolutionary tradition which was reinforced in a part of their rank and file by the absence of reform. Nor could they prepare their followers for revolution because they were the prisoners of the trade-unions which represented the interest of the workers in the existing order. They followed the only course open: to exploit the great safety-valve which Bismarck had created to hold his state together: elections to the virtually impotent Reichstag.

As the dissatisfaction with this course mounted on the left, the leadership, driven further right, moved toward the use of its power over the organization to hold the revolutionary incubus in check. We have seen the first indication of this development in 1910: the exercise of censorship on the mass strike question in *Vorwärts* and *Neue Zeit*. Yet in 1910 the principal conflict was still one over tactics. It remained for a new crisis on the international scene to transform the tactical conflict into an organizational struggle, and thus to usher in the penultimate phase in the development of the schism.

PART IV

THE DEEPENING CRISIS AND THE
RECONSOLIDATION OF THE RADICALS
1911–1914

Chapter VIII

THE MOROCCO CRISIS AND PARTY REFORM

On 1 July 1911 the cruiser "Panther" sailed into the harbor of
Agadir to protect German interests in Morocco. Under the strange
illusion that this show of force would result in a speedy and mutually satisfactory accord with France, Germany's foreign office
therewith unleashed a diplomatic crisis which solidified the Entente
Cordiale, increased Germany's isolation, and strengthened the war
parties of both France and Germany.[1] If the second Morocco crisis
was a harbinger of worse to come in the arena of international politics, it also precipitated another crisis in the German Social Democratic Party. Under its impact the factional conflict over policy became a struggle for control over party institutions. Out of that
struggle the executive, whose power was threatened for the first
time in the history of the party by a frontal attack, would emerge
strengthened against its radical opposition. The crisis would show
too that the center faction, whose differentiation from the left radicals had become so clear in 1910, was an unstable group and that
a significant portion of it was ready, under certain circumstances,
to align itself with the smaller and more aggressive left radical

---

[1] Johannes Ziekursch, *Politische Geschichte des neuen deutschen Kaiserreiches*
(Frankfurt a. M., 1930), III, 229–234; Theobald von Bethmann-Hollweg, *Betrachtungen zum Weltkrieg* (Berlin, 1919), I, 30–31; Erich Eyck, *Das persönliche Regiment Wilhelms II* (Erlenbach-Zürich, 1948), 560–594.

wing. The year 1911 marked the beginning of the reconsolidation of the left at a far remove from the party leaders, a reconsolidation which, after many interruptions, would one day culminate in the absorption of the left center into the Communist Party.

i. The Morocco Crisis: Ballot Box versus Creed

On 6 July 1911 Camille Huysmans, secretary of the International Socialist Bureau, dispatched to the secretaries and delegates of the socialist parties of all countries a note which called attention to the crisis created by the German action in Morocco. Huysmans asked each national executive to inform him by return mail if they thought that the time had come to call a meeting of the delegates of the socialist parties of Germany, France, Spain and Great Britain.[2]

Edouard Vaillant answered on behalf of the French executive that it felt a meeting desirable, but would not wish formally to instigate its convocation without prior consultation with the Spanish party. On the other hand the French executive felt that, should the outbreak of war threaten, the International Bureau should be called together by the secretary without further correspondence with the national executives. The Spanish leadership expressed less concern and felt that the first step would be a meeting of the French and Spanish parties. The British favored a conference.[3]

When Huysmans' note arrived in Berlin, Bebel was away in Zürich. Hermann Molkenbuhr, one of the paid secretaries of the executive, informed Bebel of the communication, but meanwhile sent off his personal views on the question to Huysmans.

Molkenbuhr saw little danger in the Agadir incident. While recognizing that the Mannesmann steel interest was involved, he pointed to counter-tendencies in capitalist circles which militated against a Franco-German war, the chief of which was the participation of Krupp, Thyssen, and other German interests in the French mine syndicate which competed with Mannesmann in Morocco. He felt these would counterbalance the influence of Mannesmann at the German foreign office. In a rather crude economic interpretation of Germany's Moroccan policy, Molkenbuhr expressed confi-

---

[2] The correspondence of the International Bureau with the national sections is reprinted as Appendix I in *Prot. S. P., 1911,* 464ff.

[3] *Ibid.,* 465, 467–468.

dence that Germany's leaders would not move further toward war because it "could injure the interests of the greatest capitalists, who have a sharp eye for [their interests] and will order a halt in time." [4]

Behind this argumentation lay a more immediate anxiety, which Molkenbuhr stated as follows:

I see in the whole coup something with which our government wishes to divert public attention from internal conditions and to create an atmosphere for the Reichstag elections . . .

If we should prematurely engage ourselves so strongly [as to go on record through an International meeting] and even give precedence to the Morocco question over questions of internal policy, so that an effective electoral slogan could be developed against us, then the consequences will be unforeseeable . . . It is a vital interest for us not to permit the internal developments: taxation policy, the privileges of the agrarians . . . etc., to be pushed into the background. But that could happen if we ourselves were to speak on the Morocco question in every hamlet, and were thus to strengthen the [chauvinistic] counter-tendency.[5]

The lesson of 1907 had evidently not been forgotten. With elections only six months away, the party executive wished to take no chances. Though it subsequently denied that Molkenbuhr's answer to Huysmans represented its position, the executive did nothing to encourage a meeting of the International Bureau.

Meanwhile, the crisis became exacerbated by Germany's failure to answer an English demand for admittance to the Franco-German negotiations. A tough speech delivered on 21 July by Lloyd George, who was at that time still reckoned in the "Potsdam Party" which sought accord with Germany, was the occasion of a new chauvinistic outbreak in Germany.[6] At the behest of the party executive, Bebel wrote to Huysmans that he hoped a meeting of the Bureau would be called if the necessity should arise. He himself did not think that war would result, as he wrote to Molkenbuhr, for "the French government will consider well before it permits itself to be pushed by the English government into a war with Germany over Morocco, the costs of which France would doubtless have to bear." One can detect here an anti-British tone which Bebel absorbed from

[4] *Ibid.*, 466.
[5] *Ibid.*, 466–467.
[6] Ziekursch, *Politische Geschichte*, III, 231; Eyck, *Wilhelm II*, 576ff.

the then hysterical atmosphere in Germany. Indeed, the executive was not inclined to have an International Bureau meeting, as it later reported to the party congress, until it had reports "that the Morocco question had assumed a character unfriendly to Germany in the British cabinet." [7] As long as it appeared that Germany might extract concessions from France without danger to herself, the party leaders did not wish to make an issue of the question.

As usual, certain of the urban party organizations were more radical than the leadership. The Berlin comrades immediately took action. They used a series of meetings scheduled for 4 July on the suffrage question to protest against the "Panther" incident. Similar action was taken in the major cities of Prussia.[8]

While local protest was gaining strength, the question suddenly took a new turn. Fiery Rosa threw one of her bombshells. As a member of the International's secretariat, she had received a copy of Molkenbuhr's letter to Huysmans, in which he had given primacy to electoral considerations over the fight against imperialism. On 24 July, after the crisis reached a new height with Lloyd George's speech, Luxemburg published the letter, along with a vigorous denunciation of its content, in the *Leipziger Volkszeitung*. In a clear breach of confidence, she exposed for all to see the reluctance of the executive to act vigorously in the face of imminent danger.[9]

The publication of the Molkenbuhr letter caused a real upheaval in the party. Coming as it did when the international crisis was at its height, and when the executive had as yet done nothing to assume leadership in the anti-war demonstrations inaugurated from below, Luxemburg's disclosure brought discontent with the leadership to the boiling point. The executive's belated decision to launch an agitation on the Morocco question on 9 August did not help its position.[10] Only a few days earlier, on 5 August, the German government had issued a communiqué indicating that its intentions were not belligerent. It had already reduced its demands to the French. In fact, the executive seems to have been precipitated by

[7] *Prot. S. P., 1911*, 469.

[8] *Vorwärts*, 4 July 1911; *Prot. S. P., 1911*, 193, 243–244.

[9] The executive charged Luxemburg with disloyalty and misrepresentation. These charges are to be found in *ibid.*, 192–195, 214–218; her answer, 204–206.

[10] For its manifesto, see *Vorwärts*, 9 Aug. 1911.

Luxemburg's revelation into an action which could only stir up public opinion when it was already quieting down.[11]

It was not merely the revolutionary extremists who were now aroused. War was an issue of principle. The centrists too were upset. The control commission, whose function it was to check the activities of the party executive, met immediately after the publication of the Luxemburg article. Its majority, composed of centrists, expressed its conviction that the executive had been negligent in the Morocco affair, that it should have acted more quickly and more decisively, and that it should launch an agitation to make up for lost time. The executive was thus forced into a position of acute embarrassment.[12]

At the same time, but in a very different quarter, the executive created difficulty for itself in 1911. At the request of the general commission of the trade-unions, it issued a so-called "secret circular" to party district leaders to moderate the attacks of the party press on the trade-unions. Again there was a leak. A bourgeois paper in Saxony published the circular, and a great hue and cry arose over the attempted censorship.[13]

The two issues flowed together during the late summer and gave rise to a general demand for a reform of the party executive.

ii. The Demand for the Reform of the Executive

When the party congress opened in Jena on 10 September, the leaders were for the first time rather fearful of their position. Bebel laid on all his charm in his opening speech, but beneath his homely diction lurked a note of insecurity:

[The last speaker] thought that a certain dissatisfaction was noticeable in the party during recent weeks. Yes indeed, party comrades, some of you are discontented with your government and find that it hasn't done what it should 'n' ought, that a fire will have to be built behind it to push it forward . . . [W]e will cheerfully admit that it's a sign of vitality when the party bestirs itself and isn't satisfied with everything . . . On the whole, you've always been satisfied with us; after all, you've always elected us again. But let's let it come to the test; go ahead and

[11] Compare Ziekursch, *Politische Geschichte*, III, 231–232, and *Prot. S. P., 1911*, 244.

[12] *Ibid.*, 220.

[13] *Ibid.*, 190–192, 209–211, 226–227.

criticize, suggest improvements, . . . then let the majority decide; and when it's decided, then we work on together as we worked together before . . .[14]

To forestall difficulties, the executive, with Hermann Müller as its spokesman, went over to the offensive on the Morocco question. The leaders tried to turn the Morocco affair into the "Luxemburg affair," to obscure the politics of the question by stressing the personal aspect.[15] They accused Luxemburg of disloyalty and indiscretion, of playing into the hands of the opposition by criticizing the leadership in the midst of a crisis, etc.

The maneuver did not succeed. The discontented centrists joined with the left radicals to focus attention on the substantive issue: what would the leadership do in the event of war? Thus Georg Ledebour:

Everything is now being done [by the executive] to hide the core of the question. Comrade Luxemburg and I have often been in conflict; and as I know Comrade Luxemburg, and as I know myself (laughter), we will often come into conflict again in what I hope will be a long period of activity in the party for both of us . . . But if [her] criticism had not been forthcoming, you [leaders] would still be sitting there and wouldn't have lifted a finger.[16]

Ledebour's deep concern was that the Morocco crisis had shown the party's unpreparedness to meet a real war situation. Raising hands in a demonstration, he said, even if there were 200,000 hands raised, would not be enough. An action to be effective must be international. The executive should have seized the initiative to plan an international strategy with parties of other countries. Since an international crisis could recur at any moment, the party must "push the executive forward to fulfill the greatest and most significant current task of the militant revolutionary proletariat." [17] As another delegate phrased it, the Moroccan crisis raised "in the last analysis a question of the capacity for action of our party executive in its present composition." [18]

[14] Ibid., 173.
[15] Ibid., 192–195, 214–218.
[16] Ibid., 212.
[17] Ibid., 213.
[18] Ibid., 209.

The executive's assault on Luxemburg backfired because the dissatisfied delegates felt that, whatever her indiscretion, Luxemburg's disclosure had brought about such action as the executive finally undertook. The argument that the party executive had not stood in the way of a "radical Jeremiad" did not satisfy the opposition. What was needed was an executive that could and would act. The Morocco question thus led directly to the problem of the reform of the executive.[19]

The issue of the secret circular against criticism of the trade-unions by the party press became interwoven with the Moroccan problem to the same end. Here too the executive had tried to limit criticism. The criticism out of which the incident had arisen had been directed against the Book Printers' Union, a union whose leaders and press regularly attacked the party in the sharpest terms, and whose Berlin rank and file, to the jubilation of the leftist party press, had revolted in a wild-cat strike.[20] The party journalists felt not only that their criticisms were justified in terms of party principles, but that their own leaders were letting them down in curbing the discussion. "Not pretty," one irate radical editor called the role of the executive. "The general commission," he complained, ". . . always defends the interests of its officials, while the party executive disavows the party press." [21]

How far the power position of the left had changed since 1906! In that year it still fought for the subordination of the trade-unions to the discipline of the party on the basis of socialist principle.[22] In 1911 it had to take its stand on the Mannheim agreement and try to preserve its freedom of expression against its own leadership which was acting as the executor of the trade-unions' will.[23] Not "discipline" now, but "democracy" and "free speech" were the instruments which the radicals had to use against the trade-unions and their own leadership.

How had the trade-unions persuaded the party leadership to impose restrictions on its press? Legien made the mechanism of

---

[19] *Ibid.*, 242–245.

[20] *Ibid.*, 209–211; Emil Döblin, "Die Lehren des Berliner Buchdruckerstreiks," *S.M.*, XV (XVII), ii, 1069–1073; *ibid.*, iii, 1255–1266.

[21] *Prot. S. P., 1911*, 211.

[22] See above, Ch. II, sec. vi.

[23] Cf. *Prot. S. P., 1911*, 234.

power entirely clear. The general commission had decided to
proceed against the party press attacks "without regard to consequences [*mit aller Rücksichtslosigkeit*]." But in view of the Reichstag elections, the general commission "considered itself obligated,
in accordance with the Mannheim agreement," to inform the party
executive of its intention. The executive was cowed by the threat.
According to Legien, it answered, " 'Don't do it! We'll have a gigantic scandal on our hands. We think that, if we send a circular
to the press, the whole matter will be settled.' " [24] It was a kind
of blackmail in which, in effect, the general commission threatened
withdrawal of electoral support. Since the trade-unions had approximately two and one-half times the membership of the party,
that is, since they controlled the less politically minded workers
who gave the party its strength at the polls, this was a powerful
threat. Thus the same aspect of the party executive's thought — one
might call it "electionism" — which rendered it indecisive in the
Morocco crisis also made it powerless to resist the pressure of the
trade-unions to censor the party press.

If the radicals were impelled by these developments to call for
a more determined and effective executive, they had devoted little
attention to the methods for acquiring it. Only five local organizations submitted motions on the question to the 1911 congress, and
of these, four advocated as the solution the appointment of more
paid secretaries to the executive. All of the five locals were to the
left of center in the party: Berlin I, Niederbarnim, Königsberg,
Bremen, and Göppingen. The thinking of the radicals on organizational problems had become so atrophied that they could offer no
better solution than the enlargement of the executive. [25] Wilhelm
Dittmann of Solingen, one of the leaders of the reorganization
drive, likewise had no better suggestion to offer. The accusation
by a conservative speaker that Dittmann wanted an executive "constituted by the grace of Dittmann" was unfair in its personal impu-
tations but correct in its political substance. [26] It was unthinkable
that the incumbent members of the executive be replaced; the
only hope for the radicals lay in adding more members of their

[24] *Ibid.*, 227.
[25] *Ibid.*, 151.
[26] *Ibid.*, 236; Dittmann's answer, 240–241.

own kind. Alfred Henke, spokesman of the Bremen organization, promised the radicals much from the enlargement of the executive: two new secretaries would relieve the executive of its burdens sufficiently to restore the contact between the leaders and the masses; as a consequence, "at next year's party congress, those who stand behind it [the executive] today on the Morocco question will no longer do so; it will have instead the support of the old majority [a radical one] . . . which cannot . . . be satisfied with it today." [27]

Neither the executive nor the revisionists could stand idly by while the radicals moved to pack the party's leadership. Hermann Müller announced to the Jena congress (1911) that the executive would in any case have requested one additional secretary, and would be willing to accept two, simply to meet the growing burdens which an expanded organization had imposed.[28] The motion for party reorganization to which the executive gave its support was made not by the radicals who had started the movement for changes in the executive, but by a revisionist, Dr. Max Quarck of Frankfurt. His motion recommended: (1) the immediate appointment of two more paid secretaries to the executive, that is, an increase of the bureaucratic element; and (2) the election of a commission of twenty-one to consider a reorganization of the party executive and control commission, and to report its findings to the next congress. The commission was to consult with the party executive in the course of its work.[29] It was to be composed of representatives of the various regions. In their appointment, however, an effort seems to have been made to have the factions equitably represented.[30] The motion satisfied the demands of the radicals and was carried without further discussion.

iii. The New Executive

The proposal to enlarge the executive was acted upon at once at the Jena congress. To meet the dissatisfaction on the left halfway, the executive nominated for the two new secretarial posts men who were not professional party secretaries, but journalists and

[27] Ibid., 252.
[28] Ibid., 196.
[29] Ibid., 160, 473.
[30] Ibid., 374.

agitators: Otto Braun and Philipp Scheidemann. For the co-chair-manship of the party, left vacant by the death of Paul Singer, Bebel proposed Hugo Haase, a prominent left centrist. Could these "politicals" really fulfill the hopes of the radicals? Let us examine their records and characters.

Born in 1872, Otto Braun had been an ultra-radical in his youth. He belonged to the Berlin *"Jungen,"* a group of extremists who, during the nineties, fought the Erfurt program as a counter-revolutionary document.[31] From the late nineties on, Braun was active in Königsberg Social Democracy. He served as an editor of the Königsberg *Tribüne* (after 1901 called the *Königsberger Volkszeitung*). He developed propaganda techniques to win over the peasants of the hostile East Prussian countryside. The constant and unavoidable financial difficulties of the Königsberg party paper and rural calendar may have helped Braun to establish personal connections with the executive.[32] The Junker officialdom of East Prussia subjected the Königsberg Social Democrats to constant persecution. Hugo Haase alone represented the Königsberg Social Democratic newspaper in no less than sixty-four court trials in seventeen years.[33] Braun worked to spread the Social Democratic gospel in this difficult atmosphere. In 1904 he drew nation-wide attention as one of nine defendants in a trial for smuggling revolutionary literature across the East Prussian border into Russia.[34]

Despite the arduous conditions of Social Democratic life in Königsberg, Otto Braun lost the radicalism of his youth. When he became the first secretary of the local sickfund, he entered one of the main portals to the practical, administrative, and conservative side of Social Democracy. At the party congresses, he was generally a modest and silent participant, even after he was elected to the control commission in 1906. He seems to have kept aloof from intraparty fights. During the last great budget-voting scandal, he proposed the establishment of a committee to make recommendations on budget-voting policy to the congress on the basis of the

---

[31] Harry J. Marks, "Movements of Reform and Revolution in Germany, 1890–1903" (Ph.D. Dissertation, Harvard University, 1937), 27.

[32] Gustav Noske, *Erlebtes aus Aufstieg und Niedergang einer Demokratie* (Offenbach, 1947), 15–16; *Prot. S. P., 1908*, 232.

[33] Ernst Haase, *Hugo Haase, sein Leben und Wirken* (Berlin, n. d. [1929?]), 10.

[34] *Ibid.*, 12–13.

factual situation in each state.[35] This reasonable suggestion was eagerly seized upon by the revisionists who made it one of the bases of their position at the Magdeburg congress (1910).[36] He did not support the motion for automatic expulsion of the revisionists if they should act again in defiance of the party. Here he stood to the right of the majority of the Königsberg delegates.[37] Aside from this incident, Braun did not participate in political debate at any party congress between 1906 and 1911, the year of his election to the executive.[38] Braun had become a loyal party servant standing above faction. His radical past, however, and his record as a victim of East Prussian "class justice" made it possible for his appointment to the executive to be "generally regarded as a victory of the tendency which Ledebour represents" — at least by those who were not of Ledebour's persuasion.[39]

The party career of Philipp Scheidemann began, like Braun's, in journalism. A type-setter by trade, he joined the party in his eighteenth year. Three years later, in 1886, he began to work actively for an illegal paper in his native Kassel. One of the leaders of the Kassel party was Wilhelm Pfannkuch, later a member of the executive.[40] The connection would stand Scheidemann in good stead.

Scheidemann's career in Hessen, like Braun's in East Prussia, was devoted to propaganda in hostile terrain. The small peasant population was no better disposed to Social Democracy than the servile laborers of East Prussia. For more than a decade, Scheidemann eked out a penurious existence by writing for Eduard David's

---

[35] Otto Braun, "Ein Vorschlag zur Budgetfrage," *N.Z.*, XXVIII, ii, 919–924.

[36] *Prot. S. P., 1910*, 180 (motion no. 94); 368–369.

[37] Five out of six Königsberger, including Haase and the regional secretary Hermann Linde, signed the motion for expulsion. Braun, as a member of the control commission, was not a member of the delegation, but was free to sign motions. Cf. *Prot. S. P., 1910*, 179–180, with "Präsenzliste," *ibid.*, 491–497.

[38] In 1908, he spoke in defense of the use of paid advertisements in propaganda calendars for the rural districts. (*Ibid., 1908*, 232.) In 1909, he presented the control commission's defense of a decision to expel a Stuttgart revisionist who had published the proceedings of a secret party meeting in an anti-Social Democratic newspaper. (*Ibid., 1909*, 482–483.) These were his only appearances on the congress rostrum, other than that of 1910, until he delivered the treasurer's report in 1912.

[39] *Ibid., 1912*, 321.

[40] Philipp Scheidemann, *Memoiren eines Sozialdemokraten* (Dresden, 1928), I, 17–23, 50ff.

Mitteldeutsche Sonntagszeitung, the *Kasseler Volksbote,* and the
Offenbach organ of Karl Ulrich, the "Red Duke" of Hessen.[41]
Although Scheidemann's years of training were thus spent in a
reformist milieu, he was by nature and temperament an agitator
and never seems to have been troubled by theoretical questions.
The ideas of Dr. David appear to have rolled off him like water
off a duck's back; his memoirs reveal no interest in the great revisionist debate which raged in those years.

In 1898, on the initiative of Pfannkuch and party treasurer
Gerisch, the executive invited Scheidemann to stand for the Reichstag in Solingen. The party in this cutlery center had been riven
by dissension arising out of the unwillingness of localist trade-
unions to enter the Central League of Metal Workers. The party
congress of 1897 resolved that, in view of the hopeless factionalism
prevailing in the district organization, the executive should name
a Reichstag candidate who would be above the local conflict.[42] Thus
began Scheidemann's reputation as a man capable of standing above
faction — a useful qualification for entry into the highest posts of
the party.

Defeated in 1898, Scheidemann stood again in Solingen in 1903,
and was returned. He became in the Reichstag the party's expert
on agriculture and live-stock raising — matters over which burning
controversy was scarcely likely to arise.[43]

The Social Democratic delegation in the Reichstag was divided,
even more clearly than the party as a whole, into well-defined
revisionist and radical wings. Each held its separate sessions to
determine its line on any important question and to name its
candidates to represent the party in debate. When the whole delegation convened in caucus, the issues would be fought out between
the wings and compromises arranged where necessary.[44] Scheidemann, as a man of the center, deplored the necessity of a choice,
but decided to associate himself with the radical wing which
generally enjoyed the support of the co-chairmen, Bebel and

[41] *Ibid.,* I, 59–98, *passim.*
[42] *Ibid.,* I, 144–159.
[43] *Ibid.,* I, 166–167.
[44] The separate sessions, until the great financial reform controversy in 1909, rarely
concerned matters of policy. Cf. W. Heine, "Sonderkonferenzen," *S.M.,* XVI (XVIII),
iii, 1144.

Singer. Scheidemann asserted in his memoirs that he joined the radicals only because he disliked "the overweening manner in which the revisionists treated the delegates of the opposite color." He prided himself on having repeatedly prevented "foolish resolutions" and on having finally split the radical wing. When the latter occurred is not clear.[45]

Until his election to the executive, Scheidemann seems to have remained deliberately aloof from party controversy. From 1906 to 1911 he attended only three of the six party congresses. At none of those three did he speak.[46] This was not due to any reticence on Scheidemann's part. No Social Democrat was more eager to cut a figure as a speaker than he. None ever dwelt more fondly — not to say vainly — on his oratorical successes.[47] One suspects that careerist considerations contributed to Scheidemann's reluctance to speak up in the vital party controversies of the period. A rather primitive desire for important positions and a scarcely concealed urge to "rate" both in the party and, later on, in the ruling circles of the Empire differentiate Scheidemann's character sharply from that of all his colleagues in the executive, whatever their political persuasion. Intra-party neutrality was the safe course for a man with Scheidemann's ambitions. His appointment to the executive was no windfall for the radicals.

At the opposite pole from Scheidemann in temperament and outlook stood Hugo Haase (1863–1919), the third new member of the executive and co-chairman of the party. Where Scheidemann was a facile agitator, Haase was soft-spoken and lacking in histrionic gift. Devoid as man can be of personal ambition, he was motivated by a deep sense of justice and right. Although a professed follower of Marx, Haase was by temperament and intellectual affinity closer to his fellow-Königsberger, Kant.[48] Social Democracy was for him perhaps less a political movement than a vehicle for moral protest and the assertion of humanistic principles.[49]

Haase was the only member of the executive who was of bour-

[45] Scheidemann, *Memoiren*, I, 175–176.
[46] Cf. "Präsenzliste" and "Sprechregister" in *Prot. S. P., 1906–1911*, inclusive.
[47] Scheidemann, *Memoiren*, I, 94–97, 139–141, 163–165, 180–187.
[48] He had numerous first editions of Kant's writings in his library. Cf. Haase, *Haase*, 26.
[49] Cf. Hilferding's evaluation, in *ibid.*, 85.

geois origin and who had university training. He made his career
in the party as a lawyer and legal thinker. For all the Marxist
jargon with which he surrounded his legal discourse, Haase adhered
to the classical ideal of the *Rechtsstaat*. He believed that the working class acquired, as it grew in strength, a "new world of thought
and feeling" different from that of the ruling class, and that, correspondingly, a gulf opened up between the prevailing form of law
and the sentiment of the people. It thus became both the interest
and the duty of Social Democracy to intercede for a system of law
which would "respect individual freedom and endow the accused
with stronger legal guarantees." [50] The "new world of thought and
feeling" in the field of law, which Haase attributed to the proletariat, was in fact little different from the world of thought and
feeling of the great humanitarian legal reform movement of the
eighteenth century. "Modern penal law must be filled with the
spirit of humanity," he wrote.[51] Haase saw the working class as
the instrument wherewith the reign of law and justice would be
established. He represented in his life and work the unique characteristic of German Social Democracy as protagonist of the uncom-
pleted bourgeois revolution.

Haase was more than a political opponent of the prevailing system of law and justice. He dedicated himself as a lawyer to the
defense of its victims. For three decades before the revolution he
defended individual workers, trade-unions, party officials, and party
editors in hundreds of legal actions brought against them. He became the most prominent trial lawyer of the German working class.
He took on the greatest cases of Social Democracy, such as that of
the alleged smugglers of revolutionary literature to Russia in 1904,
and the Liebknecht treason trial in 1907. He always refused on principle to accept payment for his services.[52]

The nomination of Haase to the executive in 1911 could well be
called a victory for the left center. Here was a tried and true
representative of the Erfurt ideology, a man for whom deviation
from principle was a source of pain. Although no revolutionary

---

[50] See his address to the Mannheim Congress, "Strafrecht, Strafprozess und Straf-
vollzug," *Prot. S. P., 1906*, 360–377.

[51] In the resolution on penal law which he drafted for the party, *ibid.*, 141.

[52] Haase, *Haase*, 8ff. Cf. also Noske, *Erlebtes*, 19.

in his tactical ideas, he never attacked the revolutionary wing. His record in the intra-party debates included defense of the pure anti-colonial tradition at Stuttgart in 1907, defense of the youth movement, and consistent hostility toward revisionism in theory and practice.[53] In political behavior as in temperament, Haase was *Prinzipienfestigkeit* incarnate.

If Haase was a staunch defender of principles, he was likewise an ardent advocate of party unity. Dissension in the party caused him almost as much pain as deviation from the traditional program.[54] It was characteristic that he should have taken the lead in formulating the compromise resolution on youth at the Nürnberg congress of 1908, wherein the independent youth organization was affirmed in principle but made well-nigh impossible in practice; or that in 1910, on behalf of those who had originally wished to exclude the revisionists if they should again violate party rules, he should have accepted the milder compromise resolution offered by Bebel. If a principle was clearly reaffirmed, Haase was inclined to make concessions to the right in the sphere of action, little aware of the dangerous dilemma into which this type of concession would one day bring him and his colleagues of the center. As long as there was even a remote chance to maintain the traditional party principles within the organization, Haase would strive for compromise. But when compromise was no longer possible, his radical conscience would prove stronger than his loyalty to the organization.

Such a man was not for the trade-unionists and revisionists. At the congress of 1911 they supported the candidacies of Braun and Scheidemann but not of Haase, though the latter was Bebel's candidate for co-chairman. Carl Legien nominated for that office his friend Friedrich Ebert. Ebert, he said, was better qualified by virtue of his skill in arbitrating "the serious and numerous differences in the several *Land* organizations." Moreover, Ebert, unlike Haase, had had wide administrative experience, and would thus be better able to guide the pending party reorganization.[55] Ulrich, the Hessian revisionist leader, was more explicit: he urged that the

---

[53] Cf. Hasse, *Haase*, 96; above, Ch. IV, n. 65 and text; Ch. VII, n. 81 and text.
[54] Cf., e.g., letter to Thea (his wife), 17 Sept. 1908, in Haase, *Haase*, 98.
[55] *Prot. S. P., 1911,* 371–372.

party avoid committing itself, through the election of Haase, "to a specific tendency" before the reorganization were completed. "In view of the tremendous task of holding the party together and united," Ebert would make a "more reliable" chairman.[56] Despite Ebert's refusal to run, the right wing cast 102 votes for him. Haase was nonetheless elected, and took his place as co-chairman of the party.[57]

The addition of Haase to the executive did not greatly strengthen the position of the radicals. Haase accepted membership in the executive only on a part-time basis so that he might continue his law practice.[58] Even had he had the time and inclination to modify the executive's policy, he was virtually without allies. Only Luise Zietz, the women's representative on the executive, was, like him, an ethical radical, devoted to maintenance of party principles and of intransigent opposition to the *status quo*.[59] Her time was largely occupied with her work as head of the women's organization. Of the six paid secretaries, only the septuagenarian Wilhelm Pfannkuch had any centrist — let alone radical — sympathies. Bebel, to be sure, for all his drift to the right, was still sensitive to leftist sentiment in the party. When he felt strongly, he would pull his full weight in the executive, often to the annoyance of the bureaucratic majority.[60] For the most part, however, the aging and ailing leader dwelt with his daughter in Switzerland, returning to Berlin only for the Reichstag sessions. He took little part in the decisions of the executive.

The real power in the executive had, by 1911, passed into Ebert's hands. According to Scheidemann, Ebert "ruled dictatorially — it is meant in the best sense — in this democratic corporation." Highly skilled in procedure and familiar with the business at hand, Ebert

---

[56] *Ibid.*, 373.

[57] *Ibid.*, 410.

[58] *Ibid.*, 373; Scheidemann, *Memoiren*, I, 103.

[59] Zietz was one of the few radical leaders who was not an intellectual. The wife of a Hamburg worker, she early developed a remarkable skill as an agitator and organizer. When her talent became manifest, she and her husband agreed that she should dedicate herself to the party while he continued as a common laborer to support her. Cf. Robert Michels, "Die deutsche Sozialdemokratie," *Archiv für Sozialwissenschaft und Sozialpolitik*, XXIII: 536, n. 81 (1906).

[60] Scheidemann, *Memoiren*, I, 119.

as acting chairman "almost always put through what he wanted." [61]
If in 1911 the effort of the revisionists and trade-unionists to give
Ebert the honor of the party co-chairmanship had to await Bebel's
death in 1913, the political power which went with the office was
already in his hands. Haase's presence as co-chairman changed
nothing in the power alignment. It merely enhanced the executive's
claim to represent the totality of the party, and could not fully
satisfy the radical leaders who pinned their hopes in 1911 and 1912
on more far-reaching reorganization of the party leadership.

iv. The Deflection of Reform and the Radical Revolt

No one at the Jena congress in 1911 seemed to have observed
that the Quarck resolution on party reorganization introduced an
element which had nowhere figured in the discussion arising after
the Morocco crisis: the reorganization of the control commission.
Yet this feature was to become the instrument for the frustration
of the movement for organizational reform. What was the control
commission, and why should it have been brought under review?

According to the party statute, the control commission, composed
of nine members elected annually by the congress, was empowered
to conduct a quarterly review of the executive's activities, and to
report to the congress on the executive's behavior. It also served
the party members as a court of appeal and complaint against
actions of the executive. It had the not inconsiderable competence
to elect the two unpaid associate members (*Beisitzer*) to the executive and to fill any vacancy in the executive which should arise
between congresses.[62] In fact, the control commission's powers went
beyond those stipulated in the organization statute. Considered part
of the *"Parteileitung,"* and consulting with the executive on all
important administrative and political matters, it participated actively in policy formation.[63]

Though the control commission had stronger radical representation than the executive, relations between the two bodies were,

---

[61] *Ibid.,* I, 103.

[62] The power to fill vacancies was the only one not exercised. Auer (d. 1909) and
Singer (d. 1911) were not replaced until the succeeding congresses.

[63] See above, Ch. V, n. 9 and text.

to all outward appearances, smooth enough.[64] I have found only one instance between 1906 and 1910 where the control commission overruled an action of the executive.[65] There may have been frictions which, out of a common interest in maintaining an appearance of leadership solidarity, would have been withheld from the party public. Before 1911, however, the discord could not have been great.

Quite unexpectedly, at the Jena congress of 1911, August Kaden, chairman of the control commission, revealed that its relations with the executive had become strained during the year. Kaden referred only vaguely to "certain occurrences." Undoubtedly the disagreement over action to be taken in the Morocco crisis, noted above, was among the chief of these. As a result of the friction, the two bodies entered into consultation concerning the extent of the commission's powers. They agreed that "in view of the extent of the administrative activity of the party executive, it would be better for the mutual relations [of the two organs] if the control commission should give up all active participation in the leadership (*mitleitende Tätigkeit*), and confine itself solely to the exercise of the rights and duties laid down in . . . the organization statute." Henceforth, said Kaden, the executive would report quarterly on its activity in a joint session "for the orientation" of the control commission — a formulation not very promising for the future powers of that body. At the same time, "the control commission deemed it necessary for the more effective fulfillment of its functions to be represented by one of its members at all the more important conferences called by the party executive." [66]

It was no doubt at the behest of the executive that the Quarck

[64] The members of the commission were predominantly centrist. Only two revisionists were members at any one time from 1906 on: Ehrhardt (replaced by Timm, another Bavarian revisionist, after 1907) and Brühne. Klara Zetkin was the only representative of the extreme left, though she would no doubt find a frequent ally in Wilhelm Bock, the veteran radical leader of Gotha and later patriarch of the Independent Social Democrats.

[65] In 1907 the radical organization of the Berlin suburban district of Teltow-Beeskow-Storkow petitioned the executive to institute proceedings against certain of its members who had failed to vote in the 1907 elections. The executive's refusal to do so was overruled by the control commission on appeal by the local. Cf. *Prot. S. P., 1907*, 203.

[66] *Ibid., 1911*, 202–203.

motion had included the control commission in the proposed reorganization. The delegates voted the motion without a moment's
discussion as to why the control commission's functions and structure were to be reviewed.

In the first issue of the *Sozialistische Monatshefte* to appear after
the congress, Eduard Bernstein addressed himself to the reorganization question. For him, the executive was quite satisfactory in its
present composition. How things had changed since 1905! It had
but one flaw: its failure to represent the regional differentiation of
the party. To remedy this defect, Bernstein said, the executive ought
to be constructed of representatives of the federal units of the
party.[67] Bernstein recognized, however, that a federal structure of
the executive would again give rise to the demand for proportional
representation. An executive built on the proportional principle
would be both unwieldy in size and have the disadvantage of the
Bundesrat; that is, Prussian preponderance.[68] Translated into the
terms of Social Democratic political demography, this could mean
radical dominance.

If the territorial or federal principle was therefore impractical
for the executive, said Bernstein, let it be applied to the control
commission. Let the control commission be elected by the federal
(regional) units of the party. "The important [point] is that this
grouping would not have a party-factional character," he argued.[69]
This was a half-truth. Bernstein admitted that, "depending on the
region, the radical element would predominate in one, the reformist
in another"; hence all factions would be represented. As we know,
the reformist elements were stronger at the regional than at the
local level. Bernstein too recognized this, if only obliquely, when
he commended a "healthy democratic federalism" to counteract
the "factional passion" which could play into the elections of the
control commission "through the brusque application of the majority principle."[70] In terms of the political composition of the
party institutions, the federal principle would represent a conservative check on the majority principle.

[67] Eduard Bernstein, "Reorganization der Parteileitung," *S.M.*, XV (XVII), iii,
1326.
[68] *Ibid.*, 1326–1327.
[69] *Ibid.*, 1327–1328.
[70] *Ibid.*, 1327–1328.

Bernstein had advanced this idea during the reorganization discussions of 1905, but at that time it had fallen on barren soil.[71]
The executive, then close to the radicals, had no wish to favor
federal control over its activities. But now that regional organizations had been established throughout the country, largely in the
hands of a conservative bureaucracy, and now that the executive
was on the opposite side of the political fence from the radicals,
the federal principle could be used to buttress the conservatism of
the central authorities. Federalism was transformed by politics from
a defensive weapon of the revisionists into an offensive weapon of
the executive and its allies. The revisionist advocates of the *Staaten-
bund* in 1905 were the supporters of the *Bundesstaat* in 1911.

To the intense annoyance of the radicals, the executive exercised
firm control over the work of the reorganization commission established by the second Jena congress. It not only prepared the first
draft of the statutory changes, but joined the sessions of the commission in full strength and voted in its decisions. The balance
between right and left in the twenty-two man commission was, by
the addition of ten members of the executive, shifted in favor of the
right.[72]

Completing its deliberations on 14 May 1912, the commission
shortly thereafter released its proposals. In every respect they
represented a defeat for the radicals. The executive was left exactly
as it had been — though to change it somehow was the *raison d'être*
of the commission. The control commission was confined to re-
viewing only the administrative activity of the executive and to
acting as a court of appeal. The remainder of its former functions,
including the previously unwritten right of participation with the
executive in "deciding important political questions affecting the
party as a whole," were turned over to a new institution, the party
council (*Parteiausschuss*).[73] This body was, in all essentials, built
to Bernstein's specifications. It was to be composed of thirty-two
representatives of the *Land* or regional organizations, nominated

[71] *Ibid.*, IX (XI), ii, 728–729.

[72] These complaints were registered by Georg Ledebour in "Die Reorganisierung
des Parteivorstandes," *N.Z.*, XXX, ii, 457–458.

[73] The literal translation of *Ausschuss*, "committee," conveys the character of the
institution less adequately than our word "council."

by the latter, and elected by the party congress. As a further rebuff
to the radicals, the Social Democratic Reichstag members, among
whom were most of the prominent radical leaders, were to be deprived of their ex-officio right to participate in the party congress.
Henceforth, only one-third of the deputies were to be permitted
to attend as voting delegates.[74]

The Reichstag session had just closed when the reorganization
commission's proposals were released. The radical deputies were
furious over the content of the "reform." Under the leadership of
Georg Ledebour and Gustav Hoch — the latter was a member of
the reorganization commission — a conference of some thirty dissatisfied radical deputies and certain minority members of the
commission was called at Eisenach on 16 June 1912. The conference
discussed plans to accomplish the radicals' original purpose, the
politicization of the executive, and to combat the proposed party
council.

If the radicals could have done as they pleased, they no doubt
would have recommended the replacement of certain paid secretaries on the executive with men of their own kind. Deposing a
member of the executive, however, was politically impossible.[75] The
Eisenach conference therefore proposed the enlargement of the executive by seven to nine unpaid members who would give the
"political" element a majority. This suggestion went beyond the
feeble recommendations of the radical locals to the congress of
1911, which were confined to the addition of two more paid secretaries. The Eisenachers now formulated their proposal in overt
opposition to paid secretaries as political leaders. The latter would
provide administrative continuity, but the transient, unpaid members would reflect in the executive the changing political will of the
party congress which would elect them.[76]

The proposed party council could find no favor with the radicals.

---

[74] The May draft is reproduced in *Prot. S. P., 1912,* 154–158. The smaller regional
organizations were to be fused to bring the number in the party council down from
43 to 32.

[75] The *Magdeburger Volksstimme* accused the participants in the Eisenach conference of plotting to change the personnel of the executive, which the conference
members denied. *Prot. S. P., 1912,* 383–384. Cf. also Ledebour in *N.Z.,* XXX, ii,
458.

[76] *N.Z.,* XXX, ii, 459–461, 920–925; *Prot. S. P., 1912,* 314–316.

Far from solving the problem of political control by the bureau-crats, they said, the council would only aggravate it since its mem-bers would be drawn from the regional organizations.[77] It would be merely a conference of the regional leaders (*Bezirkskonferenz*) under another name.[78] Moreover, the council members would be chosen by regional organizations of which some, like Württemberg, had constitutions incompatible with the party principle of equal representation.[79] Above all, the radicals felt that the party council was designed to give "a disproportionately strong representation to the regions with weak organizations," and thus to accord to the revisionists "a position of power beyond their actual [numerical] strength." [80]

The revisionists held firmly to the federal principle, insisting that the new council was a counter-measure against excessive centraliza-tion and its threat to liberty in the party.[81] This argument was a hold-over from the days of 1900–05 when the revisionists had indeed to fight for their political life. The party council of 1912, however, was not a federalizing, but a centralizing institution. Its federal composition was but a means to strengthen its conservative charac-ter. Not to protect a hapless minority from the tyranny of the majority was the new institution devised, but to strengthen the executive in the pursuit of policies unpopular in the metropolitan strongholds of Social Democratic radicalism.

In the urban centers, resentment ran high against the distortion of the reform from its original purpose. An unusually large number of local organizations submitted to the Chemnitz party congress (1912) motions against the party council and in favor of enlarging the executive by from five to nine members.[82]

The strength of the protest raised by the cities and by the radical leaders who had conferred at Eisenach led in September 1912 to certain revisions in the statutory proposals drafted for the Chemnitz congress. The party council was no longer to "decide" but only to

[77] *N.Z.*, XXX, ii, 923.
[78] *Prot. S. P., 1912,* 311.
[79] *Ibid.,* 308.
[80] Georg Ledebour, "Parteiausschuss, Kontrollkommission und Fraktionsvertretung," *N.Z.*, XXX, ii, 510.
[81] *S.M.*, XVI (XVIII), ii, 832, 910–913.
[82] *Prot. S. P., 1912,* 161–164, 173, 176.

"consult" with the executive on important political matters. The clause restricting the control commission's competence to the review of the executive's administrative activity was dropped in favor of the traditional more general powers of review. The election of the two associate members of the executive was transferred from the party council (it had previously been vested in the control commission) to the party congress. Such were the concessions — all minor — to radical opinion. At the same time, the procedure for the election of the members of the party council was clarified. In the May draft of the reorganization committee's report, the regional organizations were to nominate the candidates, the party congress to elect them. The party congress was now removed from the process.[83]

At the congress itself the debate was heated but the changes few.[84] Ledebour succeeded in restoring the right of all Reichstag deputies to attend the congresses. He failed to secure acceptance of a modest amendment which would have left open the number of unpaid members of the executive. The number remained fixed at two.[85] The many motions to abandon the idea of a party council and to enlarge the executive were not put to a vote. The radicals, conforming to the tradition of party unity by voting in favor of a measure which was sure to win, abandoned the field in the end. The official reform was adopted with only eight dissenting votes.[86]

Actually, the radical reform efforts were not realistic. Even assuming acceptance of their proposal to build a non-bureaucratic majority in the executive, that majority would never have been composed purely of radicals. The executive would have thrown its full weight against their election. It could quite properly have represented the packing of the executive with radicals as a threat to party unity, and the congress would have responded to such an argument.

Thus the radicals' campaign for party reform ended in a rout. The bureaucratic majority on the executive remained unchanged.

[83] The two drafts appear in *ibid.*, 154–158 (May version), and 520–524 (September version). For the changes, cf. sections 14, 20, 21 and 23.
[84] *Ibid.*, 296–327, *passim.*
[85] *Ibid.*, 182 (motion no. 203); 327.
[86] *Ibid.*, 327.

The control commission, which had dared to cross the executive on the Morocco question, had its wings duly clipped. The commission's essential functions and more were taken over by the party council, an institution which would serve as an impressive rubber-stamp for the executive's actions and policies. The conservative federalism of an earlier day became transformed, through the party council, into a conservative centralism. The tables had been well turned on the would-be reformers. The institutional changes of 1912 secured the power of the executive more firmly than ever against the mounting radical opposition.

v. The Political Significance of the Reform Movement

The organization crisis of 1911–12 represents a milestone in the development of the great schism in Social Democracy. That the demand for reform should have arisen out of the Morocco crisis, out of a question of action in the face of the threat of war, was in itself of great significance. How many times had the executive failed to satisfy the left radicals or the center with no one turning a thought to a change in the leadership! In the Morocco crisis of 1905–06, Liebknecht, Eisner, and a handful of others had stood virtually isolated in their Cassandra-like demands to intensify the fight against war. In the Noske debate and at the Stuttgart congress of 1907, the issue had become more pressing and the division on policy clearer. In both cases, a polarizing tendency had manifested itself: on the one hand the executive, with trade-union support, moved closer to the revisionist position[87] on the national question; on the other, the radicals pushed for a stronger agitation against war and imperialism than had been the party's wont. Still there was no thought in 1905 or 1907 of changing the leadership. Not until the second Morocco crisis did a substantial portion of the radicals come to the conviction that the executive could not be trusted to execute the policies which they held dear. Where in 1907 the question of war and imperialism arose as an issue of policy, in 1911 it became transformed into an issue of intra-party power, a struggle for control over institutions.

The crisis of 1911 gave a new cohesiveness to the radical opposi-

[87] Eisner always excepted.

tion. We have used the word "radical" throughout the discussion of this episode since the factional line between the left radicals and the center, so clear on the mass strike issue in 1910, was, though perceptible, not pronounced. The political divide ran through the center. Kautsky, Hilferding, and Lipinski stayed aloof from the movement against the executive, as did the bulk of the centrist bureaucracy: such men as Wels, Ernst, and König.[88] The leadership of the opposition was in the hands of the left center: the Reichstag deputies Ledebour, Dittman, Hoch, Stadthagen, Albrecht, and Emmel. The clique which they now formed, the "Eisenacher" group, was the nucleus of the later parliamentary opposition which broke off in 1917 to form the Independent Social Democratic Party. Veteran parliamentarians, they belonged to the second, parliamentary level of party leadership. There was nothing novel in their siding with each other on matters of party policy. We have met them frequently as defenders of radical tradition. What was new was that they should, in effect, plot against the executive.

"*Sonderkonferenzler!*" — that term of opprobrium was hurled at Ledebour and his company again and again at the Chemnitz congress. *Sonderkonferenz* meant, roughly, a factional caucus, a meeting held by a group of party members outside the framework of the party institutions in order to put one over on the party. For years the *Sonderkonferenz* had been resorted to by the revisionists in order to work out their plans for voting budgets in the federal states.[89] The radicals had been the ones to condemn the practice then, to raise the cry of conspiracy. Now the tables were turned. The leftist opposition was the group plotting outside the framework, sinning against the party's political ethic. As in 1911 there had been an effort to turn the Morocco question into a "Luxemburg affair," so in 1912 the reorganization discussion was diverted into a debate on the admissibility of *Sonderkonferenzen*. The proposals of the radicals could, at least in part, be discredited by the method which they had used in formulating and promoting them.[90]

[88] Kautsky took the view that the question was one for the party practitioner, not for the theorist. Cf. *N.Z.*, XXX, ii, 884. Hilferding, who celebrated the Chemnitz congress as marking the end of revisionism, completely supported the executive's position on the reorganization. *Ibid.*, 1005.

[89] Cf. Bebel's historical review of *Sonderkonferenzen*, *Prot. S. P., 1912*, 391–392.

[90] Cf. *ibid.*, 380–403, *passim*.

Feeling against the procedure of the Ledebour group was by no means confined to the party's conservative elements. Even the organizations of Lübeck, Köln, and Niederbarnim, which were anything but reformist, offered resolutions condemning the *Sonderkonferenz*.[91] The radical oppositon suffered from its offenses against the party's ethos and its myth of unity, as the revisionists had in an earlier day.[92] The ethos had remained intact; but those who were impelled to violate it for a higher cause had exchanged roles with their erstwhile prosecutors.

Thus the question of party discipline became a problem for the radical opposition. The very men who had upheld discipline against the revisionists now were victims of their own principle. There was, however, a difference between the revisionist breaches of discipline and that of the *Sonderkonferenzler* of 1912. The former had broken organizational discipline in order to pursue aims or actions not sanctioned by the party; the latter broke it in order to create the conditions for the observance in practice of a policy on war accepted by the party.[93] Once the leadership ceased to represent in action the professed principles of the party, the radicals had to choose between loyalty to the organization and loyalty to principle. In 1911–12, this phenomenon of divided loyalty, which was to be a major psychological problem for many a Social Democrat after the outbreak of war, first manifested itself in serious form. To men for whom, through years of combat with the revisionists, party discipline had become a cardinal virtue, the decision to take

[91] Nine other organizations offered similar motions. Cf. *Prot. S. P., 1912,* 168–169; 174–175. At least one revisionist, Wolfgang Heine, opposed the interdiction of *Sonderkonferenzen* as contrary to party democracy. He made an exception, however, for the left radicals. If they should ever begin to resort to "secret conventicles," the party must expose them. He felt that the Eisenach conference, while not promoted by the left radicals, played into their hands by assaulting the leadership. See Heine, "Sonderkonferenzen," *S.M.,* XVI (XVIII), iii, 1139–1146.

[92] The motions condemning the Eisenach conference were not adopted, however; Bebel threw his weight in the balance to this end. The resolution on the question simply expressed the "urgent wish" that *Sonderkonferenzen* be avoided in future. Cf. *Prot. S. P., 1912,* 391–392, 529.

[93] Ströbel argued on behalf of the *Sonderkonferenzler* that their action was no breach of discipline at all, since their conference was held to discuss a matter not yet decided, rather than to break from established policy. See Heinrich Ströbel, "Sonderkonferenzen," *N.Z.,* XXX, ii, 926–927; also Hoch, *Prot. S. P., 1912,* 382–385.

up the cudgels for an idea against the organizational leaders could not have been easy. That the old guard radicals found it hard to take such action was revealed by their complete retreat in the voting. Despite that retreat, however, they showed that they would not follow blindly wherever the executive led. Through their movement for organizational reform, they contributed to their own psychological preparation for the deeper crisis to come.

Chapter IX

THE ELECTORAL ALLIANCE OF 1912 AND
THE LEFT RADICAL OFFENSIVE

"While the storm-clouds gathered ever more heavily on the world horizon, an almost inexplicable pressure weighed on the political life of Germany," wrote Chancellor Bethmann-Hollweg of the last prewar years. There was, he rightly observed, no sense of gratification in Germany's economic prosperity and in her national achievements. "Instead, malaise and dejection imparted a depressing tone to political party activity, which lacked any progressive impulse. The word *'Reichsverdrossenheit'* [dissatisfaction with empire] rose up out of the darkness of an earlier time of troubles."[1]

The chancellor shared the frustration engendered by the hopeless condition of unresolved tension into which the German body politic had fallen. He aimed to satisfy all social strata by minor concessions to each, and thus to weld the nation into a greater unity. It was his tragic lot that the society of his time had passed the point where a policy of uniformly distributed concessions could succeed. The long era of stagnation had made all classes and parties, except perhaps the Center, rigid beyond the possibility of compromise. The most needed reform, that of the Prussian constitution, could be achieved only at the expense of the Junkers. The chancellor's effort in 1910 to approach the problem in a gradualist spirit had proved satisfying to no parties, exasperating to all; he had been forced to give up the entire idea. Even his reforms of the year 1911, the last in which any progress was achieved, failed of their political intent. The Reich Insurance Act, designed to cement the working classes to the crown, not only fell far short of labor's hopes, but was so loaded with provisions to curtail the influence of the trade-unionists and Social Democrats in its administration that it only

---

[1] Theobald von Bethmann-Hollweg, *Betrachtungen zum Weltkrieg* (Berlin, 1919), I, 95.

exacerbated their hostility to the state.[2] The effort to allay Franco-German antagonism through Alsatian constitutional reform was turned to dross by the second Morocco crisis, the Kaiser's repeated threats to smash the new constitution, and the high-handed behavior of the military against the Alsatian population in the Zabern affair.[3] The government's introduction of direct, universal suffrage in Alsace-Lorraine in 1911, moreover, made the more glaring its unwillingness to grant the same right to the citizens of Prussia. The only successful reform was the introduction of a personal property tax in 1913 to cover enormous new military expenditures. Otherwise, there was complete atrophy of public policy and rigid maintenance of the uneasy *status quo*. Stagnation on the surface, tension and ferment beneath it, these were the outstanding characteristics of the Reich's politics in the last prewar years.

Reichsverdrossenheit had is parallel in *Parteiverdrossenheit*. By 1912 the Social Democratic party numbered nearly a million members. Yet it stood powerless in the German political arena: powerless to win the fundamental constitutional reform upon which in turn further social reforms depended; powerless to stop the armaments race and the recurrent threats of war; powerless to resist increasing pressure upon the labor movement from the employers, the bureaucracy, and the courts.

The problem of the party, posed in its broadest terms, was how to break out of the closing ring of its hostile environment, how to achieve some success commensurate with its numerical strength. The political patience of the party had been easy enough to maintain when it was small. Now that it was great, patience was running out under the impact of the cumulative frustration of years. And the impatience to which it gave place was not of one variety but of two: reformist and revolutionary. Each wing had its answer to the tactical problem. In the elections of 1912, the reformist policy of alliance with the Liberal parties was tried in earnest for the first time on a national scale. This effort and its failure to

[2] Cf. Karl Severing, "Politische Tendenzen in der Reichsversicherungsordnung," *S.M.*, XV (XVII), ii, 675–685; Robert Schmidt, "Die Reichsversicherungsordnung," *ibid.*, iii, 1225–1229.

[3] Johannes Ziekursch, *Politische Geschichte des neuen deutschen Kaiserreiches* (Frankfurt, 1930), III, 226–229; *N.Z.*, XXX, ii, 258; Erich Eyck, *Das persönliche Regiment Wilhelms II* (Erlenbach-Zürich, 1948), 606–607, 665–672.

realize the hopes placed in it revitalized the left radicals once again in that dialectical process which has become so familiar to us. The left radicals' theoretical structure acquired its final pre-revolutionary form, and their agitation for a new tactic brought the division within the party to a new level of maturity. This process of polarization, a reenactment at a deeper and more fateful level of the reformist drive and the radical counterdrive which followed the dissolution of the Bülow Bloc in 1909-10, will be our concern in the present chapter.

i. The Electoral Alliance of 1912

Ever since the mass movement for the suffrage had been suspended in 1910, the party had been busily preparing for the elections of 1912. "At the next Reichstag elections," the leaders had promised, "we shall deliver the next great blow." [4] The elections would give Social Democracy the chance to reverse the defeat of 1907 and to resume its march of progress. Internecine rancor would be forgotten while all factions joined in the common cause. For the leaders of Social Democracy, as for those of the German state, the Reichstag elections had come to serve as a lightning rod for the deflection of discontent which might otherwise, as in 1905-06 and 1910, seek its outlet in more dangerous forms of political expression.

At the congress of Jena in September 1911, Bebel laid down the plan for what he bellicosely called the *Wahlschlacht*. [5] He focussed attention on domestic issues: the inequitable taxation system, the high cost of living, the threats to the right of association, the possibility of new and higher tariffs and greater military expenditures. The mounting danger of war had only a minor place in Bebel's address. He attacked armaments expansion rather for the financial burdens it imposed than for its meaning to the peace of Europe. At the very congress at which a significant portion of the secondary party leadership, in the controversy over Morocco and party reorganization, was according primacy to the problems of foreign policy and war, the executive placed domestic questions in the forefront for the election campaign.

[4] Paul Frölich in Luxemburg, *Werke*, III, 491.
[5] *Prot. S. P., 1911*, 376-392.

Corresponding to this emphasis, the executive concentrated on the Blue-Black Bloc as the main enemy at the polls. It was therefore necessary to soft-pedal those problems — such as foreign policy and the Reich Insurance Act — where the political watershed lay between Social Democrats and Progressives rather than between National Liberals and Centrists. The leadership mapped its campaign not on the basis of socialist isolation, which had prevailed from 1907 to the break-up of the Bülow Bloc and again during the mass movement of 1910, but on the assumption of coöperation with the bourgeois parties. The new campaign strategy, in all respects the opposite of that of 1907, marked a victory for the revisionists who had been advocating such a course ever since the collapse of the Bülow Bloc.[6] The Jena congress accepted the change with little opposition.[7] The Social Democrats thus resolved to try to break the stalemate of German politics with the help of the Liberal parties.

In conformity with past policy, the congress laid down a set of conditions for supporting the candidates of other parties in run-off elections from which the Social Democrats would have been eliminated. The conditions were less stringent than those of 1903.[8] In 1903 the Social Democrats demanded of other candidates opposition to existing tariffs on food products; in 1912, merely opposition to further increase in tariffs on consumer goods. The condition of opposition to all "exceptional laws" against the working class and its organizations in 1903 was now, in view of current proposals to limit the right of coalition and to sharpen the penal code against labor, narrowed and made more specific. The party demanded in 1898 opposition "to every increase in the standing army and navy"; in 1903, "to every military and naval bill which would require increased taxes." Of these conditions, nothing remained in 1912 but a requirement to oppose indirect taxes on consumer goods.[9]

---

[6] See *S.M.*, XIII (XV)–XV (XVII), *passim*.

[7] One speaker complained that Bebel had concentrated his fire exclusively against the Center Party, and insufficiently against the Liberals. Bebel's answer, that the Liberals, sinners though they were, were the lesser of two evils, satisfied the congress. *Prot. S. P., 1911*, 398.

[8] No uniform national conditions were laid down in 1907.

[9] Cf. Walter Croll, *Die Entwicklung der Anschauungen über soziale Reform in der deutschen Sozialdemokratie* (Berlin, 1915), 50–51.

Had the party held on to the anti-military conditions, it could have found no Progressive candidates to support; its concentration of the campaign against the Blue-Black Bloc required that the old demand be jettisoned. The change in the Progressives' attitude toward armaments after 1906 was thus acting back upon Social Democracy. The pursuit of allies for domestic reform on the one hand, and opposition to Germany's foreign and military policy on the other, were increasingly incompatible aims.

When the long-awaited elections were held on 12 January 1912, Social Democracy scored a resounding victory. The results of the first ballot showed how well adapted was the campaign strategy to the mood of the voters, and how splendidly the fully developed organization had proven itself as a vote-getting machine. Every third voter cast his ballot for Social Democracy. The party polled 4,250,329 votes — nearly a million more than in 1907 and over twice as many as the Center, its nearest contender.[10]

Together, the anti-Blue-Black parties (Social Democratic, Progressive, and National Liberal) polled 61.4 per cent of the popular vote on the first ballot. With respect to mandates, however, the situation was less favorable. Of the 206 seats (out of 397) settled in the first ballot, the three anti-Blue-Black parties had won only sixty-eight. Of those, the Social Democrats captured sixty-four seats, the National Liberals only four, and the Progressives, despite their 1,528,886 votes, none at all.[11]

Under these circumstances, the Social Democratic executive entered into negotiations with the Progressive party leadership for a nation-wide agreement on mutual support in the run-off elections. Kautsky later described the bright hopes which the party leaders attached to securing the agreement:

There was the prospect of forcing the Blue-Black Bloc into the minority, to create a determined liberal majority even without the right wing of the National Liberals, and to make a government against the left impossible. Within this left, however, our influence would have had to be dominant . . . Liberalism would have been powerless without us, the Progressives [would have been] in deepest hostility with the Blue-Black

[10] Paul Hirsch and Bruno Borchardt, *Die Sozialdemokratie und die Wahlen zum deutschen Reichstag* (Berlin, 1912), 24–25.
[11] *Prot. S. P., 1912*, 27–28.

Bloc because of their electoral deal with us, so that they would have had no choice but to fight an energetic battle with us against the right and [against] any Junker regime . . .[12]

The Progressives drove a hard bargain. They promised to support the Social Democratic candidates in thirty-one districts where the opposing candidate was an adherent of the Blue-Black Bloc. In exchange they demanded not only that the Social Democrats reciprocate, but also that they (1) withdraw the conditions of support laid down at the Jena congress; and (2) withdraw the Social Democratic candidates in sixteen districts in which Social Democrats and Progressives faced each other in run-off elections. The Social Democratic executive rejected the last condition in its original form but agreed to suspend all campaign activity in the sixteen districts — to hold no rallies, to distribute no pamphlets, and to conduct no canvassing even on the day of election. Hard as these terms were, the executive accepted them in the hope of enlarging both the number of Social Democratic mandates and the Progressive representation in the Reichstag. The executive viewed the surrender of the sixteen districts as the price necessary to prevent the Progressives from seeking "a connection on the right." Given the fundamental aim of Social Democracy in the elections, to reduce the Conservative-Centrist coalition to a minority in the Reichstag, the agreement made complete sense.[13]

To make the broad concessions demanded by the Progressives was easy enough, but to have them executed by the local Social Democratic organizations was another matter. The agreement went far beyond the stipulations of the Jena congress for the endorsement of non-socialist candidates. The executive maintained secrecy on the full content of the electoral deal lest the left radicals raise a protest even in the midst of the campaign.[14] Only the regional secretaries and the affected electoral district organizations were informed in a confidential circular of the decision to "mute" the

[12] *Vorwärts*, 6 Mar. 1912.

[13] For the full content of the agreement, see *Prot. S. P., 1912*, 29–31. The executive's formal justification is given by Kautsky in *Vorwärts*, 5, 6, and 7 March 1912; and by Scheidemann at the Chemnitz congress, *Prot. S. P., 1912*, 327–338. For less official justifications, see Bernstein, *S.M.*, XVI (XVIII), iii, 1278, and Hilferding, *N.Z.*, XXX, ii, 1006.

[14] *Prot. S. P., 1912*, 337.

campaign in the sixteen run-off elections with the Progressives. A public announcement confined itself to urging support for the liberal candidates against those further to the right.[15] Even Bebel, who was absent from Berlin at the time of the deal, was confronted with a *fait accompli*. Scheidemann tells us that Bebel had "serious worries" not only about the value of the agreement, but also about the reaction of the party to it.[16]

In the sixteen affected district organizations the reaction to the orders from on high was one of shock and surprise, where not of indignation. Precisely because the agreement covered the districts in which the Progressives were relatively strong, the local comrades had come to look upon them as the main enemy. The feelings of hostility and competition aroused in months of campaigning could not be put aside without emotional repercussions. For forty years, a leader of the Hirschberg organization complained to the executive, his district had fought a particularly reactionary Progressive party local: "Do you expect of the comrades there that they should understand the *mot d'ordre* to mute the campaign?"[17] In Hagen, formerly the seat of the "Socialist-eater" Eugen Richter, the local organization refused to go along, and the executive finally granted permission for the resumption of the campaign.[18] The party comrades in Nordhausen simply kicked over the traces and continued, over the strenuous objections of the executive, to prosecute their campaign to a successful conclusion.[19] The district of Liegnitz did not bolt, but came near to doing so.[20] In eleven of the sixteen districts pledged to the Progressives, the Social Democrats had secured a plurality over the Progressives on the first balloting; one can comprehend the difficulty of reconciling the membership in those constituencies to calling off their campaign. Although in the majority of the affected districts most of the voters for the eliminated rightist parties would have given the victory to the Progressive candidate, it was still a wrench for the comrades to surrender

---

[15] *Ibid.*, 29–30.

[16] Philipp Scheidemann, *Memoiren eines Sozialdemokraten* (Dresden, 1928), I, 109.

[17] *Prot. S. P., 1912*, 347. Cf. also the remarks of the Elberfeld delegate, *ibid.*, 346.

[18] *Ibid.*, 339–340.

[19] *Ibid.*, 332–333, 344–345. Nordhausen's deputy, Dr. Oskar Cohn, subsequently became an important figure in the Independent Social Democratic Party.

[20] *Ibid.*, 350.

without a fight. Nevertheless, discipline was maintained in fourteen districts which were duly delivered to the Progressive candidate.[21]

Beyond the districts covered by the agreement, the Social Democrats threw their votes behind the Progressives in every run-off contest where the Progressive faced a non-socialist candidate. In twenty-one such contests out of twenty-six, Social Democracy was the decisive element. The electoral statistics show that the party mobilized its voters *en bloc* for the run-offs. Even in the five contests in this category lost by the Progressives, the Social Democratic vote was fully mobilized, but was not the decisive factor in the outcome.[22]

Of their forty-two seats in the Reichstag, the Progressives owed thirty-five, over 80 per cent, to the Social Democratic Party: fourteen by concession under the secret electoral agreement, and twenty-one to the successful execution of the party policy laid down at Jena. The Progressives, in effect, owed their continuation as a political party to the electoral policy of Social Democracy and the discipline of its voters.

If we examine the electoral alliance from the opposite side, we find a striking contrast both in the attitude of the leadership and the behavior of the followers. The Progressive executive's call to its voters, while it gave primacy to "the shattering of the Blue-Black Bloc" in the run-off election, included only a negative implication that Social Democratic candidates were to be supported against the Conservatives and their allies. Social Democracy was not mentioned by name, while the voters were told: "The National Liberal

[21] The run-off returns in the fourteen districts show almost no increase in Social Democratic vote. The returns for both first ballot and run-off are given in Hirsch and Borchardt, *Sozialdemokratie und Wahlen*, 76–154, *passim*. The districts involved were Oberbarnim, Liegnitz, Schönau-Hirschberg, Apenrade-Flensburg (where the anti-German Danes seem to have voted Social Democratic despite the lack of a campaign), Lauenburg, Merseburg-Querfurt, Ditmarschen, Calw (Nagold), Balingen-Rottweil, Meiningen, Schaumburg-Lippe, Lippe-Detmold, Oldenburg I and II.

[22] *Ibid.*, 68–158, *passim*, for the returns for the constituencies won by the Progressives: Landkreis Königsberg, Tilsit, Gumbinnen, Züllichau-Krossen, Rügen-Franzburg-Stralsund, Grimmen-Greifswald, Glogau, Lüben-Bunzlau, Löwenberg, Schleswig-Eckernförde, Tondern-Husum (where the Danes were co-responsible with the Social Democrats for the Progressive victory), Oldenburg-Plön, Emden-Norden, Minden-Lübbecke, Freudenstadt-Oberndorf, Ulm, Freiburg i. Br., Parchim-Ludwigslust, Malchin-Waren, Zabern, Schweinitz-Wittenberg. The lost constituencies were Labiau-Wehlau, Fraustadt, Hall-Oehringen, Bingen, and Waldeck.

Party, which is allied with us, is to be supported against all opponents." [23] This although the National Liberals opposed equal suffrage for Prussia, a cardinal feature in the Progressive program! It was a far cry from the hopes of a leftward orientation of the Progressives cherished by many Social Democrats. Where the choice lay between Bebel and Bassermann, the Progressive executive chose Bassermann as a matter of principle. Its support to Social Democracy under the agreement was confined to areas where the opponent stood for the Conservative Party or one of its allies.

For the voters of the Progressive Party, even the preference which its leaders expressed for Social Democracy over the Blue-Black Bloc went too far. They honored their leaders' pledges to the Social Democrats more often in the breach than in the observance. Of the thirty-one districts where support was promised the Social Democrats, the Progressive voters were decisive in twenty-five. In twenty-one of these, a majority of the Progressives threw their vote to the Conservative contender, agreement or no; only in four districts did the Progressives give Social Democracy a majority of their votes. The wholesale defection of the Progressive voters from their leaders' policy cost the Social Democrats fourteen seats: eleven to the Junkers, two to the *Reichspartei,* and one to the *Wirtschaftliche Vereinigung.*[24] In eleven districts the limited support given by the Progressive voters was sufficient (though a majority of their vote on the first ballot in only three cases) to give victory to the Social Democrat.[25] The Social Democrats won four more seats covered

---

[23] *Prot. S. P., 1912,* 31.

[24] The districts were: (1) to the Junkers: Ruplin-Templin, Zauch-Belzig, Königsberg (Neumark), Uckermünde-Isedom, Sagan-Sprottau, Landshut-Jauer, Rothenburg-Hoyerswerda, Mühlhausen-Langensalza, Bielefeld-Wiedenbrück, Hagenow, and Gustrow; (2) to the *Reichspartei:* Westpriegnitz, and Mansfeld; (3) to the *Wirtschaftliche Vereinigung:* Giessen. See Hirsch and Borchardt, *Sozialdemokratie und Wahlen,* 76–148, *passim.*

[25] Potsdam-Osthavelland, Kottbus-Spremberg, Striegau-Schweidenitz, Grünberg-Freistadt (where the Progressives voted three to two for the Social Democrat), Jerichow I and II, Bitterfeld-Delitzsch, Eschwege-Schmalkalden, Heilbronn (three to two for the Social Democrat), Jena, Altenburg, and Strassburg-Land. Strassburg was the only place where the Progressives offered solid support (five to one of their votes on the first ballot) to the Social Democratic candidate. Since the rival candidate in this constituency was an Alsatian irredentist, nationalist motives may explain this departure from the norm. *Ibid.,* 77–158, *passim.*

by the agreement, but in these (as in two of those lost) the Progressive vote was either not measurable or not decisive.[26]

The final results reflected the difference in the behavior of the voters of the two parties. The Social Democrats surrendered to the Progressives fourteen of the sixteen districts promised. In addition, through supporting the Progressives solidly in all other districts where the latter were engaged in the run-offs, they were responsible for another twenty-one Progressive seats — thirty-five in all. In no case did the Social Democrats cost the Progressives a seat. By contrast, the Social Democrats won only eleven districts of the twenty-five pledged to them by the Progressives, where the latter were the decisive element. The majority of the Progressive voters, except in four of those twenty-five districts, voted for Blue-Black candidates rather than the Social Democrats, whatever the disposition and advice of their leaders. Rosa Luxemburg had said of the same trend in the 1911 by-elections, that the Progressive Party "strikes out to the left and falls over to the right." [27] Her words applied equally well to the elections of 1912.

The details of the working of the electoral agreement reveal an ominous discrepancy between parliamentary politics and popular opinion. At the level of parliamentary politics, the Socialist executive's tactic succeeded: an anti-Blue-Black majority was created by throwing the Social Democratic machine in to the task of returning the Progressive Party to the Reichstag. The Social Democrats won 110 seats, the National Liberals, forty-four, and the Progressives, forty-two; with the help of a few votes from oppositionists in the splinter parties, they could together control the Reichstag. There were thus grounds for hope that the political divide in parliament would lie between the Center and the National Liberals with the Blue-Blacks on one side and the Liberal-Social Democratic alliance on the other. Outside parliament, however, the dividing line lay rather between Progressives and Social Democrats. The majority of Progressive voters had demonstrated their preference for Conserva-

[26] The successes were in Kalau-Luckau, Stadt Köln, Elberfeld-Barmen, and Düsseldorf, where the Progressives were too weak to put up their own candidates in the first election. The losses were in Landkreis Danzig and Landsberg-Soldin.

[27] Luxemburg, *Werke*, III, 489.

tives over Social Democrats as their Reichstag deputies, and for the old order of things over a reform created at the price of a strengthened Social Democracy. Thus the elections of 1912 revealed that the real cleavage in public opinion followed the divide of middle class and workers, not that of Junkers and middle class.

These considerations could not dim the luster of the Reichstag victory, the great "shift to the left." In an article entitled "The New Liberalism and the New Middle Class," Kautsky opened encouraging vistas of a transformation in middle-class political attitudes. Ignoring the actual behavior of the Progressive voters, he emphasized the new-found willingness of the Progressive leadership to enter into an electoral agreement with Social Democracy. He explained this sociologically through the rise of the "new middle class," the salaried workers who were neither independent entrepreneurs nor proletarians proper. Their middle position gave them a mediating role between Social Democracy and Liberalism. Kautsky stressed the numerical increase in the new middle class: from 295,957 (2.42 per cent of the earning population) in 1882 to 1,130,839 (6.6 per cent) in 1907.[28] In raising the new middle class to the position of a politically decisive force, Kautsky was following an argument which had been used by Bernstein and his followers for over a decade.[29] Not until 1912 had Kautsky's position shifted sufficiently to make the fact of lower-middle-class growth useful to his political argumentation. "All the plans of the reactionaries" were ruined by revitalized Liberalism, which was now "ready to struggle against the right." The power relations among the parties and classes as revealed in the elections had "produced a political situation unprecedented in the previous history of Germany." Kautsky felt that substantial political progress could once more be achieved through parliamentary action. Never had Kautsky evaluated the possibilities of reform more optimistically.[30]

To be sure, no one expected a really firm Left Bloc in the

[28] Karl Kautsky, "Der neue Liberalismus und der neue Mittelstand," *Vorwärts*, 25 Feb. 1912; cf. also *idem*, "Unser Stichwahlabkommen," *ibid.*, 6 Mar. 1912.
[29] The most recent statement had been given by Ludwig Quessel, "Der alte und neue Liberalismus," *S.M.*, XV (XVII), ii, 898–906.
[30] *Vorwärts*, 25 Feb. 1912.

Reichstag; the differences between Social Democracy and Liberalism on German military and world policy were too great to permit it. But the centrist and revisionist commentators anticipated marked progress over the previous Reichstag. Ludwig Quessel looked forward to a reform of the Reichstag suffrage, the establishment of a constitutional regime, alleviation of the tax burden, and more enlightened commercial treaties. Bernstein, less optimistic, saw in the formation of left and right party groupings at least an indispensable substitute for a two-party system on which any constitutional reform would have to be based. Kautsky felt that the Social Democratic victory was such that the party's four millions could no longer be ignored. Whatever the parliamentary alignment, the ruling regime would "either have to make concessions or declare war to the knife." At the very least, the commentators outside the left radical camp were agreed that the new Reichstag would prove a viable defensive mechanism to prevent a more rightward course in German policy.[31] Even Franz Mehring sanctioned the electoral alliance and was pleased, after his own fashion, with the results.[32]

To understand the hopes of the party in a new era of reform after its victory, one must remember the changes in party alignment since 1906: first the Bülow Bloc, the alliance of Liberals and Conservatives created out of the election of 1907; then the Liberals forced into opposition against the Blue-Black majority of 1909–1912; finally, the transformation of the Liberal-Social Democratic minority opposition into the majority of the new Reichstag. Surely this sequence looked like political progress toward breaking the Junker strangle hold. If reforms could ever be achieved through the instrumentality of the Reichstag and with the help of the bourgeois parties, if the electoral machinery of Social Democracy was ever to vindicate itself in positive achievement, now was the time. But the bright moment had its dark side for the party: if its promise should not be realized, the revolutionary critics of the pure parliamentary tactic would surely gain strength as against the party leaders.[33]

[31] S.M., XVI (XVIII), i, 79, 141–157; N.Z., XXX, i, 581.
[32] N.Z., XXX, i, 628.
[33] Cf., e.g., S.M., XVI (XVIII), i, 555.

ii. Failure of the Reform Coalition: The
National Liberals Move Rightward

At the opening session of the new Reichstag, the anti-Blue-Black parties tried to collaborate in the election of the provisional praesidium. Its three officers, president, first vice-president, and second vice-president, were by tradition representative of the parties composing the dominant political grouping in the Reichstag. The Social Democrats, as the largest party, could have laid claim to the presidency, but their own symbolic etiquette forbade their participation in court ceremonies or in a *Hoch* in the Reichstag for the Kaiser, which the position demanded. Thirty of the Social Democratic deputies voted in caucus to jettison this tradition, but they remained a minority.[34] The party therefore asked the National Liberals and Progressives to support only its candidate for interim first vice-president, Philipp Scheidemann. The National Liberals first pledged their complete support, then retracted it, but the National Liberal deputies were left free to cast a majority of their votes for Scheidemann, who was thus elected provisional first vice-president. For the office of president, the Social Democrats were prepared to support a National Liberal, but the National Liberals' withdrawal of formal support for Scheidemann led them to put up their own candidate, Bebel. In a run-off contest between Bebel and the Centrist, Spahn, twenty National Liberals voted for Bebel.

In the election of the permanent praesidium four weeks later, the National Liberals changed their position, on the grounds that the Social Democrats had disavowed an alleged earlier assurance of Bebel: that a Social Democratic vice-president would attend court if the need arose. Bebel hotly denied having given such an assurance. The truth of the charges and countercharges remained wrapped in the smoke of the Reichstag caucus rooms. The significant fact was that the National Liberals in the end withdrew their support of Scheidemann and brought about his defeat. The Social Democrats were thus deprived of their prestige position in the praesidium.[35]

[34] *Prot. S. P.*, *1912*, 374–375.
[35] *Schulthess*, *1912*, 22–23, 54–58; "Bericht der Reichstagsfraktion," *Prot. S. P.*, *1912*, 100–105; *N.Z.*, XXX, i, 689ff.

The wrangle over the praesidium was a tempest in a teapot, or, as Theodor Heuss has called it, "a parliamentarism of As-if, i.e., as if the election of the three presiding officers were a question of political power." [36] And yet the incident had its significance: in its early phase it gave grounds for hope that a viable working arrangement of National Liberals, Progressives, and Social Democrats might be established. In its ultimate outcome, it revealed that the two wings of the hoped-for coalition were separated by an unbridgeable chasm. Not merely the persistence of a sterile "petit-bourgeois radicalism" in Social Democracy was responsible for the outcome,[37] but also the strength of the right wing of the National Liberals. The humor magazine *Simplizissimus* celebrated the National Liberals' ambivalent behavior in satiric doggerel:

The National Liberal Hussy

Bedecked in scarf of workers' red,
Begging for votes as though for bread,
The scrawny hussy danced her way
Through smoked-filled pubs 'fore polling day.

Second thoughts came with election:
"Excuse, Herr Scheidemann, my defection;
But how would folks at court upbraid
Were I to be your chambermaid!

"Ah me! You do not comprehend?
Bowing, scraping year on end
Affects the angle of one's spine;
A lackey cannot change, in fine.

"Elected by a narrow squeak,
We find our memory grows weak.
The Bassermann's a funny bird
Which knows not how to keep its word.

"Who cares if democrats will spurn us?
The Reichstag's fate does not concern us.
He will be pushed who does not shove;
All blessings come from up above.

[36] Theodor Heuss, *Friedrich Naumann* (Stuttgart and Berlin, 1937), 387.
[37] *Ibid.;* cf. also Eyck, *Wilhelm II*, 608–609.

" 'Watch on the Rhine' we'll loudly bray,
Today it's Yea, tomorrow Nay.
We'll change our stripes, now black, now red
Until, quite color-blind, we're dead." [38]

Indeed, the praesidium question precipitated a show-down between the left and right wings of National Liberalism in which the former suffered a decisive defeat. A thorough study of the National Liberals after the collapse of the Bülow Bloc, is not available.[39] It seems clear, however, that Bassermann's maintenance of a balance between the two wings, precarious since 1909, was very nearly upset after the elections of 1912. Chancellor Bethmann-Hollweg seized the opportunity offered by the dissension in the party to excoriate it in the Reichstag for having, by its opposition to the

[38]

Die Nationalliberale Vettel

Vor der Wahl im roten Schal
Durch das raüchige Lokal
Tänzelte die dürre Vettel
Wochenlang auf Stimmenbettel.

Nach der Wahl sie sich besann:
"Tut mir leid, Herr Scheidemann!
Doch was sagte man bei Hofe,
Würd' ich Ihre Kammerzofe?

Sie verstehn mich nicht? Ei, ei!
Hoflakai bleibt Hoflakai.
Durch ein jahrelanges Bücken
Krümmt von selber sich der Rücken.

Kaum gewählt mit Ach und Krach,
Wird man schon gedächtnisschwach.
Bassermannische Gestalten
Pflegen niemals Wort zu halten.

Tadelt uns auch der und der,
Reichstag hin und Reichstag her!
Wer nicht schiebt, der wird geschoben,
Und der Segen kommt von oben.

Singen wir die Wacht am Rhein!
Heute ja und morgen nein,
Heute schwarz und morgen rot
Leuchtet uns zu frühem Tod."

Simplizissimus, XVI, 834.
    [39] Theodor Eschenburg's *Das Kaiserreich am Scheideweg* (Berlin, 1929) covers only the Bloc period.

Blue-Black Bloc, helped Social Democracy to its election victory.[40]

In March 1912 the right wing of the National Liberal executive attempted a palace revolution against Bassermann. The veteran chairman retained his position, but 30 blank ballots were cast in protest against him out of 79 votes. The insurgents eliminated from the executive's steering committee both Dr. Fischer, the leader of the Young National Liberals, and Gustav Stresemann, who was considered too close to the *Hansabund*. The same conference laid the plans for a revision of the organization statute to break up the national organization of the Young National Liberals and to bring its members under firm control at the *Land* level. Finally, the political line of the right was embodied in a resolution pledging "positive collaboration with all bourgeois parties." The party, it was further stated, "decisively rejects the imputation that it wishes to pursue a Great Bloc policy [with Progressives and Social Democrats] in the Reich." [41] The National Liberal congress which followed in May, though marked by a softening of the intra-party fight, adhered to the basic lines laid down at the March conference.[42]

Meanwhile the National Liberals in the Reichstag had resumed their "connection to the right." They aligned themselves with Centrists and Conservatives to raise the needed funds for military and naval expansion through indirect taxes.[43] The Social Democrats and the Progressives were pressed back into a minority position. With the National Liberals supporting the right, the Reichstag again became the government's willing tool. Its only constitutional achievement was the enlargement of the Reichstag's rights of interpellation.[44] The promise of a reform parliament, such as it was, lay in ashes.

[40] His indictment included the Progressives as well. *Reichstag Debates*, CCLXXXIII (16 Feb. 1912), 64–67; (19 Feb. 1912), 146–147.

[41] *Schulthess, 1912*, 92–93; *S.M.*, XVI (XVIII), i, 467–468, 502–503.

[42] Dr. Fischer was restored to the executive committee, but the central directorate of the Young National Liberal organization was dissolved. Cf. *S.M.*, XVI (XVIII), ii, 629–630; also *Schulthess, 1912*, 147–148.

[43] *Prot. S. P., 1912*, 99.

[44] The members could henceforth pose "little questions" to the government with respect to the administration of the laws. The Reichstag was also empowered to express in a resolution its view on any question raised in interpellation — without, of course, any binding power on the government. *Schulthess, 1912*, 76, 142.

There is a paradoxical similarity in the development of the National Liberal and Social Democratic parties in 1912. The executive of Social Democracy and the party reorganization committee were in process of drafting the statutory reform designed to safeguard the party leadership against the left, and thus to free itself for the pursuit of a true parliamentary, reformist policy. At the same time, the National Liberals took similar institutional measures against their own left wing, upon which any hope of an effective reformist coalition in the Reichstag depended. Thus as the Social Democrats, growing conservative, extended a hand to the right, the National Liberals backed away still further to the right, to remain always out of reach. The gap between the two parties could not be closed.

The principal bill passed in the first session of the new Reichstag was a military and naval budget providing for additional expenditures of M. 125,000,000. In opposing this measure, the Social Democrats were, of course, in isolation. The 1912 naval budget was of particular significance, for it marked a victory of Grand Admiral Tirpitz over Bethmann-Hollweg, the foreign office, and the treasury. Bethmann-Hollweg, since his accession to the chancellorship, had striven for some agreement with England. In February 1912, the last of the conversations to this end, the Haldane mission, had failed, partly because Tirpitz had already persuaded the Kaiser of the necessity of further naval construction. The hands of the German civilian authorities were thus tied in the negotiations.[45] The supremacy of the naval over the political officials was again demonstrated in March 1912 when State Secretary of the Treasury Adolf Wermuth, who opposed increased naval expenditures without equivalent increases in state income, was forced to resign by the Bundesrat. The Reichstag lifted no finger in Wermuth's defense, although the majority parties had been elected on a platform of taxation reform. In June 1912, Count Wolff-Metternich, Germany's ambassador to the United Kingdom, offered his resignation in protest against the naval policy which made his position impossible. In foreign policy, the "shift to the left" of the 1912 elections had no meaning. All the major non-socialist parties proved themselves reliable supporters of the naval authorities against the civilian

45 Ziekursch, *Politische Geschichte*, III, 235–240.

whatever the constitutional implications of their behavior.[46] Thus the hopes in the "completely new situation" which the electoral victory would bring withered and died. The Blue-Black majority was destroyed, but Blue-Black policy still prevailed.

Among the Social Democratic advocates of the liberal alliance, an embarrassed silence fell. Bernstein sought comfort in the fact that the new Reichstag, if no better than its predecessors, was no worse, and that its work could not "simply be called reactionary." [47] It must have been with a heavy heart that the executive approved these words in the annual report of the Reichstag deputation to the party, words which reflected the bankruptcy of its campaign strategy:

Whoever assumed that the powerful demonstration of the people at the elections . . . would have as its consequence a transformation in our [Germany's] policy, would halt the mad armaments race, and would spur on political and social reforms, was thoroughly disappointed.

. . . If little has been achieved [by us in the Reichstag], the primary reason therefore is that the bourgeois parties more and more let the Reichstag sink to the level of a mere machine for approving military expenditures and [tax] burdens on the people.[48]

"There is never a lack of laughing heirs," Hegel once said, "at the deathbeds of history." The left radicals were not slow in foregathering to claim their inheritance; but to claim an inheritance is not to receive it.

iii. Imperialism and the "New Tactic"

Never happy about the party's strategy of concentrating the campaign against the Blue-Black Bloc, the left radicals were furious over the secret deal with the Progressives. The *Bremer Bürgerzeitung* condemned the agreement as "wholly purposeless" and "destructive of [the masses'] confidence in Social Democracy." "What history has condemned to death," the *Bürgerzeitung* wrote of German Liberalism, "the party executive in the Lindenstrasse, even if it were made up of much younger elements than it is, cannot

[46] Eyck, *Wilhelm II*, 610–624; *Schulthess, 1912*, 83, 106–116, 120–127, 149, 177, 179–180.

[47] *S.M.*, XVI (XVIII), ii, 650.

[48] *Prot. S. P., 1912*, 98–99.

awaken to new life.[49] The "clear lines of the principal struggle" against all capitalist parties had been blurred, complained Klara Zetkin's *Gleichheit*.[50] Luxemburg, who prepared a detailed analysis of the elections for the *Leipziger Volkszeitung*, stressed the difference between the left radical concept of the function of elections and that of the executive:

> Up to now it has been a fundamental principle of Social Democracy that an election serves first and foremost [as a vehicle of] agitation, of enlightenment concerning the aims of Social Democracy, and in this sense it was a sacred duty and a matter of honor to use every day, every hour of the campaign to perform the maximum of agitational work. [Instead] the party executive, for the sake of the Progressives, forbade our comrades to agitate for their own party . . . For the bourgeois liberal politicians, constituencies are worth consideration and agitation rewarding only if a mandate is to be won; for Social Democracy, the agitation comes first and the mandate last.[51]

Thus, where the executive was prepared to sacrifice the party's propaganda efforts for its strength in the Reichstag, the left radicals held the inverse order of values.

These initial protests of the left radicals had been drowned in the thunder of victory. But once the Reichstag's "shift to the left" had proved illusory, their voices became stronger. It was easy for Luxemburg to parody Kautsky's optimistic evaluation of the prospects of a Left Bloc:

> Within this determined left majority of the Reichstag, we Social Democrats . . . are the decisive . . . majority, and, standing like Apollo, steer the chariot of German policy toward the rosy-fingered dawn, while the snorting steeds, Wiemer and Kopsch [Progressives], draw the chariot, with Bassermann and Schönaich-Carolath [National Liberals] fluttering about it like fair muses.[52]

The debates on the electoral tactic itself were soon left behind in a broader discussion of the whole strategy of the party. In the course of it, the left radical faction hammered its theory and tactic into a

[49] *Bremer Bürgerzeitung*, 26–27 Feb. 1912, quoted in Max Schippel, "Die neuesten Vorstösse unserer Impossibilisten," *S.M.*, XVI (XVIII), i, 283.

[50] *Ibid.*, 281.

[51] Luxemburg, *Werke*, III, 500–501.

[52] *Ibid.*, 515.

synthesis which was to govern the minds of Spartacists and Communists deep into the German Revolution. The synthesis achieved its final formulation in a negative reaction against the policies pursued by the party leaders, and against the theoretical arguments advanced to support them. The ideas of the German revolutionaries must be understood in this historical context.

We have earlier watched the emergence of the several conceptual elements which were now brought together: the mass strike as the form of the twentieth-century revolution, promulgated by Rosa Luxemburg in 1906; the conception of cumulative mass actions as the proper weapon to win suffrage reform in 1910; and the growing preoccupation with the fight against imperialism and war, pioneered by Eisner and Liebknecht in 1905–06 and taken up by the radicals on a broad scale in the Morocco crisis of 1911. It was the last of these concerns which now became fundamental to the left radical view of current political development. "The question of militarism and imperialism," wrote Rosa Luxemburg shortly after the election, "form the central axis of political life; in them, and not in questions of ministerial responsibility and other pure parliamentary demands, lies the key to the political situation." [53]

How was imperialism "the key to the present situation"? Firstly, the left radical theorists were convinced that imperialism was the "last card" of capitalism as an economic system.[54] The international struggle for colonial outlets for surplus capital had reached the final phase, and war was seen as the virtually certain outcome of the intense international rivalry. War would bring confusion if not ruin to the capitalist world, and would present the great challenge to revolution. The antithesis, imperialism-socialism, which Kautsky had formulated in 1907, was the foundation stone of the left radical view of contemporary political reality.[55]

There was an apocalyptic moment in left radical thought, a conviction of the imminence of the final struggle, which helps to ac-

---

[53] *Ibid.*, 527.

[54] Rosa Luxemburg, *ibid.*, VI, *Die Akkumulation des Kapitals*, worked out a theoretical limit to the survival of capitalism, namely, the absorption of pre-capitalist economies into the capitalist orbit.

[55] Cf. e.g., Karl Radek, *In den Reihen der deutschen Revolution* (Munich, 1921), 169–175; Paul Frölich, *Rosa Luxemburg* (London, 1940), 195–196. See also above, Ch. III, note 14 and text.

count for that faction's bitterness against the party leadership, and its frenetic efforts to steer the party away from any association with the nationalistic middle class.

Typical of the apocalyptic attitude was the crusade of the left radicals against the party's advocacy of international agreements to limit armaments.[56] As imperialist rivalry was inevitable in the present stage of capitalist development, the radicals argued, so armaments were an inevitable accompaniment of imperialism. To involve the working class in the tactic of fighting for disarmament within capitalist society would be to delude it into the pursuit of a will-o'-the-wisp; the great awakening would one day come in the form of profound disillusionment. The left radicals argued that the party had never embodied in its list of immediate demands any reform economically inconsistent with capitalism, such as the right to work; armaments had come to play such a large rôle in the economy of all advanced countries that disarmament was absolutely impossible.[57] At the same time the left radicals clung to the old demand for the introduction of a militia. This they considered economically possible, since it involved no disarmament, and politically useful, since it provided a moral *point d'appui* from which to criticize the class character of the German army.

The rigidity with which the left radicals rejected any effort to stop the arms race can be understood only in terms of the circumstances in which their position was formulated, that of the general tendency to moderate the party's opposition to imperialism and militarism. We know that this tendency was not new — it was already strong before 1907, and was strengthened by the elections of that year.[58] In 1912, however, it took another step forward. In the

---

[56] Arms limitation had been the policy of the party in the Reichstag since 1909, when it arose in connection with the discussions of an Anglo-German naval accord. Cf. "Bericht der Reichstagsfraktion," *Prot. S. P., 1909,* 132; Erwin Dörzbacher, *Die deutsche Sozialdemokratie und die nationale Machtpolitik bis 1914* (Gotha, 1920), 84–85; Georg Ledebour, "Eine parlamentarische Improvisation," *N.Z.,* XXX, ii, 537–541.

[57] Anton Pannekoek, "Das Wesen unserer Gegenwartsforderungen," *N.Z.,* XXX, ii, 810–817. Cf. also Karl Radek, "Der deutsche Imperialismus und die Arbeiterklasse," reprinted in *idem, In den Reihen,* 48–155; Paul Lensch, "Miliz und Abrüstung," *N.Z.,* XXX, ii, 765–772; *idem,* "Eine Improvisation," *ibid.,* 308–313, 359–368.

[58] See above, Ch. III, *passim.*

Reichstag, the party introduced resolutions to improve pre-military youth training in the public schools,[59] and to procure for the Social Democratic coöperatives a share in the supply contracts for the army! [60] The former motion was shelved by the Reichstag, the latter rejected. For Social Democracy to strive for its cut of war orders, however, was a sign of the times.

The center's arguments for disarmament conventions likewise gave the radicals, made nervous by the sense of impending war and revolution, more cause for alarm. Kautsky abandoned his earlier position that the arms race was the inevitable accompaniment of imperialism.[61] He no longer viewed the "physical force" aspects of imperialism as of its essence. The armaments race had economic causes, but was not, like the quest for markets, an economic necessity.[62] In the case of the growth of monopoly, initial competition between national monopolies yielded to international cartel agreements; similarly in the development of imperialism, the rival nations were already reaching the point where mutual agreement was a necessity for the mitigation of the economic burden of armaments. The imperialist interest of Britain and Germany could, in fact, be better served by an agreement between them, in which the other Western European nations would have to join. With the armaments rivalry put aside, "their capitalists could open up the whole area [of the underdeveloped portions of the world], or at least the eastern hemisphere far more energetically . . . than before." Russia would be contained by this Western alliance for the mutual, rather than competitive, exploitation of the underdeveloped sectors of the globe. Such a scheme might not banish war forever, said Kautsky, but it would at least postpone it. He saw strong support for such a plan already existing in the middle classes, especially in England and France.[63]

---

[59] Cf. above, Ch. III, note 57 and text.

[60] Other proposals recommended the improvement of working conditions for labor employed by the military, and the elimination of religious and political discrimination in the armed forces. Cf. "Bericht der Reichstagsfraktion," *Prot. S. P.*, *1912*, 141–142.

[61] His earlier views were, of course, used against him by his adversaries. Cf. *ibid.*, 428; Lensch in *N.Z.*, XXX, ii, 310–311, 359–368.

[62] *N.Z.*, XXX, ii, 107.

[63] *Ibid.*, 97–109, 847–854.

Thus Kautsky added to the old Marxist tradition of a Western orientation of German policy the idea of exploiting the "pacific tendencies" which he felt to be inherent in imperialism. The armaments race was to be fought as the work of a "small clique" — or, as Bernstein called it, a "non-organic parasite on the tree of modern economic development." Bernstein was, to be sure, more optimistic than Kautsky. He looked upon the repeated international crises of the twentieth century as "occasional interruptions" or "relapses" in a general progress toward international understanding. That the increasingly severe international crises had all been overcome seemed to him proof of the validity of his position.[64]

Kautsky's views — minus the idea of the Western union for the exploitation of the eastern hemisphere — were essentially shared by Haase, Ledebour, Hilferding, and most of the other later Independent Social Democrats.[65]

At bottom, the left radicals' rather absurd opposition to any encouragement of tendencies within capitalism to lessen international tension was based on their fear of the whole course of party policy. They saw the disarmament tactic as another aspect of the attempt to reform capitalism with the help of the middle class at the very moment in history when, they believed, a policy of revolutionary isolation should have been in preparation. Radek observed correctly that Kautsky revised his conception of imperialism in 1912 not because imperialism had changed but because his Fabian "strategy of attrition" could not be sustained by his earlier analysis.[66] The left radicals viewed the party's tactic against war as the projection of the electoral strategy into the foreign sphere, a watering down of the revolutionary struggle.[67]

[64] S.M., XVI (XVIII), i, 542; ii, 651; cf. also Bernstein's address to the Chemnitz congress, Prot. S. P., 1912, 419–421.

[65] Unlike Kautsky, Hilferding considered the conflict of interest among the imperialist powers as economically necessary; he agreed, however, that Social Democracy should work for Anglo-German understanding, and not content itself with empty protests against imperialism as a whole. Cf. Hilferding, "Der Balkankrieg und die Grossmächte," N.Z., XXXI, i, 74–77. Ledebour and Liebknecht believed in leaving no stone unturned to maintain peace, but did not share Kautsky's optimism and emphasized the need for supplementary extra-parliamentary action against war. Cf. Prot. S. P., 1912, 426–427, 431–432. Hasse's position was unquestionably built on Kautsky's. Ibid., 408–415.

[66] Radek, In den Reihen, 205.

[67] Ibid., 203.

We now come to the second aspect of the left radical credo, the tactic of mass actions. Here again imperialism was "the key to the present situation." For imperialism, according to the left radicals, simultaneously reduced the effectiveness of parliamentary action and threw the working class on the defensive. It therefore made it necessary to resort to a tactic of mass action.

How did imperialism undermine parliamentarism? First, it strengthened, at parliament's expense, the power of the bureaucracy — the military authorities, the diplomatic corps, etc. — which acquired increasing control over the vital aspects of state policy. Second, by placing in the center of political interest matters which were not susceptible to parliamentary action, said Radek, imperialism "hollows out parliamentarism as a weapon of the working class." [68]

At the same time imperialism was seen to bring in its wake increasing tax burdens, a higher cost of living, cessation of social reform, and the increasing difficulty of trade-union struggles. All these tended to radicalize the masses, according to the Dutch-born Bremen theorist Anton Pannekoek. With the possibilities of reform through parliament simultaneously limited, the proletariat must "naturally" resort to mass actions in order to exert pressure on the ruling class. Mass actions, from the ordinary demonstration to the general strike, were thus placed in a neat dialectic relationship to imperialism: they were both produced by it, and were the proletarian answer to it.[69] From the premise that the only answer to imperialism and the threat of war lay in socialism, the left radical theorists deduced as a tactical consequence that mass action, rather than parliamentary action, must be the party's chief weapon, even in the struggle for domestic reform. What could be at further remove from this complex of ideas than Kautsky's answer to Pannekoek that the goal must remain "the same as it always was: the conquest of the state power by winning a majority in parliament and by making parliament the controller of the government"? [70]

Following the concepts developed earlier by Luxemburg, the left radicals regarded the masses as subject to education and direction,

[68] *Ibid.*, 144; cf. also *N.Z.*, XXX, ii, 542.
[69] *Ibid.*, 541–542.
[70] *Ibid.*, 732.

but not to manipulation or to military discipline. From the masses themselves would come the pressure to action. The duty of the party was to take the lead whenever the masses manifested any will to action, to direct them, to "transform their revolutionary energy" into politically fruitful actions when their passions were aroused.[71] Through a series of mass actions, the proletariat was expected to acquire that sense of solidarity and, thanks to the educational work of the party, that political enlightenment which would make it a closely united and self-conscious political power. As imperialism was the center of the analytic structure of the German left radicals, the masses were the center of their *mystique*.

With their boundless confidence in the judgment of the masses, the German revolutionary theorists paid little or no attention to the questions of organizing a revolution. Here their difference from the Russian Bolshevists is most pronounced. Lenin would have agreed with Luxemburg and her associates that the masses would have to make the revolution when the historical moment had arrived. But he did not share their faith in the masses. He both objectified and distrusted them, hence insisted on an organizational cadre to manipulate them. The German revolutionists by contrast, disliked and distrusted organization. They longed for the day when the party organization as then constituted would be absorbed in the revolution itself. Pannekoek distinguished the essence of proletarian organization from its transient institutional form. The essence was "something spiritual, . . . the total revolution of the character of the proletarian," which must not be confused with the contemporary, hierarchical party and trade-union "in which the still firm bourgeois order expresses itself."[72] Organization for Pannekoek was an almost Platonic sense of proletarian solidarity. Lenin would certainly have agreed with Kautsky when he called Pannekoek's formulation "a masterpiece of social alchemy."[73] But never would he have supported Kautsky's idea, entirely consistent with the latter's concept of the purpose of organization, that the party should support the mass strike "only in exceptional, extreme cases, only then and there, *where the masses can no longer be held back*"; that is,

[71] *Ibid.*, XXXI, i, 373.
[72] *Ibid.*, XXX, ii, 548.
[73] *Ibid.*, 688.

that the function of the party should be to curb the masses' will to action until it was impossible to do so any longer.[74]

Why was there no theory like Lenin's in the German left? The presence of a higher degree of civil liberties in Germany doubtless operated against the rise of those concepts of revolutionary organization which are produced by a conspiratorial existence. More important was the fact that the party organization, while more highly perfected in Germany than elsewhere, was more consistently employed to thwart the development of revolutionary radicalism. The political content of the German organization made the party's revolutionaries suspect it as a kind of counter-revolutionary instrument which the revolution would have profoundly to alter — in unspecified ways. The left radicals believed as a matter of faith that the masses, once in motion, would find the proper forms of organization.[75]

Let us recapitulate the elements of the left radical synthesis: fundamental was the conviction of the imminence of the *parousia,* based on the idea of imperialism as the last phase of capitalism. Imperialism meant too that reforms by parliamentary means were no longer possible for the working class. The greater the power of Social Democracy in the Reichstag became, the less power would be left to the Reichstag. The party must therefore encourage mass actions in order to educate the proletariat and strengthen it for the coming struggle.

These propositions involved opposition to official party policy in every respect. Where the party leaders accorded primacy to domestic reform, the left radicals derived their tactic from the primacy of foreign policy. Where the party looked to the liberal bourgeoisie for aid in the fight against the Blue-Black Bloc, the left radicals sought to mobilize the unorganized proletariat for the fight against the bourgeoisie as a whole. Where the party concentrated its efforts on the Reichstag as the appropriate instrument of its policy, the left radicals, rejecting the Reichstag as of diminishing value, demanded a tactic of mass actions. Finally, the contrast may be summarized in terms of proximate objectives: where the party struggled for equal rights for labor (*Gleichberechtigung*) in the existing order,

[74] *Ibid.,* 697. Italics mine.
[75] *Ibid.,* 549.

the left radicals sought to prepare for the decisive struggle for power. Thus the antitheses, which had slowly matured since 1905, were complete at every level. The policies pursued by the party and by the left radicals were not merely different in emphasis, they had become mutually exclusive; the pursuit of one was directly harmful to the prosecution of the other.

iv. Wormwood and Gall

As the tactical incompatibility of left-radical and party policy reached full maturity, intra-party strife became almost unbearable. The left radicals began to organize on their own to undercut the leadership while the party leaders and their supporters worked to limit the influence of the left radicals in every possible way. Fair means and foul were used by both sides.

Each side became convinced that the party could be saved only at the expense of the other. The leftist Julian Karski reflected the views of Luxemburg and Mehring when he called the internal crisis "far more serious than at the time when revisionism first arose." Convinced that the party would fall into a decline if matters went on unchanged, Karski saw "only one hope for a revolutionary party: the sharpest and most ruthless self-criticism." [76] "Self"-criticism clearly meant criticism of the leaders, their actions, and their theoretical positions. No, came the answer from the defenders of the leadership; the threat to the movement came "not from these leaders, but on the contrary from that close network of small circles and conventicles which rests on the authority of the masses, and whips up the masses against the leaders." [77] Deep into the party cut the unbridgeable gap between these two views.

The letters of Konrad Haenisch reveal the terrible nervous strain of party life at the lower echelons during the last years — constant bickering, frustration for the minority faction (usually the left radical), a life demanding tremendous expenditure of energy and yielding few psychic satisfactions. Characteristic is this excerpt from Haenisch's correspondence:

[76] Letter to Block, editor of the *Leipziger Volkszeitung* (late 1913), quoted in Frölich, *Luxemburg*, 204–205.

[77] *S.M.*, XV (XVII), iii, 1185–1186.

[You ask] whether I should like to take an editorship again? No! Thrice no! For it would have to be a 'homogeneous' editorial board; an equally 'homogeneous' press commission would have to support me; and no less homogeneous would the local party leadership have to be. And where should I still find *that* in the party today? Homogeneous *revisionist* corporations — certainly. But radical ones? And to go through the sniping warfare of internal fights once again — my nerves would no longer permit it! I went through it in Mannheim, in Dresden, in Dortmund, in Leipzig, and then again (and how!) in Dortmund: more than a dozen years almost without interruption . . .[78]

The frayed nerves and the sharpening of political differences unquestionably reinforced each other to aggravate the whole situation within the party.

The more frustrated the left radicals became, the more closely they knit the ties which bound them. In 1912, we find the radical organizations of Bremen and Stuttgart submitting similarly worded motions to the party congress.[79] In the intercourse and movement of left radical personalities, too, one can see the first efforts at consolidating forces and spreading influence where it would count.[80] Thus Arthur Crispien, until 1911 regional party secretary in backward West Prussia, was invited by Fritz Westmeyer, head of the Stuttgart city machine, to edit the *Schwäbische Tagwacht*.[81] Wilhelm Pieck, today the president of the East German Republic, who had inherited the mantle of Ebert as Bremen party secretary in 1906, moved to Berlin in 1910 as assistant business manager of the central cultural committee of the party.[82] From this position he worked to

[78] Letter to Rudolf Franz, 2 Apr. 1912, in Rudolf Franz, "Aus Briefen Konrad Haenischs," *Archiv für die Geschichte des Sozialismus und der Arbeiterbewegung,* XIV, ii: 470–471 (1929).

[79] *Prot. S. P., 1912*, 160, 162.

[80] Cf. Franz, "Aus Briefen Konrad Haenischs," *Archiv für die Geschichte des Sozialismus,* XIV, ii, 469ff. Haenisch's correspondence shows the efforts for mutual defense and for obtaining jobs for left radicals, as well as the squabbles within their own fold.

[81] Wilhelm Keil, *Erlebnisse eines Sozialdemokraten,* I (Stuttgart, 1947), 262; *Prot. S. P., 1912*, 13.

[82] Pieck is interesting as the first prominent organizer-type among the left radicals. His career resembles that of Ebert, Scheidemann, and Braun, rather than that of the intellectual left radicals. He came to Social Democracy as a young worker through the trade-union movement, was blacklisted, became head of the Woodworkers'

establish left radical control within the Berlin organization, for which activity he was ridiculed by Scheidemann and others at the party congress of 1912.[83]

The general consolidation of the left radicals was given formal expression in December 1913, when Luxemburg, Mehring, and Karski set up an organ for their wing, the *Sozialdemokratische Korrespondenz*.[84]

The closer the left radicals drew together, the greater was the pressure under which they lived. The revisionist problem, as far as the executive and its centrist supporters were concerned, played almost no role in party life. Kautsky, who in 1910 had still considered revisionism as the most dangerous deviation,[85] now shifted his view. Precisely because the class conflicts were so obviously growing sharper and the revolutionary pressure of the masses was increasing, he explained, the left radicals were now the major internal enemy.[86]

The revisionists could afford a tolerant, almost patronizing view of their erstwhile centrist foes. Wolfgang Heine saw the "so-called radicals" (the center) as occupying a useful place in the party; they balanced the pursuit of political opportunity with the maintenance of principle.[87] Another revisionist commented that the center had "knocked the bottom out of [its own] barrel" by sanctioning the alliance with the Progressives in 1912. "Who has once been seduced can regain virginity through no power of the Gods." The long-persecuted revisionists could well enjoy the division in the radical camp. As one of them expressed it, they took their seats "in the parquet . . . of the theater of war" and smilingly watched the heavy artillery of the left radicals fired "not against them but

---

Union in Bremen, whence he stepped into Ebert's shoes as party secretary after a fight in the local which was won by the left. The only prewar publication of Pieck's which I have found is an article on the most efficient method of dues collection: "Die Erhebung der Parteibeiträge," *N.Z.*, XXX, ii, 778–781. His career was that of a party bureaucrat, but his politics were revolutionary — an ideal background for his career under Stalinism. See *Wilhelm Pieck zum 70. Geburtstag* (Berlin, 1946), *passim*.

[83] *Prot. S. P., 1912*, 334–335, 351–352, 355–357.
[84] Frölich, *Luxemburg*, 205. I have been unable to obtain this important periodical.
[85] *N.Z.*, XXVIII, ii, 667.
[86] *Ibid.*, XXX, ii, 517.
[87] *S.M.*, XVI (XVIII), iii, 1145.

against the party executive, *Vorwärts,* and Karl Kautsky."[88]

The executive tended now to apply party rules and regulations with leniency to the right, with rigor against the left. Thus Kautsky was permitted to circulate a series of articles attacking Mehring through the party press bureau; but when Mehring submitted a digest of Luxemburg's *Akkumulation des Kapitals* through the same channel, the executive sent a letter to all editors of party newspapers saying that the circulation of the Mehring digest was a misuse of the press bureau. When Mehring appealed to the control commission, it held the executive was right in Mehring's case, wrong in Kautsky's; but the executive's error in Kautsky's case was too late to rectify.[89]

In 1912, when Kautsky undertook a reorganization of the editorial board of *Neue Zeit,* Mehring lost his vital post as writer of the leader. According to Ebert, Mehring had asked to be relieved of this position and to confine himself to scientific matters. Mehring, denying this, subsequently appealed his case to the control commission, which left it unresolved. The actual facts are too obscure to permit an objective judgment; for, once the left radicals became aware that discrimination was being practiced against them, they saw it in every aspect of party life.[90] Whatever the rights and wrongs of Mehring's case, Kautsky's "reorganization" of *Neue Zeit* followed hard upon the publication of articles by Mehring critical of the executive for its electoral alliance with the Progressives and, above all, for its unwillingness to take criticism.[91] But the line between criticism and subversion was becoming perilously thin as the party neared its dissolution. The unity which the executive could no longer secure by consent, it sought to impose by discipline and the exercise of its power.

[88] *Ibid.,* 1167.
[89] *Prot. S. P., 1913,* 242–243.
[90] Cf. the contradictory testimony of Ebert and Scheidemann on the one hand (*ibid., 1912,* 215, and *1913,* 275) and Haase and the control commission on the other in the Mehring case (*1913,* 242–243).
[91] See esp. his quotation from Marx against the Social Democratic executive of an earlier day: " 'They are already so much . . . under attack that they believe themselves to stand above criticism, [and] . . . thunder at criticism as a crime of lèse-majesté.' " Franz Mehring, "Einiges um Marx und Liebknecht," *N.Z.,* XXX, ii, 4. The article had the distinction of drawing an answer from Bebel himself, *q.v.* in *ibid.,* 87–89.

Where the left radicals had the power, they used it with no more scruples than the executive. Thus in the Lower Rhine district, where the revolutionaries controlled the regional organization, they expelled from the party the right-wing revisionist Gerhard Hildebrand by procedures which, even in the eyes of such convinced leftists as Mehring and Heinrich Laufenberg, were anything but fair.[92]

In the little city of Göppingen, in Württemberg, the left radicals kicked over the traces in 1912, and unleashed a national party scandal which showed how far party ethics were degenerating in the internal struggle. Here the left radicals, who controlled the local party organization, had established a newspaper, the *Freie Volkszeitung.* The paper had been printed in the presses of the *Schwäbische Tagwacht,* which was controlled until the end of 1911 by the revisionist *Land* executive. Because of difficulties arising out of this printing arrangement, the Göppingen comrades decided to establish their own press, and set up a coöperative to this end. Fearful lest their enterprise receive no sanction from above for political reasons they did not obtain the approval of the *Land* or national executive despite a party ruling which bound them to do so.[93] Proceeding on their own, they were soon deep in debt and obliged to appeal to the national executive for assistance. The latter initiated conferences between the *Land* executive and the Göppingen comrades and proposed as a settlement that, in its business management but not in its editorial aspect, the Göppingen paper should be fused with the party organ of Ulm. The *Land* leaders, however, supported a demand of the Ulm organization that its reformist editors should supersede the radical editors of Göppingen. This the good leftists of Göppingen naturally resisted, feeling that their financial embarrassment was being exploited to weaken their political position.

This typical Württemberg squabble acquired national importance. The *Land* leaders claimed, without foundation, that they had the

---

[92] The case has particular interest because the executive, Kautsky and Hilferding supported the exclusion of Hildebrand at the party congress of 1912. Hildebrand favored overt Social Democratic support to German imperialism, which went well beyond what was acceptable to the center. Cf. Gerhard Hildebrand, "Wegen groben Vorstosses," *S.M.,* XVI (XVIII), i, 523–531; Wolfgang Heine, "Autodafé," *ibid.,* 531–538; *idem,* "Die Bedeutung der Ausschliessung Hildebrands," *ibid.,* iii, 1289–1300; Ernst Heilmann, "Parteijustiz," *ibid.,* XIX, iii, 1267–1269.

[93] *Prot. S. P., 1912,* 208–209, 225.

full support of the national executive, not only for the financial fusion of the Ulm and Göppingen organs, but also for the displacement of the radical by the reformist editors. Thus the national executive, in the minds of the Göppingen comrades and their radical sympathizers throughout Germany, became identified with the *Land* leaders' policies. Just when the fight was growing hot, the relatively obscure Göppingen editor went "on vacation," and was temporarily replaced by the nationally known Karl Radek, editor of the *Bremer Bürgerzeitung,* who had come to see what profit for the left radical cause could be drawn from the affair.

With his vitriolic pen, Radek at once set the party press into commotion by accusing the executive of conniving with the revisionist state leadership to force a revisionist organ on the Göppingen radicals. There is no reason to doubt that, when he began his campaign, he acted in good faith, since the state leaders had claimed the executive's sanction for their proposals. But the executive soon made clear that it had never taken the position which the Württemberg leaders attributed to it. Radek nonetheless continued in his false allegations. The radical papers, naturally suspicious of the executive, credited the local reports above the executive's denial. From the executive's point of view, Radek had from the start simply aimed at creating a scandal.[94]

Though the presence of the misunderstanding was plain for all to see, the seething emotions unleashed by the incident could not be quieted. The left radicals would not fully retract the imprecations they had hurled at the executive, and the executive was determined to avenge itself on its principal assailant, Karl Radek.

The restraint which the executive had shown in the handling of the Göppingen case as such disappeared in its aftermath. It launched a full-scale defamation campaign against Radek with a view to his expulsion from the party. Its charges that Radek had not properly enrolled in the party and had paid no dues proved partly unfounded and were in any case inadequate to warrant Radek's expulsion. The Polish Socialist Party, however, had previously expelled Radek on charges of stealing 300 rubles of trade-union funds in his youth. The Polish Party, in early 1913, formally requested that the German

---

[94] The details, from the point of view of all contenders, are contained in *Prot. S. P., 1912,* 180, 209–215, 225–241. Cf. also Karl Radek, *Portraits and Pamphlets* (London, 1935), 49, where he persists in his distortion of Ebert's position.

party exclude him; at the same time, many Polish Socialists wrote to insist that his trial in Poland had been irregular and that he was the victim of a factional frame-up. In the end, the executive pushed through the Jena congress (1913) a resolution that anyone who had been dishonorably expelled from the party of another country could not be taken into the German party, and that this ruling should have retroactive application against Radek.[95] The executive had its revenge.

Even many of his fellow-radicals had little use for Radek personally, or for his handling of the Göppingen affair.[96] But far over into the revisionist fold, it was felt that more was at stake than Radek and his crimes. From Liebknecht and Luxemburg to the revisionists Heilmann and Katzenstein there was an awareness that the executive was behaving with no regard for the rule of law within the party. Heilmann wrote, "The party executive, driven beyond the bounds of justice by its wrath at Radek's Göppingen intrigues, could force through such a criminal law with retroactive force only with the wildest demagogy." [97] Mehring insisted that Social Democracy could at least "guard the moral existence of its members . . . with the same legal guarantees which bourgeois society has thus far maintained unbroken for all its members, including the working class." [98]

These commentators felt the real change which was coming over party life as Social Democracy moved toward division. The flouting of legal procedures, which has become a hallmark of modern communism and, increasingly, of its adversaries, was in 1913 a strange new thing, which evoked fear and disgust in the more sensitive Social Democrats of that softer era. As power questions moved to the fore, that ethical sense which had generally prevailed in the movement began to be dulled.

[95] *Prot. S. P., 1912,* 214–215, 238–239, 282–283, 515; *1913,* 536–545; also Ruth Fischer, *Stalin and German Communism* (Cambridge, Mass., 1948), 201–203. Miss Fischer erroneously maintains that the case was "never officially concluded."

[96] Franz, "Aus Briefen Konrad Haenischs," *Archiv für die Geschichte des Sozialismus,* XIV, ii, 472–483; Frölich, *Luxemburg,* 211. Fischer goes beyond the evidence in saying that the left radicals "joined in the move to expel him." Fischer, *Stalin,* 203.

[97] Ernst Heilmann, "Parteijustiz," *S.M.,* XIX, iii, 1272.

[98] Quoted in *ibid.,* 1276. For similar arguments by Katzenstein, Liebknecht, Luxemburg, and Oskar Cohn, none of whom defended Radek's behavior in Göppingen, cf. *Prot. S. P., 1913,* 540–544.

Chapter X

THE SENSE OF SICKNESS AND THE RECON-
SOLIDATION OF THE RADICALS

By 1913 the body of the party was wracked by the poison of dissension. The bright hopes in the future, which had sustained morale through all previous internal troubles, gave way to a universally
felt sense of sickness. External circumstance seemed to conspire with
internal discord to rob the party of its self-confidence and unity of
purpose.

Economic recession brought new difficulties for the trade-unions.
The entrepreneurial class manifested a greater aggressiveness on
the political as well as on the economic front. Worst of all, the
Social Democratic movement suddenly became aware of the shocking fact that its expansion had ceased. Unrest, or in its absence,
discouragement and indifference, spread through the rank and file.
In an atmosphere of malaise bordering on defeatism the factions
moved toward their final alignment, with the line of party cleavage
running its saw-toothed course through what had once been the
united radical camp. While the executive, the revisionists, and the
right center formed a solid phalanx, the left center joined forces
once more with the left radicals to heal, at least in part, the breach
of 1910, and to work for a radicalization of the party's tactic.

i. Labor on the Defensive

In March 1912, in the same month when the failure of the Reichstag coalition of the left was sealed by the National Liberals, there
broke out in the Ruhr a short but violent coal strike resulting from
the gap which had again opened up between wages and the rising
cost of living. The strike failed abysmally, partly because the Catholic unions did not wish to join in it.[1] Troops were sent into the

---

[1] For the causes and course of the strike, see O. Niehbuhr, "Der dritte grosse
Bergarbeiterstreik im Ruhrrevier," *N.Z.*, XXX, i, 934–944; Robert Schmidt, "Der
deutsche Bergarbeiterstreik," *S.M.*, XVI (XVIII), i, 356–359; *Prot. S. P., 1912*, 148–
151.

area to maintain order. Legal reprisals against workers reached unheard-of proportions with 1500 charges preferred against individual
strikers. Prison sentences exceeded the total imposed on the whole
labor movement, economic and political, in any year of the preceding decade.[2] Even the Social Democrats admitted that the strikers
were guilty of excesses; but the rigors of the law were not confined
to these. A high proportion of the sentences were imposed for "personal insults" to strike-breakers. To call *"Pfui"* and ironically tip hats
to the strike-breakers were offenses which brought prison sentences
to the pickets.[3]

Thenceforward, the legal persecution of the trade-unions and
their members increased rapidly until it became a major concern of
the leadership. The right to picket was progressively curbed by the
police on the grounds of interference with traffic. In 1912 for the
first time, union locals were stamped as political associations because of their contributions to the Social Democratic campaign
chests, and thus brought under the provisions of the Reich Law
of Associations requiring police permission for and surveillance of
meetings and — most important — forbidding membership to mi-
nors. When industrial corporations contributed to political parties,
the law was not similarly enforced. As part of its campaign for the
improvement of judicial practice and the law of association, the
general commission issued in 1914 a carefully documented compila-
tion of cases of police and judicial discrimination against the trade-
unions. The report leaves no doubt that the grievances were real —
and costly — to the unions.[4]

The efforts of the unions and the party to secure a reform of the
antiquated law of coalition were fruitless. On the contrary, growing
pressures from the business classes forced the unions into the defensive. Around the slogan "Defend the right to work," the employers'
organizations launched a campaign to limit the right of coalition
even further, especially by the elimination of picketing and the
strengthening of the penal code against the use of boycotts and
other labor weapons. Begun in 1911 by the most aggressive of all

[2] Calculated from *Prot. S. P., 1906*, 43; *1907*, 57; *1908*, 58; *1909*, 58; *1910*, 58;
1911, 59; *1912*, 57.
[3] *N.Z.*, XXX, ii, 84–87; *S.M.*, XVI (XVIII), ii, 741–742, 745; Paul Umbreit, *25
Jahre deutscher Gewerkschaftsbewegung, 1890–1915* (Berlin, 1915), 123–132.
[4] Siegfried Nestriepke, *Das Koalitionsrecht in Deutschland. Gesetze und Praxis*
(Berlin, [1914?]), *passim.*

economic associations, the *Zentralverband deutscher Industrieller,* this campaign was intensified until the outbreak of the war. In its prosecution all the economic organizations of the possessing classes were at one. The two rival employer organizations finally overcame their remaining differences to form a single association (the *Vereinigung deutscher Arbeitgeberverbände*) in early 1913.[5] Even the chambers of commerce, the banks, and the *Hansabund,* normally less anti-union than industry, supported the campaign.[6]

The political pressure generated by these groups to limit the right of coalition brought no immediate results. The attitude of Bethmann-Hollweg was decisive here. While expressing himself in favor of removing the "excessive consequences" of the right of coalition, he wished to avoid provocative measures. Even at the end of 1913, when the pressure for restrictive legislation against the unions was reaching its height, Bethmann continued to pursue a delaying tactic, urging that the time for making concrete proposals was not yet ripe. He now indicated, however, that he had ordered the collection of material on labor struggles to serve as a basis for early discussion in the Reichstag.[7]

The trade-unions, at their congress in June 1914, protested vigorously against the plans to increase the existing legal limitations on the right of coalition and against the rigorous application of existing law. Their calls for extension of legal safeguards, in the current anti-labor atmosphere, had a distinctly hollow ring.[8]

On the eve of the world war [wrote the trade-union theorist Adolf Braun in 1915] the top representatives of the trade-unions had to emphasize more strongly than for many years the antagonism of interests between worker and entrepreneur. That came about not out of any general views, not as a reflex from the socialist attitudes of the masses, but as a result of well-founded fears of grave dangers threatening the whole development of the trade-unions.[9]

[5] *N.Z.,* XXXII, i, 791.
[6] Cf. Carl Legien, "Sturmlauf gegen das Koalitionsrecht," *N.Z.,* XXX, ii, 899–907; *Der Deutsche Metallarbeiter-Verband im Jahre 1913* (Stuttgart, 1914); Hrsg., Vorstand des Deutschen Metallarbeiter-Verbandes, 31–36; Umbreit, *25 Jahre,* 131.
[7] *Reichstag Debates,* CCXCI, 6341–6343.
[8] Paul Barthel, *Handbuch der deutschen Gewerkschaftskongresse* (Dresden, 1916), 260–262.
[9] Adolf Braun, *Gewerkschaften; Betrachtungen und Ueberlegungen während des Weltkrieges* (Leipzig, 1915), 19.

. . . If we wish to summarize the facts, hopes and fears which then filled our trade unions, then we should say above all that the trade unions felt themselves forced onto the defensive against the authority of the state.[10]

ii. Internal Pressures on the Trade-Unions

The threat of an assault on its organization from without was paralleled in 1913 and 1914 by profound disturbances within the unions.

In December of 1912 the German economy entered another recession which lasted until the outbreak of war. One must use the word "recession" guardedly, however, for the whole economy was not affected by it. The First Balkan War, with the attendant European war scare, resulted in an increase in the discount rate to peacetime industries, particularly to the building and textile industries, which brought reduction in activity in these sectors of the economy. Industrial unemployment averaged 2.9 per cent during 1913 and 3.2 per cent during the first half of 1914, figures which, small though they may be by present-day depression standards, created a flexibility in the labor market unfavorable to union advances.[11] At the same time, rank and file pressure for action to keep wages abreast of the rising cost of living increased. The trade-union leaders, aware that their power to strike was weakened by the softening of the labor market, controlled the impatient rank and file only with difficulty.

In the Hamburg shipyards, a great strike broke out in July 1913 despite all efforts of the national leadership to avert it. The national union withheld strike support. The employers' organizations, whose superior strength the national union leaders had correctly evaluated, turned the strike into a general lockout which ended in a fiasco for the workers. Over 1000 workers were not returned to their positions.[12]

The strike — and especially the refusal of the union leaders to support the strikers — unleashed rank and file resentment of formidable proportions. Among the metal workers (whose union was the

---

[10] *Ibid.*, 18.

[11] Jürgen Kuczynski, *A Short History of Labour Conditions under Industrial Capitalism* (London, 1942–45), III, i, "Germany, 1800 to the Present Day," 163; *Metallarbeiter-Verband, 1913,* 1–3, 37–38.

[12] *N.Z.*, XXXII, i, 55–59; *S.M.*, XIX, iii, 1155–1162.

one concerned) arose the demand to abrogate the veto right of the union executive in wage actions, and to give autonomy of decision and control of union funds to the regional and district organizations.[13]

The pressure to widen membership control over policy spread from the Metalworkers' Union throughout the whole union movement. At union congresses in 1913 and 1914 the members wrangled over the best form of organizational statute.[14] The leadership, fearing the rank and file's overestimation of union strength, clung to its powers of decision and called for greater discipline as the only solution to the present difficulties. The situation in the unions was described by a contemporary commentator as follows:

Trade-union struggle poses ever greater demands on the discipline of its members. The conditions of trade-union life have become more complicated, because the struggles are no longer so easy to conduct as formerly. Particularly in times of crisis, the workman in the shop becomes pessimistic concerning his organization. . . . The fundamental atmosphere in broad sectors of the trade-union membership is a kind of syndicalist undercurrent. Not in the sense that sabotage is propagated openly or secretly — for that the traditional trade-union training is too deep-seated in the German worker. But it's nevertheless an atmosphere of despair: the union is not successful enough for the man in the shop, the tactic too cautious, the leaders too circumspect, and since cause and effect are not always clear to him, he is readily inclined in meetings to let himself be whipped up into opposition to the leaders.[15]

In some instances the dissatisfaction was such that the leaders, despite their better judgment, gave in to rank and file pressure to strike in order to maintain confidence.[16] Elsewhere, local rebelliousness manifested itself in breakoffs and a curious revival of "localist" unions, with their strong emphasis on local autonomy. Such unions were formed in textiles, painting, and metals. These breakoffs concerned the party too, for all persons joining them were, under a ruling of 1908, subject to expulsion from the party. The number of

[13] N.Z., XXXII, i, 59.
[14] Ibid., 704.
[15] Ibid., 988.
[16] Such was the case in the Bosch strike in 1913, where the union suffered a severe setback. Cf. Metallarbeiter-Verband, 1913, 254–279.

such expulsions cannot be estimated from sources available, since they were carried out at the regional level. The number of appeals to the party congress, however, was large enough in 1913 to require handling *en masse* rather than as individual cases. There was even a motion to lift the Nürnberg resolution providing expulsion for localists, although this proposal was not acted upon.[17]

The question of how to bridge the widening gap between leaders and rank and file became the subject of lively discussion. The trade-union leaders called for greater discipline, which, as one of them said, was "even more important than the other indispensable pre-condition for the success of union struggles — enthusiasm." In the comments of the leaders one often feels a sense of profound disgust and mistrust for the unstable and uncomprehending rank and file.[18] There was general agreement that the workers must be better educated in the conditions of trade-union struggle. With respect to organization, some, seeking the solution in greater democratization, called for the creation of action committees in which the shop stewards, who lived among the men, would have an equal voice with the higher trade-union officials. Others, stressing concentration of forces rather than democratization, advocated greater centralization and the elimination of craft unions in order to match the increased striking power of the employer organizations.[19]

The contents of the reform proposals are of less consequence than the dissatisfaction and difficulty which they reflected. Even the unions were now on the defensive, and their impotence was reflected in the discord between leaders who were powerless to produce successes and followers who clamored for them. The leaders were subject to pressure for action, not primarily from politically motivated, radical-minded Social Democrats as in 1905, but from an economically dissatisfied and impatient rank and file. The loss of self-confidence and unity in the trade-union movement thus had its own causes, but it paralleled and unquestionably aggravated the sense of sickness and division in the party.

[17] *Prot. S. P., 1913*, 183, 533–535.
[18] Cf., e.g., *N.Z.*, XXXII, i, 866–867.
[19] See the series of articles by union and non-union commentators, *ibid.*, 546–548, 634–635, 673–675, 790–792, 828–831, 862–867.

iii. *Against Imperialism or for Reform?*

Like the trade-unionists, the party leaders were caught between conflicting external and internal pressures. While the government, with the majority of the public behind it, prepared for the coming war, the pressure mounted within the party to answer the impending "last crisis of capitalism" with preparations for revolution.

At the Chemnitz congress, the long debates of 1912 with respect to imperialism and war were resolved in favor of the Kautsky view. The left radical position, that imperialism would inevitably lead to war and could be combated only by revolutionary means and in isolation from the bourgeoisie, was rejected. The resolution submitted by Haase stated that "nothing can be left undone to mitigate its [imperialism's] dangerous effects," and called for the party to work for international understanding through arms limitation and the removal of trade barriers.[20] In the debates at the congress, the four major divisions of opinion which were to appear in World War I were represented. There were the so-called "social imperialists," right-wing revisionists who, agreeing with the left radicals that the politics of force were decisive in the present era, felt that the workers' interest lay in full support of the state in the imperialist struggle. They also rationalized their nationalism on the grounds that Germany, as the most advanced capitalist country with the greatest socialist movement, was the power most ripe for socialism.[21] Bernstein supported the Haase resolution and stressed the ideological, as opposed to the economically determined, character of imperialism. His ethical revulsion against war and his love of England made it impossible for him to follow his colleagues of the *Sozialistische Monatshefte* into support of Germany's power politics. His only demand, which was not granted, was that the party support

---

[20] *Prot. S. P., 1912,* 529–530.

[21] Ludwig Quessel presented their position. Cf. *ibid.,* 429–430. The affinity which his group felt for the left radical analysis of — as opposed to tactic toward — imperialism finds expression in Max Schippel, "Radikales Durcheinander," *S.M.,* XVI (XVIII), i, 547–549. For a general discussion of the theory of the social imperialist group, see Erwin Dörzbacher, *Die deutsche Sozialdemokratie und die nationale Machtpolitik bis 1914* (Gotha, 1920), 129–195. A briefer treatment is presented in Lenore O'Boyle, "Theories of Socialist Imperialism," *Foreign Affairs,* XXVIII (1949–1950), 290–298.

international arbitration courts.[22] The third group, represented by Haase, Kautsky, Ledebour, and Liebknecht, all emphasized the need to work against war within the capitalist framework, a task which, they felt, was favored by the development of international cartels. Among them, however, there were differences in the degree to which they considered the fight against war of primary importance.[23] Finally, there were the left radicals, who condemned the encouragement of international agreements as illusionistic and urged the use of mass actions against war.[24]

The decision, as we have seen, fell in favor of the center, of that group whose leaders — Haase, Kautsky, Ledebour et al. — would later have to form the Independent Social Democratic Party to maintain the policy which they then advocated. It was anti-war, but not revolutionary — an extension of Social Democratic domestic policy into the sphere of foreign affairs. For all this, the Chemnitz resolution was a turn to the left. There was no repetition of the behavior of the executive in the Morocco crisis of 1911 until August 1914. During the Balkan Wars and at the time of the Ludendorff military budget of 1913, the Social Democrats campaigned against war through the press, pamphlets, and nation-wide mass meetings. The great demonstrations of July 1914, which so deceived the world as to the intentions of the German party with respect to war, were likewise conducted in the spirit of the Chemnitz resolution. The kind of opposition to war which the party embarked upon in 1912 was fundamentally agitational; it was the tactic which we saw Liebknecht, Eisner, and some of the radicals call for in 1905–1907. The party had caught up with them now, but it was barely abreast of the times; it embarked on its full-scale war of words against war at a time when the challenge to action lay just around the corner. Meanwhile, the left radicals had taken another step: their plea to the party now was to prepare for deeds. What the leftists failed to see was that the "masses," upon whom they pinned all their hopes, would not and could not react to the outbreak of war as they expected.

[22] Prot. S. P., 1912, 419–421.
[23] Ibid., 408–415, 425–427, 430–432.
[24] Ibid., 415–418, 421–423, 429.

Active though the party may have been in anti-war propaganda, its parliamentary deputation revealed in 1913 the limits of its anti-militarism. In March, the government introduced another record-breaking military expansion bill.[25] Behind this bill lay the compelling facts of the First Balkan War and the introduction of a three-year service term in France. As in 1909, so in 1913 the demands of the military could not be met with the existing financial resources. The government resolved once again to press for the introduction of Reich property taxes. It proposed a one-time defense levy and a continuing tax on annual increments in personal property. While not an income tax, the government measure represented a substantial advance over the previous indirect taxes.

A majority for the military bill could, of course, be obtained without Social Democratic votes. But in the tax measures the Social Democratic vote was decisive; without it, the government bill, opposed by the Conservatives, would be defeated. Thus the Social Democratic deputation was confronted again with the dilemma of 1909, but in a sharper form. In 1909, their action could not save the government tax plan; in 1913, their votes were decisive. In 1909, the international situation, grave though it was, was not as ominous as in 1913. The question, domestic reform or absolute opposition to militarism, was no longer theoretical. Whatever the Social Democrats decided would affect the course of Reich politics as well as create a precedent for their own subsequent behavior.

Division in the Reichstag delegation was correspondingly sharp. Many deputies of the Social Democratic center who had supported the executive's view of imperialism against the left radicals in 1912 nevertheless refused to compromise with imperialism for the sake of domestic reform. Under the impact of the majority's favorable attitude toward the tax bills, they were pushed closer to the left radicals. After two heated caucus sessions, a vote was finally taken: 52 favored voting for the tax; 37 opposed it; 7 abstained. It was agreed that the deputation must vote as a bloc, and that a declaration

[25] The bill was to raise the peace-time strength of the army by approximately twenty per cent. Cf. Johannes Ziekursch, *Politische Geschichte des neuen deutschen Kaiserreiches* (Frankfurt a. M., 1930), III, 256.

must be read which would do some justice to the minority position.[26]

Thus the Social Democratic Reichstag delegation forecast both its external behavior and its internal division over the war credits issue in the days of 2–4 August 1914. The left centrists, Fritz Geyer, Hoch, Stadthagen and Ledebour, headed the *recusants;* the revisionists David, Frank and Südekum led the *acceptants.* But the deputation broke into half a dozen different groups motivated by a wide variety of considerations of tactic and principle. There were also a certain number of shifts in allegiance: Bernstein deserted the reformist bloc to vote against accepting the taxes, Emanuel Wurm and other left centrists joined the majority.[27]

The tax bill, the one major domestic reform of the new Reichstag, was accomplished at a price for Social Democracy. As Fritz Geyer pointed out, the government now knew that it could get bigger and better armaments with Social Democratic support.[28] Between the party's advocates of the short-run interest in tax reduction and those of the long-run interest in intransigent anti-militarism, there was no longer any meeting of minds. An interchange between Stadthagan and Frank illuminates the difference in outlook. Stadthagen, for whom "principle," that is, anti-militarism, was paramount, described the present situation as one where the bourgeois parties voted the soldiers and the Social Democrats voted the funds. To this Frank answered that, if Stadthagen's policy had been followed, it could be said that the bourgeois parties voted the soldiers while "through the stupidity of the Social Democratic deputation, . . . the Social Democratic workers must pay for them." [29]

The revisionists were right in asserting that, if Social Democracy refused the taxes, others would be raised which hit the workers harder. No less right was Luxemburg's summary of the implications of the policy followed: "If you take the position of our deputation's resolution, then you will get yourself into the situation where, if war breaks out and this fact can't be altered, and if then the question

[26] A full account of the transactions within the deputation is given in the "Bericht der Reichstagsfraktion," *Prot. S. P., 1913,* 169–172. This report was cleared with representatives of each sector of opinion and received their approval for its accuracy.
[27] Cf. *ibid.,* 419–515, *passim.*
[28] *Ibid.,* 477.
[29] *Ibid.,* 495, 505.

arises whether the costs should be covered by indirect or direct taxes, you will then logically support the approval of war credits." [30] For the left, the lesser evil was the sacrifice of a positive reform in order that the basic opposition to militarism might be maintained. But this was no longer the view of the majority. As in the Morocco crisis, the left center found itself again in opposition to the leadership and drawn closer to the intransigents of the left radical wing.

iv. The Doldrums

Aside from the mixed blessing of the taxation reform, Social Democracy achieved nothing in the parliamentary arena in the last pre-war years. The hopes arising from the party's great success in the 1912 elections made the disappointment in the new Reichstag more difficult to bear. What had sustained the Social Democrats against discouragement from the lack of direct political achievement in the past was their belief that the natural course of history (aided and abetted by lively agitation) would feed voters and members to the party until it became invincible. The actual development of the party over three decades had steadily reënforced this nineteenth-century faith in numerically measurable progress. From the election of 1881, when Social Democracy received 6.1 per cent of the vote cast, the increase in voting strength had been unbroken, except for a slight drop in 1907, until the party received 34.8 per cent of the vote in 1912.[31] Party membership had likewise increased by leaps and bounds from 384,327 in 1906 to 907,112 in 1912.[32]

Suddenly, in 1913, in the midst of all the other difficulties which beset the party, the faith in numbers boomeranged. In the annual report of the executive to the party, there stood the shocking news that the party membership had increased by only 1.3 per cent in the

---

[30] *Ibid.*, 487.

[31] Paul Hirsch and Bruno Borchardt, *Die Sozialdemokratie und die Wahlen zum deutschen Reichstag* (Berlin, 1912), 26.

[32] Prior to 1906, there were no membership statistics. The yearly membership figures, with the annual increase in percentage, were as follows:

1906	384,327	——	1910	720,038	13.6%
1907	530,466	38.0%	1911	836,562	16.1%
1908	587,336	10.7%	1912	970,112	15.9%
1909	633,309	7.8%			

Taken from *Prot. S. P., 1913,* 10.

business year 1912–13. Only 12,000 new members, as opposed to 140,000 in the previous year. A closer inspection of the statistics revealed that 10,000 of the 12,000 new recruits were women![33] Though the period covered was only nine months, as the executive pointed out, this was still "a membership . . . increase which in its paucity borders on stagnation."[34]

"Stagnation" — the word swept through the party, dominated the press discussions through the summer and the party congress in the fall of 1913. The Prussian Landtag elections, held in May, only increased the gloom. With their "4,000,000 victory" in the Reichstag elections behind them, the Social Democrats hoped for better results in Prussia, despite the three-class system. The party did poorly; it won only four new seats — one on its own steam, the other three through a deal with the Progressives — to bring its total to ten.[35] The Social Democratic penetration of the "bastion of reaction," the Prussian parliament, was as negligible as ever, and all prospects for its reform were dead.

In the Landtag elections of Baden of October 1913, the party took an even worse beating than in Prussia. Here was the "model *Land*," where the Great Bloc of Liberals and Social Democrats, under universal suffrage, had won a majority in 1909. The Social Democrats not only lost seven of their twenty seats but suffered an absolute loss of votes. There had been relative losses before in the Baden party's history, but never an absolute decline. Even in the industrial city of Mannheim, the party lost in relative strength to its Bloc partners.[36] Baden Social Democracy had gone so far in accommo-

---

[33] *Ibid.*, 13.

[34] *Ibid.*, 10.

[35] At the Prussian party congress, the revisionists this time called upon the party to support anti-Blue-Black candidates directly where Social Democracy had no chance of winning. The congress instead made stiff conditions for the support of other candidates. As in the deal with the Progressives in 1912, the party leaders abandoned these conditions in the election itself in the hope of securing more seats. This time the Progressives would not agree to vote for the Social Democrats, but only to abstain. Progressive-Social-Democratic relations were deteriorating. Cf. *S.M.*, XVI (XVIII), ii, 1026–1031; *N.Z.*, XXXI, i, 553–557; *ibid.*, ii, 190–197, 361–365, 606–607.

[36] C. A. Lehmann, "Der Ausfall der badischen Landtagswahlen," *ibid.*, XXXII, i, 177–182, 333–335.

dating itself to its Liberal partners, especially in taxation policy, that it was making itself unnecessary.[37]

In another sector of party life, the party press, the revered statistics spoke ominous language. The number of subscribers for the year 1911–12 had been 1,478,042 — an increase over the previous year of 171,577. Now the number of subscribers fell off by 12,830. Of all the papers published under the direct auspices of the executive, only the women's periodical, Klara Zetkin's ultra-radical *Gleichheit,* showed a substantial gain. The executive was undoubtedly correct in its assertion that the depression was primarily responsible for the loss of subscribers. But to the worried party men it was another unprecedented sign of standstill.[38]

Lack of concrete achievements, loss of voters, stagnation in membership, loss of press subscribers — all these contributed to produce a profound feeling of impotence. As one old veteran expressed it, where some party members had formerly regarded an increase in votes as a turning point in world history, they now saw in a little decline in the organization "a world catastrophe, . . . the *Götterdämmerung* of Social Democracy."[39]

Criticism of the party we have seen abundantly over our period, but such a general sense of sickness as now appeared was new. Not the intellectual opposition, but the men from the lower echelons of the party hierarchy began to voice discouragement and describe the loss of morale. Their analyses, simple though they were, revealed that the loss of faith in the party was widespread and deep.

If you sit in a shop day after day, you hear how the workers talk about the agitational efforts: 'What's the good of all the resolutions and meet-

[37] In justifying his Bloc policy to his own party in 1910, the National Liberal leader Rebmann described Social Democracy's policy as follows: "It (the SPD) voted for an income tax law which went less far in disburdening the lowest income groups and in burdening the higher and highest incomes than the Center's bill, which was rejected as unacceptable by the government; for a school law which included nothing concerning free instruction and free school supplies or the abolition of religious instruction . . . ; [and] for a law on local government which included a class voting system." — Quoted in *N.Z.,* XXXI, i, 181.

[38] *Prot. S. P.,* 1912, 40; 1913, 29. In the next year (1913–14) there was a small increase of 23,000 subscribers, of which, however, 13,000 were accounted for by *Gleichheit.* Cf. *Prot. S. P.,* 1917, Appendix I, 21.

[39] *Ibid., 1913,* 246.

ings?' . . . Our movement had grown high and wide, and now it's beginning to stand still. When a pond has no outlet it begins to ferment. For us that's manifested in the discontent of the masses. I don't look on the leaders as stuffed shirts or wet blankets. But in the shops and factories they say, 'Our leaders have gotten too close to bourgeois ideals. They're trying to lay on the wet blanket.' I don't share these views, but I'm expressing the attitude of most of the comrades.[40]

One member who brushed off the decline in membership as a transient, inconsequential problem, nevertheless gave voice to the dissatisfaction which seemed to be rising to the surface everywhere:

What we have a right to be somewhat pessimistic about is that the inner life of the party has become unsatisfying . . . It's a sign that in the last years we've neglected to deepen the movement. I don't attribute the fault to particular corporations or to particular persons; we're probably all more or less guilty . . . I believe that what's dangerous for our party life is the increasing mechanization of the party, the attempt to manage everything according to set rules and regulations, in one place exactly as in the other . . . We need administrative officials of course, but we ought to consider well whether we should go on multiplying them at the same tempo as formerly . . . Through the binding together of the organization, through the centralization which we've adopted from the trade-unions, the broad view gets lost for the individual comrade, and more and more the paid official and secretary gets to be the one who alone controls the whole mechanism . . . He acquires great influence; and because he sees his chief task in organizational activity, the deeper education of the members in Social Democratic principles goes by the board. Moreover, the individual comrades come to rely on their official to do everything properly and no longer worry themselves about things. You wait for the order from the regional command, and when it comes you move, not before. Through reliance on the initiative of the administrative officials and the party executive, the initiative of the individual organizations and of the individual comrades becomes restricted. I give you this to think about, without making any specific suggestions.[41]

Thus from the ranks there came an analysis of the decline of party democracy which, in substance if not in sophistication, resembled that of the sociologist Robert Michels.

Concerning the press, there was a similar outburst of dissatisfac-

[40] *Ibid.*, 286–287.
[41] *Ibid.*, 246–247.

tion. The party press bureau, established in 1907, was accused of having increased the uniformity of the party papers. The press bureau chief refused to let his office be "the whipping boy for the whole party press." He pointed out that the bureau had to serve both radical and revisionist papers; it had been condemned by the terms of its foundation in 1907 to be "politically sexless." If seventy-eight of the party's ninety papers differed from each other only in the masthead, it was as much the fault of the locals as of the press bureau. Too often the editors were chosen not from the point of view of quality, but according to "who could use the salary most." [42]

Political frustration and the weight of the party machine was particularly felt in the youth movement, where matters had gone from bad to worse under the arrangements of 1908.[43] With assistance — and not a little prodding — from the youth central, the locals throughout the Reich had rapidly established adult-controlled youth committees, until by 1913 they numbered no less than 655.[44] Their following among the youth, which could be measured only by the number of subscribers to the party's youth periodical, numbered about 100,000 in 1913, as compared to 20,000 in 1909.[45]

The party had bent over backward to keep the youth movement unpolitical and out of the hands of the law. Sports, cultural lectures, and social activities were the staple fare provided. The youth committees operated, their official historian tells us, on Goethe's principle that "only law can give freedom." [46] His evidence, however, suggests that Goethe's principle had rather limited validity for prewar Social Democracy. He recorded page after page of police and judicial actions against even the most harmless activities of the youth committees and their young wards.[47] The Reich Law of Association, which had provided the opportunity for the trade-union and party leaders to bring the radical autonomous youth

---

[42] *Ibid.*, 256–257, 272–274. In 1914, 80.2 per cent of the party's 241 editors were of working class origin and had only a grammar school education. Most editors held one or more other jobs, as members of executive committees, city councilmen, etc. Cf. Ludwig Kantorowicz, *Die sozialdemokratische Presse Deutschlands* (Tübingen, 1922), 102–105.

[43] See above, Ch. IV, sec. iii.

[44] Karl Korn, *Die Arbeiterjugendbewegung* (2nd edition, Berlin, 1923), 247.

[45] *Ibid.*, 249.

[46] *Ibid.*, 181.

[47] *Ibid.*, 202–256, *passim*.

organizations under control, was applied with increasing rigor against the Social Democrats from 1911 on. In the same year, the Prussian Ministry of Instruction organized a "state youth culture," which extended barracks facilities, camping equipment, and other indirect financial aid to the bourgeois youth organizations. The *Jungdeutschlandbund,* formed under the leadership of General von der Goltz, was designed as a roof organization for all non-socialist youth associations. From school to garrison, the state sought to win and maintain control over the minds of the young.[48]

The state policy of carrot and stick had a double effect on the Social Democratic youth movement. The "carrot," especially the camping and para-military activities, drew away potential recruits from Social Democratic youth activities. But the "stick" radicalized those who remained Social Democrats, and thus increased the friction between adults and youth.

The radicalism of the youth made itself felt not only in the youth groups proper, but also among their alumni who, at eighteen, entered the party as full-fledged members. Scheidemann complained in 1913 that they were politically unprepared, easily bored and lacking in understanding for "the many purely business matters of the political organization." [49] Characteristically, the party sought to solve the problem by building a staff of adult youth functionaries and by educating the adults in training courses in "handling" the young; its methods were essentially copied from the state youth "culture." [50] To take care of the youth alumni, the party cultural committee established special meetings in which the young could be instructed in what interested them — "questions of *Weltan-schauung* and the like" — and in which, one suspects, they could blow off steam without interfering with the routine which occupied most party meetings.[51]

By 1913, the party knew well that its sober methods were not working. "If the party had attractions for the youth [of eighteen to twenty-one], we would have had them long ago," wrote one of

[48] *Ibid.,* 193–202; *Prot. S. P., 1913,* 258; *Schulthess, 1913,* 101.

[49] *Prot. S. P., 1913,* 221.

[50] The pamphlets issued by the Youth Central in 1912 were largely directed to parents and adults concerned with youth training, rather than to the youths themselves. See titles in *Prot. S. P., 1912,* 20; cf. also 262–263, 273.

[51] *Ibid.,* 528; *1913,* 221.

the youth leaders.[52] Adolf Braun, a sensitive trade-union journalist, told the 1913 party congress,

We don't understand youth; we've all become old codgers. We convince ourselves that youth should be as understanding, wise and sober as all of us — alas! — have become . . .

Let's not deceive ourselves with the official report; we're not going forward, but the bourgeois youth movement is. The young people in the bourgeois youth movement have the feeling of far greater freedom and independence, of much less supervision than ours have. Perhaps they're more supervised and pushed around than ours, but they don't notice it as much. With us they perceive that they're to be watered down and disciplined. We want to make the youth as wise as [Ludwig] Frank, not as he was [when he was a fiery anti-militarist youth leader in 1905/1906], but as he is now . . . Many a one of us would be thankful if he were a quarter as smart today as he thought he was when he was eighteen. We must be able to transpose ourselves into the thought and feeling of the young people if we are to . . . have more than a paper success with them.[53]

There is nostalgia in this exposition of Braun's, nostalgia for the *élan* which the party as a whole now knew it had lost, and which alone could attract the youth. If the state-sponsored youth movement was making more headway, it was perhaps because its ideal of national superiority and national power was being tangibly and actively pursued; there was no evident gap between word and deed. Social Democracy, on the other hand, had come to fear the terrible practical consequences of pursuing its own ideal. It had, as Braun observed, grown old. That was why it had brought the youth movement under wraps in 1908; why its "educational" methods failed to satisfy the young; why, in 1913, it could, despite a general awareness of the nature of the youth problem, find no solution which did not involve a basic — and dangerous — change in party policy as a whole; and why, during the war, the majority of the youth movement deserted to the opposition.

The failure with youth was but the last of the long list of discouraging experiences which bore in upon the party in 1913–14 to shatter its previously high morale. Failure in reform, gathering

[52] *N.Z.*, XXXI, ii, 942.
[53] *Prot. S. P., 1913*, 257–258.

clouds of war, a poor showing in the Prussian and Baden elections, unprecedented dissension in the ranks, cessation of membership expansion, loss of subscribers to the party press, trouble in the trade-unions: everywhere gloom, gloom, and more gloom. Every development was calculated to reveal to the party, against the bright background of the electoral victory of 1912, the dark features of its impotence.

v. What Is to Be Done?

"As the assemblies of recent times show," we read in the *Sozialistische Monatshefte* of 11 September 1913, "there is in the party a great number of people who are of the opinion that something must happen." [54] What, then? What could the party do to resume the "irresistible forward march" so long honored in socialist rhetoric and so indispensable to party morale? Two types of solution were offered: one quantitative, the other qualitative.

The quantitative solutions involved additional and more refined forms of propaganda, more organization. The party should publish an illustrated newspaper, a family journal, a fashion periodical for women. The press should stress local news more; its tone should be less highbrow. The party should spend more money on youth; it should hire trained youth specialists. Someone discovered that there were 35,000 deaf mutes in Germany; the party should issue a special paper for them (it already published literature for the blind). The farmers had been too much neglected; a commission must be appointed to work out new approaches to them. These and similar proposals, all in the well-grooved tradition of mass manipulation, were presented to the Jena party congress of 1913. [55]

The qualitative solutions were likewise no novelty: the resort to a more offensive tactic, and, above all, the psychological preparation of the proletariat for the mass strike. We shall not burden the reader with a discussion of another long mass strike debate which reached its climax in the Jena party congress of 1913. We must, however, briefly indicate the new elements in the issue which throw light on the condition of the party in that year.

The first call for consideration of the mass strike came this time

[54] *S.M.*, XIX, iii, 1134.
[55] *Prot. S. P., 1913*, 244–281 *passim*.

not from the left radicals, but from the revisionist Ludwig Frank. The failure of the party in the Prussian *Landtag* elections was the immediate cause of his appeal. Despairing of the achievement of suffrage reform from within the *Landtag,* he called upon the party, in a stirring address, to prepare for mass action.[56] An impressive Belgian strike for suffrage reform in April 1913, which achieved at least a partial success, provided Frank and those who took up his summons with a useful, dramatic example of orderly mass action.[57]

In the press discussion of Frank's proposal, a second consideration appeared which soon outweighed the first: the mass strike as a therapeutic device for combating "the contagious disease of disappointment" and for reconstructing the party's lost self-confidence. The experience of the mass strike would revive the party's revolutionary spirit and sense of power.[58] "If one recognizes that dispiritedness is spreading," wrote a contributor to *Neue Zeit,* "if one misses proletarian combative defiance in the labor movement, and if one can't point to any other means to fight for suffrage reform, then surely one ought to take the general strike [weapon] out of the revolutionary arsenal without being frightened by the bloody specter of revolution." [59]

The mass strike discussion of 1913 thus had a different source than that of 1905 or 1910. It arose neither out of a strong popular wave of radicalism nor out of the tense atmosphere of constitutional crisis, but from the worried heads of the second echelon party leaders. "One turns to it," said Kautsky, who opposed the whole discussion, "not with an idea of victory, but out of embarrassment." [60]

By the time the congress met in September the idea of the mass strike had taken hold once more. Scheidemann's insistence that the mass strike discussion was confined to intellectuals was denied not only by its protagonists, but also by some of its enemies. Thus a high trade-union official reported with regret "that the whole mass

[56] Ludwig Frank, *Aufsätze, Reden, und Briefe,* ed. Hedwig Wachenheim (Berlin, n. d.), 267–269.
[57] For the Belgian strike, see Hendrik de Man, "Der belgische Wahlrechtsstreik," *N.Z.,* XXXI, ii, 244–252.
[58] *Ibid.,* 474–475.
[59] *Ibid.,* 610.
[60] *Ibid.,* 559.

strike discussion had done great damage in the organizations, because the disgruntled workers, who earn little and who are partially unemployed, have been largely stripped of their desire to do the . . . organizational work. That's what the people tell us in our meetings when we call on them to do the little jobs which are more necessary now than ever . . ." [61] On the other hand, Gustav Bauer, vice-chairman of the general commission, stated that, in areas where thousands were organized, only 100 men and women would attend the meetings where the mass strike was discussed. His evaluation of the attendance was probably justified; the mass strike idea was now a party question rather than a general question of the working class, which was more indifferent than incendiary in the year 1913. Yet Bauer showed concern lest the mass-strike discussion become general. The trade-unionists, he said, had embarked on a regular policy of refusing to discuss or debate the mass strike in meetings. "L. S. was the slogan," he said: *"Lasst schwätzen"* (let them chatter).[62]

If it was not a mass phenomenon, the interest in the mass strike had nevertheless acquired sufficient vitality within the party to oblige the reluctant executive, which found the whole discussion "untimely," to place it on the agenda of the 1913 party congress.[63] It was through the mass strike idea that the sense of sickness which pervaded the party was transformed into a divisive force dangerous not only to the reformist tactic, but to the very integrity of the party.

vi. The Final Alignment: Reunion on the Left

At the congress of Jena in 1913, all the major problems which beset the party flowed together. The members seemed to sense that the historical future of the party was at stake in its tactical decisions. If there were still theoretical questions, they presented themselves now not abstractly, but in immediately practical form. It was a time for the exercise not so much of the understanding as of the will. And as a clash of wills is always more bitter than a clash of minds,

---

[61] *Prot. S. P., 1913,* 314.
[62] *Ibid.,* 295, 298.
[63] Cf. Scheidemann, in *ibid.,* 228, 327.

so the fights at Jena were correspondingly more acrimonious than those of previous congresses.

Two major problems lay before the congress: to express its view on the Reichstag delegation's vote for the military taxes, and to decide on the desirability of preparing the party for the use of the mass strike. In both questions the reformist tactic was at stake. The taxation issue involved the broad and burning problem of the primacy of domestic reform over the fight against war. Behind the mass strike question lay all those phenomena which have been described in this and the preceding chapters: the frustration of the labor movement by state and employer, the dissatisfaction with the results of the reform tactic of 1912, the feeling of disproportion between the party's size and its power, the sense of stagnation in party life, and — last but not least — the attempt to reaffirm the revolutionary character of the party.

The significance of the military tax bill debate lay in the new alignment of forces. The arguments were, with minor modifications, the same as those advanced in the similar, if less *actuel,* debate in 1909.[64] The point of reference which gave the 1913 debate its importance was not the earlier tax issue of 1909, but the discussion on imperialism in 1912. In the latter the line of cleavage had run between the left radicals on one side, and the center, the revisionists, and the executive on the other. The issue then was not *whether* to fight for peace, but *how;* that is, whether the party should fight for peace with other allies within the capitalist framework, or through revolutionary isolation. In 1913, however, the left center felt that the vote for the military tax bills raised the question of *whether* to fight for peace or not. They had seriously meant it when, in 1912, they had voted for the sentence in Haase's resolution which expressed the party's "determined will to devote everything to bringing about an understanding between nations and to safeguard the peace." [65] They regarded the voting of funds for Germany's record-breaking military expansion of 1913 as inconsistent with this declaration.[66] The left center, the "men of principle," once more closed

[64] See above, Ch. VI, sec. iii.
[65] *Prot. S. P., 1912,* 529.
[66] See, in *ibid., 1913,* the speeches of Geyer (474–479), Hoch (481–484), Stolle (491–492), Stadthagen (494–497), Emmel (498–499), Ledebour (502–504).

ranks with the left radicals against the executive and its followers.

The same reunion on the left occurred on the issue of the mass strike. In this case the alliance of left and center radicals was the more striking in view of the centrists' negative attitude toward Luxemburg's campaign for the mass strike in 1910.[67]

The executive, well aware that a portion of the center was growing rebellious again, as it had in the Morocco crisis, took the bull by the horns and brought forth a resolution of its own on the mass strike. It reaffirmed the mass strike as a possible weapon, but one which could be used only if all the organizations of the proletariat — the phrase would include the coöperatives, which were more conservative than the trade-unions — favored its employment, and if the masses were "inspired for the last goals of socialism." These conditions meant, in effect, the postponement of mass strikes to the point of actual revolution. The resolution concluded that, in order to create the preconditions for the mass strike itself, "the party congress makes it the duty of the party comrades to work tirelessly for the expansion of the political and trade-union organizations." [68] Thus the executive's conception was to canalize the sentiment for mass strike into normal organizational work. The trade-union leadership trumped its partner's ace when it urged that the question of Prussian suffrage, around which the mass strike discussion centered, was actually not so "extraordinarily important," for, as Gustav Bauer said, even without it the labor movement had "the possibility of strengthening the organizations, of conducting . . . political struggles." The Reichstag suffrage provided "an adequate safety valve" which enabled the proletariat "to count its forces and to keep active politically." [69]

The radicals in drafting their resolution formulated their opposition to the executive in the sharpest possible way. They paralleled the language of the executive's motion as much as possible, but added an aggressive, revolutionary twist. Granting that a strong organization was prerequisite to the mass strike, the resolution stated that the mass strike could "nevertheless not be facticiously

[67] See above, Ch. VII, *passim.*

[68] *Prot. S. P., 1913,* 192–193, 300–301; Karl Kautsky, *Der politische Massenstreik* (Berlin, 1914), 297–298.

[69] *Prot. S. P., 1913,* 295.

produced on the command of the party and trade-union officials." The first condition of successful mass actions, the radicals said, was "an offensive, determined and consistent party tactic in every sphere. Only such a tactic, which consciously transfers the center of gravity of the struggle into the masses, is calculated to keep fighting energy and idealism alive in the ranks of the organized, as well as to carry along the unorganized in decisive moments, and to win them permanently for the trade-union and political organizations." [70] Thus the radicals almost stood the executive's resolution on its head: they made mass actions and an offensive tactic the precondition of the health and progress of the organization, rather than the reverse.

The radical motion was more far-reaching than Luxemburg's mass strike resolution in 1910.[71] Yet in 1910, the left centrists had given her no support; now they drafted the resolution with her.[72] There was more than the maintenance of ancient party principle involved here: it was a question of revolutionizing the Erfurt tactic. The left center was moving leftward once more.

It was this drift which the executive had most grounds to fear. Accordingly, it concentrated its fire on the left radicals, assailing their alleged anarchism and their efforts to whip up the followers against their responsible leaders. Scheidemann's personal attack on Luxemburg, complete with purple passages from her writings, was designed to portray her and her allies as what the Stalinists today call "wreckers." [73] Luxemburg, for her part, played it cautiously in order not to alienate center support, but her attack on the timorousness of the executive was not the less blistering for that.[74] With the majority of the congress, the executive's arguments succeeded, but a substantial portion of the left center could not be satisfied.

The leftists' antagonism to the executive found expression at the congress not only in the broad policy debates, but also in organiza-

---

[70] Ibid., 194.

[71] See above, Ch. VII, n. 72 and text.

[72] Her influence is clear in the wording of the passages given, which were taken from the resolution she drafted for the Niederbarnim local. The portions emphasizing the importance of organization, however, were introduced by the left center. Cf. the Niederbarnim and final radical resolutions, Prot. S. P., 1913, 179, 194; also 306–307.

[73] Ibid., 224–225, 230–231, 328–332.

[74] Ibid., 288–293.

tional matters. The Ledebour group, the *Sonderkonferenzler* of 1912, fought the executive's desire to name a committee on the agrarian question as a "sacrifice of a constituted right of the congress." [75] The maneuvering which marked the elections to the executive had no precedent in our period. The opposition centrists tried to name a candidate of their own for membership in the executive. When they had difficulties in securing a candidate, the executive, departing from previous custom, moved the cloture of nominations back one day. In view of the left center's protest, Ebert granted the centrists a three-hour extension for filing their nomination.[76] The left opposition, breaking from the tradition of accepting the executive's nominees, proposed the candidacy of Robert Dissmann, later leader of the Metal Workers' Union and of the Independent Party in Southwest Germany. Dissmann lost to the executive's candidate by only fifty-seven votes (269 to 211). The meager evidence of the congress proceedings suggest that the executive also broke precedent by trying to remove a radical associate member, Paul Brühl, who had voted at the congress against the executive's resolutions on taxation and the mass strike. By thirteen votes, Brühl lost his place to the executive's new candidate, Otto Wels, regional secretary for Brandenburg.[77] These election maneuvers were but another sign of the sharpness of the inner antagonisms in the last prewar years. In matters of personnel, as in those of tactic, there was no longer any mutual trust between the executive's party and the left opposition.

vii. Toward the Independent Social Democratic Party

The congress of Jena was the last general congress of united Social Democracy. Friedrich Ebert, the newly elected co-chairman, was delighted with its achievements:

When we look back over our proceedings, we can say with complete justice that the party congress has done good and industrious work. The

---

[75] *Ibid.*, 268.

[76] *Ibid.*, 448–450.

[77] *Ibid.*, 549. Wels was a skilled organizer, and deserving of the executive's recognition for services rendered. He saw to it that every electoral district organization in his region was represented at the congress, including one of only 82 members. He threw his block of 23 votes solidly behind the executive, although his district contained radical Potsdam-Osthavelland, the Reichstag constituency of Karl Liebknecht.

party congress has sanctioned the activity of the party leadership and the Reichstag delegation . . .

For our enemies, our meeting was a really bitter disappointment. They put their only hope in the party's self-destruction, and they had particularly great expectations of this congress in that regard . . . Surely I do not exaggerate when I say that . . . the decisive will to party unity and coherence has seldom been more strongly expressed at any party congress than at this one. This congress has reaffirmed anew the realization [that] the summoning of all forces in the party to unified work is the root of our strength and our successes.[78]

True, the majority had supported the executive in all things. But this had ceased to be a sign of unity, let alone of strength. With a kind of uncanny precision, the party congress had pulled at the seams along which it was soon to split. There was once more a tactical unity on the left, this time as a minority opposition at the congress. Not since 1909 had there been a congress at which left radicals and left centrists were at one on all major issues. Whatever their theoretical differences, they put them by in a common fight for the radicalization of the tactic and the maintenance of the party's intransigent opposition to military credits. The left center had been brought to accept, through the frustrations and dangers of the reform policy, the substance of the left radical tactic. The division of 1910 was temporarily overcome.

The balloting revealed that 30 per cent of the congress was now in favor of an offensive tactic and opposed to the party's stand on the tax question.[79] An analysis of the roll-call vote, which we have considered before in another connection,[80] makes it possible to establish a surprising degree of continuity between the division at the congress and the later Independent Social Democratic Party, both in terms of leadership and local organizations.

The Reichstag deputies at the Jena congress divided in about the same proportion as the congress delegates as a whole. Of the eighty-seven deputies present (exclusive of the members of the executive), twenty-seven voted radical on both issues, six voted radical only on

---

[78] *Ibid.*, 554–555.

[79] On the mass strike question, the vote was 333 to 142; on the taxation resolution, 336 to 140. See *Prot. S. P., 1913,* 337–338, 515–516.

[80] See above, Ch. V, sec. iv.

the mass strike question, while three voted against the executive only on the taxation resolution.

From this group the parliamentary leadership of Independent Social Democracy was to emerge. Of the fourteen deputies who opposed voting the war credits in the famous caucus of 3 August 1914, thirteen had participated in the Jena congress; all but one had voted with the opposition, not merely against the military tax bill, but also for the offensive tactic.[81] And of the eighteen deputies who on 24 March 1916 set up the "Social Democratic Collaboration Group (*Sozialdemokratische Arbeitsgemeinschaft*)," the parliamentary embryo of the Independent Social Democratic Party, fifteen had been associated with the opposition in 1913.[82]

The records of the organizations show the same continuity from prewar dissatisfaction with the reformist tactic to secessionism during the war. By October 1917, when the Independent Social Democratic Party was six months old, it included fifty-eight electoral district organizations which had seceded from the old party. Of these, thirty-seven were included in six regional organizations which broke from the parent party.[83] The remaining twenty-one seceded from regional organizations which remained loyal.[84]

The great majority of the seceding organizations were already in radical hands in 1913, as their voting records at Jena show. Of the six regional organizations which bolted in 1917, four had had majorities for a more radical tactic and a condemnation of the party's military tax policy in 1913; one had been evenly divided between radical and conservative; only one (Greater Berlin) had shown a conservative majority (see Table III). Of the twenty-one locals which seceded in 1917 from regional organizations remaining loyal

[81] Albrecht, Antrick, Bock, Geyer, Henke, Herzfeld, Ledebour, Lensch, Liebknecht (who did not vote with the radicals on the tax question), Rühle, Vogtherr and Emmel. Cf. *Prot. S. P., 1913*, 337; and Eugen Prager, *Geschichte der U.S.P.D.* (Berlin, 1922), 26. Haase did not attend the Jena congress. Peirotes, a revisionist, voted conservative on both issues; he was presumably motivated to oppose the war credits in 1914 by his Alsatian patriotism.

[82] One (Haase) had been absent, two (Wurm and Bernstein) had voted conservative. Cf. Prager, *U.S.P.D.*, 96, with *Prot. S. P., 1913*, 337, 515–516.

[83] Ebert, in 1917, reported the number of locals in the secessionist regional organizations as 36; this figure does not correspond to the list of locals by region in 1913, which gives the figure as 37. Cf. *Prot. S. P., 1917*, 235 and *1913*, 54–71.

[84] *Ibid., 1917*, 235.

TABLE III

*Political Complexion of Later Independent Social Democratic Regional Organizations
at Jena Congress, 1913*

Regional organization	No. locals[a]	Vote on mass strike resolution			Vote on military tax resolution		
		Rad.	Conserv.	Abstain.	Rad.	Conserv.	Abstain.
Greater Berlin	8	6	28	–	15	17	2
Halle	8	7	3	1	8	3	–
Erfurt	4	2	1	–	2	1	–
Leipzig	4	7	5	2	10	4	–
Frankfurt-a-M.[b]	11	13	5	–	9	9	–
Brunswick	3	1	2	–	2	1	–

For the method of computation of this table, see above, Chapter V, note 89.
[a] Election district organizations.
[b] The city organization of Frankfurt did not follow the regional organization into the Independent Party.

only five had predominantly conservative records in the congress of 1913.[85] Not all the organizations which had indicated radicalism in 1913 became oppositionist: there were eighteen locals, radical before the war, which remained within the party.[86] These were the exceptions. The core of the Independent Social Democratic Party was provided by organizations in radical control before 1914, which came over to the new party, lock, stock and barrel.[87]

[85] The secessionist organizations, grouped by voting record at the Jena congress of 1913, were as follows:

With conservative majorities (5): Elberfeld-Barmen, Potsdam-Osthavelland, Aschaffenburg, Reuss ä.L., Reuss j.L.
With radical majorities (12): Solingen, Düsseldorf, Essen, Hagen-Schwelm, Königsberg Stadt, Königsberg Land, Randow-Greifenhagen, Pirna, Weimar I, Weimar II, Gotha, Bremen.
Evenly divided (3): Lennep-Remscheid-Mettmann, Schwarzburg-Rudolstadt, Friedberg-Büdingen.
Unidentified (1): Limbach.
[86] Mülhausen i. Els., Duisburg, Bayreuth, Nürnberg, Köln Stadt u. Land, Göppingen-Gmünd, Esslingen, Annaberg, Zschoppau, Mittweida, Stade-Bremervörde, Zwickau, Neustadt-Jena (Weimar III), München-Gladbach, Krefeld, Labiau-Wehlau, Coburg, Stuhm-Marienwerder.
[87] At the founding convention of the Independents in April 1917, 91 electoral district organizations sent representatives. The sources do not name the electoral districts, but give only the number of districts represented from each region. It may be assumed, however, that the old organizations, which seceded from the old party as units, would have done so early, and that the figure available for October (58)

If the Independent Social Democratic Party was a well-formed embryo in the organizational sense in 1913, the same was true of its political character. The Independent Party has too often been regarded as "the product of a temporary war-time situation," with opposition to the government's war policy as its *raison d'être*.[88] Here again, the 1913 Congress throws some light. Opposition to the support of the military tax bill had, as its corollary, a rejection of the whole reformist course, a demand for an aggressive, offensive policy of mass action. Resistance to war and general political radicalism went hand in hand. Bernstein and the negligible few who shared his views in the Independent Party were but exceptions to prove the rule. The professions of those who argued that the party could pursue an anti-war course within the framework of a reformist tactic, or that the sanctioning of the 1913 tax reform in no sense compromised the party's anti-war position, were soon shown to be hollow. Those who supported the executive's position in 1913 also followed it to its logical outcome: the support of the war effort and the suspension of opposition to the state.[89] True, there were many of the 1913 opposition who could not bring themselves to break with the old party in 1916–17. This does not alter the fact, however, that there was an integral connection between the rejection of a reformist course and resistance to war after as before 1914. Though the connection was obscured by the adherence of a handful of reformists to the Independent Party during the war, it emerged again during the Revolution and in the final fate of the Independent Party in 1920: its dissolution and the entry of its majority into the Communist Party.

---

would be reasonably valid for April. In this case, about three-fifths of the new party's locals would have come from the old party, while two-fifths would have been newly formed break-offs from majority-controlled locals.

[88] Cf., for example, Arthur Rosenberg, *The Birth of the German Republic* (London, 1931), 120–122; A. Joseph Berlau, *The German Social-Democratic Party, 1914–1921* (New York, 1949), 146. Berlau over-generalizes the exceptions to the basic continuities of the prewar alignments.

[89] Among the parliamentarians who supported the executive in 1913, only six were in the wartime opposition even before the split.

Chapter XI

WAR AND SCHISM

i. August Fourth

By its unanimous vote for the war credits on 4 August 1914, the Social Democratic Reichstag delegation made its crucial contribution to the creation of national unity in defense of the existing state. The slogan, "To this system, no man and no penny," was finally abandoned for the slogan which had competed with it since 1907: "In the hour of danger, we shall not leave the Fatherland in the lurch."

To one who has followed the evolution of Social Democracy through the prewar decade, the vote for the war credits on 4 August 1914 is but the logical end of a clear line of development.[1] It was forecast in the party's attitude toward the first Morocco crisis; in the leadership's reaction to the electoral defeat in 1907, its behavior at the Stuttgart congress of the International in 1907, and its attitude in the second Morocco crisis; and, perhaps most clearly, in the vote for the military tax bill in 1913.

To those who lived through the stormy days which followed

[1] Cf., for the most recent statement of the opposing view, A. Joseph Berlau, *The German Social Democratic Party, 1914–1921* (New York, 1949), 67–69. Berlau argues that the party's consistent official rejection of revisionism before 1914 meant that the direction which the party would take in the war was at least an open question. My own view is, of course, that the command of the crucial power positions in the party had passed to the reformist forces in the preceding decade, and that this, not the official ideology of the party, was decisive in 1914.

Sarajevo, however, a Social Democratic decision to refuse the credits would have come as no surprise. When the international crisis first broke, the executive acted with a promptness and vigor which stood in sharpest contrast to its temporizing in the Morocco crisis of 1911. Its manifesto of 25 July 1914 could have been drafted by the most radical of radicals. Calling for mass demonstrations against the war, it stated:

The class-conscious proletariat of Germany, in the name of humanity and civilization, raises a flaming protest against this criminal activity of the warmongers. It insistently demands that the German Government exercise its influence on the Austrian Government to maintain peace; and, in the event that the shameful war cannot be prevented, that it refrain from belligerent intervention. No drop of blood of a German soldier may be sacrificed to the power lust of the Austrian ruling group [or] to the imperialistic profit-interests.[2]

The manifesto found swift response at the local level. Between 26 and 30 July demonstrations were held throughout Germany.[3]

The stiff stand and swift action taken by the executive in the first five days of the crisis (25–29 July 1914) was at least in part the result of a purely temporary displacement of the locus of power in that body. Scheidemann, Ebert, and Molkenbuhr, the most determined conservatives of the executive, were all away from Berlin on holiday.[4] Haase, the strongest of the remaining members, unquestionably exercised a dominant influence in framing the policy in those critical days.

The course which Haase was steering would have maintained the Erfurt policy of passive opposition to the state and the war, but the turn away from it came swiftly. Between 26 and 30 July, the missing members of the executive returned to Berlin. The sources do not reveal how many of the members had made up their minds before the 30th on the party's policy. Haase's behavior during the last week of July indicates that he opposed support to the war effort. On

<hr />

[2] Carl Grünberg, *Die Internationale und der Weltkrieg*, I, "Vor dem Kriege und während der ersten Kriegswochen" (Leipzig, 1916), 51.

[3] Edwyn Bevan, *German Social Democracy during the War* (London, 1918), 8–9.

[4] Philipp Scheidemann, *Memoiren eines Sozialdemokraten* (Dresden, 1928), I, 234; Friedrich Ebert, *Schriften, Aufzeichnungen, Reden* (Dresden, 1926), I, 309; Bevan, *Social Democracy*, 7.

Ebert's position before the 30th, there is but one bit of evidence, a letter to the executive written from his vacation spot on 27 July. He approved the demonstrations, and indicated only indirectly that he would favor the cessation of opposition when he spoke of "difficulties" which would arise within the party: "War and the powerful revitalization of the labor movement in Russia will surely fill the Rosa [Luxemburg] group with new plans." [5] Scheidemann, in his memoirs, indicates that he was vastly impressed with the power of the patriotic demonstrations in Berlin, which the Social Democratic rallies "could not outbid," but he tells us nothing of his attitude toward the party's course until 30 July. [6] That the executive had fallen into confusion in the last days of July is indicated by the fact that Hermann Müller was dispatched to Paris to consult with the French socialists (31 July) without instructions and with no decision reached on party policy toward war credits. [7]

By 30 July it was clear that war could not be averted, and that a state of siege would be declared momentarily. The executive now met to draft a second manifesto which reflected a mood neither of defiance nor of chauvinism, but one of failure and anxiety which no idealistic rhetoric could disguise:

Until the last minute, the international proletariat did its duty, here and beyond our borders, and harnessed all its power to maintain peace and make war impossible. If our earnest protests, our repeated efforts were unsuccessful, if the conditions under which we live were once again stronger than our will and that of our fellow-workers, we must nevertheless look with resolution at what the future may bring.

* * * * *

The strict prescriptions of military law strike the labor movement with dreadful severity. Ill-considered actions, needless and falsely understood sacrifices at this moment [can] harm not only the individual but our cause. Party comrades! We call upon you to hold out in the unshakeable confidence that, in spite of all, the future belongs to international socialism, justice and humanity. [8]

[5] Ebert, *Schriften*, I, 309.
[6] Scheidemann, *Memoiren*, I, 235ff.
[7] Bevan, *Social Democracy*, 13–14; Karl Liebknecht, *Klassenkampf gegen den Krieg* (Berlin, n. d. [1919?]), 11.
[8] Grünberg, *Die Internationale und der Weltkrieg*, I, 63–64.

Out of this manifesto there speaks the worst enemy of logically conducted politics: fear. Perhaps we should say "fears," for there was more than one source of anxiety.

First and foremost was the fear of state action against the Social Democratic leaders and the party's institutions. In the application of a state of siege, German law accorded to the commanders of military districts virtually dictatorial powers against any actions which might stimulate the use of force against the authority of the state. The military were responsible to no civilian authority except the King-Emperor. In 1911, in view of the mounting internal and international tension, it was decided that even if war only threatened, a state of siege would be proclaimed for all corps districts whether there was unrest or not. A few weeks before the outbreak of World War I, Bethmann-Hollweg tried to have the enormous political powers of the army under the state of siege curtailed, lest the stringent regime rather incite than allay dangerous opposition. He succeeded only in securing from the military a pledge that the Social Democratic leaders would not be arrested and their press suppressed as a matter of course at the outset of war.[9]

Under the rigorous law of siege, Social Democracy, if it were to continue in its oppositional position, might have to pay the price in a return to the conditions of the Bismarckian era, and the suppression of its organizations. This threat was a powerful force in determining the Social Democratic attitude.[10] On the evening of 30 July, Ebert and Otto Braun were dispatched to Zürich with the treasury, so that the party might have some continuity if the other leaders were seized and the party dissolved.[11] The trade-union leaders, likewise fearful for their organizations under the state of siege, took a different form of precaution. Shortly before 1 August (the exact date is not clear), the leaders went to the Reich Office of the Interior to ask what the status of their organizations would be in the war. According to Paul Umbreit, official historian of the trade-unions, the government's answer was "reassuring in every respect:

[9] E. O. Volkmann, *Der Marxismus und das deutsche Heer im Weltkriege* (Berlin, 1925), 50–52.
[10] Untersuchungsausschuss der . . . verfassungsgebenden deutschen Nationalversammlung und des deutschen Reichstages, *Vierte Reihe. Die Ursachen des deutschen Zusammenbruches im Jahre 1918* (Berlin, 1925–1929), IV, 277. (Hereinafter cited as Untersuchungsausschuss, *4. Reihe.*)
[11] Scheidemann, *Memoiren,* I, 245.

'We do not think of going after you, provided that you make no difficulties for us, for we are glad to have great labor organizations which can help the administration in necessary social work.'" [12] A conference of representatives of the trade-union leagues on 2 August called off all strikes pending or in progress. To make assurance doubly sure, it declared the suspension of all strike support payments for the duration. Trade-union funds were henceforth to be devoted to unemployment relief and to the support of war victims. The trade-unions also reached an accord with the employers' associations for the automatic extension of wage contracts and the banning of strikes and lockouts for the duration.[13] Characteristically, the trade-unions acted even before the party in ending all opposition to state and employer and throwing their weight behind the war effort. Their action could not have been without influence on the decision of the Social Democratic Reichstag delegates, of whom one-fourth were trade-union officials.[14]

The fear of the severity of the law of siege might have been enough to determine the vote for the war credits. But to this factor, two others, quite as real, were added: the fear of defeat, especially at the hands of the Russians, and that of the loss of working-class support. These can be grouped under one head: the identification of the working class with the destiny of the nation. Friedrich Stampfer expressed the party's alternatives as the majority of its leaders saw them: either with the German people upward to power, or against the people down into the abyss of impotence.[15] The party

[12] Paul Umbreit, *Die deutschen Gewerkschaften im Weltkrieg*, Sozialwissenschaftliche Bibliothek, I (Berlin, 1917), 21.

[13] *Ibid.*, 20–21; cf. also Paul Umbreit and Charlotte Lorenz, *Der Krieg und die Arbeitsverhältnisse*, Wirtschafts- und Sozialgeschichte des Weltkrieges, Deutsche Serie (Stuttgart and New Haven, 1928; ed. James T. Shotwell) 158–160; Richard Müller, *Vom Kaiserreich zur Republik* (Vienna, 1924), I, 36–37; Paul Frölich, *Zehn Jahre Krieg und Bürgerkrieg* (2nd edition, Berlin, 1924), I, 90–91.

[14] Willy Kremer, *Der soziale Aufbau der Parteien des deutschen Reichstages von 1871–1918* (Emsdetten, 1934), 62–65; John L. Snell, "Socialist Unions and Socialist Patriotism in Germany, 1914–1918," *American Historical Review*, LIX: 67 (1953).

[15] *N.Z.*, XXXV, ii, 20. Cf. also Bevan, *Social Democracy*, 15; Berlau, *Social Democratic Party*, 73. The role of patriotic enthusiasm in the working class is perhaps too heavily stressed in Evelyn Anderson, *Hammer or Anvil. The Story of the German Working Class Movement* (London, 1945), 19–20, 22–25. William Maehl places primary emphasis on the fear of Russia. Cf. Maehl, "The Triumph of Nationalism in the German Socialist Party on the Eve of the First World War," *Journal of Modern History*, XXIV: 40 (1952).

confronted in magnified form the situation of 1907 where the national idea governed the imaginations of the majority of the people.

In the confused atmosphere of the week preceding August 4 there appeared a psychological factor of great importance to the subsequent evolution of the schism. That was what one might call the desire to belong, or, negatively stated, the urge to escape from the pariah position in which the Social Democrats had been held by the pressure of the ruling class and by the political philosophy with which they sought to meet that pressure. The reformist component in the party's prewar policy, the quest not for power but for *"Gleichberechtigung,"* was bound up with the desire for status and recognition within the existing order. How the socialist ethos of perennial opposition and the desire to belong were brought into a final conflict at the outbreak of the war was revealed in a confession of the erstwhile left radical, Konrad Haenisch:

The conflict of two souls in one breast was probably easy for none of us. May the author try to overcome a certain inner embarrassment and speak for a moment of himself . . . ? Well, then I'd like to say: not for everything in the world would I like to live through those days of inner struggle again! [On the one hand] this driving, burning desire to throw oneself into the powerful current of the general national tide, and, on the other, the terrible spiritual fear of following that desire fully, of surrendering oneself to the mood which roared about one and which, if one looked deep into one's heart, had long since taken possession of the soul. This fear: will you not also betray yourself and your cause? Can you not feel as your heart feels? [Thus it was] until suddenly — I shall never forget the day and hour — the terrible tension was resolved; until one dared to be what one was; until — despite all principles and wooden theories — one could, for the first time in almost a quarter century, join with a full heart, a clean conscience and without a sense of treason in the sweeping, stormy song: *'Deutschland, Deutschland über alles'.*[16]

The decision of the Social Democratic Reichstag delegation to vote the war credits was taken in an atmosphere somewhat reminiscent of that of another August 4 — that of 1789, when the nobility of France, seized by a paroxysm of fear, voted away its privileges and, in effect, publicly renounced its own principles of social organization. As in 1789 the hard facts of political life — above all the

[16] Quoted in Eugen Prager, *Geschichte der U.S.P.D.* (Berlin, 1922), 34.

threat of force against the nobility — operated to strengthen the left wing of the second estate, so in 1914 the cold facts favored the right wing of the German Social Democratic Party.

In the critical caucus of the Reichstag deputation of 3 August, only the revisionists were clearheaded and determined; the radicals were divided, uncertain, and confused. Eduard David gave a strong and clear recommendation for voting the credits, urging that the moment of national danger demanded that the party "free itself of outworn concepts" that it "unlearn and re-learn." [17] The trade-unions had already taken their stand. Twenty to thirty members who favored the credits had agreed to break discipline if the majority in the caucus decided to vote against them.[18] The fourteen opponents of the credits, overwhelmed by the situation, could not muster similar resolution. The degree of their confusion was revealed in the fact that they insisted excitedly that Haase, an opponent of the credits, read the majority's declaration in support thereof in the Reichstag.[19] Expecting that the party, despite its about-face on the war credits, would soon resume its oppositional position, the minority felt that it should not separate itself publicly from the majority.[20] Confronted by the ultimate test of their relationship to state and nation, the Social Democratic deputies unanimously cast their vote in the Reichstag in support of the national war effort.

ii. The New Position of the Labor Leaders

The advent of war created an atmosphere of national solidarity, nay jubilation, which had no precedent in our period. The internal tensions of German society seemed to find their release in the prospective struggle against the external enemy. For Bethmann-Hollweg, who was anything but warlike by temperament, the "spirit of 1914" was the realization of a long-cherished dream:

This wonderful spirit, which welds the hearts of the German people into an unprecedented unity, — it must and will remain victorious . . . As if by magic, the barriers have fallen which, through a barren and de-

---

[17] Liebknecht, *Klassenkampf*, 14.

[18] *Ibid.*, 55, 87; Grünberg, *Die Internationale und der Weltkrieg*, I, 73.

[19] Scheidemann, *Memoiren*, I, 257–258.

[20] Liebknecht, *Klassenkampf*, 16, 87–88; Grünberg, *Die Internationale und der Weltkrieg*, I, 73.

pressed period, have separated the sectors of the people from each other, [barriers] which we erected against each other in misunderstanding, ill-favor, and mistrust. It is a liberation and a blessing that at last all this trash has been swept away, that only the individual person counts, one equal to the other, one stretching out his hand to the other for a single, holy goal.[21]

If, as Clausewitz said, "war is an extension of politics by other means," this dictum was applicable to the domestic as well as the foreign policy of the German government in World War I. The regime was ready to utilize the advantages which the national mood offered it. The stagnation by stalemate which prevailed before the war could now be lifted to a new plane: stagnation by consent. Such was the meaning of the *Burgfrieden,* the voluntary suspension by the political parties of all struggle among themselves and against the government. All parties, even the Social Democratic, accepted the *Burgfrieden,* which gave the government "a dictatorial right to decide all military, political and economic questions." [22]

It can readily be understood that the *Burgfrieden* implied a greater change in policy for the Social Democratic Party, with its tradition of pure opposition, than for any other. Bethmann-Hollweg was resolved to do what he could to reconcile the Social Democrats to it. He cautioned army and bureaucracy to accord Social Democratic persons equal treatment with others, and relieve them of the feeling that they stood under special police and judicial controls. He held out the possibility of a "new orientation" of domestic policy after the war and promised, in the meantime, to introduce certain minor social and political innovations. The most fundamental reform, that of the Prussian suffrage, was not to be taken up for the duration.[23]

The "new orientation" unquestionably exercised a strong influence on the attitude of the Social Democratic leaders. No reader of Scheidemann can miss the genuine pleasure which he felt in being invited to discuss matters on an equal footing with the ministers of state. Parliamentary junkets to the front, where high officers played

[21] Address to the Reichstag, 2 Dec. 1914, *Schulthess, 1914,* I, 437.

[22] Arthur Rosenberg, *The Birth of the German Republic* (New York, 1931), 77.

[23] Volkmann, *Marxismus,* 75–79, 275–277; cf. also Scheidemann, *Memoiren,* I, 310–313.

host to Social Democratic deputies, heightened their feeling of being in the club.[24]

Particularly striking was the new role of the trade-unionists in the war economy. Having voluntarily abandoned the right to strike, they had to concentrate their efforts on securing a recognized position in public or semi-public bodies concerned with welfare and economic administration. In certain of these, such as the boards for the economic rehabilitation of disabled veterans, the administration of labor exchanges, and the labor arbitration boards, the union officials frequently won a considerable measure of influence.[25]

Having accepted the *Burgfrieden*, the labor movement could only defend its interest "at the green table," as the Germans say. It was of vital importance that its leaders establish good relations with the state bureaucracy and penetrate the institutions dealing with labor's problems. Yet inevitably in this process the meaning and function of the labor leaders changed. Their responsibility was now dual: to the state as well as to the workers. Once they accepted the primacy of foreign policy, the leaders of the labor movement assumed the function of disciplining the labor movement in the interest of the state. In national government, the *Burgfrieden* strengthened the civil and military bureaucracy at the expense of the Reichstag; within the labor movement it increased the power of the leaders as mass participation in public agitation and labor struggle declined. Before the war, the gap between leaders and followers, especially in the trade-unions, had been a serious problem. Even the sweet side of the *Burgfrieden,* the new recognition accorded labor leaders and their organizations, would tend to widen that breach unless the political and economic concessions extracted at the green table were far-reaching enough to destroy the powerful legacy of lower-class hostility to the upper orders.

Its full subscription to the *Burgfrieden*, then, had three major effects on the labor movement. First, it drew the leaders psychologically closer to the ruling groups. Second, it raised the importance

[24] Gustav Noske, *Erlebtes aus Aufstieg und Niedergang einer Demokratie* (Offenbach, 1947), 39–40, 44–45, 55–58; Scheidemann, Memoiren, I, 274–277.
[25] Umbreit and Lorenz, *Krieg und Arbeitsverhältnisse,* 79–80, 113–118; cf. also Vorstand des Deutschen Metallarbeiter-Verbandes, *Der Deutsche Metallarbeiter-Verband im Jahre 1916* (Stuttgart, 1917), 10–12, 403–409.

of the leaders within the labor movement by confining political and economic action essentially to the negotiating level. Third, it compelled Social Democracy to adhere fully, in word as in deed, to a strict reformist course.[26] With respect to the second and third points, the *Burgfrieden* was backed up by the state of siege, whose military executors stood always ready to enforce the reformist course upon the Social Democratic Party should it show signs of wavering. The government's iron hand in a velvet glove lifted the reformists of Social Democracy to a total victory which they could not have won of their own strength.

iii. The New Discipline and the Re-emergence of the Opposition

When we recall the strength and solidity of the radical opposition to the leadership in 1913, we cannot be surprised at its swift re-emergence after the initial shock of August 4. But as the radicals set to work to bring the party back to its oppositional policy, they quickly found that the conditions under which they had to propagate their views, even inside the party, were drastically altered. Heretofore the pressure of the state, however much it increased the tension within the party, had been a force for holding its dissident wings together; now it became a force for driving them apart. It was of the essence of the party's new position that any basic opposition to its policy was *ipso facto* an attack on the national war effort and the state, and vice versa. If Social Democracy's subscription to the *Burgfrieden* was to be meaningful, then the *Burgfrieden* would have to be enforced within the party itself. At its first wartime meeting, on 27 September 1914, the party council ruled accordingly.[27]

In the new historical situation, then, party discipline changed both in form and political content. We have seen an increasing need

---

[26] Particularly striking is the address of Scheidemann at the 1917 party congress, where he insisted that the war created an "alliance" between the classes which would make forever impossible a return to pure opposition and agitation. Cf. *Prot. S. P., 1917*, 404–413. A literary monument to the hope of bourgeois intellectuals and majority Socialist leaders in a transcendence of class struggle through the war effort is a volume of essays published by Friedrich Thimme, Prussian archivist, and Carl Legien under the title, *Die Arbeiterschaft im neuen Deutschland* (Leipzig, 1915).

[27] *Prot. S. P., 1917*, 29.

for discipline and a sharper application of it as the polarization of the party developed in the prewar years. The iron-bound wartime discipline of Social Democracy was a projection of this tendency to such a degree that the change in quantity became a change in quality. Before the war, discipline had applied largely to actions; the right to oppose the leadership's policies in the press and in meetings had been sometimes infringed but never denied in principle. Now that opposition to the party leaders became a menace to national unity, freedom of discussion had to be sharply curtailed. Even at the level of freedom of action, which involved primarily the tradition of unanimous voting in parliamentary bodies, discipline had been regarded before the war as a means to enforce resolutions and principles adopted by the party congresses. Now this concept was stood on its head: Karl Liebknecht and those who joined him later in voting against war credits were condemned and ultimately expelled for adhering to the decisions of the congresses which the parliamentary majority violated.[28]

The methods and content of the new discipline at both the organizational and the parliamentary level became fully apparent as early as 1914. Necessary to the maintenance of party unity in the new situation, discipline paradoxically became a major factor in the rapid maturing of the split. Let us examine briefly its concrete operation.

The executive knew its party well enough to realize that there would be trouble over the new policy: certainly from the "Rosa group," as Ebert had predicted, and perhaps beyond.[29] Official censorship, much as the Social Democrats detested it, would naturally help to keep the opposition within bounds, and the executive counseled strict observance of its regulations.[30] Since the oppositionists, such as the editors of *Vorwärts,* at first feared the consequences of violating the censor's regulations, they readily complied.[31] But by

[28] Cf. Liebknecht, *Klassenkampf,* 53.

[29] See above, Ch. XI, n. 5 and text; also Haase's view, quoted in Bevan, *Social Democracy,* 20.

[30] This was first hinted at in the 30 July warning against rash behavior under the state of siege, *q.v.* above, Ch. XI, n. 8 and text. Cf. also Scheidemann, *Memoiren,* I, 266–271.

[31] Cf. *Vorwärts'* declaration to readers, 1 Aug. 1914, reprinted in Grünberg, *Die Internationale und der Weltkrieg,* I, 64–65. For its oppositionist position, see Curt Schoen, *Der Vorwärts und die Kriegserklärung, vom Fürstenmord in Sarajevo bis zur Marneschlacht* (Berlin, 1929), *passim;* also Prager, *U.S.P.D.,* 30–32.

mid-September 1914 they began to venture an expression of their real views. The military censors twice suspended publication of *Vorwärts* before the end of 1914. Each time the executive interceded through the Reich Office of the Interior for its release, which followed after pledges of good behavior, including a promise to refrain from mentioning the class struggle. Soon the problem began to spread to other party organs. Scheidemann reports that, "day after day," the executive had to intercede for one newspaper or another.[32]

In Berlin the position of the executive rapidly became impossible. The press commission of the Berlin organization, like the Berlin organization as a whole, supported the *Vorwärts* editors in their policy of opposition. Press commission and national executive were thus in a constant feud. The executive, fearing the effect on the party of drastic action against the *Vorwärts* editors, continued for a time to use its good offices with the government on the paper's behalf. Thus it was involved in supporting an opposition which might be fatal to its own policy. Normally, of course, a dispute between executive and press commission would be carried to the control commission, the party's superior court, for settlement. But the left was still strongly represented on that body. For the executive to appeal to it, said Scheidemann, "would have meant no more than filing a complaint against the devil with his grandmother, namely Klara Zetkin."[33] In January 1915 Scheidemann tried obliquely to raise sentiment for a change in *Vorwärts* editors on the grounds of the paper's poor journalistic quality, which no one who has suffered through its dull pages could honestly deny.[34] This was the first groping for the solution to which the executive was ultimately driven by the logic of its own position: the confiscation of the Berlin party's paper in October 1916.[35]

Karl Liebknecht was the first parliamentarian to test the meaning of the "party *Burgfrieden*." He had voted for the credits on 4 August and expected, as did the other oppositionists, that the mood of that time would pass and that the party could by internal means be brought back at least to its oppositional course. He therefore began

[32] Scheidemann, *Memoiren*, I, 271; cf. also 266–270.
[33] *Ibid.*, I, 268.
[34] *Ibid.*, I, 271–272.
[35] Prager, *U.S.P.D.*, 116–120.

at once, with his friends Luxemburg, Mehring, and Zetkin, to work for a reversal of the party's policy.[36]

At the end of August Liebknecht wrote to the executive to suggest the holding of meetings for peace and against annexations. According to his account the executive rejected this proposal because it feared that some of the comrades would express themselves in favor of annexations.[37] In September Liebknecht revealed to the public the existence of differences of opinion in the Reichstag delegation on the approval of the credits, journeyed to Belgium and Holland to inform the foreign comrades of the existence of an opposition within the German party, and went to Stuttgart to mobilize sentiment against the action of the Reichstag deputation.[38]

The reaction of the party leadership to Liebknecht's activities was perhaps of more importance for the schism than his actions in themselves. Attacked for his behavior in the party council, Liebknecht was summoned before the executive to explain himself. He averred that he was defending the interest of the party in revealing that the deputation had been divided on the credits. The executive insisted, with the concurrence of the party council, that the protection of the interest of the party was "the exclusive task of the party leadership."[39] Liebknecht defended himself in terms of a democratic theory of membership responsibility, asserting that every party comrade shared the duty of defending the party's interests. "We are still so damned democratic," he wrote to the executive, "that every party comrade may take a stand even against the highest party authorities."[40] Liebknecht's conceptions were simply anachronistic. The changed relationship of the party to the state demanded that it keep its opposition under control, that it maintain the *Burgfrieden* within the labor movement.

What the majority leaders wished, or, rather, were compelled to

[36] Ossip K. Flechtheim, *Die KPD in der Weimarer Republik* (Offenbach a. M., 1948), 11. Cf. Mehring's letter to the *Labour Leader,* Dec. 1914, in Ernst Drahn and Susanne Leonhard, *Unterirdische Literatur im revolutionären Deutschland während des Weltkrieges* (Berlin-Fichtenau, 1920), 15–16.

[37] Liebknecht, *Klassenkampf,* 16.

[38] Ibid., 17; Wilhelm Keil, *Erlebnisse eines Sozialdemokraten* (Stuttgart, 1947), I, 309–310.

[39] Letter from Scheidemann, on behalf of the executive, to Liebknecht, 7 Oct. 1914, in Liebknecht, *Klassenkampf,* 23.

[40] Letter from Liebknecht to the executive, 10 Oct. 1914, *ibid.,* 24.

wish, was an end to all discussion in the party. On 5 August 1914 the annual congresses were declared postponed *sine die*.[41] At the local level, at least in some localities where the conservatives were in control, membership meetings were rarely held. Thus in Hamburg the nascent opposition could reach the party membership openly only in one district where initiative in summoning meetings rested with the rank and file rather than with the local executive.[42] The opposition maintained that the leadership had a duty to consult the membership on the party line, and in early 1915 began to agitate for a revised organization statute. Thus the inability of the opposition to secure a hearing in the party at once led into the organizational question, with all its schismatic implications.[43]

Nowhere did the problem of the new discipline come to a head more rapidly than in Württemberg. Here, as we know, the rightist regional bureaucracy and Stuttgart's radical machine had been at each other's throats for years. In August 1914 the trouble began anew when the Stuttgart local and the *Schwäbische Tagwacht,* the organ of both the city and the *Land* organizations, launched a campaign for peace without annexations. In November the *Land* party authorities installed the conservative Wilhelm Keil as editor of the *Tagwacht* to bring the paper's policy into harmony with the party line. The national executive, fearing that a split in Stuttgart might have national repercussions, sent Braun and Ebert to urge the *Land* organization not to go through with the *Tagwacht* seizure. The *Land* authorities stuck to their previous decision and were well aware of the implications of their action for the national party. Keil told Ebert that he would soon recognize "that we in Stuttgart were trail-blazers." [44]

Trail-blazers the Württemberg reformists were, during as before the war. The vigor of their methods, which had evoked one of the

[41] Grünberg, *Die Internationale und der Weltkrieg,* I, 77.

[42] Heinrich Laufenberg, Fritz Wolffheim and Carl Herz, *Organisation, Krieg und Kritik. Dokumente zu den Hamburger Parteidebatten* (Hamburg, n. d. [1915?]), 37.

[43] *Ibid.,* 74–77. For another variant of the same problem see the experience of the Frankfurt opposition described in Toni Sender, *The Autobiography of a German Rebel* (New York, 1939), 68–70.

[44] Keil, *Erlebnisse,* I, 317; for the entire affair, *ibid.,* 306–317; Bevan, *Social Democracy,* 34–35.

most radical urban organizations before the war, now rapidly led
to a split. Stuttgart, Esslingen, and Göppingen supported the opposition as of yore. Cannstatt, formerly a radical district, swung over
to the reformists, while the previously conservative cities and little
country towns stood "as good as solidly" behind the *Land* executive.[45] The conservative minority in Stuttgart set up its own organization as an "Association for the Advancement of the *Tagwacht*"
on 6 December 1914. Shortly thereafter the opposition erected its
own *Land* organization.[46] The final consummation of the schism
thus came first where the prewar cleavage ran deepest.

Not everywhere was the break as sharp or as rapid as in Württemberg. Where the local leadership was on the side of the opposition, as in Halle, Brunswick, Bremen, and Leipzig, the tension
over policy could not so rapidly become transformed into a determination to make an open break. There the oppositionists could
continue to cherish the hope of changing the party's policy. On the
other side, the national executive and the less determined anti-radi-
cal functionaries hoped to win over the radicals. Their first reaction
to the "hateful machinations" within the party was not to force out
the opposition, but to loosen the restraints on discussion. In January 1915, before six months of war had passed, the party leaders had
to suspend the party's internal *Burgfrieden*, requesting that discussions of party policy be conducted only within the party organizations.[47] The relaxation of the new discipline was a recognition of
the real situation in the party and was probably undertaken in the
hope that it would provide a safety valve for the opposition. When
it became clear that the latter was only emboldened by a measure
of restored freedom, the new discipline was reimposed so drastically
as to split the party.

iv. The Division of the Opposition Leadership; the Annexation Question

If it was difficult for the opposition at the lower echelons of the
party to find its voice, how much more so at the parliamentary
level! Here party discipline (*Fraktionsdisziplin*), requiring unani-

---

[45] Keil, *Erlebnisse*, I, 317–318.
[46] *Ibid.*, I, 321–322.
[47] *Prot. S. P., 1917*, 29.

mous voting and the presentation of a single, solid front in the Reichstag, was no wartime innovation; it was a well-established tradition, a symbol of the irrefragable unity of the working-class party. Hence the oppositionists in parliament had to suffer through a terrible *crise de conscience*. They were torn between their loyalty to principle and their loyalty to the party as the institutional embodiment of proletarian solidarity. To grasp the magnitude of the decision to go into open opposition, we must understand that the party was almost life itself to these individuals. The party had given them that psychological security, that ethical satisfaction which they had not found in society as a whole. On its unity were founded their hopes of building the new order. Is it to be wondered that Luxemburg, Zetkin, and Mehring were physically ill much of the time? Or that Haase complained in his letters of frayed nerves and depression? [48] No matter how advanced had been the radicals' disillusionment with the party's course before the war, it had not brought them to the point of breaking the powerful emotional ties that bound them to the party. The bright hue of resolution was sicklied o'er by more than the pale cast of thought.[49]

It was natural that Karl Liebknecht, who had been the earliest and most steadfast critic of the party's policy toward war, should have been the first to cut the Gordian knot which bound the opposition to the war policy of state and party. He resolved to vote against the second war credits bill of 3 December 1914 in order, as he tells us, to provide a rallying-point for all the anti-war forces. Behind his decision stood his whole experience of the party's *Burgfrieden*, the frustration and condemnation of his effort to rally the party from within.[50] Liebknecht tried in vain to line up others who opposed the credits to join him in a negative vote. Ten opposition

[48] Paul Frölich, *Rosa Luxemburg,* trans. Edward Fitzgerald (London, 1940), 241, 243; Ernst Haase, *Hugo Haase, sein Leben und Wirken* (Berlin, n. d. [1929?]), 112–113, 130.

[49] We cannot do more here than to sketch the outlines of the crystallization of the parliamentary opposition. For the fullest account of the internal discussions of the deputation, the reader is referred to Liebknecht's *Klassenkampf gegen den Krieg,* the accuracy of which has not been questioned even by his most bitter antagonists.

[50] He indicated the impact of this experience in a letter to the *Fraktionsvorstand,* 3 Dec. 1914: "Every other activity through which I could have given expression to my dissenting opinions . . . was denied me no less than a negative vote." See Liebknecht, *Klassenkampf,* 41.

deputies, meeting at Ledebour's house on the night of 1 December, failed to reach agreement.[51]

This little caucus at Ledebour's marked a fatal turning point in the history of the opposition. Until then the radical minority had maintained the unity which it had built up through the organizational reform efforts of 1912 and the common fight for a radical tactic in 1913. Now its potential leadership was split wide open. The latent theoretical and tactical differences between the two radical groups flared up anew in the most doctrinaire form. To these were added the harshest personal judgments. To the left centrists — particularly to Ledebour — Liebknecht was a purist fool, guilty of the political error of drawing the line prematurely, of converting an issue of substance into a question of discipline, and thus of passing the political initiative to the party conservatives. For Liebknecht, those who dragged their feet were merely playing into the hands of the "credit-approvers." The time had passed for compromise: "External agitation and clarification were needed now, not agreement on some middle position." [52] The executive committee of the Reichstag delegation moved skilfully in exploiting the cleavage on the left. Instead of firing Liebknecht outright, as Carl Legien proposed, it merely censured his action. At the same time it laid down a new ruling, which granted to a deputy "whose conviction would not permit him to participate in the unanimous vote of the deputation . . . the right to absent himself from the session in which the vote was taken; but his abstention might not have a demonstrative character." [53] Under this formula, the oppositionists were to have a means of self-expression which would have no damaging effect on the party's policy. This decision, taken on 3 February 1915, was the counterpart at the parliamentary level of the lifting of the intraparty *Burgfrieden* in January at the organizational level. It removed from the less determined oppositionists the temptation to defy the majority openly in a separate vote. In the next two credit votes, on 20 March and 20 August 1915, the centrist opposition abstained from the balloting while Liebknecht continued on his lonely road.[54]

[51] *Ibid.*, 89.
[52] *Ibid.*, 51–52.
[53] Prager, *U.S.P.D.*, 53–54.
[54] *Ibid.*, 60, 81–82. Rühle voted with Liebknecht on 20 March, but abstained on 20 August.

From December 1914 until January 1917 the two sectors of the opposition leadership lived in mutual hostility. During those two crowded and critical years the left radicals outside the Reichstag developed their innate distrust for organization to a blind passion, no longer restrained by the cooler minds of the center. The left centrists, bereft of the revolutionary insight of the left radicals which had served to goad them on, relapsed into their prewar tendency of letting themselves be pushed by events rather than keeping one jump ahead of them. It was perhaps inevitable that the differences of 1910–1912 should re-emerge; but for the future of the German Revolution, it was fatal that they should have reappeared among the leaders so soon. Each faction was freed to cultivate its vices to the detriment of their common cause.

After the break of December 1914 Liebknecht and his group began at once to unfold a systematic agitation not only against the *Burgfrieden,* but against the war itself.[55] Between the two wings of the opposition, the debate of 1912 was resumed. The left radicals rejected out of hand the party declaration of August 4 which called for peace "as soon as the objective of security is achieved." In a speech of January 1915, Liebknecht asked:

What kind of security? Merely that of the territory or of the state's independence, or, in addition, that elbow-room which capital deems necessary for the economic development of the German Empire? And what sort of elbow-room would that be . . . ? Can it be won without conquests, without subjection of other peoples? [56]

Liebknecht denied the possibility of a peace without annexations, just as the left radicals had denied the possibility of arms reductions and a "peaceful imperialism" in the debate of 1912. Not by supporting the war as one of defense, said Liebknecht, but only by opposing it *in toto* could the proletariat achieve its real security: the destruction of imperialism. The only effective struggle for peace was the struggle for socialism itself in every belligerent nation. By May 1915 this view was given expression in the slogan, "The chief enemy is at home." [57] The left radicals thus embarked on the policy called

[55] Frölich, *Zehn Jahre,* I, 139–142; Berlau, *German Social Democracy,* 139–143.
[56] Drahn and Leonhard, *Unterirdische Literatur,* 17.
[57] See the pamphlet which appeared under this title, *ibid.,* 24–27.

for by the 1907 resolution of the International which Luxemburg herself had helped to formulate: "to work for [the war's] speedy termination, and to exploit with all their might the economic and political crisis created by the war to arouse the population and to hasten the overthrow of capitalist rule." [58] The fight for peace, against annexations and against capitalism itself was welded into an indissoluble whole. It was to be conducted, as Mehring declared in December 1914, "with the leaders if they wish; without the leaders if they remain passive; despite the leaders if they resist." [59]

By contrast, the left centrists tried until mid-1915 to uphold the ambiguous prewar position of the party. On the one hand, they recognized the right of the German nation to defend itself; up to that point, they were prepared to support the war effort.[60] On the other hand, they regarded the war as imperialist in origin, and fought against any expansion of Germany's territory. They wanted neither victory nor defeat, but a peace based on the *status quo ante*.[61] Thus they neither supported the war in principle, as did the majoritarians, nor opposed it in principle, as did the left radicals; theirs was a relativistic position subject to variation with the course of the war itself and with the aims for which, at any given moment, it was fought.

It was characteristic of these loyal men of Erfurt that their first venture into open opposition in the Reichstag was on domestic questions. Not the war, but, as Ebert later observed, "our attitude toward the state was for the most part the point of departure for our differences." [62] In March 1915 left centrist spokesmen attacked the state of siege and censorship (Haase and Stadthagen), the mistreatment of national minorities (Ledebour), and the absence of political and social equality (Haase). Far from attacking the war effort, Haase justified his call for reforms on the basis of the need

---

[58] See above, Ch. III, n. 84 and text.

[59] Letter to the *Labour Leader*, Dec. 1914; reprinted in Drahn and Leonhard, *Unterirdische Literatur*, 15–16.

[60] Untersuchungsausschuss, *4. Reihe*, VI, 259.

[61] Cf. the first left centrist manifesto, "Das Gebot der Stunde," drafted by Haase, Kautsky, and Bernstein (June 1915), in Prager, *U.S.P.D.*, 72–74; also the statement by Gustav Hoch who, though he did not join the secessionists in their final break, shared their views on the war, in *Prot. S. P., 1917*, 339–351.

[62] *Prot. S. P., 1917*, 230; cf. also Untersuchungsausschuss, *4. Reihe*, VI, 259.

to maintain the morale of the Fatherland's defenders in the field.[63]
Similarly, the first wholesale abstention from a vote for credits, in
March 1915, was represented not as a rejection of the war effort, but
as a return to party tradition on budget-voting in order not to reg-
ister a "vote of confidence for the government." [64]

It was only when the annexation question became central in German politics that the left center leaders in the Reichstag began to
oppose the party's war policy explicitly. At the outbreak of war the
official statements of the German government, designed in part with
an eye to Social Democratic opinion, emphasized the purely defensive character of Germany's war and denied any intention to conquer new territory. Bethmann-Hollweg went so far as to promise
that the wrong which Germany had done to Belgium would be
righted "as soon as our military purpose is achieved." [65] Germany's
victories in the West, represented in the official communiqués as far
more significant than they actually were,[66] inevitably released a
flood of annexationist sentiment which, soon fed by the successes
on the eastern front, continued to rise throughout 1915.[67] Though
Bethmann maintained a cool attitude toward annexationist agitators, he fell more and more under the spell of their ideas as the
military situation seemed to promise the possibility of a "German
peace." [68] Where the Social Democratic opposition altered their position on the war in the light of the aims for which it was fought,
Bethmann changed his ideas of war aims in the light of the progress
of the war. His first public pronouncement in favor of annexations,
though very vague in character,[69] galvanized the Social Democratic
opposition. In June 1915 the minority submitted a petition to the
party executive and the Reichstag delegation stating that the imperialist character of the war was now an established fact, and that

[63] *Reichstag Debates,* CCCVI, 46. Prager, the official historian of the Independent
Social Democrats, makes no reference to the nationalistic content of Haase's speech.
Cf. his *U.S.P.D.,* 56–57.

[64] Cf. Haase, Letter to Ebert, 5 Mar. 1915, in Haase, *Haase,* 105; Prager
U.S.P.D., 56.

[65] E. O. Volkmann, *Die Annexionsfragen des Weltkrieges,* in Untersuchungsausschuss, *4. Reihe,* XII, i, 32–33.

[66] Cf. Rosenberg, *Birth of the German Republic,* 82.

[67] Hans Gatzke, *Germany's Drive to the West* (Baltimore, 1950), 7–67.

[68] Volkmann, *Annexionsfragen,* 37, 53, 193ff.

[69] Gatzke, *Germany's Drive,* 16.

the time had come to break with the policy of August 4. Bearing the signatures of over a thousand party and trade-union functionaries, the petition was the first nationwide action of the Social Democratic opposition.[70] Upon its heels followed the less radical public manifesto of Bernstein, Haase, and Kautsky, *The Demand of the Hour,* which, while eschewing all language of the class struggle (it was first drafted by Bernstein), urged that the party answer the annexationist threat by taking the national lead in a campaign for a peace of understanding. Although the manifesto was pale in formulation, the prestige of its three signatories was sufficient to make it carry real weight in the party. The government considered it sufficiently dangerous to suspend the *Leipziger Volkszeitung* for a time for publishing it.[71]

The aggressiveness of the annexationists on the one hand, and the concomitant increase of oppositionist and peace sentiment in the party on the other hand, forced the majority leaders to clarify their own position. In the opinion of E. O. Volkmann, the leaders at this time would have gone along with Bethmann toward moderate annexation, were it not that the pressure of their internal minority made this course too dangerous to party unity.[72] Their manifesto on war aims, issued in August 1915 after clearance with the government, reflected the ambivalence resulting from the effort to satisfy both the government and the party minority. On the one hand, the manifesto enunciated the principle of self-determination of peoples; on the other, it called for the retention of Alsace-Lorraine by Germany and the maintenance of the territorial integrity of Turkey and Austria-Hungary. Belgium was to be restored, but no mention was made of Germany's eastern neighbors. The uncertainty of the minority at this stage is reflected in the fact that it approved the manifesto.[73]

In December 1915 the party felt it necessary to interpellate the government on the peace question. Scheidemann discussed the con-

---

[70] For the text, see Prager, *U.S.P.D.,* 69–72; cf. also Bevan, *Social Democracy,* 51.

[71] For the text, see Prager, *U.S.P.D.,* 72–74; cf. also Bevan, *Social Democracy,* 51–52. For Bernstein's evolution, see Peter Gay, *The Dilemma of Democratic Socialism* (New York, 1952), 274–283.

[72] Volkmann, *Annexionsfragen,* 64.

[73] Philipp Scheidemann, *Der Zusammenbruch* (Berlin, 1921), 28.

tent of his interpellation beforehand with the chancellor and most differences between them were ironed out.[74] The interpellation provided the occasion not only for the chancellor's most annexationistic pronouncement to date, but also for its qualified acceptance by the Social Democratic spokesman.[75] Instead of quieting the fears of the opposition, as it was designed to do, the interpellation goaded the minority to a new fury. In the vote on the war credits which followed, twenty left centrists finally took the plunge: instead of quietly abstaining as they had done in March and August, they voted openly against the credits.[76]

While this action of December 1915 brought the left center closer to its final break from the majority, it did not produce, as one might have expected, a rapprochement with the left radicals. The theoretical differences between the two groups were perhaps never more sharply drawn than in the winter of 1915-16. The center opposition based its rejection of the credits explicitly on the fact that Germany's military situation was favorable. Therefore Germany had the duty "to make the first step toward peace" by clearly abjuring all conquests and offering a peace without annexations.[77] The left center's campaign for a "peace of understanding" was a logical continuation of its prewar tactic.

Instead of rejoicing that the left center was growing bolder, the left radicals were enraged that the target of its opposition was annexationism rather than the war itself. Rosa Luxemburg, analyzing the minority declaration of 29 December, fastened on the premise of the centrists' peace demand, "Our boundaries are secured," to demonstrate that the only difference between majority and minority lay in a different evaluation of the strategic situation.[78] In a biblical quotation which she placed at the masthead of her

[74] *Ibid.*, 30–32. The disagreement lay only in the question of whether specific German peace terms should be offered. Cf. *Reichstag Debates*, CCCVI, 443.

[75] *Reichstag Debates*, CCCVI, 442–445; for Bethmann's position, cf. Gatzke, *Germany's Drive*, 70–71.

[76] Prager, *U.S.P.D.*, 87–88; Flechtheim, *Die KPD*, 15.

[77] The declaration which accompanied the credit vote is given in Prager, *U.S.P.D.*, 87. It was read by Friedrich Geyer, who had been the leader of the radicals in the party controversy over the military tax bill in 1913.

[78] Rosa Luxemburg, "Entweder-Oder," cited in Untersuchungsausschuss, *4. Reihe,* IV, 102–103. Cf. also "Die Dezembermänner von 1915," Spartakusbrief No. 1a, reprinted in Drahn and Leonhard, *Unterirdische Literatur*, 29–33.

indictment, Luxemburg revealed the depth of her bitterness against the centrist opposition: "I know thy works, that thou art neither cold nor hot: I would that thou wert cold or hot. So then because thou art lukewarm, and neither cold nor hot, I will spew thee out of my mouth." [79]

In January the majority party leaders helped foster the cleavage between the opposition groups by formally expelling Liebknecht from the Social Democratic Reichstag delegation — a warning to the moderate oppositionists, whose desire to maintain party unity was still great.[80] On New Year's Day 1916 the left radicals (now beginning to be known as "Spartacists") held a national conference and adopted a program in which the immediate task of the socialist movement was stated to be "the intellectual liberation of the proletariat from the subservience to the bourgeoisie which expresses itself in the nationalist ideology." Any unity of the opposition "on the 'Marxist center's' broad and crooked path of compromise" with national defense was rejected:

Not unity, but rather clarity on every point. No gentle tolerance — not even in the 'opposition'; rather the sharpest criticism, an accounting down to the last penny. Through merciless disclosure and discussion of differences, to unanimity on principles and tactics, and therewith to capacity for action and to unity. Not at the beginning of the fermentation process which is taking place in the socialist parties and in the 'opposition', [but] only at its end may unity be achieved.[81]

Thus the Spartacists flung down the gauntlet at the very moment when the time seemed ripe for a consolidation of the opposition forces. And yet the course of events was swiftly to produce some measure of unity. As German state policy and the sentiment of the masses moved in opposite directions from 1916 onward, the Spartacists, standing firm and adamant, saw the center opposition moving leftward to the point where, despite remaining differences, they could join forces for the final blow to the united party. The evolution of the radicals from the division of 1910 to the reconsolidation of 1913 was being played over again.

[79] Untersuchungsausschuss, 4. Reihe, IV, 102.
[80] Prager, U.S.P.D., 90.
[81] Drahn and Leonhard, Unterirdische Literatur, 34.

v. Economic Hardships and Political Persecution

With the deterioration of the food situation the first signs of mass discontent began to appear. The year 1916 saw a drop in the bread ration, a severe rationing of the already scarce fat and potato supplies, and, finally, the failure of the potato crop which led to the terrible "turnip winter" of 1916–17.[82] Simultaneously, real wages began to drop rapidly.[83] In 1916 the trade-unions, despite their earlier pledges to maintain the wage contracts in force at the outbreak of the war, had to press for upward revisions which, in view of the no-strike policy, could be achieved only with difficulty.[84] In such an atmosphere the demand for peace became widespread.[85]

The same economic difficulties which stimulated the will to peace in the masses — peasantry as well as workers — aroused the right-wing parties to demand a more vigorous prosecution of the war. Where the Social Democratic opposition propagated a peace of understanding, the Conservatives and National Liberals spearheaded the drive for unrestricted submarine warfare which, in the eyes of the oppositionists, would make peace the more remote. The submarine warfare question, which dragged on through 1916, slowly brought the Reichstag into a *de facto* alliance with the navy against the chancellor, and thus paved the way for Bethmann's fall and the military dictatorship of Ludendorff in 1917.[86] With the parties of the later Weimar coalition generally siding with the right on the questions of war and foreign policy, and with the left on domestic issues, the *Burgfrieden* was rent to shreds and prewar conflicts were resumed with unprecedented intensity.

In the first half of 1916 the growth of the opposition to war and the government was answered by the military authorities with a broader application of the state of siege law. In many corps areas,

---

[82] August Skalweit, *Die deutsche Kriegsernährungswirtschaft*, in Wirtschafts- und Sozialgeschichte des Weltkrieges, Deutsche Serie, ed. James T. Shotwell (Stuttgart, Leipzig, and New Haven, 1927), 185, 210–216.

[83] Jürgen Kuczynski, *A Short History of Labour Conditions*, III, i, "Germany, 1800 to the Present Day" (London, 1945), 215–218.

[84] Umbreit and Lorenz, *Der Krieg und die Arbeitsverhältnisse*, 118–119.

[85] Untersuchungsausschuss, *4. Reihe*, V, 100–101; IV, 281.

[86] Bredt, *Der Reichstag im Weltkrieg*, in Untersuchungsausschuss, *4. Reihe*, VIII, 64–68.

pre-censorship of the Socialist press was introduced. Some corps area commanders prohibited even closed membership meetings of the Social Democratic Party, while others forbade individual Social Democrats from making speeches in their district. House searches of opposition leaders became increasingly frequent, and their mail was subjected to censorial inspection.

Not only the opposition, but the majority party felt the new rigors of the state of siege. *Vorwärts* was placed under pre-censorship for publishing a statement of the party executive calling for better control of food distribution and food speculators. Even the loyal Otto Braun, scheduled to speak on the high cost of living, was warned not to wander into the political aspects of the question.[87]

Governmental repression in the mounting atmosphere of unrest played into the hands of the opposition. The sentencing of Karl Liebknecht to over two years imprisonment for treasonable utterances on May Day 1916 evoked the first political demonstration strikes since 1906[88] and served as a catalyst for the unification of the opposition. Haase, whose profound belief in civil liberties was outraged by the treatment of Liebknecht, defended him both in the Reichstag and in the courts. The experience drew Haase closer to Liebknecht politically as well as personally.[89] The protest strikes against Liebknecht's arrest provided the occasion for the Berlin party organization to expel the majority officials in its executive. The first meeting of Berlin's new "action committee," Haase joyfully reported, resulted in a "full understanding . . . with the Rosa group."[90] Haase himself now threw his considerable weight into the consolidation of the opposition throughout the country.[91]

The more the opposition came into the open, the harder the authorities clamped down. In the second half of 1916, "military protective custody," that is, jailing without the preferment of legal charges, was applied on a broad scale. The ailing Franz Mehring, now over seventy, Rosa Luxemburg, Käthe Duncker, and countless

---

[87] For these and other details, see *Reichstag Debates*, CCCVI, 716–725; CCCVII, 943–947, 1244–1250.

[88] Bevan, *Social Democracy*, 106, 118; Haase, letter to Gottschalk, 2 July 1916, in Haase, *Haase*, 124.

[89] *Reichstag Debates*, CCCVII, 1028–1032; Haase, *Haase*, 120–124.

[90] *Ibid.*, 125.

[91] *Ibid.*

lesser figures of the radical opposition were jailed with little hope of trial. Haase, Kurt Rosenfeld, Oskar Cohn, and the other lawyers of the left center were overwhelmed with civil liberties cases. In the Reichstag the left center gave the fullest publicity to the worst episodes, using them as weapons in their vigorous campaign for the lifting of the state of siege.[92] The government was now too nervous to consider such a measure. As Helfferich, State Secretary of the Interior told the Reichstag, "It is better that one or another innocent person suffer than that a guilty one be left at large to create harm for the Fatherland."[93]

The majority Social Democrats were placed in an impossible position by the offensive of the military against the opposition. Their own civil liberties, which were being curtailed with those of the minority, had to be defended. The opposition attacked the majority policies fully as bitterly as those of the government. The maintenance of those policies now demanded that the majority free itself from the incubus of the opposition. In March 1916, after the left centrists had voted against war credits for the second time, the majority expelled them from the Reichstag delegation.[94] The executive began a systematic house-cleaning in the party press. Where the executive or its local adherents enjoyed property rights over the newspapers, these were used to discharge opposition editors.[95] In September 1916 the executive summoned a party conference to consider measures to "prevent the party's being torn apart." Here all the differences were brought into the open and the policies of the majority sustained. The minority, which had denied the competence of the conference in the first instance, was only alienated further by it.[96]

With the strengthening of discipline in the party organization proceeding *pari passu* with the more rigorous application of the siege law by the state, the minority needed little further encouragement to complete the secession. The final impetus was

[92] *Reichstag Debates,* CCCVIII, 1875–1883, 1947–1955; Prager, *U.S.P.D.,* 100.
[93] *Reichstag Debates,* CCCVIII, 1884.
[94] Parteivorstand (der S.P.D.), *Material zur Fraktionsspaltung* (Berlin, 1916), 9–16.
[95] Prager, *U.S.P.D.,* 103–104.
[96] *Ibid.,* 108–114; N.Z., XXXIV, ii, 673–677.

given at the close of 1916 by two measures of the government: its "peace offer" of 12 December and the passage of the *Hilfsdienstgesetz*, the compulsory labor mobilization law, on 2 December. The peace note of the Central Powers, which contained no specific terms of settlement, was viewed by the opposition as a mere device to reconcile public opinion to the continuation of the war.[97] The *Hilfsdienstgesetz*, with its tight labor controls, was seen as a kind of final enslavement of the worker to the war machine. In the Reichstag, the oppositionists proposed a nationalization of war industries as the only fair counterpart to the regimentation of labor which the new law represented.[98] Denouncing the bill as a second anti-Socialist law, Haase told the Reichstag that it would only make the masses more conscious of the true nature of the war, raise their will to peace, and pave the way for the "expropriation of the expropriators." [99] The majoritarians, in line with the primacy of foreign policy, supported the bill after some of their proposed improvements had been adopted, and saw the new law as a triumph of *Gleichberechtigung*. Haase's group, with its diametrically opposed conception of the means to defend labor's interest, considered it an unprecedented outrage that party and trade-unions should "help to forge the shackles of the proletariat" by voting for the bill.[100]

The majority Social Democrats were indeed in a difficult position now since their previously cogent argument, that the support of the war effort would safeguard the material interests of labor, could no longer be convincingly maintained. The inequities of the *Hilfsdienstgesetz*, felt in the setting of a rapidly deteriorating economy, became a contributing factor to the revolutionization of

[97] For the contents of the note, see *Reichstag Debates*, CCCVIII, 2332; for the opposition reaction, cf. "Bericht über die gemeinsame Konferenz der Arbeitsgemeinschaft u. der Spartakusgruppe vom 7. Januar, 1917," in *Protokoll über die Verhandlungen des Gründungsparteitages der U.S.P.D., vom 6. bis. 8. April, 1917 in Gotha*, ed. Emil Eichhorn (Berlin, 1921), 87 [Hereafter cited as *Prot. U. S. P.*]; Haase, *Haase*, 137; Bevan, *Social Democracy*, 143–144.
[98] See, in *Reichstag Debates*, CCCVIII, 2183–2191 (Vogtherr), 2221 (Dittmann).
[99] *Ibid.*, 2290–2294.
[100] Albrecht Mendelssohn-Bartholdy, *The War and German Society*, in Economic and Social History of the World War, German Series, ed. James T. Shotwell (New Haven, 1937), 81–86; "Bericht," *Prot. U. S. P., 1917*, 88.

the working class and hence to the loss of control by the majority party and trade-unions.[101]

In looking back over the year 1916, one is impressed at the way in which the military stalemate and the economic difficulties polarized German society. The basic pattern of division, on both foreign and domestic policy, was that of the prewar era. But the war had ripped what Burke called "the decent draperies of life" from the German body politic. The ruling groups were impelled by the mounting tide of discontent to hold their power by siege law. The tentative gestures toward a "new orientation" (which, to be sure, did not reach their height until 1917) were generally frustrated by the Conservatives while real power was passed by the patriotic Reichstag — almost in a fit of absent-mindedness — to the military authorities. Under these circumstances the unstable coalition which was the Social Democratic Party fell apart. With the workers' coöperation in the war effort rewarded neither by a successful termination of hostilities nor by any tangible political and social reforms, but only by economic misery and political oppression, the party's war policy became discredited. Reformism had had its day; the party had gone the whole way, as it had never been able to do before the war, to meet the state and the ruling class on their own terms in the hope of some concessions. As the failure of the policy became manifest, the hour of the intransigents struck.

vi. The Schism Consummated

In January 1917, in the depth of the "turnip winter," Haase, Ledebour, and Vogtherr called the first conference of the opposition, Spartacist and left centrist. The purpose of the conference was ostensibly to take measures to protect the minority and its organizations against the expulsions and confiscations undertaken by the majority.[102] Neither the left centrists nor Spartacists advocated a break with the party. The former wished to establish "continuous, close contact" among the opposition locals to assist them in spreading their views "within the framework of the organization stat-

[101] Cf. Ludwig Bergsträsser in Untersuchungsausschuss, *4. Reihe,* IV, 138; Müller, *Vom Kaiserreich zur Republik,* 75–77.
[102] "Bericht," *Prot. U. S. P., 1917,* 97–98.

ute." [103] The Spartacists remained in the party "only to cross up and combat the policy of the majority in every way, to protect the masses from the imperialist policy pursued under the cloak of Social Democracy, and to use the party as a recruiting-ground for the proletarian, anti-militarist class struggle." [104] The Spartacists wished the opposition locals to withhold dues payments from the executive. Their proposals were rejected in favor of the left center's more conservative course. Ernst Meyer, spokesman for the Spartacists, was not much disturbed by the outcome: "I am convinced that, however you decide today, you will in a few months all approve what we have today proposed." [105]

The situation matured even more quickly than the Spartacists expected. Within ten days of the minority's conference the hope of the opposition to remain within the party was shown to be vain. On 16 January 1917 the party council declared that the opposition, by the very act of holding a conference, "had separated itself from the party." The party's organizations were instructed to take the necessary organizational measures against the "wreckers of the party." [106] Under the party statutes, separate opposition conferences were not punishable by expulsion; but the time for legalities, on which the left center counted, had passed. The executive could no longer permit the minority to utilize the party machinery against its policies. If the break was now certain, the executive presumably reasoned that it must conduct a purge before the minority could do any further damage. Where the opposition was in a minority, it was now expelled; where it controlled the locals, new organizations were set up by the majority.[107] Thus the split was carried out by the old party before the new one was actually organized. The Social Democratic leaders had again followed the lead of the state in its policy toward its opposition: where the state suppressed, the party purged.

The oppositionists, some enthusiastically, some reluctantly, drew the only possible consequence. At Easter 1917 they held a congress

[103] *Ibid.*, 98.
[104] *Ibid.*, 99.
[105] *Ibid.*, 114.
[106] Prager, *U.S.P.D.*, 129–130.
[107] *Ibid.*, 130–131.

in which the schism was finally institutionalized by the establishment of the Independent Social Democratic Party. Gotha was the site of the secessionist congress — the same Gotha where, forty-two years earlier, the Lassalleans and Eisenacher had joined to form the party which was now being broken up.

The Russian Revolution was already a month old when the Gotha congress met. Germany's revolution, toward which the founding of the Independent Party was a material if not entirely a conscious contribution, was but a year and a half away. Those who were forgathered at Gotha were to provide such leadership as the revolution would enjoy. They were now freed from the necessity of compromise with the old party, freed to chart a new and bolder course. With what ideas, with what organizational weapons would they go to work?

The ideas put forward at Gotha were all drawn from the past. Haase's observation in 1914, that "the times seem . . . to deepen rather than to change one's views," [108] was still applicable to most of the secessionists.

On the far right was a small group headed by Kautsky, Bernstein, and Emanuel Wurm whose essential concern was a "peace of understanding." As long as the government refused to work sincerely and concretely for this aim, they wished to vote against war credits as a measure of pressure and protest. This issue alone divided them from the majority party. They had no desire to bring about the end of the war through revolutionary insurrection, which in any case appeared to them "unlikely." [109] Despite the fact that the majority had already expelled the minority, the Kautsky-Bernstein group vigorously opposed the establishment of a separate party.[110] When the sentiment at Gotha proved to be overwhelmingly for a new party, Kautsky and Bernstein very nearly withdrew, especially

---

[108] Letter to his son, 30 Oct. 1914, in Haase, *Haase*, 103.

[109] Karl Kautsky, *Mein Verhältnis zur Unabhängigen Sozialdemokratischen Partei* (Berlin, 1922), 5; Gay, *Dilemma*, 285–286.

[110] Eichhorn states that "a good part" of the Reichstag opposition hoped to stay in the old party under the name, "Opposition in the Organization." See his account in *Prot. U. S. P., 1917*, 4. When the decision to set up a new party was taken, Kautsky, Bernstein, and Eisner favored retention of the old name, Kautsky arguing that it was the "governmental Socialists" who had deserted the program and thus forfeited the right to the name. Haase and Luise Zietz supported the Kautsky wing in this, though they favored a new party. Cf. *ibid.*, 49.

as they feared the strengthening of Spartacist influence in an independent organization. After a private discussion they decided to go along, in view of the primacy of the peace problem.[111]

At the other end of the spectrum were the Spartacists. Their program was that of 1912: that imperialism could be answered only by revolution. The tactical consequences of this position were (1) to abandon any effort to secure a "peace of understanding" which was impossible under imperialism; and (2) to displace the center of gravity in party policy from parliamentary to mass action.[112]

The bulk of the Independent leaders stood between the reformists and the Spartacists, some leaning toward the former, some toward the latter. Ledebour, although he was later to prove himself the most active revolutionary of the old left centrist leadership, stood to the right of the others of his wing at Gotha. He adhered to the doctrine of national defense and to the tactic of forcing the government by popular pressure to a negotiated peace. His peace program included self-determination, arbitration courts, general disarmament, and open diplomacy, the program of the International's congress of 1910, or — it was much the same thing — the Wilsonian program.[113] Ledebour likewise sustained parliamentarism against the Spartacist attack: "We are democrats. Not only socialists but democrats. We seek to introduce democracy in state and society." [114]

Haase, intent upon welding Spartacists and centrists into a truly united party, was closer to the Spartacists. Completely repudiating his group's espousal of the principle of national defense in December 1915, he virtually asked the Spartacists for forgiveness: "Heaven rejoices more over one repentant sinner than over a thousand righteous [souls]. Our later declaration was so sharp that this error, if such it was, was relegated to the attic." In contrast to Ledebour, Haase declared that the capitalist governments were "no more capable of ending the war than they were of preventing

---

[111] Kautsky, *Mein Verhältnis*, 8; *idem*, "Eduard Bernsteins 75. Geburtstag," *Die Gesellschaft*, II, i (1925), 19–20.

[112] In explaining his program, the Spartacist spokesman leaned heavily on Radek's writings of 1911–12. Cf. *Prot. U. S. P., 1917*, 62–67.

[113] *Ibid.*, 56.

[114] *Ibid.*, 52–53.

it." [115] Haase pleaded with the factions to desist from attacks on each other. The main task, he said, was "to unite in order to conduct the class struggle with vigor and might." [116] And yet Haase's objectives in the "class struggle" were not clear beyond the termination of the war.

The debates at Gotha terminated in the readoption of the Erfurt program with the proviso that it should be revised at the close of hostilities. [117] For the Spartacists, this was entirely unsatisfactory: the Erfurt program was unsuited to the period of the struggle for power, "the socialist epoch." [118] Most party members at that time could scarcely understand such a criticism; revolution in Germany seemed still remote despite the recognized "ferment" in the masses. Above all, the years of preoccupation with the idea of the passive revolution, the revolution made "objectively" by the collapse of the ruling classes, relegated the whole problem of the seizure of power into the background of centrist thought. The chief concern of the Independents was to resurrect the tradition of pure opposition. As expressed in the preamble of the Gotha organization statute, the party stood "in fundamental opposition to the ruling governmental system, to the war policy of the Reich government and to the policy of the old party which the executive has steered into a governmental course." [119] So much, and no more. Objectively, the establishment of the new party was a major contribution to the development of the revolution for it provided both a galvanic of opposition sentiment and a rallying point for it. But the greater part of the leading actors in the drama had little intention, in 1917, of "making" — or even leading — a proximate social revolution. They were merely trying to resuscitate the *principles* of the old party which had been abandoned, as they believed, to the detriment of the working class.

Nowhere was the legacy of the old party's stormy prewar history more fateful for the new one than in the problem of organization. In matters of program and policy, opinion was graduated between

[115] *Ibid.*, 39–40.
[116] *Ibid.*, 39.
[117] *Ibid.*, 47.
[118] *Ibid.*, 62.
[119] *Ibid.*, 47.

the extremes of right and left;[120] in matters of organization it was more clearly divided between Spartacist and left centrist. Both groups adhered to the ideas developed in the prewar fight for organizational reform, but reinforced and hardened by the war.

The left centrist proposals were founded on the notion that a hierarchical organization was both necessary and desirable in order to guarantee unity of action. For the central authority, they suggested at first the name "action committee" — a designation reminiscent of their reform effort of 1911–12 with its emphasis on making the executive "capable of action." Its paid members were to have only a consultative voice; real control was vested in the political, nonbureaucratic element.[121] "In the new organization," said Dittmann, one of the old *Sonderkonferenzler* of 1912, "the officialdom may not dominate." [122] To forestall the creation of another centrally controlled bureaucratic machine, the executive was to have no power to appoint regional or local secretaries; these were to be hired and paid by the organizations which they served.[123] The executive was to be forbidden to acquire "property rights in any form in the business enterprises of the party, particularly in party newspapers or presses." [124] Here spoke the bitter experience of confiscations of the minority press — from the *Schwäbische Tagwacht* in 1914 to *Vorwärts* in 1916.

The party council of the old party, that corporation of regional officials which the executive had erected as a bulwark against these same reformers in 1912, was to have no counterpart in the new party. Here, to be sure, the left centrists were involved in a contradiction: on the one hand, they sought to curtail the executive's power over the regional and local organizations; on the other, their prejudice against the party council was too deep for them to use the regional organizations, freed of their centrally dominated bureaucracy, as a control on the executive. An intermediate solution was

[120] Lenore O'Boyle has drawn a more monochrome picture of the Independents, whom she regards as largely sharing Kautsky's views. See her article "The German Independent Socialists during the First World War," *American Historical Review*, LVI (1951), 824–831.

[121] *Prot. U. S. P., 1917*, 48.

[122] *Ibid.*, 18.

[123] *Ibid.*, 18, 48.

[124] *Ibid.*, 31, 48.

found by obliging the executive to call together the representatives of the regional organizations for consultation on all "major political measures" without vesting the latter with permanent status or powers.[125]

Moderate decentralization and de-bureaucratization: these were the principal characteristics of the left center's proposals. In 1905, when the left centrists (then known simply as the "radicals") had dominated the party, they had favored both centralization and bureaucracy. In 1911-12, when control had passed to the reformists, they had sought to weaken the influence of the bureaucracy in the central executive. In 1917 they wished to weaken not only the bureaucratic element within the executive, but also the executive's control over the bureaucracy at the lower echelons. The left centrists conceived the structure of their new organization in terms of a problem which, though it had dominated the last decade of their lives in the party, was in reality terminated by their own secession: control by a reformist leadership through a bureaucratic machine built in its image. The impending problem of performance in a revolutionary situation, where centralization of forces would be required, played no part in their thinking.

Even more bitterly anti-bureaucratic and anti-centralist than the left center were the Spartacists. Some of them wanted no paid employees at all, partly because of their unspoken axiom that wealth corrupts, partly out of fear that the new party would become an institution for the support of employees expelled from the old for their views.[126] The powers of the central authority they sought to cut to the bone. They wished to starve the executive economically by limiting to five per cent its receipts of the dues collected at the local level.[127] The regional and local organizations were to be accorded absolute freedom of action regardless of the attitude of the central leadership.[128] With such insistence did the Spartacists press the last point that the left center finally succumbed to a far-

[125] Dittmann, who drafted the left center's original proposals, suggested a consultative council (*Beirat*) of regional representatives, but this was abandoned as too close to the old party council. Cf. *ibid.*, 17, 35, 48.

[126] *Ibid.*, 22, 24-26.

[127] *Ibid.*, 29.

[128] *Ibid.*, 29.

·reaching compromise embodied in the following clause of the
statute:

The proper democratic application of the organization statute is . . . a
matter for the localities, districts and regions, which are to have far-
reaching independence and freedom of action on condition that actions,
[once] decided upon by the appropriate organization, will be executed
in unity. In every locality, district or region there may be only one organization.[129]

The Spartacists were partly motivated by their distrust of the
left centrists as feeble and unreliable revolutionaries. They did not
conceal the fact that no authority could bring them to pursue any
but their own course, and only on these terms would they join the
new party:

The opposition should unite on a common ground [said one of their
spokesmen]. But we must be free to continue our own particular policy.
No longer can matters go on according to the old scheme of majority
and minority. The minority may no longer be suppressed . . . We must
keep our independence. We demand protection against the majority . . .
We wish to join our own methods of agitation to those of the left center.[130]

Their fear of left centrist control of the new organization only
reinforced the Spartacists' antipathy toward organization as such. As
we have seen in their prewar theoretical development, their concept
of the nature of revolution left little place for organization. The
revolution would be made by the masses who, out of their own
revolutionary resourcefulness, would devise the organizational forms
appropriate to the historical moment. The role of the party was to
stimulate the masses to act, to show them, not to rule them or to
wield power in their behalf. Had the Spartacists not had this extreme democratic concept of revolution, they would either have
built their own party outside the Independent Party or at least have
constructed a tighter organization of their own within the broader
party. They did neither. Staying within the Independent fold they
strengthened its centrifugal tendencies with their insistence on local

[129] *Ibid.*, 49.
[130] *Ibid.*, 22.

autonomy and on the masses themselves as the organizational center of gravity. Thus those who were most eager for revolution resisted in principle the construction of an institution which might have consolidated the revolutionary forces into a politically effective striking force.

When the smoke of factional battle had cleared, a new party stood ready, whatever its weaknesses, to enter the political arena. The Erfurt synthesis, resurrected as the program of Independent Social Democracy, had a meaning in 1917–18 different from that which it had had in the long period of peace. A policy of pure opposition to the state and the war, launched in the face of the majoritarians who had abandoned it, and conducted in an atmosphere of hunger, war-weariness, and political oppression, had increasingly revolutionary consequences as the hour of defeat approached. That most of the left centrist leaders of the new party were not eager to precipitate a revolution is clear. But their political ethic, their negation of the existing order, their readiness to follow if not to lead mass insurrections — all these made them a major factor in the revolutionizing of Germany during 1917 and 1918. They declared their solidarity with all the great mass strike movements of 1917–18; they did not, like the majoritarians, try to hold back the revolutionary wave, but rode with it.[131]

If the organizational division of the German working class opened a new and darker chapter of labor history, the nature and outlook of the new party itself represented rather an end than a beginning. The Independents, of whatever faction, prepared to face the future by devising solutions to problems already past. The Erfurt program was designed for a period in which the state still held its power and the masses, though discontented, were not revolutionary. The year 1917 was such a moment, to be sure, but a rapidly fleeting, transitional one, between *Burgfrieden* and revolution. The Erfurt program was soon overtaken once more, as it had been in 1914, by sweeping changes in the historical situation.

The organizational measures taken at Gotha, anti-centralist and anti-bureaucratic, were designed to solve the problems of a left-wing

---

[131] Untersuchungsausschuss, *4. Reihe*, V, 243–244.

minority in a reformist party. The Independents thus deprived themselves of any organizational instrument by which the spontaneous mass actions of the revolution, once begun, could be unified and consolidated into a single political striking force. The frustrating experience of yesterday had blinded the revolutionary leaders of tomorrow.

Chapter XII

CONCLUSION: THE GREAT TRANSFORMATION

With the formal division of the Social Democratic Party our story is at an end. We have traced the development of the split from the level of ideas, through tactical conflict and the struggle for power in the organization, to final institutional division. The process whereby the schism matured was not always clear and neat, but it was relentless. From 1905 on, the external pressures, economic and political, on the German working class were such as to strengthen the determination of the revolutionaries while simultaneously urging on, by carrot and stick, the forces of reform. Within the labor movement, the polarization process acquired a dynamic of its own. The war merely delivered the final blow to complete the division which had fully matured before 1914.

With the revolution itself the years of fraternal dispute found their bitter end in fratricidal warfare. Ours is not the task to describe this period of violence. Yet in order to indicate the relationship of our problem to the modern political scene, we must say a word on the transformation of the secessionist Social Democrats into the formidable Communist Party we know today.

"Transformation" — we use the word advisedly. For if the modern Communists and their left radical forbears in the prewar Social Democratic Party have a common core of faith in the salvation of man through revolution and socialism, their respective concepts of the means to that salvation are radically different.

The left radicals who pioneered the twentieth-century revolution in Germany after 1905 developed their concepts, as we hope to have shown, partly in negative reaction to the other dynamic element of prewar Social Democracy: trade-unionist reformism. Where the reformists feared the fractious masses as revolutionary, and regarded them as incapable of pursuing their own interest, the left radicals glorified the masses as capable of everything. Where the reformists constructed the party machine in part to hold down the revolutionary element within the party, the left radicals drew the conclusion that a great party apparatus was incompatible with revolutionary aims. Where the party leaders preached democracy without and based their power on semi-autocracy within the party, the left radicals preached social revolution without and democracy within. Where the reformists held to an eighteenth-century progressivist optimism, to the belief that the ruling class could be brought to see the need for the rule of reason and justice in the social order, the left radicals propounded the dialectic, rationalistic optimism of Marx: the belief that with historical conditions as their goad and the party as their teacher the proletarian masses *as a whole* would shatter the old, irrational social order to build the new one out of their own spontaneously released rational capacity.

It was partly in terms of these antitheses that the German Revolution was fought out, a fratricidal combat within the working class. The old Social Democratic Party, extending its discipline as well as might be over the workers, fought to maintain the purely bourgeois-parliamentary character of the Revolution, to preserve the capitalist economy which was the bread and butter of the working class. Where control of the masses through peaceful means failed, the Social Democratic Party combated the social revolution with the help of the Imperial Army and the Free Corps.

The form of the German Revolution was as the left radicals had predicted: mass actions and mass strikes, largely spontaneous in character. The institutional instrument of the revolution was the workers' and soldiers' councils; in them the left wing of the Independents and the Communists (who broke from the Independents in December 1918) sought to concentrate all public powers. The councils represented democracy in its most extreme form, virtually direct rule by the *demos*. But these institutions were not bound together by any centralizing authority and their very members were often ready to surrender their powers to the reconstituted authorities of the old order. Here the prewar radical theory of the spontaneous revolution, the reliance on the democratic will and institutional ingenuity of the masses proved a fatal weakness. There was no central leadership which, like Lenin's in Russia, pursued a conscious strategy in the interest of the *single* aim of the seizure of power, no cold political planning in which the masses were viewed not solely as the subjects of politics, but as its objects. Nor was there on the left any disciplined organization like Lenin's which could coördinate and concentrate the revolutionary forces. The whole evolution of radical ideas on organization, crowned in the Independent Party's loose constitution of 1917, militated against any such authoritarian structure. The radical leadership could not, overnight, break from the intellectual equipment which it had acquired through a decade of bitter experience in the old party.

Even with respect to the use of force itself the radical leaders as a whole differed from their Russian counterparts. As late as 14 December 1918 Luxemburg could write:

In all bourgeois revolutions bloodshed, terrorism, and political murder have always been weapons in the hands of the rising classes, but the proletarian revolution needs no terrorism to attain its ends, and its supporters abominate murder. It needs none of these weapons because it fights against institutions, not against individuals. Because it does not enter the struggle with naïve illusions, it needs no bloody terror to avenge its disappointments. The proletarian revolution is not the desperate attempt of a minority to shape the world by violence according to its own ideals. It is the action of the overwhelming majority of the working people called upon to fulfil a historic mission and to make historical necessity into a historical reality.[1]

Criticizing the suppression of civil liberties by the Russian Bolsheviks, she commented:

Freedom for supporters of the government only, for members of one party only — no matter how big its membership may be — is no freedom at all. Freedom is always freedom for the man who thinks differently. This contention does not spring from a fanatical love of abstract 'justice', but from the fact that everything which is enlightening, healthy and purifying in political freedom derives from its independent character, and from the fact that freedom loses all its virtue when it becomes a privilege . . .

The suppression of political life throughout the country must gradually cause the vitality of the Soviets themselves to decline. Without general elections, freedom of the press, freedom of assembly, and freedom of speech, life in every public institution slows down, becomes a carica-

[1] *Rote Fahne,* 14 Dec. 1918, quoted in Paul Frölich, *Rosa Luxemburg,* trans. Edward Fitzgerald (London, 1940), 299.

ture of itself, and bureaucracy rises as the only deciding factor. No one can escape the workings of this law. Public life gradually dies, and a few dozen party leaders with inexhaustible energy and limitless idealism direct and rule. . . . In the last resort cliquism develops a dictatorship, but not the dictatorship of the proletariat: the dictatorship of a handful of politicians; i.e., a dictatorship in the *bourgeois* sense, in the Jacobin sense . . .[2]

Such democratic humanism, such profound faith in the masses were little calculated to bring success to the revolutionaries when the counter-revolution had no hesitation in restoring and maintaining order by force of arms. In the young democratic republic the revolutionaries acquired their first thorough schooling in violence. From the suppression of the sailor's mutiny in December 1918 to the Kapp Putsch in March 1920, the Imperial Army and the Free Corps, at first at the behest of the Social Democratic government, later on their own initiative, demonstrated again and again their superiority in arms. When some of the revolution's finest leaders — Haase, Luxemburg, and Liebknecht — fell to assassin's bullets; when the revolution was being crushed locally with no centralized direction of resistance; when in the name of democracy War Minister Noske used troops against defenseless demonstrators, the outlook of a large portion of the Independent Party underwent a change. Finally, when "Social Democrat" became, for the Independent rank and file, a synonym for "cop," [3] its faith in democracy in society and in the party, and its concept of the revolution as made and won by the masses themselves, were shaken. In their majority the masses indeed were on the side of the forces of order. By 1920, the Independents were sufficiently disheartened by their own failure to look elsewhere for support and guidance, to Russia, where the revolution had succeeded.

In June 1920, on authorization of its congress, the Independent Party dispatched a delegation to Russia to negotiate terms for affiliation with the Third International. The delegation was confronted with twenty-one conditions which, taken together, spoke a

[2] Quoted in *ibid.,* 276–277.
[3] Ruth Fischer, *Stalin and German Communism* (Cambridge, 1948), 415–416. Miss Fischer speaks of this attitude as characteristic of the Communist rank and file in 1924, but this same rank and file came largely from the former Independent Party.

language not yet heard in left-wing German Social Democracy, the
language of Lenin's "hards":

1. The general propaganda and agitation shall bear a really Communist
character, and should correspond to the program and decisions of the
Third International . . . All periodicals and other publications are subject to the control of the central committee . . . 2. Every organization
desiring to join the Communist International shall be bound systematically and regularly to remove from all the responsible posts in the labor
movement (party organization, editorship, labor unions, parliamentary
fractions, cooperatives, municipalities, etc.) all reformists and followers
of the 'center', and to have them replaced by Communists . . . 3. Communists shall everywhere create a parallel illegal apparatus, which at the
decisive moment should be of assistance to the party in its duty toward
the revolution . . . 6. Every party desirous of affiliating to the Third
International shall renounce not only avowed social patriotism, but also
the hypocrisy of social pacifism. It shall systematically demonstrate to
the workers that without a revolutionary overthrow of capitalism no international arbitration, no talk of disarmament, no democratic reorganization of the League of Nations, will be capable of saving mankind
from new imperialist war . . . 12. All the parties belonging to the Communist International shall be formed on the basis of democratic centralism . . . 13. The Communist parties of those countries where Communist activity is legal shall clean out their members from time to time, in
order systematically to free the party from petty-bourgeois elements that
have penetrated into it. 15. Those parties that have stood for the old
Social Democratic programs shall as soon as possible draw up a new
Communist program in conformity with the special conditions of the
country and the resolutions of the Communist International . . .[4]

These few articles will suffice to show how alien were Lenin's
concepts to the traditional ultra-democratism of the German left.
Seen in the light of German Social Democratic history, Lenin's
terms represented a synthesis of the revolutionary aims of the left
radicals with the concepts of centralization, hierarchy, and discipline
of the reformist Social Democratic leadership, with the latter elements heightened and intensified far beyond anything Social
Democracy, even in the war years, had ever seen. The synthesis
focussed on the one question which the German party, reared in a

[4] *Ibid.*, 141–142.

world different from Lenin's, had never fundamentally faced: the seizure and organization of power.

Ruth Fischer describes the discussion of the twenty-one points carried on in the Independent Party:

[The] discussion's central point was how to organize a militant party . . . All the questions of the Russian Revolution were, for the first time, brought to large worker audiences and compared and collated with their own experiences since 1918. It was not a discussion where a standpoint could be accepted or rejected on academic grounds; decisions had consequences in the lives of the disputants . . . [T]he workers discussing the affiliation or non-affiliation to the Moscow center correctly interpreted their decision as one determining the revolutionary policy to be carried out immediately after a regrouping of their cadres.

Thus, in spite of the form of the discussion, which referred to the relation between the Russian center and the Communist parties, the fight within the U. S. P. D. was essentially concerned with Germany.[5]

The centrist leaders of the Independent Party protested in vain against the "slavish imitation of Russian methods" in the German party, argued in vain that the entry into the Third International would mean the subordination of the German Revolution to the needs of Russian state policy.[6] The contrast between the success of the revolution in Russia and its failure in Germany was decisive for the majority at the Halle congress which in October 1920 voted to affiliate with the Third International.

Whatever the real causes of the failure of the German social revolution — the vitality of German capitalism and the strength of the trade-union movement were certainly not the least of these — the majority of the Independents felt that their own inadequacy had played a large role in the fiasco. The decision to accept the principles embodied in the twenty-one demands represented a sharp and final break from their own past. In it the Independents paid a terrible tribute not merely to the successes of the Bolsheviks, but also to those of Ebert, Noske and Groener who had taught them that centralization and bureaucracy, force and violence are stronger in the hard world of social crisis than the masses' unorganized effort to bring about the good society.

[5] *Ibid.,* 144.
[6] Prager, *Geschichte der U.S.P.D.* (Berlin, 1922), 227.

With the entry of the Independent majority into the Communist Party, the latter was raised from the position of an impotent sect (it had polled only 441,995 votes in June 1920) to a great mass party. Within a few years it was transformed into an authoritarian organization manned by professionals totally dedicated to the world revolution as the Russian leaders of the Comintern construed it. The old problems of "principle" — budget voting, alliance with bourgeois parties, rank and file control of party policy, intra-party democracy — were no more. The first two of these had meaning for the revolutionaries only so long as a reformist tactic was an instrument of men with reformist intentions; the last two had meaning only so long as the masses were believed to be the decisive element of the revolutionary process. The break-up of the old party removed the first condition; the experience of the revolution, the second. In the Communist Party the strategy of revolution, conceived in politico-military terms, admitted every tactic, be it reformist or revolutionary, fair or foul. The Communists reversed the famous statement of Eduard Bernstein to read, "The movement [and, let us add, the human beings who compose it] is nothing; the goal is everything." The weapon of the purge, developed by the right in the last years of the old party, became the normal, everyday instrument of leadership control and policy enforcement in the transformed left.

Having helped to rescue the principal elements of the old order — bureaucracy, army, and capitalism itself — from the social revolutionary threat, the old Social Democratic Party was soon deprived of its position of primacy in the affairs of the republic. Committed to a docile and unimaginative trade-union policy, the party lost the political initiative, and also the tremendous attractive power which its innocent promise of a brighter future had given it among the people before the war. With the radicals gone from the fold, the terrible tension of prewar party life was no more. Gone too was the dynamic, energetic tone of a party whose leaders had always to answer challenges from within. *"Bonzentum,"* self-satisfied and comfortable bureaucracy, well equipped under Weimar with sinecures, proliferated freely. At the same time the Social Democratic left was too weak in the postwar party to be an earnest threat to the leadership; this fact permitted a degree of tolerance, nay, generosity, to the opposition not known in the years from 1910 to 1917. Former Independents and expelled Communists could find not only a cordial reception, but even employment in the reformist party.

Whereas the radicals came out of the revolution as a hard, authoritarian party, and the reformists emerged more cohesive and more tolerant but less alive than the prewar party, the center met its death in the revolutionary period. The centrists who had stayed in the old party when their brethren had seceded in 1917 lost what little influence they had had. Those who seceded, though they provided the bulk of the Independent leadership, were drawn, as Kautsky had predicted, into the orbit of left radical policy. Committed equally to socialism and parliamentary democracy, the left centrists were trapped in a historical situation where the forces supporting each opposed the other. Supporting both the councils and their rival institution, the National Assembly, the Independent leaders sought to maintain an impossible dual power in the Reich. When the Independent party was at the height of its electoral power (after the Kapp Putsch, with 4,895,317 votes in the June 1920 elections), the left center leaders were deserted by their army which, no longer satisfied to face the armed power of counter-revolution with the gentle voice of reason, entered the Communist Party. For two years after the Halle congress the rump Independent Party lived on in weakness and futility until its majority returned to the parent party in 1922. The fate of the centrists had been adumbrated long in advance. We have seen them, the true men of Erfurt, trying through the years to sustain revolutionary principles against the reformist practice of the old party, drawn apart between the two magnets of revolution and reform. We have seen the left center, from 1910 to 1917, following the left radicals into one position after another which they, the hesitant ones, had at first condemned. Never until the facts nearly engulfed their principles did they resort to oppositional action; but they did so in the end and continued to do so as long as the aims of socialism and democracy could be jointly pursued. The break-up of the old party had destroyed the center's role as mediating agent between right and left; the collapse of the Empire and the form of the revolution destroyed the compatibility between socialism and parliamentary democracy in Germany into our own time. The twenty-one conditions of the Comintern in effect demanded a recognition of that incompatibility, and a clear subordination of democratic values to the achievement of socialism by authoritarian-revolutionary means. Whether it gave or withheld that recognition, the old center faced its end. Not Ledebour, but Ebert and Lenin were the grim heirs of the old party's divided legacy, the keepers of the keys to the tragic future of the German working class.

BIBLIOGRAPHICAL ESSAY

This essay is designed as an introduction to the literature on Social Democracy in the years 1905–1917. It offers a selection of works which, positively or negatively, are basic to work in the subject. This aim has led me both to exclude some titles which are cited in the footnotes to the text, and to include others to which I have had no access but which appear to be significant. Wherever possible I have maintained the traditional distinction between primary and secondary sources. The line between these classes of materials, however, becomes perilously thin in a field of study so recent and so charged with political passion as Social Democratic history. A topical approach has seemed on balance more suitable to the purpose at hand. Within this framework I have tried to indicate not only the utility of each work for the researcher, but also the political outlook within which it was conceived.

The student wishing further bibliographical guidance should consult the excellent article by Arkadij Gurland, "Die Strömungen im modernen Sozialismus," in Reichsausschuss für sozialistische Bildungsarbeit, *Sozialistischer Literaturführer,* 3 vols. (Berlin, 1926–1930), III, 5–22. Gurland's essay incidentally offers the best brief description of the main currents in socialist thought. More comprehensive but less selective bibliographies will be found in Ernst Drahn, *Führer durch das Schrifttum der deutschen Sozialdemokratie* (Berlin, 1919) and in the catalogue of the book-dealer R. L. Prager, *Marx, Engels, Lassalle. Eine Bibliographie des Sozialismus* (Berlin, 1924). A. Joseph Berlau, *The German Social Democratic Party, 1914–1921* (New York, 1949) contains a useful list of works on the war period, while Peter Gay offers a comprehensive Bernstein bibliography in *The Dilemma of Democratic Socialism* (New York, 1952). John L. Snell has prepared a guide to "Some German Socialist Newspapers in European Archives," *Journal of Modern History,* XXIV: 380–382 (1952).

i. Documentary Sources

For blocking out problems in the history of Social Democratic politics, no source is more useful than the annual *Protokoll über die Verhand-*

lungen des Parteitages der Sozialdemokratischen Partei Deutschlands
(Berlin, 1890–1913, 1917). The reporting of the debates, initially weak
and selective to the detriment of the less important party personalities,
grows fuller with the years, thus providing progressively greater insight
into the attitudes of the lower echelons of the party. The value of the
protocols extends beyond the congress debates: the annual reports of
the executive include rich statistical material on the party's institutions,
while the reports of the Reichstag delegation constitute a handy summary of the party's parliamentary policy. In his *Handbuch der Sozialdemokratischen Parteitage, 1863–1913,* 2 vols. (Munich, 1910–1915),
Wilhelm Schröder has made convenient excerpts of motions, resolutions, and speeches at the congresses and arranged them topically.
Other indispensable party proceedings are: Emil Eichhorn, ed., *Protokoll über die Verhandlungen des Gründungsparteitages der U.S.P.D.
vom 6. bis 8. April 1917 in Gotha. Mit Anhang: Bericht über die
gemeinsame Konferenz der Arbeitsgemeinschaft und der Spartakusgruppe vom 7. Januar 1917 in Berlin* (Berlin, 1921); and *Internationaler
Sozialisten-Kongress zu Stuttgart, 1907* (Berlin, 1907).

The development of party division over the issue of war is illuminated
by the documents, oral testimony, and special studies contained in Das
Werk des Untersuchungsausschusses der verfassungsgebenden deutschen
Nationalversammlung und des deutschen Reichstages, 1919–1928, *Die
Ursachen des deutschen Zusammenbruches im Jahre 1918,* 4. Reihe, ii.
Abteilung, *Der innere Zusammenbruch,* 12 vols. (Berlin, 1925–1929).
Since many of the witnesses are concerned with justifying their earlier
behavior in terms of a political outlook acquired only after the event,
their testimony must be treated circumspectly. The same strictures apply
to the oral testimony appearing in the proceedings of two political
trials: *Der Ledebour Prozess* (Berlin, 1919), and *Der Dolchstossprozess
in München, Oktober-November 1925. Eine Ehrenrettung des deutschen
Volkes. Zeugen- und Sachverständigenaussagen. Eine Sammlung von
Dokumenten* (Munich, 1925).

The most useful collection of anti-war resolutions and actions taken
by the Socialist International (1867–1914) and the national parties
(1912–1914) is Carl Grünberg's *Die Internationale und der Weltkrieg,*
Part I, "Vor dem Kriege und während der ersten Kriegswochen"
(Leipzig, 1916). S. Grumbach has brought together Social Democratic
and other statements pertinent to German annexationism in the first
war years in *Das annexionistische Deutschland* (Lausanne, 1917). Ernst
Drahn and Susanne Leonhard, *Unterirdische Literatur im revolutionären Deutschland während des Weltkrieges* (Berlin-Fichtenau, 1920)

contains the principal manifestos and programmatic statements of the Spartacist opposition.

The development of the trade-union movement is summarized, with excellent statistical material, in the annual report of the Internationaler Sekretär der gewerkschaftlichen Landeszentralen, *Internationaler Bericht über die Gewerkschaftsbewegung* which I have used for the years 1905 *et seq.* Unable to procure the proceedings of the triennial trade-union congresses, I have found Paul Barthel's *Handbuch der deutschen Gewerkschaftskongresse* (Dresden, 1916) a convenient substitute. Like Schröder in his handbook of party congresses, Barthel presents abstracts from speeches, motions, and resolutions on all major questions and conscientiously includes different points of view.

Particularly useful in placing the development of Social Democracy in its German political context is *Schulthess' europäischer Geschichtskalender* (Munich, 1861, *et seq.*). Its annual volumes contain not only excerpts from press editorials on all major events, but also abstracts of proceedings of the most important German party conferences and of *Landtag* sessions. In the absence of substantial monographic literature on Imperial Germany's internal history, *Schulthess* acquires particular significance as an instrument of research. The value of the *Stenographische Berichte der Verhandlungen des deutschen Reichstages* (Berlin, 1871 *et seq.*) requires no special comment. Election statistics through 1912 are conveniently broken down by district and by voting phases in Paul Hirsch and Bruno Borchardt, *Die Sozialdemokratie und die Wahlen zum deutschen Reichstage* (Berlin, 1912).

ii. Periodicals and Newspapers

Neue Zeit (Stuttgart, 1893 *et seq.*), the party's official theoretical organ, and the revisionist *Sozialistische Monatshefte* (Berlin, 1898 *et seq.*) illuminate the crosscurrents of socialist thought better than any other pair of sources. *Neue Zeit* contains more information on the party and covers a wider sector of the Social Democratic political spectrum, while *Sozialistische Monatshefte* provides more insight into the trade-union attitude on all issues. The *Monatshefte's* "Rundschau" is a mine of information on detailed developments, especially at the regional level. *Vorwärts* (Berlin, 1891 *et seq.*), the daily of the party and the Berlin organization, while incredibly dull is particularly useful for its news coverage of Social Democracy in action. I have had no access to other Social Democratic dailies. Although most of them are composed of syndicated stories which appear in *Vorwärts,* the *Leipziger Volkszeitung* has unique value for understanding the left radical position.

Significant special articles are contained in *Archiv für die Geschichte des Sozialismus und der Arbeiterbewegung, Archiv für Sozialwissenschaft und Sozialpolitik,* and *Die Gesellschaft,* successor to *Neue Zeit.* Where relevant to the topic under discussion such articles will be listed below. The doggerel and cartoons of *Simplizissimus* provide a light but often penetrating obligato in the cacophony of German prewar politics.

iii. Memoirs, Biographies, Letters, Speeches

Prewar Social Democracy boasted few outstanding personalities and those who might lay claim to some distinction too rarely kept journals or published their memoirs and papers. Even the work of mediocre figures, however, can afford unusual insights into the mentality and political development of the party, or into the behind-the-scenes activities where the real decisions were so often made. One can only lament that this class of material is not larger and that the biographies of Social Democratic leaders which supplement it rarely transcend the level of official encomia.

Eduard Bernstein's sketch, *Entwicklungsgang eines Sozialisten* (Leipzig, 1930), is the only autobiography to emerge from the political wing of revisionism. Its contents have been absorbed and evaluated in a larger historical frame in Peter Gay's excellent political biography, *The Dilemma of Democratic Socialism. Eduard Bernstein's Challenge to Marx* (New York, 1952). Ludwig Frank's *Aufsätze, Reden und Briefe,* ed. Hedwig Wachenheim (Berlin, n.d.) illuminates the sense of impending victory with which the revisionists waged their intra-party battles in the prewar years. The ebullient and intelligent Frank deserves a better biography than S. Grünebaum's *Ludwig Frank. Ein Beitrag zur Entwicklung der deutschen Sozialdemokratie* (Heidelberg, 1924), of which the subtitle is particularly misleading. Robert Michels' "Kurt Eisner," *Archiv für die Geschichte des Sozialismus und der Arbeiterbewegung,* XIV: 364–391 (1929), though an interesting appreciation based on intimate personal acquaintance, suffers, like much of Michels' work, from an excess of intuition.

The ethos of German trade-unionism did not encourage the movement's leaders to develop highly individualized public personalities in the manner of John L. Lewis. The few biographies of union leaders, such as Theodor Leipart's *Carl Legien. Ein Gedenkbuch* (Berlin, 1929), are official encomia thin in political content. Carl Severing's *Mein Lebensweg,* 2 vols. (Köln, 1950) is the only full-scale autobiography of a prewar union leader. While it illuminates the impact of the German apprenticeship training system on the trade-union mentality, it does not, as one would hope, show how Severing built the machine which gave him control of the party in Bielefeld.

The party leaders, thanks to their political and parliamentary functions less reticent than the trade-unionists, have left the richest block of memoirs. August Bebel's *Aus meinem Leben,* 3 vols. (Berlin, 1910–1914), however, does not reach into our period, nor is there among the handful of Bebel biographies one sufficiently scholarly to fill the gap. With respect to the younger members of the executive, we are better off. Friedrich Ebert's *Schriften, Aufzeichnungen, Reden,* 2 vols. (Dresden, 1926) throws some light on his activities, supplemented in Paul Kampffmeyer's biographical introduction. Ebert's *Kämpfe und Ziele* (Dresden, n.d.) is less valuable for its collection of speeches than for the sidelights thrown on his character by the appended reminiscences of various of Ebert's associates. Karl Radek's essay on Ebert in *Portraits and Pamphlets,* trans. anon. (London, 1935), despite its hostility and inaccuracy, contains a few useful insights. The irrepressible vanity of Philipp Scheidemann happily takes the form of candor rather than concealment in his *Memoiren eines Sozialdemokraten,* 2 vols. (Dresden, 1928), where he reveals facts which his more cautious colleagues in the executive would have left unsaid. A translation by J. E. Mitchell is entitled *The Making of New Germany. The Memoirs of Philipp Scheidemann,* 2 vols. (New York, 1929). Most but not all of the material in Scheidemann's earlier work, *Der Zusammenbruch* (Berlin, 1921), which is based on his wartime diary, has been absorbed into his *Memoiren.* Otto Braun, *Von Weimar zu Hitler* (New York, 1940), contains nothing of interest on his pre-Weimar party career. Erich Kuttner has added little in his brief and laudatory *Otto Braun* (Leipzig, 1932). Hermann Müller, *Die November-Revolution* (Berlin, 1931) tells us something about the executive in the war years, but not before.

Gustav Noske, *Erlebtes aus Aufstieg und Niedergang einer Demokratie* (Offenbach-am-Main, 1947) and Wilhelm Keil, *Erlebnisse eines Sozialdemokraten* (Stuttgart, 1947), vol. I, contain material on party life at the regional level as seen by right-wing leaders. Noske's information on Königsberg and Chemnitz and Keil's more extensive but highly colored account of party squabbles in Württemberg must be used with caution. Keil's autobiography is, however, an excellent case study in the evolution of a socialist leader from radical to reformist. Noske's *Von Kiel bis Kapp. Zur Geschichte der deutschen Revolution* (Berlin, 1920), while lying beyond our period, is revealing of the author's political attitudes.

Material on the left center's leading personalities is scarce and thin. Ernst Haase, in *Hugo Haase, sein Leben und Wirken* (Berlin, n.d. [1929?]), presents a revealing but not voluminous selection of his father's letters and speeches and a biographical introduction. Kautsky's brief autobiographical sketch in Felix Meiner, ed., *Die Volkswirtschaftslehre der Gegenwart in Selbstdarstellung* (Leipzig, 1924) is less useful than the more limited but illuminating pamphlet, *Mein Verhältnis zur Unabhängigen Sozialdemokratischen Partei* (Berlin, 1922). Karl Renner's *Karl Kautsky. Skizze zur Geschichte der geistigen und politischen Entwicklung der deutschen Arbeiterklasse* (Berlin, 1929) is useful for its skeletal data on the theorist's life. Kautsky's papers, which were not accessible to me, are reported to be in the archives of the Institute for Social History in Amsterdam. Another important centrist figure, Wilhelm Dittmann, now residing in Zürich, has prepared a manuscript entitled *Wie Alles kam: Deutschlands Weg seit 1914* which would presumably be a welcome addition to the sparse memoir material from the left center wing. Tony Sender's *The Autobiography of a German Rebel* (New York, 1939), while concerned primarily with the Weimar period, casts light on the extraordinary fluidity of the line between the Spartacists and centrist Independents at the local level.

Among the left radicals, Rosa Luxemburg has, by virtue of her extraordinary personality, received the most attention from editors and biographers. Three collections of letters have appeared, all interesting but none rich in political content: Rosa Luxemburg, *Letters to Karl and Luise Kautsky from 1896 to 1918,* ed. Luise Kautsky, trans. Louis P. Lochner (New York, 1925); *Letters from Prison,* trans. Eden and Cedar Paul (Berlin, 1923); and *Briefe an Freunde,* ed. Benedikt Kautsky (Hamburg, 1950). A selection of Luxemburg's speeches has been published with an introduction by Paul Frölich in the series *Redner der Revolution,* vol. XI (Berlin, 1928). Paul Frölich's *Rosa Luxemburg. Gedanke und Tat* (Paris, 1939), a devotional but scholarly work, remains the best political biography of any German Social Democratic leader (English translation by Edward Fitzgerald, *Rosa Luxemburg* [London, 1940]). Henriette Roland-Holst, *Rosa Luxemburg, ihr Leben und Wirken* (Zürich, 1937) adds some personal touches to Frölich's portrait. Luxemburg's theory and political life are criticized in the dissertation of Anne Baier, *Rosa Luxemburg* (Würzburg, 1933). Karl Liebknecht, *Klassenkampf gegen den Krieg* (Berlin, n.d. [1919?]), with its appended "Betrachtungen und Erinnerungen aus grosser Zeit," is the richest single source on the conflicts in the wartime Reichstag delegation. It also includes a valuable account of Liebknecht's efforts to mobilize the opposition. Julian Gumperz has edited Liebknecht's *Reden und Aufsätze* (Hamburg, 1921) which will prove especially useful to the student of anti-militarism both before and after 1914. Karl Liebknecht, *Briefe aus dem Felde, aus der Untersuchungshaft und aus dem Zuchthaus* (Berlin, 1920) reveals more of the person than of his politics. Klara Zetkin's pamphlet, *Rosa Luxemburg, Karl Liebknecht, Franz Mehring* (Moscow-Leningrad, 1934), does not transcend the level of hagiography. A sensitive essay on Mehring's position in the intellectual history of Social Democracy is Jan Romein, "Franz Mehring," *Archiv für die Geschichte des Sozialismus und der Arbeiterbewegung*, XIII: 80–103 (1928). The left radicals' conflict with a rightist bureaucracy receives dramatic documentation in Rudolf Franz, "Aus Briefen Konrad Haenischs," in the same *Archiv*, XIV: 444–484 (1929). A very few interesting bits on the prewar years are to be gleaned from a collaborative eulogy to a former comrade of Haenisch's who has since risen to fame: *Wilhelm Pieck, dem Vorkämpfer für ein neues Deutschland, zum 70. Geburtstag* (Berlin, 1946).

iv. Contemporary Writings on Social Democratic Theory and Tactics

The period of our study produced few major theoretical works. The best thinkers of Social Democracy devoted much of their energy to day-to-day political practice. New departures in theory, arising out of political controversy, usually found their expression in article form in *Neue Zeit* or *Sozialistische Monatshefte*. For these the reader is referred to the text and footnotes above.

The books which exercised the most influence in Social Democracy after 1905 were largely written before that year. Karl Kautsky's *Das Erfurter Programm* (11th edition, Stuttgart, 1912), originally published in 1892, was the basic, official interpretation of the party program. For the party tactic in a non-revolutionary era, Friedrich Engels' expurgated introduction to Karl Marx, *The Class Struggles in France,* trans. anon. (New York, 1935) was equally decisive. Eduard Bernstein's epochmaking *Die Voraussetzungen des Sozialismus und die Aufgaben der Sozialdemokratie* (12th thousand, Stuttgart, 1906) originally appeared in 1899. Edith Harvey's translation of this work under the title, *Evolutionary Socialism* (New York, 1909) contains an interesting English introduction by Bernstein. The two classic orthodox answers to Bernstein were Karl Kautsky, *Bernstein und das sozialdemokratische Pro-*

gramm. Eine Antikritik (Stuttgart, 1899) and Rosa Luxemburg, *Sozialreform oder Revolution,* included in volume III of her *Gesammelte Werke* (see below).

Eduard Bernstein, *Die heutige Sozialdemokratie in Theorie und Praxis* (3rd edition, Munich, 1912) offers the best summary statement of the moderate revisionist position for our period. Kurt Eisner, *Gesammelte Schriften,* 2 vols. (Berlin, 1919), while primarily literary and philosophical contain valuable material on the national question, though Eisner's views were not representative of revisionist thinking on the issue. Extreme nationalism in the revisionist camp finds expression in Richard Calwer, *Das sozialdemokratische Programm* (Jena, 1914). Typical of the many theoretical justifications of the party's war policy are: Eduard David, *Die Sozialdemokratie im Weltkrieg* (Berlin, 1915); Konrad Haenisch, *Die deutsche Sozialdemokratie in und nach dem Weltkriege* (2nd edition, Berlin, 1919), interesting for the conversion experience of an apostate from radicalism; and Wolfgang Heine, *Zu Deutschlands Erneuerung* (Jena, 1916), a volume rich in promise of reward to labor for its coöperation in the war effort. The wartime attempt of right-wing Social Democrats and middle-class intellectuals to work together toward a Germany of class harmony and national might is symbolized in a work edited jointly by Friedrich Thimme and Carl Legien, *Die Arbeiterschaft im neuen Deutschland* (Leipzig, 1916). Its contributors include such luminaries as Meinecke, Natorp, Tönnies, and Noske. Gustav Schmoller hailed the labor bureaucracy as a synthesis of aristocratic and democratic principles in "Der Weltkrieg und die Sozialdemokratie," *Schmollers Jahrbuch,* XXXIX: 1103–1114 (1915). Schmoller's essay is redeemed by some useful statistics on the party bureaucracy.

The classic centrist statement on Social Democratic theory and practice in the last prewar decade and the first larger effort at analyzing the political implications of imperialism for the party is Karl Kautsky, *Der Weg zur Macht* (2nd edition, Berlin, 1910), English translation by A. M. Simons, *The Road to Power* (Chicago, 1909). In 1910, Rudolf Hilferding published the first major Marxist economic analysis of imperialism in *Das Finanzkapital* (Vienna, 1923). Rosa Luxemburg showed similar power in her now famous "Juniusbroschüre," *Die Krise in der Sozialdemokratie* (Zürich, 1916), the classic Spartacist analysis of the economic and diplomatic origins of World War I.

Much but not all of Luxemburg's writing is collected in Paul Frölich's scholarly edition of her *Gesammelte Werke* (Berlin, 1925–1928). Only three of the six volumes planned by the editor were published:

volume III, containing Luxemburg's writings and speeches against reformism; volume IV, those on trade-unions and the political mass strike; and volume VI, *Die Akkumulation des Kapitals*. Luxemburg set forth in 1918 her last criticism of Lenin's ideas of party organization and of the nature of proletarian dictatorship in *Die russische Revolution. Eine kritische Würdigung* ("Neuer Weg" edition, Paris, n.d.), English translation by Bertram D. Wolfe, *The Russian Revolution* (New York, 1940). Karl Liebknecht's principal theoretical work was never completed. His drafts were published under the title, *Studien über die Bewegungsgesetze der gesellschaftlichen Entwicklung*, ed. Dr. Morris (Munich, 1922). A landmark in the history of the new revolutionism is Karl Liebknecht's pamphlet of 1907, *Militarismus und Antimilitarismus unter besonderer Berücksichtigung der internationalen Jugendbewegung* (Berlin, n.d. [1919?]). An introduction "by a friend" to the anonymous translation, *Militarism* (New York, 1917), provides a brief survey of Liebknecht's anti-militarist record.

The extensive debates on the political mass strike, although carried on largely in periodicals, found expression also in Karl Kautsky, *Der politische Massenstreik. Ein Beitrag zur Geschichte der Massenstreikdiskussion innerhalb der deutschen Sozialdemokratie* (Berlin, 1914); Rosa Luxemburg, *Massenstreik, Partei und Gewerkschaften*, reprinted in *Gesammelte Werke*, IV; Henriette Roland-Holst, *Generalstreik und Sozialdemokratie* (2nd revised edition, Dresden, 1906). The last-named work surveys the theory and practice of the general strike in all countries from a Marxist point of view. Emil Vandervelde, the Belgian socialist leader, contributed an important article to the discussion, "Der Generalstreik," *Archiv für Sozialwissenschaft und Sozialpolitik*, XXVI: 539–558 (1908). The best general introduction to the complexities of the mass-strike question is a scholarly study by a contemporary non-socialist, Elsbeth Georgi, "Theorie und Praxis des Generalstreiks in der modernen Arbeiterbewegung" (Ph.D. dissertation, Zürich, 1908).

Of the numerous general critiques of German Social Democracy by hostile contemporaries, two stand out for their insight and knowledge-ability. Robert Brunhuber, *Die heutige Sozialdemokratie* (Jena, 1906), by virtue of its well-founded predictions of a split in the party, caused no little uneasiness in the Social Democratic camp. In response to this work, Bernstein wrote *Die heutige Sozialdemokratie in Theorie und Praxis* (see above). An equally able analysis of the internal division of Social Democracy is that of the Catholic trade-unionist, Joseph Joos, *Krisis in der Sozialdemokratie* (München-Gladbach, 1911).

v. History and Sociology of the Social Democratic Party

There is no general history of Social Democracy in our period to correspond to Franz Mehring, *Geschichte der deutschen Sozialdemokratie,* 4 vols. in 2 (12th edition, Stuttgart, 1922). Harry J. Marks, "Movements of Reform and Revolution in Germany, 1890–1903" (Ph.D. dissertation, ms., Harvard University Library, Cambridge, Mass., 1937) takes up the development of the party with the end of the Anti-Socialist Laws, where Mehring left it. Marks' exhaustive and scholarly study, although somewhat weakened by the author's excessively normative approach, is an excellent introduction to the problems of the years after 1903. General surveys of the period 1903 to 1914 are all embedded in works devoted to other purposes. Paul Frölich's introductory articles and explanatory notes in Rosa Luxemburg *Gesammelte Werke* (see above, Sec. iv), despite the author's primary focus on a single figure, represent the only serious effort to treat the period on the basis of detailed research. Frölich's viewpoint is Leninist. Meagre in content, pedestrian in tone, is Richard Lipinski, *Die Sozialdemokratie von ihren Anfängen bis zur Gegenwart. Eine gedrängte Darstellung für Functionäre und Lernende,* 2 vols. (Berlin, 1927–28). A brief, revisionist survey of party history is offered by Eduard Bernstein in "Die Entwicklung der deutschen Sozialdemokratie," *Die Entwicklungsgeschichte der grossen politischen Parteien in Deutschland,* Schriften der Deutschen Gesellschaft für Politik an der Universität Halle-Wittenberg, II (Bonn and Leipzig, 1922). English readers will find a convenient though sketchy introduction to the subject in the first chapter of Evelyn Anderson, *Hammer or Anvil. The Story of the German Working Class Movement* (London, 1945).

I have found scarcely a handful of regional and local histories of the party. Paul Hirsch, *Der Weg der Sozialdemokratie zur Macht in Preussen* (Berlin, 1929) concentrates primarily on the position and policy of the Social Democratic deputation in the Prussian Landtag of which the centrist Hirsch was a member. Ernst Heilmann, *Geschichte der Arbeiterbewegung in Chemnitz und dem Erzgebirge* (Chemnitz, n.d. [1912?]), describing the growth of the party and trade-unions in membership and property, glosses over the acute internal conflicts in this reformist-controlled area. Eduard Bernstein scarcely touches our period in his *Geschichte der Berliner Arbeiterbewegung,* 3 vols. (Berlin, 1907–1910). A few sidelights on the history of the party in Württemberg are contained in the work of the right-wing reformist Wilhelm Blos, *Von der Monarchie bis zum Volksstaat. Zur Geschichte der Revo-*

lution in Deutschland, insbesondere in Württemberg, 2 vols. (Stuttgart, 1922–23). Two local histories to which I have not had access are: Heinrich Laufenberg, *Geschichte der Arbeiterbewegung in Hamburg, Altona und Umgebung,* 2 vols. (Hamburg, 1911, 1931); and Hermann Müller, *Geschichte der Arbeiterbewegung in Sachsen-Altenburg* (Jena, 1923).

The sociology of the prewar party has been more thoroughly explored than its history. The brilliant and eccentric Robert Michels broke ground in this field with his penetrating work, *Zur Soziologie des Parteiwesens in der modernen Demokratie* (Leipzig, 1911). Although his strange amalgam of Rousseau's individualism and Max Weber's institutionalism prevented Michels from comprehending the dialectic aspect of the party's development, his typology of Social Democratic bureaucracy remains unsurpassed. His earlier effort at analyzing the sociological composition of the party, though limited in scope, is still of value: Robert Michels, "Die deutsche Sozialdemokratie. Parteimitgliedschaft und soziale Zusammensetzung," *Archiv für Sozialwissenschaft und Sozialpolitik,* XXIII: 471–556 (1906). G. Sinowjev, *Der Krieg und die Krise des Sozialismus* (Vienna, 1924) and N. Lenin and G. Sinowjev, *Gegen den Strom. Aufsätze aus den Jahren 1914–1916* (Hamburg, 1921) present supplementary views or, more frequently, Marxist alternatives to Michels' analysis of the sociological development of the prewar party. Harry J. Marks utilizes the contributions of both in "The Sources of Reformism in the Social Democratic Party, 1890–1914," *Journal of Modern History,* XI: 334–361 (1939), but emphasizes the economic basis of reformist bureaucracy in the party's "labor aristocracy." The Michels and Lenin-Zinoviev views on the sociology of Social Democratic bureaucracy are penetratingly criticized in Rudolf Schlesinger, *Central European Democracy and Its Background,* International Library of Sociology and Social Reconstruction (London, 1953). Schlesinger looks upon the bureaucracy as a faithful reflection of the German working class mind. This somewhat oversimplified view leads him to the untenable corollary that the party conflicts of the years 1905–1914 were purely ideological and essentially divorced from any social or organizational basis. Theodor Buddeberg, "Das soziologische Problem der Sozialdemokratie," *Archiv für Sozialwissenschaft und Sozialpolitik,* XLIX (1922) suggests a theoretical framework for understanding the fate of socialist ideology and the party at the hands of the trade-unions.

I am inclined to doubt that further advances in the understanding of the sociology of Social Democracy can be made through speculation on data already available. Only close regional and local analyses can open new horizons. The approaches through mass psychology have not yet provided usable intellectual tools to the political sociologist who is so frequently confronted with two areas of the same social composition but widely differing political behavior. Typical of the speculative efforts of the mass psychologist are Kurt Geyer, *Der Radikalismus in der deutschen Arbeiterbewegung. Ein soziologischer Versuch* (Jena, 1923) and Robert Michels, "Psychologie der antikapitalistischen Massenbewegung," *Grundriss der Sozialökonomik*, IX, i (Tübingen, 1926), ch. VII, works in which the empirical loci of political radicalism and conservatism are blandly disregarded. Two brief political sociologies of the S.P.D., though explicitly focussed on Weimar, are useful for understanding the party in the last prewar years: Siegfried Marck, *Sozialdemokratie, Die geistige Struktur der politischen Parteien Europas* (Berlin, 1931); and Sigmund Neumann, *Die deutschen Parteien. Wesen und Wandel nach dem Kriege,* Fachschriften zur Politik und staatsbürgerlichen Erziehung (Berlin, 1932). To these must be added a short but penetrating historical survey by an independent Marxist, Boris Goldenberg, "Beiträge zur Soziologie der deutschen Vorkriegssozialdemokratie" (Ph.D. dissertation, Heidelberg, 1932).

The knotty problem of the sociology of the Social Democratic electorate has been the subject of two studies of which the first, though narrow in its statistical basis, is the more illuminating: R. Blank, "Die soziale Zusammensetzung der sozialdemokratischen Wählerschaft Deutschlands," *Archiv für Sozialwissenschaft und Sozialpolitik,* XX: 507–553 (1905); and Emil Eichhorn, *Parteien und Klassen im Spiegel der Reichstagswahlen* (Halle, 1925). Eichhorn attempts a statistical correlation of political behavior and occupational status for the elections between 1907 and 1924. Willy Kremer analyzes the Reichstag delegates in search of a correlation between party allegiance and occupation in *Der soziale Aufbau der Parteien des deutschen Reichstags von 1871–1918* (Emsdetten, 1934). For his biographical data, Kremer relies on Joseph Kürschner, ed., *Deutscher Reichstag. Biographisch-statistisches Handbuch,* in which the occupational material on many Social Democratic Reichstag members is necessarily unreliable as a guide to social origins and status.

The only history of Social Democratic party organization is the nonanalytical but accurate work of the revisionist Wilhelm Schröder, *Geschichte der sozialdemokratischen Parteiorganisation in Deutschland,* Abhandlungen und Vorträge zur sozialistischen Bildung, IV–V, ed. Max Grunwald (Dresden, 1912), to which is appended a complete collection of party statutes from 1863 to 1912. A group of left-wing Social

Democrats produced a provocative critical study of the party organization in the late Weimar period, when the problems grounded in prewar party history became acute once more. The student of prewar party history will find conceptual utility in this work, by Fritz Bieligk and others, *Die Organisation im Klassenkampf,* Rote Bücher der "Marxistischen Büchergemeinde," II (Berlin, n.d. [1931?]). Ludwig Kantorowicz illuminates the nature and impact of the party apparatus on Socialist journalism in *Die sozialdemokratische Presse Deutschlands. Eine soziologische Untersuchung* (Tübingen, 1922).

The Social Democratic youth movement is comprehensively surveyed in Karl Korn, *Die Arbeiterjugendbewegung* (2nd edition, Berlin, 1923). As editor of the party's official youth journal, Korn presents the majority view. While generally accurate, Korn minimizes the degree of tension between youth and adults in the years 1911–1914. Willy Münzenberg, *Die sozialistische Jugendorganisation vor und während des Weltkrieges* (Berlin, 1919), is a rather stormy Communist treatment of the subject. Social Democratic youth organization is considered in the wider setting of the German youth movement as a whole in Viktor Engelhardt, *Die deutsche Jugendbewegung als kulturhistorisches Phänomen* (Berlin, 1923). The socialist author draws his material on Social Democratic youth largely from Korn.

Of the special studies devoted to the development of revisionism, the most comprehensive is Erika Rikli, *Der Revisionismus. Ein Revisionsversuch der deutschen marxistischen Theorie, 1890–1914,* Zürcher volkswirtschaftliche Forschungen, XXV (Zürich, 1935). Karl Vorländer, one of the leading exponents of Kantian socialism has described Kant's position in revisionist thought in *Kant und Marx. Ein Beitrag zur Philosophie des Sozialismus* (2nd revised edition, Tübingen, 1926). The student of revisionism should also consult Peter Gay's study of Bernstein's intellectual development (see above, Sec. iii). Walter Croll, *Die Entwicklung der Anschauungen über soziale Reform in der deutschen Sozialdemokratie, nach den sozialdemokratischen Parteitagsprotokollen von 1890 bis 1912* (Berlin, 1912) is an objective but rather superficial description of changes in party attitudes toward social reform. The revitalization of anti-reformist elements is treated in Richard W. Reichard, "The German Working Class and the Russian Revolution of 1905," *Journal of Central European Affairs,* XIII: 136–153 (1953).

The problem of nationalism in Social Democracy has received more attention from non-socialist scholars than any other topic. Nationalism, after all, proved to be the ideological key to the domestication of Marxian socialism. How German Social Democracy retraced the course of mid-nineteenth-century liberalism and was similarly shattered on the rock of nationalism provides the theme of an interesting discussion by Eduard Wilhelm Mayer, "Parteikrisen im Liberalismus und in der Sozialdemokratie," *Preussische Jahrbücher*, CLXXII: 171–179 (1918).

The best survey of the evolution of the party's international policy is Max Victor, "Die Stellung der deutschen Sozialdemokratie zu den Fragen der auswärtigen Politik (1896–1914)," *Archiv für Sozialwissenschaft und Sozialpolitik*, LX, i: 147–179 (1928). A pioneering effort in the American historiography of German socialism, Carlton J. H. Hayes' "German Socialism Reconsidered," *American Historical Review*, XXIII: 62–101 (1917), still ranks among the better descriptions of the party's position on war and foreign policy. In "The Internationalism of the Early Social Democrats of Germany," *American Historical Review*, XLVII: 245–258 (1942), Sinclair W. Armstrong discloses the existence of a Wilsonian ideology in the party before 1890. William Maehl traces "The Triumph of Nationalism in the German Socialist Party on the Eve of the First World War," *Journal of Modern History*, XXIV: 15–41 (1952). While he assigns to nationalism more autonomous political force than I should do, Maehl relates it fruitfully to the development of the schism before 1914. The "social patriotic" current is fully described but little analyzed in Erwin Dörzbacher, *Die deutsche Sozialdemokratie und die nationale Machtpolitik bis 1914* (Gotha, 1920). In a stimulating examination of "Theories of Socialist Imperialism," *Foreign Affairs*, XXVIII: 290–298 (1949–1950), Lenore O'Boyle draws formal parallels between German prewar "social imperialist" theory and modern Stalinist expansionism. The party's resistance to any kind of revolutionary commitment against war is surveyed in Richard Hostetter, "The S.P.D. and the General Strike as an Anti-war Weapon, 1905–1914," *The Historian*, XIII: 27–51 (1950–1951).

The effect of nationalism on the position of the German Social Democratic Party in the Second International is discussed in two contemporary essays: Robert Michels, "Die deutsche Sozialdemokratie im internationalen Verbande," *Archiv für Sozialwissenschaft und Sozialpolitik*, XXV: 148–231 (1907); and Paul Feucht, "Der internationale Sozialistenkongress in Stuttgart," *Preussische Jahrbücher*, CXXX: 102–110 (1907).

The history of Social Democracy during World War I has been more frequently studied than the less dramatic prewar period. The most systematic and comprehensive survey of the subject is A. Jospeh Berlau, *The German Social Democratic Party, 1914–1921* (New York: Columbia University Studies in History, Economics and Public Law, No. 557, 1949). Friedrich Herbach provides useful summaries of the divisions in party opinion on specific issues in "Die Strömungen des Marxismus in Deutschland während des Weltkrieges und die Grenzen zwischen seinen einzelnen Richtungen nach Ideologie und Praxis" (Ph.D. dissertation, Würzburg, 1933). Edwyn Bevan, *German Social Democracy during the War* (London, 1918), for its time a remarkably complete account of the split, retains the flavor of immediacy through the fulsome utilization of parliamentary debates and local newspaper sources. Hans Herzfeld, writing on the basis of the *Dolchstossprozess* proceedings — and in their spirit — excoriates the traitorous Social Democrats in *Die deutsche Sozialdemokratie und die Auflösung der nationalen Einheitsfront im Weltkriege* (Leipzig, 1928). Charles Andler carries on the French right-wing socialists' war against the Teuton in *La décomposition politique du socialisme allemand, 1914–1919* (Paris, 1919). A more useful study of the final schism will be found in Eugen Prager, *Die Geschichte der U.S.P.D., Entstehung und Entwicklung der Unabhängigen Sozialdemokratischen Partei Deutschlands* (2nd edition, Berlin, 1922). The author faithfully reflects the centrist point of view. His inclusion of many documents and excerpts from speeches not elsewhere available makes his work of unique value to the researcher. Lenore O'Boyle, in a sympathetic evaluation, "The German Independent Socialists during the First World War," *American Historical Review,* LVI: 824–831 (1951), derives the character of the party exclusively from the outlook of its most prominent parliamentary leaders. Her view that the Independents were essentially revisionist does not hold for the majority of its local organizations. Paul Frölich, *Zehn Jahre Krieg und Bürgerkrieg,* I, "Der Krieg" (Berlin, 1924), presents the Communist view of the breakdown of Social Democracy. Frölich overestimates the purely pacifist ingredient in the left center's oppositional attitude. The first chapter of Ossip K. Flechtheim, *Die Kommunistische Partei Deutschlands in der Weimarer Republik* (Offenbach a. M., 1948), summarizes the wartime split with the emergence of the Spartacist opposition as its focus.

Of the numerous works dealing with socialism in or after the German Revolution, a few contribute to our knowledge of the break-up of the party. Two highly colored accounts by left-wing union leaders show the difficulty of precising the line between Spartacists and Independents: Emil Barth, *Aus der Werkstatt der deutschen Revolution* (Berlin, 1919); and Richard Müller, *Vom Kaiserreich zur Republik, ein Beitrag zur Geschichte der revolutionären Arbeiterbewegung während des Weltkrieges,* Wissenschaft und Gesellschaft, III (Vienna, 1924). Ruth Fischer, *Stalin and German Communism. A Study in the Origins of the State*

Party (Cambridge, Mass., 1948), is particularly valuable for its account of the relations between Communists and Independents in the wake of the Revolution. In social discernment and historical vividness, no account of the meaning of the schism for the life of the factory worker can compare with Erik Reger's *Union der festen Hand* (Berlin, 1930), a novel on the great strikes in the Krupp works.

Outstanding among the studies of special aspects of wartime Social Democracy are two works of Erich Otto Volkmann: *Der Marxismus und das deutsche Heer im Weltkriege* (Berlin, 1925), and "Die Stellung der oppositionellen sozialdemokratischen Parteigruppen im Weltkrieg zum nationalen Staat und zur Frage der Landesverteidigung," in Das Werk des Untersuchungsausschusses, *Die Ursachen des deutschen Zusammenbruches im Jahre 1918*, 4. Reihe, ii. Abteilung, VI: 284–306 (1928). Though a nationalist and a militarist, Volkmann analyzes the complex currents in Social Democracy with mastery and discrimination. The student of the party's hour of decision at the outbreak of the war will find little assistance in the monograph of P.-G. La Chenais, *Die sozialdemokratische Reichstagsfraktion und die Kriegserklärung* (Lausanne, 1918). The opening round in the fight for control of the party organ during the war is described in Curt Schoen, *Der "Vorwärts" und die Kriegserklärung, vom Fürstenmord in Serajevo bis zur Marneschlacht 1914* (Berlin-Charlottenburg, 1929). Schoen employs virtually no sources except *Vorwärts* itself.

vi. Trade-Unions

The student wishing a general introduction to the German trade-union movement will be best served by Theodor Cassau, *Die Gewerkschaftsbewegung*, Soziale Organisationen der Gegenwart, ed. Ernst Grünfeld (Halberstadt, 1925). An earlier, careful but more pedestrian study based on extensive use of the trade-union press and congress proceedings concentrates on the period of union expansion and centralization: Otto Heilborn, *Die "freien" Gewerkschaften seit 1890; ein Überblick über ihre Organisation, ihre Ziele und ihr Verhältnis zur sozialdemokratischen Partei* (Jena, 1907). The Free Trade Unions produced two official histories which convey the union leaders' image of the movement as well as useful historical data: Paul Umbreit, *25 Jahre deutscher Gewerkschaftsbewegung, 1890–1915* (Berlin, 1915); and Siegfried Nestriepke, *Die deutschen Gewerkschaften bis zum Ausbruch des Weltkrieges*, 3 vols. (Stuttgart, n.d. [1923?]). The researcher will find deeper insight into the problematics of German unionism in two collections of essays by the sensitive and intelligent trade-union journalist, Adolf Braun: *Die*

Gewerkschaften, ihre Entwicklung und Kämpfe (Nürnberg, 1914), and *Gewerkschaften. Betrachtungen und Überlegungen während des Weltkrieges* (Leipzig, 1915).

Alexander Wende, *Die Konzentrationsbewegung bei den deutschen Gewerkschaften* (Berlin, 1913), examines the relationship between the centralization of trade-unions and the concentration of industry. The employers' attempt to organize against the unions is comprehensively treated in Gerhard Kessler, *Die deutschen Arbeitgeberverbände,* Schriften des Vereins für Sozialpolitik, CXXIV (1907). Another useful monograph on employer-union relations is the construction workers' official history of their great strike in 1910: August Winnig, *Der grosse Kampf im deutschen Baugewerbe, 1910* (Hamburg, 1911).

Franz Neumann, *European Trade Unionism and Politics* (New York, 1936), is a *tour d'horizon* which places German unionism in its wider, European context. Neumann's sound and original system of periodization for the trade-unions' relation to political life is of lasting value. In *Koalitionsfreiheit und Reichsverfassung. Die Stellung der Gewerkschaften im Verfassungssystem* (Berlin, 1932), a work dealing primarily with the Weimar Republic, Franz Neumann provides some interesting theoretical discussion which has relevance to the prewar period. Background on the origin, nature and practical application of the German laws of association down to 1899 will be found in Theodor Loewenfeld, "Koalitionsrecht und Strafrecht," *Archiv für soziale Gesetzgebung und Statistik,* XIV: 472–602 (1899). On the eve of World War I, when the unions were threatened with further legal restrictions, Siegfried Nestriepke compiled his comprehensive case study of legal discrimination against the unions, *Das Koalitionsrecht in Deutschland, Gesetze und Praxis,* Im Auftrag der Generalkommission der Gewerkschaften Deutschlands (Berlin, n.d. [1914?]).

The policies, aspirations, and problems of the trade-unions during the war are most fully but uncritically described in Paul Umbreit and Charlotte Lorenz, *Der Krieg und die Arbeitsverhältnisse,* Wirtschafts- und Sozialgeschichte des Weltkrieges, Deutsche Serie, ed. James T. Shotwell (Stuttgart, Berlin, Leipzig, and New Haven, 1928). In most respects inferior to the foregoing work, Paul Umbreit, *Die deutschen Gewerkschaften im Weltkriege,* Sozialwissenschaftliche Bibliothek, I (Berlin, 1917), contains a better discussion of the impact of the Social Democratic opposition on the trade-union movement. Carl Legien set forth the union strategy of counterattack against the opposition in a significant pamphlet, *Warum müssen die Gewerkschaftsfunktionäre sich mehr am inneren Parteileben beteiligen?* (Berlin, 1915).

vii. General Studies of Socialism and the International Socialist Movement

There is no comprehensive history of prewar international socialism which takes account of the massive specialized literature appearing in the last quarter century. Werner Sombart, *Socialism and the Social Movement,* trans. M. Epstein (New York, 1909), describes the movement country by country and can still serve as an introduction to the national typology of socialism. Arthur Rosenberg, *Democracy and Socialism. A Contribution to the Political History of the Past 150 Years,* trans. George Rosen (New York, 1936), lacks the arresting interpretative power which one has learned to expect from its author. Rudolf Schlesinger, *Central European Democracy and Its Background* (see above, Sec. v) contains illuminating comparisons between the German and Austrian socialist movements.

On socialist political theory, two studies deserve particular attention: Hans Kelsen, *Sozialismus und Staat. Eine Untersuchung der politischen Theorie des Marxismus* (Leipzig, 1923), analyzes the evolution of the socialist idea of the state from Marx to Bolshevism, and devotes a chapter to the *étatisme* of German Social Democracy. A remarkable conservative-nationalist study of Marx's attitude toward the German problem is Hans Rothfels, "Marxismus und Aussenpolitik," *Deutscher Staat und deutsche Parteien,* ed. Paul Wentzcke (Munich and Berlin, 1922), 308–341.

Among the general interpretations of the socialist movement, Joseph A. Schumpeter, *Capitalism, Socialism and Democracy* (3rd edition, New York and London, 1942), is surely the most original. The author views socialism as the revolt of the herd against the creative destructiveness of capitalism. Paul A. Sweezy, in *The Theory of Capitalist Development. Principles of Marxian Political Economy* (New York, 1942), presents a penetrating analysis of the "breakdown" controversy and the rise of the Marxian theory of imperialism.

There is still need for a scholarly history of the Second International. The unpublished M.A. thesis of Patricia A. M. Mitchell, "The Second International, 1889–1914" (Bryn Mawr College, Bryn Mawr, Pa., 1947), illuminates its organizational structure and contains interesting observations on the atmosphere of the international congresses. William E. Walling in *The Socialists and the War* (New York, 1915) compiled the most important statements and resolutions of the national parties after 1890 on the war problem and connected them with running commentary. The break-up of the International during the war has received more attention than its prewar history. The best brief study is Merle Fainsod's *International Socialism and the World War* (Cambridge, Mass., 1935). Alfred Rosmer *Le mouvement ouvrier pendant la guerre. De l'union sacrée à Zimmerwald* (Paris, 1936) presents a more detailed treatment, strongly Leninist in tone. Especially useful for the complex divisions in the German anti-war opposition is Angelica Balabanoff, *Die Zimmerwalder Bewegung, 1914–1919*, Die Internationale und der Weltkrieg, Part II, ed. Carl Grünberg (Leipzig, 1928).

Three works on Bolshevism deserve mention for the light they throw on the comparative history of German and Russian left radicalism: Franz Borkenau, *World Communism. The History of the Communist International* (New York, 1939); Arthur Rosenberg, *A History of Bolshevism from Marx to the First Five Years' Plan*, trans. Ian F. D. Morrow (London, 1934); and Bertram D. Wolfe, *Three Who Made a Revolution* (New York, 1948).

viii. The German Background

One of the most difficult problems confronting the student of German Social Democracy under the Empire is to acquire an adequate understanding of the socio-political setting in which the party's life took shape. Preoccupied with problems of foreign policy, German historians have produced only a handful of significant monographic studies on the internal development of the Empire of William II. The political histories of the separate federal states, so important to an understanding of Social Democracy, have yet to be written. Sociological analyses of the growth of cities are lacking. Even the histories of most of the political parties have not been studied in detail.

A number of competent general histories of the Reich will introduce the reader to the main lines of political development. Arthur Rosenberg, *The Birth of the German Republic*, trans. Ian F. D. Morrow (London, 1931), stands out for the originality of its presentation of the political consequences of the Bismarckian constitution in terms of Germany's social structure. Solid, reliable, and richer in political detail is the work by the liberal Johannes Ziekursch, *Politische Geschichte des neuen deutschen Kaiserreiches*, vol. III, *Das Zeitalter Wilhelms II, 1890–1918* (Frankfurt a. M., 1930). Erich Eyck, *Das persönliche Regiment Wilhelms II. Politische Geschichte des deutschen Kaiserreiches von 1890 bis 1914* (Erlenbach-Zürich, 1948), adds little to Ziekursch's presentation of domestic developments except fuller and more sensitive political portraiture. A conservative analysis of the Wilhelminic Empire, stronger on the cultural aspect than the foregoing works, is the fourth volume of

Adalbert Wahl, *Deutsche Geschichte von der Reichsgründung bis zum Ausbruch des Weltkrieges,* 4 vols. (Stuttgart, 1926–1936).

Three studies in political sociology, none of them primarily concerned with the period 1905–1917, indirectly illuminate aspects of its history. The relation between the economic position of the Junkers and their prewar policies is discussed in Part I of Alexander Gerschenkron, *Bread and Democracy in Germany* (Berkeley and Los Angeles, 1943). Eckart Kehr, *Schlachtflottenbau und Parteipolitik* (Berlin, 1930), provides a conceptual framework for understanding the later failure of the Social Democratic Party either to consummate an alliance with the Progressives or to compete successfully with the appeal of the "world-political idea." While Kehr's work analyzes the socio-political background for the Bülow-Bethmann era, Edmond Vermeil assesses its aftermath in his brilliant study, *L'Allemagne contemporaine (1919–1924). Sa structure et son évolution politiques, économiques et sociales* (Paris, 1925). Albrecht Mendelssohn Bartholdy, *The War and German Society. The Testament of a Liberal,* Economic and Social History of the World War, German Series, XII, ed., James T. Shotwell (New Haven, 1937) is disappointingly impressionistic but contains useful observations on the relations of government and labor.

Turning to more specialized studies, the student of Social Democracy will find an exemplary analysis of a crucial Reichstag campaign in George Dunlap Crothers, *The German Elections of 1907* (New York: Columbia University Studies in History, Economics and Public Law, No. 479, 1941). The history of the Bülow Bloc has not been studied in comparable detail. Johannes Haller, *Die Aera Bülow. Eine historisch-politische Studie* (Stuttgart and Berlin, 1922) is a slim volume in which foreign affairs take precedence over domestic politics. Theodor Eschenburg, *Das Kaiserreich am Scheideweg. Bassermann, Bülow und der Block* (Berlin, 1929), describes the development of National Liberal policy during the Bloc period from the viewpoint of Bassermann. A broader political study is available for the period between the collapse of the Bloc and the elections of 1912: Walter Koch, *Volk und Staatsführung vor dem Weltkriege.* Beiträge zur Geschichte der nachbismarck-ischen Zeit und des Weltkrieges, Heft 29 (Stuttgart, 1935). A clear analysis of the Reich taxation system, so important to an understanding of prewar politics, will be found in Edwin R. A. Seligman, *Essays in Taxation* (8th edition, New York, 1919). For the role of the Social Democratic problem in the thinking of the policy makers, the writings of two chancellors are of value: Theobald von Bethmann-Hollweg, *Betrachtungen zum Weltkriege,* 2 vols. (Berlin, 1919); and Prince Bernhard von Bülow, *Imperial Germany,* trans. Marie A. Lewenz (New York, 1914). Bülow's *Denkwürdigkeiten,* 4 vols. (Berlin, 1930–31), contain little touching our subject.

Of the non-socialist parties, the National Liberals and Progressives were most important to the development of Social Democracy in our period. Ludwig Bergsträsser, *Geschichte der politischen Parteien in Deutschland* (5th edition, Mannheim, 1928), briefly surveys their evolution in his study of the German party system. The only history of the Liberal parties is Oskar Stillich, *Die politischen Parteien in Deutschland,* vol. II, *Der Liberalismus* (Leipzig, 1911). Rochus Freiherr von Rheinbaben, *Stresemann. Der Mensch und der Staatsmann* (Dresden, 1928), casts light on the development of the Young National Liberals and the Hansabund in which Stresemann played an important part. Theodor Heuss, *Friedrich Naumann. Der Mann, das Werk, die Zeit* (Stuttgart and Berlin, 1937), though chaotic in its organization, contains invaluable material on left-wing liberalism in the prewar period.

The shifting party constellation and the constitutional developments during World War I are searchingly examined in Viktor Bredt, *Der deutsche Reichstag im Weltkrieg,* Das Werk des Untersuchungsausschusses, 4. Reihe, vol. VIII (Berlin, 1926). Two excellent studies have been made of the war aims problem, so significant for the final break-up of Social Democracy: Hans Gatzke, *Germany's Drive to the West* (Baltimore, 1950); and Erich O. Volkmann, *Die Annexionsfragen des Weltkrieges,* Das Werk des Untersuchungsausschusses, 4. Reihe, vol. XII (Berlin, 1929).

Sartorius von Walterhausen, *Deutsche Wirtschaftsgeschichte, 1815–1914* (2nd edition, Jena, 1923) remains the most comprehensive introduction to Germany's economic development. A more sophisticated study of the institutional structure and ideology of German capitalism is W. F. Bruck, *Social and Economic History of Germany from William II to Hitler, 1888–1938. A Comparative History* (Cardiff, 1938). For socialist history, particular importance attaches to changes in the workers' standard of living. These are best described in Jürgen Kuczynski, *A Short History of Labour Conditions under Industrial Capitalism* (London, 1945), III, 1, "Germany, 1800 to the Present Day." While Kuczynski's doctrinaire Leninist explanations of changes in labor conditions are often questionable, his tables on wages, hours, and cost of living are conscientiously compiled from government and trade-union statistics and from the local studies of living standards published by the Verein für Sozialpolitik. Die Wirtschafts- und Sozialgeschichte des Weltkrieges, Deutsche Serie, edited by James T. Shotwell, contains two volumes on the food crisis which contributed to the final schism: Friedrich Aeraboe, *Der Einfluss des Krieges auf die landwirtschaftliche Produktion in Deutschland* (Stuttgart, Berlin, Leipzig, and New Haven, 1927), reveals the agrarian producer point of view of the food crisis; August Skalweit, *Die deutsche Kriegsernährungswirtschaft* (Stuttgart, etc., 1927), shows the problem of production, distribution and control in its full politico-economic complexity.

INDEX

Anarcho-socialism, 35
Annexation question, 304–306
Anti-militarism, *see* Militarism
Anti-Semitic Party, 61
Anti-Socialist Laws, 3, 4, 9, 119
Arms limitation, 161, 244–246, 263
Association, laws of, 120; Prussia, 98, 102, 104; Reich, *1907*, 102–104, 107, 258, 271–272

Baden: budget-voting, 185, 188–189, 190–191, 194; Social Democratic Party organization, 25, 190. *See also* Elections, Baden
Baden Great Bloc, 156, 157, 186, 188
Barth, Theodor, 152, 154–155
Basserman, Ernst, 156–158, 175–176, 237, 238, 239
Bebel, August, 2, 42–44, 100, 161, 169, 198, 213, 226, 236; budget-voting, 24, 194–195; mass strike, 42–44; militarism, 70, 72–77, 78, 81–83, 160, 226; nationalism of, 75–77, 85, 86, 199–200; party aims and strategy, 42–44, 226; radicalism, 24, 206, 208, 212, 230
Belgian Socialist Party: influence in Germany, 33–34, 72–73, 99
Belgian Young Guard, 99–101
Bernstein, Eduard, 16–20, 23, 41, 85, 187, 188, 235, 241, 305; federalism, 215–216; imperialism and war, 85, 246, 263–264, 266, 284; Independent Social Democratic Party (U.S.P.D.), 284, 314–315; mass strike, 34, 35; suffrage reform, 34, 163, 173–174, 175, 178; theory, 16–20
Bethmann-Hollweg, Theobald von, 171–172, 224–225, 238, 240, 259, 288, 291–292, 304, 305–306, 308; suffrage reform, 171–172, 177, 178

Bismarck, Otto von, 2, 3. *See also* Anti-Socialist Laws
Blue-Black Bloc, 172, 186, 187, 227, 228, 233, 241
Bolsheviks, Russian: German radicals compared, 248–249, 323–327
Bömelburg, Theodor, 39–40, 52
Braun, Adolf, 259–260, 273
Braun, Otto, 126, 206–207, 211, 288, 298, 309
Budget, military, 76, 240, 264, 265. *See also* Military tax bill
Budget-voting, 111–112, 185, 188–191, 194–195, 206–207, 328; party policy on, 7–8, 111, 194–195
Bülow, Bernhard von, 59–60, 102, 103, 150–151, 152, 159, 171
Bülow Bloc, 89, 148, 149, 150, 152, 156
Bureaucracy, 116–118, 122–127, 270, 317–318, 328
Burgfrieden, 292–294, 308; intraparty, 294, 297–298, 299, 300, 301

Center Party, 59, 60, 62, 148, 149–150, 173, 178, 224, 227, 228, 233, 239. *See also* Blue-Black Bloc
Center, Social Democratic: emergence of, 185–187, 188, 189–190, 191, 194, 195–196; imperialism, arms limitation, war, 245–246, 263, 264; Reichstag, *1912*, 234–235; dissolution, 329–330. *See also* Left center; Radicals
Coalition, laws of, 258–259
Colonialism, 59–60, 84–85, 87, 108–110 *and notes*
Communist Party of Germany, 133, 322–324, 328. *See also* Bolsheviks, Russian; Spartacists
Congress, Independent Social Democratic Party: *1917*, Gotha, 313–321; *1920*, Halle, 327

72 73 74   12 11 10 9 8 7 6 5 4 3 2 1

Revised January, 1970

hARpER ✦ ᴛoRChbooks

American Studies: General

HENRY ADAMS Degradation of the Democratic Dogma. ‡ *Introduction by Charles Hirschfeld.* TB/1450

LOUIS D. BRANDEIS: Other People's Money, *and How the Bankers Use It. Ed. with Intro. by Richard M. Abrams* TB/3081

HENRY STEELE COMMAGER, Ed.: The Struggle for Racial Equality TB/1300

CARL N. DEGLER: Out of Our Past: *The Forces that Shaped Modern America* CN/2

CARL N. DEGLER, Ed.: Pivotal Interpretations of American History
Vol. I TB/1240; Vol. II TB/1241

A. S. EISENSTADT, Ed.: The Craft of American History: *Selected Essays*
Vol. I TB/1255; Vol. II TB/1256

LAWRENCE H. FUCHS, Ed.: American Ethnic Politics TB/1368

MARCUS LEE HANSEN: The Atlantic Migration: 1607-1860. *Edited by Arthur M. Schlesinger. Introduction by Oscar Handlin* TB/1052

MARCUS LEE HANSEN: The Immigrant in American History. *Edited with a Foreword by Arthur M. Schlesinger* TB/1120

ROBERT L. HEILBRONER: The Limits of American Capitalism TB/1305

JOHN HIGHAM, Ed.: The Reconstruction of American History TB/1068

ROBERT H. JACKSON: The Supreme Court in the American System of Government TB/1106

JOHN F. KENNEDY: A Nation of Immigrants. *Illus. Revised and Enlarged. Introduction by Robert F. Kennedy* TB/1118

LEONARD W. LEVY, Ed.: American Constitutional Law: *Historical Essays* TB/1285

LEONARD W. LEVY, Ed.: Judicial Review and the Supreme Court TB/1296

LEONARD W. LEVY: The Law of the Commonwealth and Chief Justice Shaw: *The Evolution of American Law, 1830-1860* TB/1309

GORDON K. LEWIS: Puerto Rico: *Freedom and Power in the Caribbean. Abridged edition* TB/1371

RICHARD B. MORRIS: Fair Trial: *Fourteen Who Stood Accused, from Anne Hutchinson to Alger Hiss* TB/1335

GUNNAR MYRDAL: An American Dilemma: *The Negro Problem and Modern Democracy. Introduction by the Author.*
Vol. I TB/1443; Vol. II TB/1444

GILBERT OSOFSKY, Ed.: The Burden of Race: *A Documentary History of Negro-White Relations in America* TB/1405

CONYERS READ, Ed.: The Constitution Reconsidered. *Revised Edition. Preface by Richrd B. Morris* TB/1384

ARNOLD ROSE: The Negro in America: *The Condensed Version of Gunnar Myrdal's* An American Dilemma. *Second Edition* TB/3048

JOHN E. SMITH: Themes in American Philosophy: *Purpose, Experience and Community* TB/1466

WILLIAM R. TAYLOR: Cavalier and Yankee: *The Old South and American National Character* TB/1474

American Studies: Colonial

BERNARD BAILYN: The New England Merchants in the Seventeenth Century TB/1149

ROBERT E. BROWN: Middle-Class Democracy and Revolution in Massachusetts, 1691-1780. *New Introduction by Author* TB/1413

JOSEPH CHARLES: The Origins of the American Party System TB/1049

HENRY STEELE COMMAGER & ELMO GIORDANETTI, Eds.: Was America a Mistake? *An Eighteenth Century Controversy* TB/1329

WESLEY FRANK CRAVEN: The Colonies in Transition: 1660-1712† TB/3084

CHARLES GIBSON: Spain in America † TB/3077

CHARLES GIBSON, Ed.: The Spanish Tradition in America + HR/1351

LAWRENCE HENRY GIPSON: The Coming of the Revolution: 1763-1775. † *Illus.* TB/3007

JACK P. GREENE, Ed.: Great Britain and the American Colonies: 1606-1763. + *Introduction by the Author* HR/1477

AUBREY C. LAND, Ed.: Bases of the Plantation Society + HR/1429

JOHN LANKFORD, Ed.: Captain John Smith's America: *Selections from his Writings* ‡ TB/3078

LEONARD W. LEVY: Freedom of Speech and Press in Early American History: *Legacy of Suppression* TB/1109

PERRY MILLER: Errand Into the Wilderness TB/1139

PERRY MILLER   T. H. JOHNSON, Eds.: The Puritans: *A Sourcebook of Their Writings*
Vol. I TB/1093; Vol. II TB/1094

† The New American Nation Series, edited by Henry Steele Commager and Richard B. Morris.
‡ American Perspectives series, edited by Bernard Wishy and William E. Leuchtenburg.
a History of Europe series, edited by J. H. Plumb.
§ The Library of Religion and Culture, edited by Benjamin Nelson.
‖ Researches in the Social, Cultural, and Behavioral Sciences, edited by Benjamin Nelson.
Σ Harper Modern Science Series, edited by James A. Newman.
° Not for sale in Canada.
+ Documentary History of the United States series, edited by Richard B. Morris.
# Documentary History of Western Civilization series, edited by Eugene C. Black and Leonard W. Levy.
Λ The Economic History of the United States series, edited by Henry David et al.
¶ European Perspectives series, edited by Eugene C. Black.
** Contemporary Essays series, edited by Leonard W. Levy.
* The Stratum Series, edited by John Hale.

VERNON LANE WHARTON: The Negro in Mississippi, 1865-1890   TB/1178

American Studies: The Twentieth Century

RICHARD M. ABRAMS, Ed.: The Issues of the Populist and Progressive Eras, 1892-1912 +   HR/1428
RAY STANNARD BAKER: Following the Color Line: American Negro Citizenship in Progressive Era. ‡ Edited by Dewey W. Grantham, Jr. Illus.   TB/3053
RANDOLPH S. BOURNE: War and the Intellectuals: Collected Essays, 1915-1919. ‡ Edited by Carl Resek   TB/3043
A. RUSSELL BUCHANAN: The United States and World War II. † Illus.
          Vol. I TB/3044; Vol. II TB/3045
THOMAS C. COCHRAN: The American Business System: A Historical Perspective, 1900-1955   TB/1080
FOSTER RHEA DULLES: America's Rise to World Power: 1898-1954. † Illus.   TB/3021
JEAN-BAPTISTE DUROSELLE: From Wilson to Roosevelt: Foreign Policy of the United States, 1913-1945. Trans. by Nancy Lyman Roelker   TB/1370
HAROLD U. FAULKNER: The Decline of Laissez Faire, 1897-1917   TB/1397
JOHN D. HICKS: Republican Ascendancy: 1921-1933. † Illus.   TB/3041
ROBERT HUNTER: Poverty: Social Conscience in the Progressive Era. ‡ Edited by Peter d'A. Jones   TB/3065
WILLIAM E. LEUCHTENBURG: Franklin D. Roosevelt and the New Deal: 1932-1940. † Illus.   TB/3025
WILLIAM E. LEUCHTENBURG, Ed.: The New Deal: A Documentary History +   HR/1354
ARTHUR S. LINK: Woodrow Wilson and the Progressive Era: 1910-1917. † Illus. TB/3023
BROADUS MITCHELL: Depression Decade: From New Era through New Deal, 1929-1941 ʌ   TB/1439
GEORGE E. MOWRY: The Era of Theodore Roosevelt and the Birth of Modern America: 1900-1912. † Illus.   TB/3022
WILLIAM PRESTON, JR.: Aliens and Dissenters: Federal Suppression of Radicals, 1903-1933   TB/1287
WALTER RAUSCHENBUSCH: Christianity and the Social Crisis. ‡ Edited by Robert D. Cross   TB/3059
GEORGE SOULE: Prosperity Decade: From War to Depression, 1917-1929 ʌ   TB/1349
GEORGE B. TINDALL, Ed.: A Populist Reader: Selections from the Works of American Populist Leaders   TB/3069
TWELVE SOUTHERNERS: I'll Take My Stand: The South and the Agrarian Tradition. Intro. by Louis D. Rubin, Jr.; Biographical Essays by Virginia Rock   TB/1072

Art, Art History, Aesthetics

CREIGHTON GILBERT, Ed.: Renaissance Art ** Illus.   TB/1465
EMILE MALE: The Gothic Image: Religious Art in France of the Thirteenth Century. § 190 illus.   TB/344
MILLARD MEISS: Painting in Florence and Siena After the Black Death: The Arts, Religion and Society in the Mid-Fourteenth Century. 169 illus.   TB/1148
ERWIN PANOFSKY: Renaissance and Renascences in Western Art. Illus.   TB/1447
ERWIN PANOFSKY: Studies in Iconology: Humanistic Themes in the Art of the Renaissance. 180 illus.   TB/1077

JEAN SEZNEC: The Survival of the Pagan Gods: The Mythological Tradition and Its Place in Renaissance Humanism and Art. 108 illus.   TB/2004
OTTO VON SIMSON: The Gothic Cathedral: Origins of Gothic Architecture and the Medieval Concept of Order. 58 illus.   TB/2018
HEINRICH ZIMMER: Myths and Symbols in Indian Art and Civilization. 70 illus. TB/2005

Asian Studies

WOLFGANG FRANKE: China and the West: The Cultural Encounter, 13th to 20th Centuries. Trans. by R. A. Wilson   TB/1326
L. CARRINGTON GOODRICH: A Short History of the Chinese People. Illus.   TB/3015
DAN N. JACOBS, Ed.: The New Communist Manifesto and Related Documents. 3rd revised edn.   TB/1078
DAN N. JACOBS & HANS H. BAERWALD, Eds.: Chinese Communism: Selected Documents   TB/3031
BENJAMIN I. SCHWARTZ: Chinese Communism and the Rise of Mao   TB/1308
BENJAMIN I. SCHWARTZ: In Search of Wealth and Power: Yen Fu and the West   TB/1422

Economics & Economic History

C. E. BLACK: The Dynamics of Modernization: A Study in Comparative History   TB/1321
STUART BRUCHEY: The Roots of American Economic Growth, 1607-1861: An Essay in Social Causation. New Introduction by the Author.   TB/1350
GILBERT BURCK & EDITORS OF Fortune: The Computer Age: And its Potential for Management   TB/1179
JOHN ELLIOTT CAIRNES: The Slave Power. ‡ Edited with Introduction by Harold D. Woodman   TB/1433
SHEPARD B. CLOUGH, THOMAS MOODIE & CAROL MOODIE, Eds.: Economic History of Europe: Twentieth Century #   HR/1388
THOMAS C. COCHRAN: The American Business System: A Historical Perspective, 1900-1955   TB/1180
ROBERT A. DAHL & CHARLES E. LINDBLOM: Politics, Economics, and Welfare: Planning and Politico-Economic Systems Resolved into Basic Social Processes   TB/3037
PETER F. DRUCKER: The New Society: The Anatomy of Industrial Order   TB/1082
HAROLD U. FAULKNER: The Decline of Laissez Faire, 1897-1917 ʌ   TB/1397
PAUL W. GATES: The Farmer's Age: Agriculture, 1815-1860 ʌ   TB/1398
WILLIAM GREENLEAF, Ed.: American Economic Development Since 1860 +   HR/1353
J. L. & BARBARA HAMMOND: The Rise of Modern Industry. || Introduction by R. M. Hartwell   TB/1417
ROBERT L. HEILBRONER: The Future as History: The Historic Currents of Our Time and the Direction in Which They Are Taking America   TB/1386
ROBERT L. HEILBRONER: The Great Ascent: The Struggle for Economic Development in Our Time   TB/3030
FRANK H. KNIGHT: The Economic Organization   TB/1214
DAVID S. LANDES: Bankers and Pashas: International Finance and Economic Imperialism in Egypt. New Preface by the Author TB/1412
ROBERT LATOUCHE: The Birth of Western Economy: Economic Aspects of the Dark Ages   TB/1290

W. ARTHUR LEWIS: Economic Survey, 1919-1939
TB/1446
W. ARTHUR LEWIS: The Principles of Economic
Planning. *New Introduction by the Author*°
TB/1436
ROBERT GREEN MC CLOSKEY: American Conserva-
tism in the Age of Enterprise   TB/1137
PAUL MANTOUX: The Industrial Revolution in
the Eighteenth Century: *An Outline of the
Beginnings of the Modern Factory System in
England*°   TB/1079
WILLIAM MILLER, Ed.: Men in Business: *Essays
on the Historical Role of the Entrepreneur*
TB/1081
GUNNAR MYRDAL: An International Economy.
New Introduction by the Author   TB/1445
RICHARD S. WECKSTEIN, Ed.: Expansion of World
Trade and the Growth of National Econ-
omies **   TB/1373

Historiography and History of Ideas

HERSCHEL BAKER: The Image of Man: *A Study
of the Idea of Human Dignity in Classical
Antiquity, the Middle Ages, and the Renais-
sance*   TB/1047
J. BRONOWSKI & BRUCE MAZLISH: The Western
Intellectual Tradition: *From Leonardo to
Hegel*   TB/3001
EDMUND BURKE: On Revolution. Ed. by Robert
A. Smith   TB/1401
WILHELM DILTHEY: Pattern and Meaning in His-
tory: *Thoughts on History and Society.*°
Edited with an Intro. by H. P. Rickman
TB/1075
ALEXANDER GRAY: The Socialist Tradition: *Moses
to Lenin* °   TB/1375
J. H. HEXTER: More's Utopia: *The Biography of
an Idea. Epilogue by the Author*   TB/1195
H. STUART HUGHES: History as Art and as
Science: *Twin Vistas on the Past*   TB/1207
ARTHUR O. LOVEJOY: The Great Chain of Being:
A Study of the History of an Idea TB/1009
JOSE ORTEGA Y GASSET: The Modern Theme.
Introduction by Jose Ferrater Mora TB/1038
RICHARD H. POPKIN: The History of Scenticism
from Erasmus to Descartes. *Revised Edition*
TB/1391
G. J. RENIER: History: *Its Purpose and Method*
TB/1209
MASSIMO SALVADORI, Ed.: Modern Socialism #
HR/1374
BRUNO SNELL: The Discovery of the Mind: *The
Greek Origins of European Thought* TB/1018
W. WARREN WAGER, ed.: European Intellectual
History Since Darwin and Marx   TB/1297
W. H. WALSH: Philosophy of History: In Intro-
duction   TB/1020

History: General

HANS KOHN: The Age of Nationalism: *The
First Era of Global History*   TB/1380
BERNARD LEWIS: The Arabs in History TB/1029
BERNARD LEWIS: The Middle East and the
West °   TB/1274

History: Ancient

A. ANDREWS: The Greek Tyrants   TB/1103
ERNST LUDWIG EHRLICH: A Concise History of
Israel: *From the Earliest Times to the De-
struction of the Temple in A.D. 70*° TB/128

THEODOR H. GASTER: Thespis: *Ritual Myth and
Drama in the Ancient Near East*   TB/1281
MICHAEL GRANT: Ancient History °   TB/1190
A. H. M. JONES, Ed.: A History of Rome
through the Fifgth Century # *Vol. I: The
Republic*   HR/1364
Vol. II The Empire: HR/1460
SAMUEL NOAH KRAMER: Sumerian Mythology
TB/1055
NAPHTALI LEWIS & MEYER REINHOLD, Eds.:
Roman Civilization *Vol. I: The Republic*
TB/1231
Vol. II: The Empire   TB/1232

History: Medieval

MARSHALL W. BALDWIN, Ed.: Christianity
Through the 13th Century #   HR/1468
MARC BLOCH: Land and Work in Medieval
Europe. *Translated by J. E. Anderson*
TB/1452
HELEN CAM: England Before Elizabeth TB/1026
NORMAN COHN: The Pursuit of the Millennium:
*Revolutionary Messianism in Medieval and
Reformation Europe*   TB/1037
G. G. COULTON: Medieval Village, Manor, and
Monastery   HR/1022
HEINRICH FICHTENAU: The Carolingian Empire:
*The Age of Charlemagne. Translated with an
Introduction by Peter Munz*   TB/1142
GALBERT OF BRUGES: The Murder of Charles the
Good: *A Contemporary Record of Revolu-
tionary Change in 12th Century Flanders.
Translated with an Introduction by James
Bruce Ross*   TB/1311
F. L. GANSHOF: Feudalism   TB/1058
F. L. GANSHOF: The Middle Ages: *A History of
International Relations. Translated by Rémy
Hall*   TB/1411
DENYS HAY: The Medieval Centuries °   TB/1192
DAVID HERLIHY, Ed.: Medieval Culture and So-
citey #   HR/1340
J. M. HUSSEY: The Byzantine World TB/1057
ROBERT LATOUCHE: The Birth of Western Econ-
omy: *Economic Aspects of the Dark Ages* °
TB/1290
HENRY CHARLES LEA: The Inquisition of the
Middle Ages. || *Introduction by Walter
Ullmann*   TB/1456
FERDINARD LOT: The End of the Ancient World
and the Beginnings of the Middle Ages. *In-
troduction by Glanville Downey*   TB/1044
H. R. LOYN: The Norman Conquest   TB/1457
GUIBERT DE NOGENT: Self and Society in
Medieval France: *The Memoirs of Guilbert de
Nogent.* || *Edited by John F. Benton* TB/1471
MARSILIUS OF PADUA: The Defender of Peace.
*The Defensor Pacis. Translated with an In-
troduction by Alan Gewirth*   TB/1310
CHARLES PETET-DUTAILLIS: The Feudal Monarchy
in France and England: *From the Tenth to
the Thirteenth Century* °   TB/1165
STEVEN RUNCIMAN: A History of the Crusades
*Vol. I: The First Crusade and the Founda-
tion of the Kingdom of Jerusalem. Illus.*
TB/1143
*Vol. II: The Kingdom of Jerusalem and the
Frankish East 1100-1187. Illus.*   TB/1243
*Vol. III: The Kingdom of Acre and the
Later Crusades. Illus.*   TB/1298
J. M. WALLACE-HADRILL: The Barbarian West:
The Early Middle Ages, A.D. 400-1000
TB/1061

4

ALBERT GOODWIN, Ed.: The European Nobility in the Enghteenth Century   TB/1313
ALBERT GOODWIN: The French Revolution   TB/1064
ALBERT GUERARD: France in the Classical Age: *The Life and Death of an Ideal*   TB/1183
JOHN B. HALSTED, Ed.: Romanticism #   HR/1387
J. H. HEXTER: Reappraisals in History: *New Views on History and Society in Early Modern Europe* °   TB/1100
STANLEY HOFFMANN et al.: In Search of France: *The Economy, Society and Political System In the Twentieth Century*   TB/1219
H. STUART HUGHES: The Obstructed Path: *French Social Thought in the Years of Desperation*   TB/1451
JOHAN HUIZINGA: Dutch Civilisation in the 17th Century and Other Essays   TB/1453
LIONAL KOCHAN: The Struggle for Germany: *1914-45*   TB/1304
HANS KOHN: The Mind of Germany: *The Education of a Nation*   TB/1204
HANS KOHN, Ed.: The Mind of Modern Russia: *Historical and Political Thought of Russia's Great Age*   TB/1065
WALTER LAQUEUR & GEORGE L. MOSSE, Eds.: Education and Social Structure in the 20th Century. ° *Volume 6 of the* Journal of Contemporary History   TB/1339
WALTER LAQUEUR & GEORGE L. MOSSE, Ed.: International Fascism, 1920-1945. ° *Volume 1 of the* Journal of Contemporary History   TB/1276
WALTER LAQUEUR & GEORGE L. MOSSE, Eds.: Literature and Politics in the 20th Century. ° *Volume 5 of the* Journal of Contemporary History.   TB/1328
WALTER LAQUEUR & GEORGE L. MOSSE, Eds.: The New History: *Trends in Historical Research and Writing Since World War II*. ° *Volume 4 of the* Journal of Contemporary History   TB/1327
WALTER LAQUEUR & GEORGE L. MOSSE, Eds.: 1914: *The Coming of the First World War.* ° *Volume3 of the* Journal of Contemporary History   TB/1306
C. A. MACARTNEY, Ed.: The Habsburg and Hohenzollern Dynasties in the Seventeenth and Eighteenth Centuries #   HR/1400
JOHN MCMANNERS: European History, 1789-1914: *Men, Machines and Freedom*   TB/1419
PAUL MANTOUX: The Industrial Revolution in the Eighteenth Century: *An Outline of the Beginnings of the Modern Factory System in England*   TB/1079
FRANK E. MANUEL: The Prophets of Paris: *Turgot, Condorcet, Saint-Simon, Fourier, and Comte*   TB/1218
KINGSLEY MARTIN: French Liberal Thought in the Eighteenth Century: *A Study of Political Ideas from Bayle to Condorcet*   TB/1114
NAPOLEON III: Napoleonic Ideas: *Des Idées Napoléoniennes, par le Prince Napoléon-Louis Bonaparte. Ed. by Brison D. Gooch* ¶   TB/1336
FRANZ NEUMANN: Behemoth: *The Structure and Practice of National Socialism, 1933-1944*   TB/1289
DAVID OGG: Europe of the Ancien Régime, 1715-1783 ° *a*   TB/1271
GEORGE RUDE: Revolutionary Europe, 1783-1815 ° *a*   TB/1272
MASSIMO SALVADORI, Ed.: Modern Socialism #   TB/1374
HUGH SETON-WATSON: Eastern Europe Between the Wars, 1918-1941   TB/1330

DENIS MACK SMITH, Ed.: The Making of Italy, 1796-1870 #   HR/1356
ALBERT SOREL: Europe Under the Old Regime. *Translated by Francis H. Herrick*   TB/1121
ROLAND N. STROMBERG, Ed.: Realism, Naturalism, and Symbolism: *Modes of Thought and Expression in Europe, 1848-1914* #   HR/1355
A. J. P. TAYLOR: From Napoleon to Lenin: *Historical Essays* °   TB/1268
A. J. P. TAYLOR: The Habsburg Monarchy, 1809-1918: *A History of the Austrian Empire and Austria-Hungary* °   TB/1187
J. M. THOMPSON: European History, 1494-1789   TB/1431
DAVID THOMSON, Ed.: France: Empire and Republic, 1850-1940 #   HR/1387
ALEXIS DE TOCQUEVILLE & GUSTAVE DE BEAUMONT: Tocqueville and Beaumont on Social Reform. *Ed. and trans. with Intro. by Seymour Drescher*   TB/1343
G. M. TREVELYAN: British History in the Nineteenth Century and After: 1792-1919 °   TB/1251
H. R. TREVOR-ROPER: Historical Essays   TB/1269
W. WARREN WAGAR, Ed.: Science, Faith, and MAN: *European Thought Since 1914* #   HR/1362
MACK WALKER, Ed.: Metternich's Europe, 1813-1848 #   HR/1361
ELIZABETH WISKEMANN: Europe of the Dictators, 1919-1945 ° *a*   TB/1273
JOHN B. WOLF: France: 1814-1919: *The Rise of a Liberal-Democratic Society*   TB/3019

Literature & Literary Criticism

JACQUES BARZUN: The House of Intellect   TB/1051
W. J. BATE: From Classic to Romantic: *Premises of Taste in Eighteenth Century England*   TB/1036
VAN WYCK BROOKS: Van Wyck Brooks: The Early Years: *A Selection from his Works, 1908-1921 Ed. with Intro. by Claire Sprague*   TB/3082
ERNST R. CURTIUS: European Literature and the Latin Middle Ages. *Trans. by Willard Trask*   TB/2015
RICHMOND LATTIMORE, Translator: The Odyssey of Homer   TB/1389
SAMUEL PEPYS: The Diary of Samual Pepys. ° *Edited by O. F. Morshead. 60 illus. by Ernest Shepard*   TB/1007
ROBERT PREYER, Ed.: Victorian Literature **   TB/1302
ALBION W. TOURGEE: A Fool's Errand: *A Novel of the South during Reconstruction. Intro. by George Fredrickson*   TB/3074
BASIL WILEY: Nineteenth Century Studies: *Coleridge to Matthew Arnold* °   TB/1261

Philosophy

HENRI BERGSON: Time and Free Will: *An Essay on the Immediate Data of Consciousness* °   TB/1021
LUDWIG BINSWANGER: Being-in-the-World: *Selected Papers. Trans. with Intro. by Jacob Needleman*   TB/1365
H. J. BLACKHAM: Six Existentialist Thinkers: *Kierkegaard, Nietzsche, Jaspers, Marcel, Heidegger, Sartre* °   TB/1002
J. M. BOCHENSKI: The Methods of Contemporary Thought. *Trans. by Peter Caws*   TB/1377
CRANE BRINTON: Nietzsche. *Preface, Bibliography, and Epilogue by the Author*   TB/1197

ERNST CASSIRER: Rousseau, Kant and Goethe. *Intro. by Peter Gay* TB/1092
FREDERICK COPLESTON, S. J.: Medieval Philosophy TB/376
F. M. CORNFORD: From Religion to Philosophy: *A Study in the Origins of Western Speculation* § TB/20
WILFRID DESAN: The Tragic Finale: *An Essay on the Philosophy of Jean-Paul Sartre* TB/1030
MARVIN FARBER: The Aims of Phenomenology: *The Motives, Methods, and Impact of Husserl's Thought* TB/1291
MARVIN FARBER: Basic Issues of Philosophy: *Experience, Reality, and Human Values* TB/1344
MARVIN FARBERS: Phenomenology and Existence: *Towards a Philosophy within Nature* TB/1295
PAUL FRIEDLANDER: `Plato: *An Introduction* TB/2017
MICHAEL GELVEN: A Commentary on Heidegger's "Being and Time" TB/1464
J. GLENN GRAY: Hegel and Greek Thought TB/1409
W. K. C. GUTHRIE: The Greek Philosophers: *From Thales to Aristotle* ° TB/1008
G. W. F. HEGEL: On Art, Religion Philosophy: *Introductory Lectures to the Realm of Absolute Spirit.* || *Edited with an Introduction by J. Glenn Gray* TB/1463
G. W. F. HEGEL: Phenomenology of Mind. ° || *Introduction by George Lichtheim* TB/1303
MARTIN HEIDEGGER: Discourse on Thinking. *Translated with a Preface by John M. Anderson and E. Hans Freund. Introduction by John M. Anderson* TB/1459
F. H. HEINEMANN: Existentialism and the Modern Predicament TB/28
WERER HEISENBERG: Physics and Philosophy: *The Revolution in Modern Science. Intro. by F. S. C. Northrop* TB/549
EDMUND HUSSERL: Phenomenology and the Crisis of Philosophy. § *Translated with an Introduction by Quentin Lauer* TB/1170
IMMANUEL KANT: Groundwork of the Metaphysic of Morals. *Translated and Analyzed by H. J. Paton* TB/1159
IMMANUEL KANT: Lectures on Ethics. § *Introduction by Lewis White Beck* TB/105
WALTER KAUFMANN, Ed.: Religion From Tolstoy to Camus: *Basic Writings on Religious Truth and Morals* TB/123
QUENTIN LAUER: Phenomenology: *Its Genesis and Prospect. Preface by Aron Gurwitsch* TB/1169
MAURICE MANDELBAUM: The Problem of Historical Knowledge: *An Answer to Relativism* TB/1198
H. J. PATON: The Categorical Imperative: *A Study in Kant's Moral Philosophy* TB/1325
MICHAEL POLANYI: Personal Knowledge: *Towards a Post-Critical Philosophy* TB/1158
KARL R. POPPER: Conjectures and Refutations: *The Growth of Scientific Knowledge* TB/1376
WILLARD VAN ORMAN QUINE: Elementary Logic *Revised Edition* TB/577
WILLARD VAN ORMAN QUINE: From a Logical Point of View: *Logico-Philosophical Essays* TB/566
JOHN E. SMITH: Themes in American Philosophy: *Purpose, Experience and Community* TB/1466
MORTON WHITE: Foundations of Historical Knowledge TB/1440
WILHELM WINDELBAND: A History of Philosophy *Vol. I: Greek, Roman, Medieval* TB/38
Vol. II: Renaissance, Enlightenment, Modern TB/39

LUDWIG WITTGENSTEIN: The Blue and Brown Books ° TB/1211
LUDWIG WITTGENSTEIN: Notebooks, 1914-1916 TB/1441

Political Science & Government

C. E. BLACK: The Dynamics of Modernization: *A Study in Comparative History* TB/1321
DENIS W. BROGAN: Politics in America. *New Introduction by the Author* TB/1469
CRANE BRINTON: English Political Thought in the Nineteenth Century TB/1071
ROBERT CONQUEST: Power and Policy in the USSR: *The Study of Soviet Dynastics* ° TB/1307
ROBERT A. DAHL & CHARLES E. LINDBLOM: Politics, Economics, and Welfare: *Planning and Politico-Economic Systems Resolved into Basic Social Processes* TB/1277
HANS KOHN: Political Ideologies of the 20th Century TB/1277
ROY C. MACRIDIS, Ed.: Political Parties: *Contemporary Trends and Ideas* ** TB/1322
ROBERT GREEN MC CLOSKEY: American Conservatism in the Age of Enterprise, 1865-1910 TB/1137
MARSILIUS OF PADUA: The Defender of Peace. *The Defensor Pacis. Translated with an Introduction by Alan Gewirth* TB/1310
KINGSLEY MARTIN: French Liberal Thought in the Eighteenth Century: *A Study of Political Ideas from Bayle to Condorcet* TB/1114
BARRINGTON MOORE, JR.: Political Power and Social Theory: *Seven Studies* || TB/1277
BARRINGTON MOORE, JR.: Soviet Politics—The Dilemma of Power: *The Role of Ideas in Social Change* || TB/1222
BARRINGTON MOORE, JR.: Terror and Progress—USSR: *Some Sources of Change and Stability*
JOHN B. MORRALL: Political Thought in Medieval Times TB/1076
KARL R. POPPER: The Open Society and Its Enemies *Vol. I: The Spell of Plato* TB/1101
Vol. II: The High Tide of Prophecy: Hegel, Marx, and the Aftermath TB/1102
CONYERS READ, Ed.: The Constitution Reconsidered. *Revised Edition, Preface by Richard B. Morris* TB/1384
JOHN P. ROCHE, Ed.: Origins of American Political Thought: *Selected Readings* TB/1301
JOHN P. ROCHE, Ed.: American Political Thought: *From Jefferson to Progressivism* TB/1332
HENRI DE SAINT-SIMON: Social Organization, The Science of Man, and Other Writings. || *Edited and Translated with an Introduction by Felix Markham* TB/1152
CHARLES SCHOTTLAND, Ed.: The Welfare State ** TB/1323
JOSEPH A. SCHUMPETER: Capitalism, Socialism and Democracy TB/3008

Psychology

ALFRED ADLER: The Individual Psychology of Alfred Adler: *A Systematic Presentation in Selections from His Writings. Edited by Heinz L. & Rowena R. Ansbacher* TB/1154
LUDWIG BINSWANGER: Being-in-the-World: *Selected Papers.* || *Trans. with Intro. by Jacob Needleman* TB/1365
HADLEY CANTRIL: The Invasion from Mars: *A Study in the Psychology of Panic* || TB/1282
MIRCEA ELIADE: Cosmos and History: *The Myth of the Eternal Return* § TB/2050
MIRCEA ELIADE: Myth and Reality TB/1369

7

MIRCEA ELIADE: Myths, Dreams and Mysteries: *The Encounter Between Contemporary Faiths and Archaic Realities* § TB/1320
MIRCEA ELIADE: Rites and Symbols of Initiation: *The Mysteries of Birth and Rebirth* § TB/1236
HERBERT FINGARETTE: The Self in Transformation: *Psychoanalysis, Philosophy and the Life of the Spirit* ‖ TB/1177
SIGMUND FREUD: On Creativity and the Unconscious: *Papers on the Psychology of Art, Literature, Love, Religion.* § *Intro. by Benjamin Nelson* TB/45
J. GLENN GRAY: The Warriors: *Reflections on Men in Battle. Introduction by Hannah Arendt* TB/1294
WILLIAM JAMES: Psychology: *The Briefer Course. Edited with an Intro. by Gordon Allport* TB/1034
C. G. JUNG: Psychological Reflections. *Ed. by J. Jacobi* TB/2001
KARL MENNINGER, M.D.: Theory of Psychoanalytic Technique TB/1144
JOHN H. SCHAAR: Escape from Authority: *The Perspectives of Erich Fromm* TB/1155
MUZAFER SHERIF: The Psychology of Social Norms. *Introduction by Gardner Murphy* TB/3072
HELLMUT WILHELM: Change: *Eight Lectures on the I Ching* TB/2019

Religion: Ancient and Classical, Biblical and Judaic Traditions

W. F. ALBRIGHT: The Biblical Period from Abraham to Ezra TB/102
SALO W. BARON: Modern Nationalism and Religion TB/818
C. K. BARRETT, Ed.: The New Testament Background: *Selected Documents* TB/86
MARTIN BUBER: Eclipse of God: *Studies in the Relation Between Religion and Philosophy* TB/12
MARTIN BUBER: Hasidism and Modern Man. *Edited and Translated by Maurice Friedman* TB/839
MARTIN BUBER: The Knowledge of Man. *Edited with an Introduction by Maurice Friedman. Translated by Maurice Friedman and Ronald Gregor Smith* TB/135
MARTIN BUBER: Moses. *The Revelation and the Covenant* TB/837
MARTIN BUBER: The Origin and Meaning of Hasidism. *Edited and Translated by Maurice Friedman* TB/835
MARTIN BUBER: The Prophetic Faith TB/73
MARTIN BUBER: Two Types of Faith: *Interpenetration of Judaism and Christianity* ° TB/75
MALCOLM L. DIAMOND: Martin Buber: *Jewish Existentialist* TB/840
M. S. ENSLIN: Christian Beginnings TB/5
M. S. ENSLIN: The Literature of the Christian Movement TB/6
ERNST LUDWIG EHRLICH: A Concise History of Israel: *From the Earliest Times to the Destruction of the Temple in A.D. 70* ° TB/128
HENRI FRANKFORT: Ancient Egyptian Religion: *An Interpretation* TB/77
ABRAHAM HESCHEL: The Earth Is the Lord's & The Sabbath. *Two Essays* TB/828
ABRAHAM HESCHEL: God in Search of Man: *A Philosophy of Judaism* TB/807
ABRAHAM HESCHEL: Man Is not Alone: *A Philosophy of Religion* TB/838
ABRAHAM HESCHEL: The Prophets: *An Introduction* TB/1421

T. J. MEEK: Hebrew Origins TB/69
JAMES MUILENBURG: The Way of Israel: *Biblical Faith and Ethics* TB/133
H. J. ROSE: Religion in Greece and Rome TB/55
H. H. ROWLEY: The Growth of the Old Testament TB/107
D. WINTON THOMAS, Ed.: Documents from Old Testament Times TB/85

Religion: General Christianity

ROLAND H. BAINTON: Christendom: *A Short History of Christianity and Its Impact on Western Civilization. Illus.* Vol. I TB/131; Vol. II TB/132
JOHN T. MCNEILL: Modern Christian Movements. *Revised Edition* TB/1402
ERNST TROELTSCH: The Social Teaching of the Christian Churches. *Intro. by H. Richard Niebuhr* Vol. TB/71; Vol. II TB/72

Religion: Early Christianity Through Reformation

ANSELM OF CANTERBURY: Truth, Freedom, and Evil: *Three Philosophical Dialogues. Edited and Translated by Jasper Hopkins and Herbert Richardson* TB/317
MARSHALL W. BALDWIN, Ed.: Christianity through the 13th Century # HR/1468
W. D. DAVIES: Paul and Rabbinic Judaism: *Some Rabbinic Elements in Pauline Theology. Revised Edition* ° TB/146
ADOLF DEISSMAN: Paul: *A Study in Social and Religious History* TB/15
JOHANNES ECKHART: Meister Eckhart: *A Modern Translation by R. Blakney* TB/8
EDGAR J. GOODSPEED: A Life of Jesus TB/1
ROBERT M. GRANT: Gnosticism and Early Christianity TB/136
WILLIAM HALLER: The Rise of Puritanism TB/22
GERHART B. LADNER: The Idea of Reform: *Its Impact on the Christian Thought and Action in the Age of the Fathers* TB/149
ARTHUR DARBY NOCK: Early Gentile Christianity and Its Hellenistic Background TB/111
ARTHUR DARBY NOCK: St. Paul ° TR/104
GORDON RUPP: Luther's Progress to the Diet of Worms ° TB/120

Religion: The Protestant Tradition

KARL BARTH: Church Dogmatics: *A Selection. Intro. by H. Gollwitzer. Ed. by G. W. Bromiley* TB/95
KARL BARTH: Dogmatics in Outline TB/56
KARL BARTH: The Word of God and the Word of Man TB/13
HERBERT BRAUN, et al.: God and Christ: *Existence and Province. Volume 5 of Journal for Theology and the Church, edited by Robert W. Funk and Gerhard Ebeling* TB/255
WHITNEY R. CROSS: The Burned-Over District: *The Social and Intellectual History of Enthusiastic Religion in Western New York, 1800-1850* TB/1242
NELS F. S. FERRE: Swedish Contributions to Modern Theology. *New Chapter by William A. Johnson* TB/147
WILLIAM R. HUTCHISON, Ed.: American Protestant Thought: *The Liberal Era* ‡ TB/1385
ERNST KASEMANN, et al.: Distinctive Protestant and Catholic Themes Reconsidered. *Volume 3 of Journal for Theology and the Church,*

edited by Robert W. Funk and Gerhard
Ebeling   TB/253
SOREN KIERKEGAARD: On Authority and Revela-
tion: *The Book on Adler, or a Cycle of
Ethico-Religious Essays. Introduction by F.
Sontag*   TB/139
SOREN KIERKEGAARD: Crisis in the Life of an
Actress, *and Other Essays on Drama. Trans-
lated with an Introduction by Stephen Crites*
                                           TB/145
SOREN KIERKEGAARD: Edifying Discourses. *Edited
with an Intro. by Paul Holmer*   TB/32
SOREN KIERKEGAARD: The Journals of Kierke-
gaard. ° *Edited with an Intro. by Alexander
Dru*   TB/52
SOREN KIERKEGAARD: The Point of View for My
Work as an Author: *A Report to History.* §
Preface by Benjamin Nelson   TB/88
SOREN KIERKEGAARD: The Present Age. § *Trans-
lated and edited by Alexander Dru. Intro-
duction by Walter Kaufmann*   TB/94
SOREN KIERKEGAARD: Purity of Heart. *Trans. by
Douglas Steere*   TB/4
SOREN KIERKEGAARD: Repetition: *An Essay in
Experimental Psychology* §   TB/117
SOREN KIERKEGAARD: Works of Love: *Some
Christian Reflections in the Form of Dis-
courses*   TB/122
WILLIAM G. MCLOUGHLIN, Ed.: The American
Evangelicals: 1800-1900: *An Anthology*
                                           TB/1382
WOLFHART PANNENBERG, et al.: History and Her-
meneutic. *Volume 4 of* Journal for Theol-
ogy and the Church, *edited by Robert W.
Funk and Gerhard Ebeling*   TB/254
JAMES M. ROBINSON, et al.: The Bultmann
School of Biblical Interpretation: New Direc-
tions? *Volume 1 of* Journal for Theology
and the Church, *edited by Robert W. Funk
and Gerhard Ebeling*   TB/251
F. SCHLEIERMACHER: The Christian Faith. *Intro-
duction by Richard R. Niebuhr.*
        Vol. I TB/108;   Vol. II TB/109
F. SCHLEIERMACHER: On Religion: *Speeches to
Its Cultured Despisers. Intro. by Rudolf
Otto*   TB/36
TIMOTHY L. SMITH: Revivalism and Social Re-
form: *American Protestantism on the Eve
of the Civil War*   TB/1229
PAUL TILLICH: Dynamics of Faith   TB/42
PAUL TILLICH: Morality and Beyond   TB/142
EVELYN UNDERHILL: Worship   TB/10

---

*Religion: The Roman & Eastern Christian
Traditions*

A. ROBERT CAPONIGRI, Ed.: Modern Catholic
Thinkers II: *The Church and the Political
Order*   TB/307
G. P. FEDOTOV: The Russian Religious Mind:
*Kievan Christianity, the tenth to the thir-
teenth Centuries*   TB/370
GABRIEL MARCEL: Being and Having: *An Ex-
istential Diary. Introduction by James Col-
lins*   TB/310
GABRIEL MARCEL: Homo Viator: *Introduction to
a Metaphysic of Hope*   TB/397

Religion: Oriental Religions

TOR ANDRAE: Mohammed: *The Man and His
Faith* §   TB/62

EDWARD CONZE: Buddhism: *Its Essence and De-
velopment.* ° *Foreword by Arthur Waley*
                                           TB/58
EDWARD CONZE: Buddhist Meditation   TB/1442
EDWARD CONZE et al, Editors: Buddhist Texts
through the Ages   TB/113
ANANDA COOMARASWAMY: Buddha and the Gos-
pel of Buddhism   TB/119
H. G. CREEL: Confucius and the Chinese Way
                                           TB/63
FRANKLIN EDGERTON, Trans. & Ed.: The Bhaga-
vad Gita   TB/115
SWAMI NIKHILANANDA, Trans. & Ed.: The
Upanishads   TB/114
D. T. SUZUKI: On Indian Mahayana Buddhism.
° *Ed. with Intro. by Edward Conze.* TB/1403

Religion: Philosophy, Culture, and Society

NICOLAS BERDYAEV: The Destiny of Man TB/61
RUDOLF BULTMANN: History and Eschatology:
The Presence of Eternity °   TB/91
RUDOLF BULTMANN AND FIVE CRITICS: Kerygma
and Myth: *A Theological Debate*   TB/80
RUDOLF BULTMANN and KARL KUNDSIN: Form
Criticism: *Two Essays on New Testament Re-
search. Trans. by F. C. Grant*   TB/96
WILLIAM A. CLEBSCH & CHARLES R. JAEKLE: Pas-
toral Care in Historical Perspective: *An
Essay with Exhibits*   TB/148
FREDERICK FERRE: Language, Logic and God.
New Preface by the Author   TB/1407
LUDWIG FEUERBACH: The Essence of Christianity.
§ *Introduction by Karl Barth. Foreword by
H. Richard Niebuhr*   TB/11
ADOLF HARNACK: What Is Christianity? § *Intro-
duction by Rudolf Bultmann*   TB/17
KYLE HASELDEN: The Racial Problem in Chris-
tian Perspective   TB/116
MARTIN HEIDEGGER: Discourse on Thinking.
*Translated with a Preface by John M. Ander-
son and E. Hans Freund. Introduction by
John M. Anderson*   TB/1459
IMMANUEL KANT: Religion Within the Limits of
Reason Alone. § *Introduction by Theodore
M. Greene and John Silber*   TB/FG
WALTER KAUFMANN, Ed.: Religion from Tol-
stoy to Camus: *Basic Writings on Religious
Truth and Morals. Enlarged Edition* TB/123
H. RICHARD NIERUHR: Christ and Culture TB/3
H. RICHARD NIEBUHR: The Kingdom of God in
America   TB/49
ANDERS NYGREN: Agape and Eros. *Translated by
Philip S. Watson* °   TB/1430
JOHN H. RANDALL, JR.: The Meaning of Reli-
gion for Man. *Revised with New Intro. by
the Author*   TB/1379
WALTER RAUSCHENBUSCHS Christianity and the
Social Crisis. ‡ *Edited by Robert D. Cross*
                                           TB/3059

Science and Mathematics

JOHN TYLER BONNER: The Ideas of Biology. Σ
Illus.   TB/570
W. E. LE GROS CLARK: The Antecedents of
Man: *An Introduction to the Evolution of
the Primates.* ° *Illus.*   TB/559
ROBERT E. COKER: Streams, Lakes, Ponds. *Illus.*
                                           TB/586
ROBERT E. COKER: This Great and Wide Sea: *An
Introduction to Oceanography and Marine
Biology. Illus.*   TB/551
W. H. DOWDESWELL: Animal Ecology. *61 illus.*
                                           TB/543